Praise for *And All Their Glory Past...*

"Donald E. Graves, the dean of Canadian scholars of the War of 1812, makes a comprehensive examination of the final months of fighting on the American–Canadian border, when territorial sovereignty was still very much in question. His study is a balanced and valuable contribution to the scholarship and is a sheer pleasure to read!"
Richard V. Barbuto, author of *Niagara 1814: America Invades Canada*

"Donald Graves's study, *And All Their Glory Past*, concerns the last months of the War of 1812 in the Canadian–United States borderlands and is an outstanding example of unbiased military history. Graves provides a strong grasp of the geo-political context, careful consideration of logistics, strategic and tactical considerations, and the military and naval personalities of the opposing sides. This book includes critical comments on leadership performance based on a deep knowledge of the primary and secondary sources."
William S. Dudley, editor, *The Naval War of 1812: A Documentary History,* and former Director, Naval Historical Center

"In this masterfully written concluding volume to his magnificent trilogy on the northern theatre, Donald E. Graves confirms once again that he is the *doyen* of War of 1812 historians." **John R. Grodzinski, author of *Defender of Canada: Sir George Prevost and the War of 1812***

"This work demonstrates why Donald E. Graves is Canada's most accomplished military historian and without peer as a student of campaigns of the War of 1812. His compelling analysis is surpassed only by his talent for constructing a sparkling narrative. *And All Their Glory Past* will entertain and educate those who read it and will almost surely remain the standard treatment of the subject for generations to come." **Donald R. Hickey, author of *Don't Give Up the Ship! Myths of the War of 1812***

"An object lesson in the writing of military history, *And All Their Glory Past* brings the War of 1812 on the Canadian border to a dramatic close and follows the fortunate warriors home. Donald E. Graves allows the soldiers to speak, sets their actions in context, while his judgements are as sharp as the bayonets they wielded." **Andrew Lambert, author of *The Challenge: Britain Against America in the Naval War of 1812***

"Donald E. Graves once again challenges established wisdom, exposes new sources, shoots sacred cows. As a result he tells a compelling and convincing story, in fact a real page-turner. But he also makes us see the human side of events by looking through the eyes of those who were there, in person, on those bloody fields. Their words give us no doubt that the War of 1812 in the north was a hard fight between two determined and capable opponents." **Jonathon Riley, author of *A Matter of Honour: The Life, Campaigns and Generalship of Isaac Brock***

"Donald E. Graves confirms his reputation as the pre-eminent scholar of early Canadian military history. His account of the battles along the Canadian–American frontier in 1814–15 brings to a triumphant conclusion his trilogy on the major engagements of the War of 1812. Graves combines extensive research and a keen eye for detail with an unrivalled skill in untangling the complexities of the battlefield. Essential reading for all students of early Canadian and American military history." **John Stagg, author of *Mr. Madison's War* and *The War of 1812: Conflict for a Continent***

OTHER BOOKS WRITTEN OR EDITED BY DONALD E. GRAVES

Blood and Steel: The Wehrmacht Archive: Normandy 1944
Frontline Books, 2013

First Campaign of an A.D.C.: The War of 1812 Memoir of Lt. William Jenkins Worth, U.S. Army
Old Fort Niagara Press, 2012

Dragon Rampant: The Royal Welch Fusiliers at War, 1793-1815
Frontline Books & Robin Brass Studio, 2010

Fix Bayonets! A Royal Welch Fusilier at War, 1796-1815
Robin Brass Studio & Spellmount Publishing, 2007

"Reading Maketh a Full Man!": Military Literature in the Napoleonic Wars. An Annotated Bibliography of the Military Titles Pubished by the London Firm of Egerton, 1782-1832
Ken Trotman Ltd. 2007

Century of Service: The History of the South Alberta Light Horse
The South Alberta Light Horse Regiment Foundation & Robin Brass Studio, 2005

More Fighting for Canada: Five Battles, 1760-1944
Robin Brass Studio, 2004

Another Place, Another Time: A U-boat Officer's Wartime Album
(with Werner Hirschmann) Robin Brass Studio, 2004, 2011

In Peril on the Sea: The Royal Canadian Navy and the Battle of the Atlantic
Canadian Naval Memorial Trust & Robin Brass Studio, 2003

C. P. Stacey. *Quebec, 1759: The Siege and the Battle*
Edited and with new material by Donald E. Graves. Robin Brass Studio, 2002

Guns Across the River: The Battle of the Windmill, 1838
Friends of Windmill Point & Robin Brass Studio, 2001, 2013

Fighting for Canada: Seven Battles, 1758-1945
Robin Brass Studio, 2000

Field of Glory: The Battle of Crysler's Farm, 1813
Robin Brass Studio, 1999

J. Mackay Hitsman. *The Incredible War of 1812: A Military History*
Updated by Donald E. Graves. Robin Brass Studio, 1999

South Albertas: A Canadian Regiment at War
South Alberta Regiment Veterans Association & Robin Brass Studio, 1998, 2004

Where Right and Glory Lead! The Battle of Lundy's Lane, 1814
Robin Brass Studio, 1997

Soldiers of 1814: American Enlisted Men's Memoirs of the Niagara Campaign
Old Fort Niagara Press, 1996

Redcoats and Grey Jackets: The Battle of Chippawa, 1814
Dundurn Press, 1994

Merry Hearts Make Light Days: The War of 1812 Journal of Lieutenant John Le Couteur, 104th Foot
Carleton University Press, 1993. Robin Brass Studio, 2012

Normandy 1944: The Canadian Summer
(with W. J. McAndrew and M. J. Whitby) Art Global, 1993

"The Rocket's Red Glare:" Sir William Congreve and His Weapon System
Museum Restoration Service, 1989

The American soldier, 1814. By the third year of the War of 1812, the United
States Army in the north, having learned some hard lessons in a hard school,
was able to meet its British opponent on equal terms. This fine portrait by artist
Don Troiani portrays a confident and competent infantryman of the Left Division
wearing the modest grey jacket that American soldiers would make famous in the
Niagara campaign of 1814, the longest and bloodiest military operation of the war.
(Painting by Don Troiani, www.historicalartprints.com. Collection of James Kochan)

Donald E. Graves

AND ALL THEIR
GLORY
PAST

*Fort Erie, Plattsburgh and
the Final Battles in the North, 1814*

*The light of the other days is faded,
And all their glory past.*
– ALFRED BUNN, *THE MAID OF ARTOIS*, ACT II

ROBIN BRASS STUDIO

Published 2013 by Robin Brass Studio Inc.
www.robinbrassstudio.com

Website for Donald E. Graves: www.ensigngroup.ca

ISBN-13: 978-1-896941-71-4
ISBN-10: 1-896941-71-0

Printed and bound in Canada by Marquis Imprimeur Inc., Montmagny, Quebec

Library and Archives Canada Cataloguing in Publication

Graves, Donald E. (Donald Edward), author
        And all their glory past : Fort Erie, Plattsburgh and the final battles in the north, 1814 / Donald E. Graves.

Includes bibliographical references and index. ISBN 978-1-896941-71-4 (pbk.)

        1. Canada – History – War of 1812. 2. United States – History – War of 1812. 3. United States – History – War of 1812 – Campaigns. 4. Fort Erie (Fort Erie, Ont.) – Siege, 1814. 5. Plattsburg, Battle of, Plattsburgh, N.Y., 1814. I. Title.

FC442.G72 2013   971.03'4   C2013-905272-0

This book is dedicated to the memory
of the following persons who contributed
to the history of the War of 1812
or who touched the life of the Author
being
Shawn Cafferky (1958-2008)
Colonel John R. Elting (1911-2000)
Sherry Dolores Greaves (1951-2013)
Robert Malcomson (1949-2009)
John Morris (1932-2009)
Ruth Redmond (1903-1999)
Barry Rich (1930-2012)
and, in particular,
Brigadier-General J. L. Summers, CMM, MC, CD (1919-1994),
who set me on the path,

and

To the memory of the men and women
of the American, British and Canadian armed forces
who have died fighting for civilization during the war on terrorism.

At the going down of the Sun,
And in the Morning
We WILL Remember Them

Contents

Maps

Preface and Acknowledgments

It is one thing to write about men who fought and died nearly two centuries ago; it is quite another to gaze at their mortal remains. I had this unique (and sobering) experience in October 1987 when I visited the archaeological excavations being conducted at the site of an American military burial ground dating from the 1814 siege of Fort Erie. This site contained the remains of thirty-one men who had died during August and September 1814 in a military operation that forms a major part of the work that follows.

At the time I was a staff historian with the Department of National Defence in Ottawa and my visit to that grave site was an official one. It triggered something in my mind, however, and shortly afterward, I began researching and writing a manuscript on the Niagara campaign of 1814, which was eventually published (first in 1993 and later in a revised edition in 1997) as *Where Right and Glory Lead! The Battle of Lundy's Lane, 1814*. Two years later, I brought out *Field of Glory: The Battle of Crysler's Farm, 1813*, which is an account of the autumn 1813 offensive against Montreal, the largest American offensive of the war, and the two battles that brought it to a close. I then decided that I would write a third book which, carrying on from the narrative of these two volumes, would complete a trilogy that I decided to call "Forgotten Soldiers: The War of 1812 in the North." At least that was the plan in 1999 but few writing plans survive first brush with reality – that is to say the necessity of making a living – and it took more than a decade before I found the time to begin serious work on this book, which is the final volume of the trilogy. Long overdue, it is finished at last and I have given it the title *And All Their Glory Past: Fort Erie, Plattsburgh and the Final Battles in the North, 1814*.

Although they are all loosely connected, the books in the "Forgotten Soldiers" trilogy can be read as individual volumes. *And All Their Glory Past* is largely an expansion of Chapter 13 of *Where Right and Glory Lead* but it differs from its companion volumes, which dealt with a single battle or a single geographic area. In this book I am examining two major military (and naval) operations, separated by hundreds of miles and fought by five different land formations and four different naval squadrons. This has required the inclusion of certain "gear change" chapters when I have to switch the focus of the book. Another difference is that, while the first two volumes concentrate on the operational and tactical level of war, this last volume – while not ignoring those levels – of necessity touches on the strategic level of war. Blending the three and the various campaigns into one readable narrative has been a rather tricky task and one that I hope I have successfully accomplished – but that is for the reader, not me, to judge.

Some of my readers will know that a secondary theme runs through all the books in the "Forgotten Soldiers" trilogy. That sub-theme is the story of how the United States Army, poorly led, supplied and trained, survived two gruelling years of war while learning tough lessons in a hard school until it reached the point where it was able to fight a very professional opponent on equal terms. "Bootstrap soldiers" is my personal term for the regular American army of the War of 1812 because what they accomplished, they accomplished through their own efforts, with precious little help and not a little hindrance from Washington. Most of the "forgotten soldiers" in this trilogy are therefore Americans because, for some reason that I have never been able to completely fathom, American historians have paid scant attention to the U.S. Army of this often overlooked conflict – it really does deserve better.

As these words are being written, two events are taking place simultaneously. The Bicentennial of the War of 1812 is being commemorated and the struggle against Islamic terrorism continues, a struggle that commenced in earnest (for want of a better date) on 11 September 2001. On both sides of the border, the Bicentennial has witnessed numerous commemorations of the heroes and heroines of that rather strange conflict. But while celebrating in North America, we must not forget that American, British and Canadian soldiers are still battling a very elusive and difficult enemy in Afghanistan and other places around the globe. We must ensure that the servicemen and women of all three nations are honoured in their time and that they do not become "forgotten" in the future as was the case with so many of their 1812 counterparts.

It is now my pleasant duty to thank all those who helped with the research and writing of this book. I must pay particular tribute to four individuals, three American and one Canadian, who rendered special assistance.

For more than a decade Jim Hill of the Niagara Parks Commission relentlessly prodded me to write a study of the siege of Fort Erie and I have finally completed it. When I first met Jim he was an animator at the Fort Erie historic site and a bombardier in a reserve artillery unit – he is now the Director of

Heritage for Niagara Parks and a captain commanding his own battery. Jim also took the trouble to read and comment on early drafts of this book.

Pat Kavanagh of Kenmore, New York, is well known on both sides of the Niagara River as a serious student of the War of 1812. For years Pat has been sending me material on the siege of Fort Erie that he has industriously collected – in fact so much material that I finally had to beg him to stop as I was being overwhelmed. I am particularly grateful to Pat for taking the hours to sit in front of a microfilm photocopier and produce a hard copy of the 600 pages of the court-martial transcript of Brigadier-General E. P. Gaines, which is an indispensable source for the fighting at Fort Erie that took place on 15 August 1814.

Jack Bilow of Plattsburgh, New York, has spent years researching the names of the fatal casualties on both sides in the northern theatre of the War of 1812, research that culminated in his recent publication A War of 1812 Death Register. I am indebted to Jack for much assistance in the location of graves and the correct spelling of names.

My friend Joseph Whitehorne of Front Royal, Virginia, while a lieutenant-colonel on the staff of the Inspector-General in Washington, was the historian tasked with the research relating to the wartime burial ground discovered at Fort Erie in 1987, research that culminated in his 1992 book While Washington Burned: The Battle for Fort Erie, 1814. In a very generous gesture, Joe gave me all his research for both the burial ground and his book, all beautifully typed or written and carefully organized, attributes that my own research files will never possess. This act of mercy certainly reduced my labours.

Next I must thank those who agreed to my request to read the manuscript of this book in draft. These eight brave souls are all distinguished historians of the War of 1812 in their own right. My thanks go to Dr. Richard Barbuto of the Command and General Staff College, Fort Leavenworth, Kansas; Dr. William Dudley, former Director, Naval Historical Center, Washington; Professor John R. Grodzinski, Royal Military College of Canada, Kingston; Keith Herkalo of Plattsburgh; Professor Donald R. Hickey, Wayne State College, Nebraska; Professor Andrew Lambert, King's College, University of London; Lieutenant-General Jonathon Riley, CB, DSO, Phd, Visiting Professor, War Studies, King's College, University of London; and Professor John Stagg, University of Virginia. All the members of this select jury had suggestions and advice which, if I ignored it, I did so at my own peril.

My gratitude must also go to Peter Rindlisbacher, Canada's premier maritime artist (who, naturally enough, lives in Texas). Peter generously gave me the choice of any of his many fine paintings of the naval War of 1812 and I took full advantage of this splendid gift.

In a similar generous vein, Richard Feltoe offered me many of the base maps which grace this book and for that I am truly grateful.

I must also thank René Chartrand, North America's leading expert on musket period military uniforms, who was generous with his time, knowledge and items in his extensive archival collections.

There are dozens of other people and institutions who have helped me over the years that this book has been in progress – too many, I am afraid, to list here. The best I can do is to issue a blanket expression of gratitude and appreciation.

I must again acknowledge my debt to Robin Brass, who listens patiently to my intelligent and perceptive advice on book design and then completely ignores it. This is the fourteenth book we have produced together and our working relationship verges on the smoothness of, say, Laurel and Hardy, or other show business duos.

Closer to home there are the cats – Miss Becky and Skinny Ned (once known as Fat Edward but now sadly reduced in old age) – whose continuing cold war within the house frequently provided an unwelcome distraction from the onerous task of writing history.

And, finally, of course there is my beautiful wife, Dianne, who has received so many encomiums in so many books that I have nearly run out of compliments. Frankly, I am amazed that she did not leave me years ago.

DONALD E. GRAVES
"Maple Cottage"
Valley of the Mississippi
Upper Canada
Dominion Day, 1 July 2013

A Note to the Reader

The physical setting of the events studied in this book is the Great Lakes Basin and its attendant lakes and waterways. Readers not familiar with this area may not realize that this basin drains into the St. Lawrence River, which flows northeast to the Atlantic. The Niagara River (it is actually a strait but do not spread that around) is part of this system and it flows north to drain Lake Erie into Lake Ontario. Also part of the system, Lake Champlain drains into the Richelieu River, which then flows north, and the foot of that lake is therefore its north end. The upper part of the St. Lawrence flows from Kingston to Montreal and the lower part from Montreal down to beyond Quebec – hence the names of the two Canadian provinces of Upper and Lower Canada.

Place names can be a problem as there was, and still is, much variance in spelling. I have opted to standardize with Sackets Harbor and Chippawa. I have also determined to call the waterway Conjocta Creek, as it was called in 1814, rather than its modern and nearly unpronounceable name.

In 1814 both the British and American armies used numerical designations written in figures for their units. To avoid confusion, I have used figures for British units and formations and words for American units and formations so it is the 3rd Regiment of Foot (or 3rd Foot) of the British 3rd Brigade but the Twenty-Fifth Infantry Regiment (or Twenty-Fifth Infantry) of the American First Brigade.

During the War of 1812 an American regiment and a British battalion were much the same thing, a permanent unit with an authorized strength of between 500 and 1,000 men. When discussing British units, I have used the terms "battalion" and "regiment" interchangeably as they were used in 1814. During the war, the British army consisted of 104 regiments of foot, each regiment having at least one and some as many as six battalions, Thus the 1/3rd Foot is the first battalion of the 3rd Regiment of Foot and the 6/95th Foot is the sixth battalion of the 95th Regiment of Foot (Rifles).

It gets worse. The book discusses a British Left Division fighting an American Right Division and an American Left Division fighting a British Right Division. If the reader has not already guessed, these terms derive from the way the two armies faced on the map, the British left formation being its easternmost formation and the American right being the equivalent opposing force. It may be confusing but the reader should try and muddle through.

Ascertaining time in a period when there were no set time zones is always difficult. In almost all cases, the times given below are a consensus based on the most reliable witnesses but it must be stressed that they are approximate.

In 1814 the average value of the British pound sterling (£) was about five

American dollars ($). It has been estimated, however, (see *Measuring Worth,* www.measuringworth.com) that £1 in 1800 was the equivalent of £56.80 in 2008 in terms of retail price, and no less than £837.62 in the same year in terms of earnings. Using these standards, it is possible to work out how much a pound sterling or dollar were actually worth in terms of what they could buy or in payment for labour. Again, the emphasis has to be on approximate and there are regional differences.

I have retained the traditional imperial measure in this book (feet versus meters and miles versus kilometers, etc.) because that system of measurement was in use in 1814 and still is in modern Britain and the United States. Canada, on the other hand, officially uses the metric system except for unrepentant obstructionists like the present author, who mentally translates all metric measurements to their imperial equivalent and will continue to do so until he falls off his perch.

D.E.G.

AND ALL THEIR

GLORY PAST

British infantryman, 1814. With the end of the greater war in Europe, more British troops were available for the American war. This fine study by artist Don Troiani shows a soldier of the 104th Foot in marching order with his shako protected by an oilskin cover. (Painting by Don Troiani, www.historicalartprints.com)

"A complete drubbing before peace is made"

QUEBEC: MAY–AUGUST 1814

The drums do beat in the army and loud the cannons roar,
And adieu to old England, adieu for ever more.
King George he has commanded us and his orders we must obey
To go and face the Yankees in North Americay.

We marched out of Plymouth the fourteenth day of June,
The meadows being in blossom and the trees were in full bloom;
See all the pretty girls from the streets come running down,
The colour in their faces – to Americay we're bound.

Now for to conclude and make an end to my song,
We're bound for North Americay, and then it is not long.
We'll show them British play, then, from seaport town to town,
And with our heavy batteries we'll tumble them all down.[1]

The people of Quebec first heard the news on 20 June 1814. Rumours had been floating around the capital of British North America for weeks but only when the ship *Everetta* arrived that day from London with recent newspapers was it confirmed that Napoleon Bonaparte had abdicated, a treaty had been signed and after nearly two decades of war, Britain was at peace with France. The Quebec *Courier* was quick to remind its readers, however, that she was still at war with the United States but added the cheering information that transports had been dispatched to pick up 10,000 of the Duke of Wellington's veteran troops for deployment against the republic to the south. Such "energetic measures," the *Courier* stressed, were "strong symptoms of a determination on the part of Great Britain of commanding such terms" from the United States "as she may think herself entitled to."[2] The great war in Europe was finally over and many Britons believed it was time to teach Cousin Jonathan – that uncouth

1

Jack Frenchman on the march, 1814. For more than two decades the British army had fought its French counterpart and it took years before well-led British troops were able to obtain victory in battle. Once they did, they were rarely defeated, and in the end, along with the Royal Navy, they brought Bonaparte's empire to the ground. (Painting by Edouard Detaille, from *L'Armée française,* 1885)

American country bumpkin who had had the impudence to declare war on his betters – a stern lesson.

Toward that end, in the seven months following the close of the European war, Britain shifted one regiment of cavalry, thirty-three battalions of infantry and ten companies (batteries) of artillery across the Atlantic.[3] The vanguard of this wave of reinforcements, the 16th Regiment of Foot, arrived at Quebec from Ireland in late May and was followed by the 97th, also from Ireland, a battalion of the 1st Foot from Holland and the 90th from Grenada. But it was the regiments from the Duke of Wellington's Peninsular army that were most eagerly awaited. Although there had been a war on their doorstep for two years, Canadian newspapers had always carried lengthy accounts of Wellington's campaigns in Europe and the deeds of his soldiers were known and admired throughout British North America.[4]

As a result, there was great celebration when the first Peninsular unit, the 6th Regiment of Foot, landed at Quebec on 26 June after a seven-week voyage from Bordeaux. Eleven months before, at Echelar in the Pyrenees, the 6th (known as "The Saucy Sixth") was part of a brigade that had mounted a bayonet assault against a French division positioned 300 feet up a steep slope and put it to flight, causing Wellington to comment: "I never saw such an attack."[5] The 6th was shortly followed by the 3rd Foot. Traditionally called the "Buffs," the 3rd had acquired a new name at the 1811 battle of Albuera, where it had suffered horrendous casualties after being broken by French cavalry. In the days that followed, however, nearly two hundred missing men returned to the ranks, causing the 3rd to be re-christened "The Resurrectionists." Next to arrive was the 5th Foot, known as "The Fighting Fifth," which had added new laurels to its fine reputation at El Bodon in September 1811 when it carried out a very dangerous withdrawal across six miles of plain in the face of superior numbers of enemy cavalry. And so, throughout late June, July and into August 1814, up the St. Lawrence they came: a battalion of the 27th, or Enniskilling, Regiment of Foot ("The Skins"); the 37th Foot ("The Tigers"); the 39th ("Sankey's Horse"); 57th ("Fighting Villains"); 58th ("The Steelbacks"); 76th ("Seven and Sixpence"); 81st ("Loyal Lincolns") and 82nd Foot ("The Powos").[6]

One of the last of the Peninsular units to arrive was not only one of the most famous but also the most notorious regiment in Wellington's army. The 88th Foot or Connaught Rangers, "a parcel of wild rattling" Irishmen, always "ready for a row," disembarked on 3 August.[7] The Rangers were renowned not only for their valour in battle but also for their light-fingered ability to acquire or "liberate" anything valuable, edible or useful. As a result, they were known as the "Devil's Own" or the "Connaught Footpads" and frequently appeared in the army court-martial reports. Wellington once complained that he had hanged and shot more men from the 88th Foot than from the rest of his army combined but he was quick to add that "when anything very gallant, very desperate is to be done, there is no corps in the army I would sooner employ."[8]

For nearly six years, the men in these regiments had routinely beaten Jack Frenchman or Johnny Crappo* – their names for the enemy – in a dozen major battles and countless minor actions, They had absolutely no doubt that they could whip the Yankees but most were unhappy about being sent to North America as the orders to embark had brought an abrupt end to the idyll they had been enjoying in southwestern France where the weather was fine, the wine flowing and the women were all friendly.

At the end of the European war, Wellington's army was stationed in and around Bordeaux in the Gironde. A traditional Royalist stronghold, the Gironde had been glad to see the collapse of Bonaparte's ramshackle empire, which had nearly destroyed the local economy, and the backside of his ill-disciplined soldiers, who had routinely committed depredations against civilians. In contrast, their British invaders were not only well behaved but paid for what they wanted in solid gold or silver, not the worthless paper currency of imperial France.

---

* From *Jean le crapaud* or "John the frog."

The result was that the Gironde greeted the redcoats with enthusiasm and after years of hard marches, short rations and bad weather, Wellington's soldiers found themselves in heaven – or a reasonable facsimile thereof.

There was so much good cheap wine in the Gironde, one drummer recalled, that he and his comrades cooked their potatoes and meat in it. The enlisted men made their own entertainment while the officers enjoyed a seemingly never-ending succession of dances, balls, parties, dinners, plays, promenades, horse races and other events. In later years, however, what officer and man alike fondly remembered about the Gironde was the local pulchritude – the area simply abounded "with beautiful females of exquisite symmetry, promenading with the most graceful deportment" and displaying "great vivacity, piercing sparkling eyes, and much animation of countenance."[9] The inevitable result was "such an abundance of kissing, as probably the like of it was never seen before," – there was "kissing in the valleys, and kissing upon the hills, ... there was embracing, kissing, and counter-kissing, from Toulouse to Bordeaux."[10] It was not long before, one officer noted, "most of our gallant fellows were in love or fancied themselves so."[11]

This being the case, there were strong (but not loud) complaints in the ranks of those regiments chosen – and only the strongest units were selected – to cross the Atlantic and thrash the Yankees. Morale was not improved when Wellington ordered that only a few of the women who had accompanied these regiments throughout their campaigns would be allowed to embark with their menfolk and those only "who had proved themselves useful and regular ... with a view to their being ultimately married."[12] Of the women left behind, the British females were returned home but the Portuguese and Spanish ladies were relegated to the care of the Portuguese army, which escorted them back to their native villages. It being almost a certainty that the women who did not embark would never again see their menfolk, there were many distressing scenes when couples had to be separated by force. One officer never forgot the melancholy sight of these "faithful and heroic women" standing abandoned on shore "while they witnessed with bursting hearts" the loading of the ships "that were to separate them for ever from those to whom they had looked for protection and support."[13] A sergeant of the 95th Foot recalled that it was too much for some men who, "bound by the charms of the Signorettas," deserted "their country's cause, to take up that of their Dulcineas."[14] Wellington's men apparently had a similar effect on French womanhood. Captain John Cooke of the 43rd Foot remembered that, when his regiment boarded boats at Bordeaux for embarkation, numbers of French girls ran "crying after their lovers – so much for female patriotism – and one, more desperate than the rest, floundered into the river to drown herself" but the soldiers fortunately "succeeded in rescuing and hauling her into the boat" and she was eventually "united in holy wedlock to the happy sergeant for whom she had risked so much."[15]

When they came ashore at Quebec, some of the Peninsular units were wearing new uniforms but others were clad in rags so tattered that "they were at first taken for so many convicts."[16] As Lieutenant William Grattan of the 88th Foot put it, the worn and patched uniforms of the veterans did not have

> the slightest pretension to uniformity; their bronzed faces, huge whiskers, and their general bearing, were of that character that inspired feelings of awe more than admiration. Their old trowsers, some black, some green, and their caps, some perforated with three or four bullet holes, while others, with a portion of them shot away altogether, most unquestionably did not mark them out to the eye of the general and ignorant spectator as a body of men that had trampled under their tread the greatest warriors in the world.[17]

The contrast between these heroes of the Peninsula and the "pipe clay" soldiers of the Quebec garrison was striking and it was noted that all the newcomers displayed the white cockade of the Spanish Bourbons rather than the regulation black cockade of the British Hanoverian Royal House.[18]

If the uniforms of some of the enlisted men were ragged, the dress of their officers verged on the fantastic. A strict disciplinarian in most matters, Wellington never took much notice of how his officers dressed – except that he forbade the carrying of umbrellas in battle. Provided they brought their men "into the field well appointed and with sixty rounds of good ammunition each," one recalled, the Duke never looked to see "whether their trousers were black, blue, or grey" while his officers "might be rigged out in all the colours of the rainbow if we fancied it."[19] The result of such licence was ludicrous. Peninsular officers disdained wearing the regulation headgear but opted for round hats (a squatter version of the top hat) or cocked hats severely cut down to a width about the size of the span of a hand and usually topped by a large white plume. Others sported forage caps "of all fancies and shapes" in a variety of colours, some resembling a "pork pie" hat, some a wedge cap, and some even a scholar's mortarboard – but usually trimmed with velvet and festooned with tassels.[20] Most officers wore what they called "slouch great coats" ("the shabbier the better," one remarked) which the French termed a *surtout* ("over all").[21] This was a bulky garment resembling a dressing gown, tailored from heavy material, decorated with braid and manufactured in a variety of colours.[22] If an officer was forced to wear his regulation scarlet coat – the "old red rag," as it was called – he was sure to complement it with a velvet or brocade vest, usually heavily

embroidered and closed with large gold or silver buttons.[23] Overalls, strapped or lined with leather along the inseam and cuffs, fastening on the outseam with large metal buttons, and held under the instep of the boot with chains, were also much favoured as were bright, brass box spurs. Heavy moustaches and sideburns were *de rigueur* but the remainder of the hair on the head was usually tightly cropped. To complete his ensemble, the well-dressed officer often added either an umbrella or a riding crop and lit up a Spanish "seegar." The only thing missing, one Peninsular officer quipped about his comrades' dress, was "the appendage of Bells."[24]

The people of Quebec did not really much care about the appearance of the new arrivals because it was clear that

> their iron frames, without an extra pound of flesh, – their muscular limbs, firm as the hough of a race horse, their arms and appointments all in order, ready for battle at a moment's notice; their knapsacks packed with a neatness that it was impossible to surpass and difficult to imitate, carried on their shoulders with as much ease as if it were a thing of no weight, pointed them out to be, in the fullest meaning of the word – SOLDIERS![25]

With men like these, commented an officer's lady, if Britain could not "make Peace on *this* side before the gates of Plattsburg or on the *other* amidst the ruins of New York" then it "may as well make the enemy a handsome present of Canada."[26] The people of British North America were fully aware that earlier in the year President James Madison had accepted London's offer to discuss a peace settlement and that diplomats from both nations would shortly meet to negotiate an end to the conflict. They welcomed this development but after two long years of war and numerous American offensives or attacks against British territory, they wanted to see their opponents humbled. The government in London felt the same and was determined, as one senior officer put it, to give the Jonathans "a complete drubbing before Peace is made" – and the veterans coming ashore at Quebec were just the men to do it.[27]

Facing page **Types of British officers, as seen in the Low Countries, 1814-1815.** The work of a Belgian artist, these cartoons show the incredible variety in officers' dress by the end of the Napoleonic wars. Note the officer carrying an umbrella, the man with the cut-down cocked hat and feather and the officer in the lower right wearing a "slouch great coat" or surtout and smoking a cigar while chatting to the lady. (Photographs by Paul Meganick in the Royal Museum of the Army and Military History, Brussels)

U.S. sergeant, 1814. The backbone of any army is its cadre of veteran NCOs. This fine drawing depicts a sergeant of the Left Division in marching order. (Drawing by G. A. Embleton, courtesy of the artist)

PART ONE

On the Niagara

26 JULY–14 AUGUST 1814

BY THE PRESIDENT
OF THE
United States of America,
A PROCLAMATION:

WHEREAS the Congress of the United States, by virtue of the Constituted Authority vested in them, have declared by their act, bearing date the eighteenth day of the present month, that WAR exists between the United Kingdom of Great Britain and Ireland, and the dependencies thereof, and the United States of America and their territories; Now, therefore, I, JAMES MADISON, President of the United States of America, do hereby proclaim the same to all whom it may concern: and I do specially enjoin on all persons holding offices, civil or military, under the authority of the United States, that they be vigilant and zealous, & discharging the duties respectively incident thereto: And I do moreover exhort all the good people of the United States, as they love their country; as they value the precious heritage derived from the virtue and valor of their fathers; as they feel the wrongs which have forced on them the last resort of injured nations; and as they consult the best means, under the blessing of Divine Providence, of abridging its calamities; that they exert themselves in preserving order, in promoting concord, in maintaining the authority and the efficacy of the laws, and in supporting and invigorating all the measures which may be adopted by the Constituted Authorities, for obtaining a speedy, a just, and an honorable peace.

IN TESTIMONY WHEREOF I have hereunto set my hand, and caused the seal of the United States to be affixed to these presents.

(SEAL.)

DONE at the City of Washington, the nineteenth day of June, one thousand eight hundred and twelve, and of the Independence of the United States the thirty-sixth.

(Signed)   JAMES MADISON.

By the President,
(Signed)   JAMES MONROE, Secretary of State.

Soldier of the 103rd Foot. One of the most junior regiments in the British army, the 103rd Foot joined the Right Division in time to fight in the battle of Lundy's Lane and the siege of Fort Erie. (Painting by Patrick Courcelle, courtesy of Parks Canada)

CHAPTER ONE

"An ugly customer"

A BLOODY BATTLE AND ITS CONSEQUENCES

Old England, forty years ago,
When we were young and slender,
She aim'd at us a mortal blow,
But God was our defender;
Jehovah saw her horrid plan,
George Washington He gave us;
His holiness inspir'd the man
With skill and power to save us.

She sent her fleet and armies o'er,
To ravage, kill and plunder;
Our heroes met them on the shore,
And drove them back with thunder;
Our independence they confess'd,
And with their hands they sign'd it,
But on their hearts 'twas ne'er impress'd,
For there I ne'er could find it.

How often Brown made Drummond fly
From scenes of desolation;
The terror of his noble eye
Struck him with consternation;
Brave Miller, Ripley, Gaines and Scott,
At Erie and Bridgewater,
At Chippewa, in battles hot,
Their bravest foes did slaughter.[1]

Drummer Jarvis Hanks of the Eleventh United States Infantry Regiment – one of the smaller Jonathans facing the armed might of an enraged Britannia – was not all that worried about receiving a drubbing at the hands of her legions. Trudging south on the road that paralleled the Canadian bank of the Niagara River during the late afternoon of 26 July 1814, 14-year-old Jarvis had more pressing concerns on his mind. First, he was dead tired; second, he was very hungry; and, third, military life was not at all what it was supposed to be. It had been bad enough to exchange his mother's cooking for army rations and a comfortable bed for the "soft side of a pine board," but Jarvis had just fought in his third major battle in nine months and he was not even supposed to go into combat. The officer who had enlisted him in Pawlet, Vermont, had promised his anxious parents that the lad would be retained on the recruiting service and never see action. Like many a young man before and since, Jarvis Hanks had come to the sad realization that recruiters tell lies.

Young drummer Hanks was a soldier in Brigadier-General Winfield Scott's First Brigade of Major-General Jacob Brown's Left Division of the United States Army. As such, the day before he had participated in the bloodiest military engagement of the war up to that time. It had commenced early in the evening of 25 July 1814 when Scott's brigade had attacked a British force deployed on a low, sand hill in front of a tree-shaded sunken country road, which local people called Lundy's Lane after a farmer of that name who lived along it. It had been a bloody, bitter, obstinate and relentless battle that had continued for six hours into the night. When it was over more than 1,700 men from both armies were dead, wounded or missing, and it had been a particularly bad evening for senior officers. Both of the British generals present were wounded and one of them was captured, while three of the four American generals were wounded, two severely.[*]

The battle of Lundy's Lane was basically a hammering match and, as young Hanks later commented, it was difficult to decide which army "had inflicted or received the greatest amount of injury."[3] Brown's Left Division had good claim to a victory, however, because, when the last shots died away, it was in possession of both the sand hill and the British artillery.[4] Unfortunately, when the division withdrew in the early hours of 26 July to its camp at Chippawa, three miles south, a combination of confusion and fatigue resulted in the captured ordnance except for one brass[†] 6-pdr. gun being left on the battlefield, where it was found at daybreak by its previous owners, who cheerfully repossessed their property.

The loss of these trophies was particularly galling to Brown. Although not a prewar regular, the 39-year-old Brown was one of the few senior commanders of the wartime United States Army to have a record of almost constant success.

---

[*] A detailed study of the 1814 battles of Chippawa and Lundy's Lane is contained in my book *Where Right and Glory Lead*, the second volume in the "Forgotten Soldiers" trilogy.

[†] "Brass" is the period British term for an alloy of copper and tin; modern Americans generally use "bronze" for the same alloy. In the early 19th century, brass, sometimes called "gun metal," was a composition of 8-10 lb. of tin and 100 lb. of copper.

The bloodiest battle, Lundy's Lane. On 25 July 1814, Brown fought Drummond at Lundy's Lane near Niagara Falls. It was a bloody, vicious, confusing action that went on into the dark and when it was over, 1,700 men lay dead or wounded. (Painting by C.W. Jeffreys, courtesy City of Toronto Archives)

As a New York militia officer, he had defeated a British raid on Ogdensburg in 1812 and had been instrumental in the successful defence of Sackets Harbor in May 1813. Brought into the regular army as a brigadier-general, Brown had proved a very able commander during the autumn 1813 offensive against Montreal. He had been responsible, along with his subordinate, Brigadier-General Winfield Scott, for turning the Left Division into the most effective fighting formation in the army and he had led it to a signal victory at the battle of Chippawa on 5 July. He had next moved against the three British-held posts at the mouth of the Niagara River – Forts George, Mississauga and Niagara – expecting to see on Lake Ontario the sails of Commodore Isaac Chauncey's USN squadron, which would transport the heavy ordnance he needed to attack these posts. But Chauncey had never appeared and, after a frustrating wait during which he had vainly tried to lure the British garrisons of the forts into open battle, Brown had withdrawn to Chippawa on 23 July to resupply in preparation for an advance against the British depot at Burlington Heights.*

---

* The location of Burlington Heights is often confused with the location of the modern Canadian city of Burlington or with Hamilton Mountain, which is that part of the Niagara escarpment behind the city of Hamilton. In fact the supply depot at Burlington Heights was located where Dundurn Castle is in the modern city of Hamilton.

Major-General Jacob Brown (1775-1822). A former militia officer, Brown was brought into the regular army in 1813 and proved to be a natural commander. Where Brown went, fighting followed as he was an aggressive leader who showed that, with proper training, the American soldier was the equal of his British counterpart. (Print after portrait by James Herring, author's collection)

Late in the afternoon of 25 July, when he learned that the British were moving south up the Niagara, Brown had dispatched Scott's brigade north down the river. Scott had encountered an enemy force at Lundy's Lane and, disobeying orders, had attacked it. The result was the vicious and costly engagement in which both Brown and Scott had been wounded.

Command of the Left Division had devolved on Brigadier-General Eleazar W. Ripley. A cautious man, so cautious that he was often accused of timidity, Ripley was much different from the incisive Brown and for some time relations between the two men had been strained. Although he had suffered a serious wound, Brown was strong enough to issue orders and, in the early hours of 26 July, he directed Ripley to withdraw from the field to the camp at Chippawa and, after making sure the troops got refreshment, to return to the battlefield at first light and "at all events bring off the captured cannon."[5]

Ripley, however, was dilatory at carrying out this order: the division did not move until 9 A.M. on 26 July and it did not go far. Finding British troops deployed between Chippawa and Lundy's Lane, Ripley halted and sought the advice of four officers as to whether he should re-engage or withdraw to the United States. These men were Brigadier-General Peter B. Porter, who commanded the non-regular volunteer brigade in the division, Majors William McRee and Eleazar D. Wood, its two senior engineer officers, and Captain Nathan Towson, an artillery officer. All four opposed any attempt to renew the action because the Left Division was not in any shape to do so, but flatly rejected any suggestion to return to American territory. They advised Ripley to withdraw to the vicinity of Fort Erie, eighteen miles to the south, where it could resupply from depots at Buffalo, just across the Niagara River.

Accepting this advice, Ripley ordered the Left Division to withdraw to Chippawa, break camp and prepare to march. He visited Brown to inform him of his

Brigadier-General Eleazar W. Ripley (1782-1839). A former Massachusetts lawyer and politician, Ripley was a good unit commander and subordinate but was too cautious and defensive to be a good formation commander. His relations with the more dynamic Brown got steadily worse as the Niagara campaign of 1814 wore on. (Courtesy, Hood Museum of Art, Dartmouth College, N.H.)

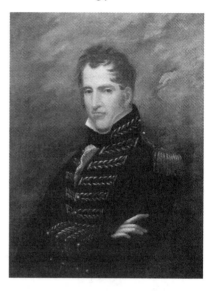

decision not to return to the battlefield – but apparently not of his intention to withdraw to Fort Erie – and when Brown remonstrated, Ripley added that Porter, the other unwounded general officer in the division, supported him. Brown's angry response was: "Sir, you will do as you please," and a curt dismissal.[6] Soon afterward, Brown was embarked on a boat for passage to Buffalo but Ripley's actions rankled him. It was not that Brown had any doubt "of the intelligence or personal bravery" of his subordinate but his confidence in him as a commander began to lessen because he realized that Ripley "dreaded responsibility more than danger" and had "a greater share of physical than moral courage."[7] This being the case, Brown immediately sent a courier to Brigadier-General Edward P. Gaines, commanding at Sackets Harbor, to come and assume command of the Left Division.[8]

For the next few hours, the division was busy breaking up its camp and preparing for a withdrawal. The seriously wounded, including Brown, were embarked on boats for a gentle water passage to Buffalo while the lightly wounded were placed on supply wagons, some forty in all, for transport by land. After destroying the fieldworks in and around Chippawa and burning the bridge over the Chippawa River, the division commenced

Brigadier-General Peter B. Porter (1773-1844). Practical and cool in action, Porter led the volunteer brigade in the Left Division. Brown liked and admired this former politician whose residence on the Niagara River was bombarded by the British in 1812. Courtesy, Buffalo and Erie County Historical Society, C-19269.

THE NORTHERN THEATRE

0 ____ 50 ____ 100 miles
0 ____ 50 ____ 100 ____ 150 km

■ fort   ● town/village or battle site

N

Lake Superior

St. Joseph I.

■ Fort Mackinac

Lake Michigan

Lake Huron

Georgian Bay

Penetanguishene

Nottawasaga Bay

L. Simcoe

Bay of Quinte

U P P E R   C A N A D A

● York

Lake Ontario

Burlington Heights ● Burlington Bay

Ft. Niagara ■

Charlotte ●

Batavia ●

Ft. George
Queenston

Malcolm's Mills ●

Grand R.

Ft. Erie ■

Niagara R.

Genesee R.

Canandaigu

M I C H I G A N

T E R R I T O R Y

St. Clair R.

Thames R.

● Moraviantown

● Port Dover
● Port Ryerse

Buffalo ●

N E W

Long Point

● Fredonia

Detroit ●

● Dolsen's Mills

Lake Erie

● Sandwich

Detroit R.

● Amherstburg (Fort Malden)

Raisin R.

● Frenchtown

Put-In-Bay

● Cleveland

Presque Isle

P E N N S Y L V A N I A

Fort Miami ■

■ Fort Meigs

Maumee River

Sandusky R.

■ Fort Stephenson

■ Fort Defiance

B L A C K
S W A M P

O H I O

Allegheny R.

● Pittsburgh

Ohio River

● Urbana

● Dayton

V A.

V A.

16

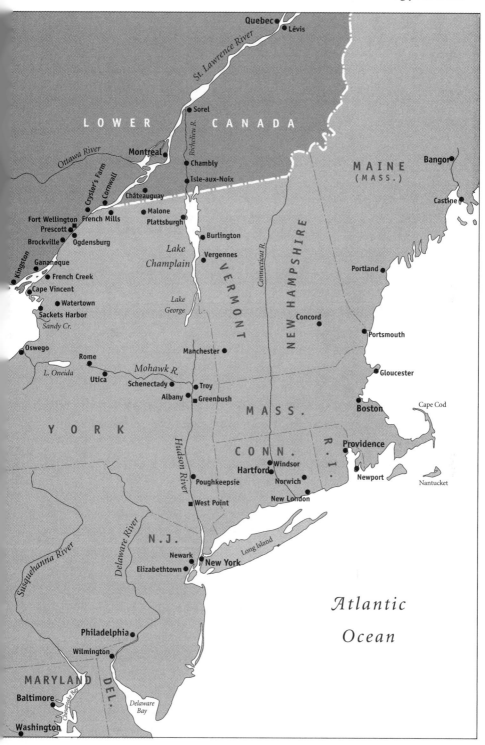

Quebec
Lévis
St. Lawrence River
LOWER CANADA
Sorel
Richelieu R.
MAINE
(MASS.)
Bangor
Ottawa River
Montreal
Chambly
Crysler's Farm
Cornwall
Isle-aux-Noix
Castine
Châteauguay
Fort Wellington
French Mills
Malone
Prescott
Plattsburgh
Brockville
Ogdensburg
Burlington
Kingston
Gananoque
Lake
Champlain
Vergennes
Connecticut R.
Portland
French Creek
VERMONT
NEW HAMPSHIRE
Cape Vincent
Watertown
Lake
George
Sackets Harbor
Concord
Sandy Cr.
Portsmouth
Oswego
Rome
Manchester
Gloucester
L. Oneida
Mohawk R.
Utica
Schenectady
Troy
Cape Cod
Albany
Greenbush
MASS.
Boston
YORK
Providence
CONN.
R. I.
Windsor
Hudson River
Hartford
Newport
Poughkeepsie
Norwich
Nantucket
West Point
New London
N.J.
Long Island
Newark
New York
Susquehanna River
Delaware River
Elizabethtown
Atlantic
Ocean
Philadelphia
Wilmington
MARYLAND
DEL.
Baltimore
Chesapeake Bay
Delaware
Bay
Washington

Captain Nathan Towson (1783-1854). A much liked and respected officer in the Left Division, Towson of the artillery was regularly consulted by Ripley in the hours following the battle of Lundy's Lane although he held a fairly junior rank. (Portrait by Rembrandt Peale, courtesy of the Maryland Historical Society)

its march about 3 P.M. When the column came to its provision store, located on Canadian Samuel Street's farm about a mile south of the Chippawa, the men were told to take whatever rations they wanted, and the remainder were dumped in the Niagara. The march then resumed but it was 10 P.M. before the division reached the ferry station two miles north of Fort Erie and directly across from the small village of Black Rock, New York. After dining on a ration of raw, greasy, salted pork, the weary men, tired from more than thirty hours of fighting, working and marching, threw themselves on the ground and promptly went to sleep under a heavy downpour of rain. Lieutenant David Bates Douglass, commanding the small company of bombardiers and sappers attached to the division, flopped onto a canvas tarpaulin on the bed of a wagon and was soon unconscious. When the 24-year-old graduate of Yale awoke the next morning, somewhat sore and bruised, he discovered that he had been sleeping on a pile of pickaxes, shovels, crowbars "and various other tools."[9]

Ripley continued to worry. A lawyer and former Massachusetts politician, the 32-year-old Ripley had been a good regimental commander but had not functioned well after he had been promoted brigadier-general early in 1814. Ripley had never been happy about the decision to invade Canada and, the day before the Left Division did so, had actually tendered his resignation to Brown, who had refused it. Now in command, he continued to be nervous and again consulted Porter, McRee, Wood and Towson in turn about withdrawing to American territory. Towson recalled that, to him, Ripley expressed his anxiety about being "placed in a very responsible situation" as he was commanding

> the skeleton of an army, that had gained reputation and fame for themselves and country, that army had not been reinforced as it should have been, but was left to struggle, in an enemy's country, against superior numbers of troops, better appointed than themselves in all the appliances of war. And although the army had surmounted all past difficulties, and had covered itself with glory, there seemed little prospect of being reinforced in season

to prevent disaster. ...... therefore, there could be no loss of reputation in retiring before vastly superior numbers, and that it might be the part of both prudence and duty to do so.[10]

Ripley added that he was a very junior general, and, if the division was defeated, it would "be ascribed to want of ability in the commander, and not to the true cause," which was "want of requisite force and supplies."[11] Again, all four officers were adamant that a withdrawal to the United States was out of the question and advised Ripley to entrench at Fort Erie. Towson gently chided his nervous superior for taking counsel of his fears and holding "too gloomy a view of the subject."[12]

But Ripley's overheated imagination gave him no peace and on the following day, 27 July, he crossed over to Buffalo to request an order from Brown to withdraw to the United States. Given the already tense relations between the two men, this was not a wise move because Brown, angered by the withdrawal from Chippawa, which he had just learned about and which "affected him greatly," was in no mood to listen to an appeal for a further retreat. In fact he was furious and, treating Ripley with what he later called "unjustifiable indignation and scorn," he refused to issue such a command.[13] When Ripley insisted that he "would not be responsible" for the Left Division if it remained in Canada, and requested a written order to that effect, Brown gave him one. It instructed Ripley to send the division's wounded and baggage across to the United States but that those soldiers "who are sound and able to fight will encamp by Fort Erie so as to defend that post."[14] Not entirely confident that this was clear enough, Brown then issued a second written order telling the nervous Ripley in no uncertain terms that he was not to contemplate surrender but, if the enemy attacked him at Fort Erie, Brown expected Ripley "to ruin him."[15]

Brown then requested one of the Left Division's senior engineers to report to him. When Major Eleazar D. Wood shortly arrived, Brown informed him that he had ordered Ripley to remain at Fort Erie and that he relied on Wood and the other divisional engineers "for the secu-

Lieutenant David Bates Douglass (1790-1849). Shown here in middle age, Douglass was a young engineer officer who played a prominent part in constructing the defences at Fort Erie in August 1814 and later wrote a memoir of his experiences. (Print after photograph, author's collection)

19

rity of the army by the erection of proper defences."¹⁶ In this Brown was not to be disappointed as, throughout the remainder of the campaign, the division's engineers "displayed a zeal and expressed a confidence which was inspiring to others and most praiseworthy at this trying moment" and "devoted an unremitted attention not only to their particular duties but to every other object connected with the honor and safety of the army."¹⁷ Ripley now had clear orders and on 28 July 1814 the Left Division began to entrench at Fort Erie.¹⁸

The engineers' first task was to survey and mark the lines of a fortified position. The small stone Fort Erie was actually the fourth such post to occupy the site. The first, built in 1764, had successively been replaced by later constructions, the current fort being approved in 1804 but still unfinished at the outbreak of war in 1812. It had been abandoned the following year by its British garrison, who exploded the powder magazine, and briefly occupied by American forces, who set it on fire before they, in turn, evacuated. The British had then reoccupied it but had surrendered it to Brown's Left Division in the first week of July. For the past three weeks the fort had been garrisoned by a small detachment of artillery under Lieutenant Patrick McDonough, who had worked steadily on improving the defences.¹⁹

Intended only for a small garrison, the stone fort was not large and consisted of two demi-bastions* each with adjoining stone buildings (usually called "mess houses" in period accounts) that were connected on their west side by a stone curtain wall† in which was placed the main gate. From the fort, the engineers laid out a trace for an earthwork extending approximately southwest for about 800 yards to a large sand mound called Snake Hill, which was levelled and transformed into an artillery position. Shorter traces were laid for lines from the stone fort and Snake Hill to Lake Erie and places were selected for artillery positions along the entire line.

Once the traces were staked out, the Left Division went to work. All men under arrest were released and handed a shovel, trained carpenters from every unit were put to work on the more complicated jobs and every soldier labouring on the construction work received an extra gill (4 ounces) of whisky per day. Work went on day and night and by the last days of July progress was evident. Each unit was ordered to construct an abattis in front of its particular sector of the line and Lieutenant Douglass of the engineers has provided an excellent definition of what might be termed the barbed wire of the early 19th century:

---

* A bastion was an angular structure that projected outward from the wall of a defence work or fortification. It consisted of two faces and two flanks. A demi-bastion was a similar projection but with only one flank and one face.
† A curtain wall was a defensive wall joining two bastions or demi-bastions in a fortification.

The Abattis is a defence constructed chiefly of rows of saplings and the tops and large branches of trees. The ends of the branches are first lopped off, so as to leave stiff points. The trees are then piled with their tops turned from the fortification; and are secured by laying heavy timbers along the trunks. The assailant, therefore, is both exposed to his enemy's fire and obliged to penetrate in the face of these innumerable bristling points, which are often made more impracticable by entwining them with thorns, cat-briars, and the like.[20]

The Left Division had four engineer officers: Major McRee, Lieutenant-Colonel Wood and Lieutenants David Douglass and Horace Story. McRee, however, was functioning as Ripley's chief of staff; Wood was temporarily serving as the commanding officer of the Twenty-First Infantry and Story had been assigned to the defences of Black Rock and Buffalo. The result was that much of the supervision of the construction fell on the shoulders of Douglass, who had only been commissioned in the engineers the previous autumn, following his graduation from Yale. He proved entirely fit for the task and also constructed for his company of sappers a battery on the north flank of the camp on top of a disused lime kiln, which came to be known as the Douglass Battery. As he recalled, "I made my bed on the platform" of that position and "for many weeks afterwards, took no rest except on one of the trailed handspikes of one of the guns, with an old tent spread upon them, and wrapped in a horseman's cloak."[21]

Despite the progress being made on the defences, Ripley continued to despond, convinced that the Left Division "could not maintain its position" in Canada.[22] He was particularly worried about its strength, which had been sapped by heavy losses at the battles of Chippawa and Lundy's Lane. When it had invaded British territory at the beginning of July, the division had numbered nearly 5,000 but on the last day of that month it could muster only 2,222 all ranks fit for duty. But morale, which had been adversely affected by the recent heavy casualties, was beginning to rebound. In a letter to New York Governor Daniel D. Tompkins, Porter assured him that the Left Division "is composed of stuff which will not yield to trifles" even though its position was "a wretched one" with "no other defences excepting such as we have erected."[23] As July turned to August, the thought on everyone's mind was: when would the British appear?

It was a good question. At daybreak on 26 July, the same day that Drummer Hanks and the remainder of the Left Division had withdrawn to the south, Lieutenant-General Gordon Drummond, commanding His Britannic Majesty's Forces in Upper Canada, had moved his troops forward to take possession of the battlefield at Lundy's Lane. He then commenced the grim but necessary task of "cleaning it up" by gathering the wounded for treatment and disposing of the human and animal dead. Late in the morning, this work was momentarily interrupted when the pickets* gave warning that the enemy were approaching and Drummond deployed for battle. It resumed, however, when the American column halted short of Lundy's Lane and then withdrew. For the next several hours, the British and Canadians buried their own dead in a series of common graves on the hillside but burned most of the American dead in three large funeral pyres. This was an unusual act as burial was the standard method of disposing of corpses but Drummond may have wanted to complete the task quickly because of the summer heat and because he had decided to withdraw. When the battlefield had been cleared and he had learned from his patrols that the Americans were moving south toward Fort Erie, Drummond gave the order for the British Right Division to march north for Queenston. Ironically, at about 3 P.M. on 26 July 1814, the two opponents were marching *away* from each other.

For the next four days, although he dated some of his official correspondence as being from "Headquarters, Falls of Niagara," Drummond was actually at Queenston, seven miles to the north of the great natural wonder and twenty-seven miles away from his opponent. He dispatched patrols down the river road to maintain contact with the Americans but did little else. There were a number of possible reasons for this inactivity. First, Drummond had been wounded during the battle of Lundy's Lane by a nearly spent musket or rifle ball that hit him beneath his right ear and lodged under the skin at the back of his neck. Although it was cut out by the surgeons, such a wound would have caused much loss of blood and hampered his mobility. Second, Drummond was suffering from a bad summer cold, which probably did nothing to improve his state of mind. Third, and most important, at Lundy's Lane he had lost more than 800 casualties out of a total strength of just over 3,600 men, and most of these losses were regular troops, which Drummond could ill afford to spare. The day after the battle, when he released the local militia from service, as

---

* Since the term "picket" or "picquet" will appear frequently below, it might be wise to explain it in greater detail. The best definition I have seen is that of David Bates Douglass, who described pickets as "small detachments of Infantry or Cavalry ... thrown out, at various points, beyond the line of camp sentinels. The pickets are often again divided into small parties, which are thrown still further forward, and which may again be subdivided into individual guards. In this method, the whole range of country, for one, two or three miles in every direction, may be completely under the surveillance of a military encampment." See David B. Douglass, "Reminiscences of the Campaign of 1814, on the Niagara Frontier," *The Historical Magazine*, vol 2 (August 1873), 69n. Pickets prevented an army being surprised by the enemy. Contrary to Douglass, however, a mounted picket is usually termed a *vedette* or *vidette*.

they were needed on their farms, he had a total strength of about 2,500 officers and men fit for duty. Reinforcements were on the way but Drummond needed time to regroup and reorganize the Right Division. When it is considered that the task of gathering and transporting the wounded from the battlefield to the military hospitals at Fort George would have utilized much of the division's transport, the delay is more understandable. Unfortunately, his inactivity in the days following the battle severely weakens any claim Drummond could make to having gained a victory at Lundy's Lane based on his repossession of the battlefield and his artillery, and the withdrawal of the enemy.[24]

Drummond was certainly not happy with the outcome of Lundy's Lane. With a quarter century of service behind him the 42-year-old British commander had fought in Holland and Egypt and had served in Canada for three years before the war. He had been brought back to North America in late 1813 to take over the command in Upper Canada, and the previous December had conducted a campaign of retribution against the American side of the Niagara in revenge for the burning of the Canadian town of Newark. He had faced only New York militia in this operation, however, and thus had acquired a very poor appreciation of American martial prowess. Drummond attributed the enemy victory at Chippawa on 5 July to "the prodigious superiority in numbers which the enemy possessed."[25] He had been confident that he could "depend upon the superior discipline" of the troops under his command "for success over an un-

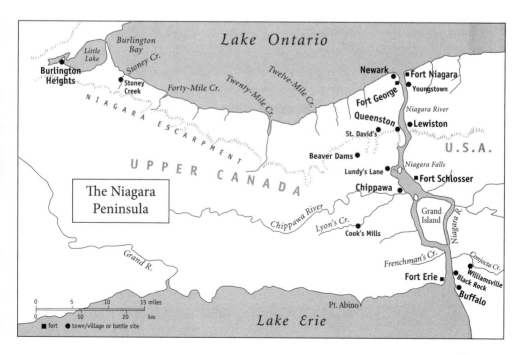

23

Lieutenant-General Gordon Drummond (1771-1854).
A career soldier who had served in North America before
the war, Drummond was a competent commander but he
faced an enemy in 1814 who was much improved from
the early years of the conflict. In addition, he suffered from supply problems throughout the campaign,
problems that were not helped by his naval counterpart,
Commodore James Yeo. (Print after painting by George
Berthon, Toronto Reference Library, T-15206)

disciplined though confident and numerous enemy."[26] The bloody action at Lundy's Lane, in which
he had actually outnumbered his opponents, had
forced him to change his mind about the quality
of his enemy.

While at Queenston, Drummond exchanged views on strategy with his
superior, Lieutenant-General Sir George Prevost, governor-general and commander-in-chief of British North America. The government in London had recently issued instructions to Prevost on how it wished him to use the reinforcements being sent across the Atlantic. For some time, the British cabinet had
been pondering the best way to bring the war in North America to a successful
conclusion and had informed Prevost that, with the reinforcements being sent
across the Atlantic, "the Canadas will not only be protected for the time against
any attack which the enemy may have the means of making," but he would also
be able to commence limited offensive operations against the American naval
bases at Plattsburgh and Sackets Harbor.[27] This being the case Prevost admitted
to Drummond that, while future moves "must depend on the success of your
operation" on the Niagara, he should not lose sight "of the principal object of
the campaign" in Upper Canada, which was "the destruction of Sackett's Harbor."[28] Drummond disagreed – he believed his objective was "the defeat and
expulsion of the enemy's force which has taken post at Fort Erie, and to this
object my sole attention must be given."[29]

Whether the primary objective was Fort Erie or Sackets Harbor, Prevost and
Drummond needed the assistance of the Royal Navy. That meant dealing with
Commodore Sir James Lucas Yeo, the naval commander on the Great Lakes,
and Yeo could be a problem. The son of a naval victualling agent, James Yeo
had joined the navy in 1792 as a 10-year-old midshipman and made remarkable
progress up the ranks, becoming an acting lieutenant at age 14 and first officer
of a frigate at 23. In 1805 he was promoted commander and given his first vessel, the 22-gun corvette HMS *Confiance*, which he had helped capture. By 1812

Commodore James Lucas Yeo, RN (1782-1818).
A successful young frigate captain who was given command on the Great Lakes because he just happened to be available, Yeo never understood that his primary task was to assist the army, not fight a separate war on the water. His reluctance to supply the army was a source of much annoyance to Drummond and Prevost. (Toronto Reference Library, T-15241)

Yeo was a captain with a Portuguese knight-hood but his career suffered a minor setback in November of that year when he lost the 32-gun frigate HMS *Southampton* in a wreck in the Bahamas after he had captured the brig USS *Vixen*. Yeo survived both the wreck and the court-martial that followed and in the spring of 1813 he was sent to the Great Lakes with the officers and ship's company of the *Southampton* when the Royal Navy took over the inland squadrons from the Provincial Marine.

Yeo was not chosen for this assignment because he had any special quali-ties deemed necessary for command on the inland seas but simply because he and his men happened to be available. The Admiralty, the Royal Navy's headquarters in London, instructed Yeo to cooperate "cordially" with Prevost and to report regularly. In fact Yeo did neither. He arrived in Kingston with 450 officers and seamen in May 1813 and within days saw his first action dur-ing the attack on Sackets Harbor, which took place on the 29th of that month. Throughout the following summer, Yeo duelled with Chauncey for control of Lake Ontario but also began to demonstrate two traits that spelled trouble for combined army–navy operations. First, after an aggressive start to his com-mand, Yeo became cautious, very cautious, and disliked seeking action unless he felt he had a clear superiority in ships and guns. As he explained to one of his subordinates,

> if he had his command on the high seas, he would risk an action at all haz-ards, because, should he be beatten, it would be but the loss of his squad-ron, but to lose it in this lake [Ontario], would involve the embarrassment, if not the discomfiture of the Western division of the army, whose depen-dence was on keeping open the channel of communication – so high a responsibility resting upon him he had to act with the more caution and prudence.[30]

These were laudable sentiments but, as we shall see, Yeo did not entirely live up to them. Indeed, he rarely reported on his actions and regarded requests or, in some cases, orders from Prevost as mere suggestions. In October 1813 he disobeyed a direct order from the commander-in-chief to station his squadron to prevent the American army under Major-General James Wilkinson, which had embarked on an armada of more than 300 boats, from entering the St. Lawrence, and the result was that the American army slipped down the river. In essence, Yeo was a frigate captain and he behaved like one, displaying an independent attitude toward higher authority and a touchy sensitivity about his independence. These were qualities necessary for frigate command but not for a senior naval command position that required inter-service cooperation. This did not bode well for the future.[31]

Drummond, of course, had more immediate concerns. On 28 July he dispatched John Norton, the Mohawk war chief, with a small band of warriors and a troop of the 19th Light Dragoons south along the Portage Road* to regain contact with the Americans. During the morning of 29 July, this detachment swam the Chippawa River as the bridge had been burned by the retreating enemy. Continuing south on the River Road, Norton shortly encountered two American officers escorted by some dragoons under a flag of truce, carrying letters from Brown to Drummond. Norton detained this party as he did not want them proceeding farther and gaining knowledge of British forces and movements. The Americans struck up a conversation, trying through "the Medium of Questions apparently indifferent," to "discover the position held by the General & the Main Body of the army" but Norton and his companions "left them in uncertainty." Seeing that it was useless, one of the Americans changed subjects and, referring to the recent battle, remarked that the conduct "there displayed on the part of the British Army certainly entitled every officer present to be knighted." Norton's reply was that "they were all benighted" – a reference to the fact that Lundy's Lane was partly fought in the dark. Accepting their letters, Norton sent the Americans back to Fort Erie.[32]

On the following day, 30 July, Norton was joined by a couple of companies of the Glengarry Light Infantry, with the main body of that unit taking post a few miles to the rear. That same day the 1st and 103rd Regiments of Foot advanced to Chippawa and over the next few days other elements began to move south. On that same day, Major-General Henry Conran arrived to assume command

---

* The road which ran along the Canadian bank of the Niagara River from Newark on Lake Ontario to Fort Erie on Lake Erie was known as the River Road from Newark to Queenston and from Chippawa to Fort Erie. The centre section from Queenston to Chippawa, which skirted the falls of Niagara and the gorge it had created, was called the Portage Road.

John Norton or the Snipe. Half Scot, half Cherokee, and one of the most effective aboriginal leaders on the British side during the war, Norton was an independent-minded man who often clashed with the white officers of the Indian Department. He fought throughout the 1814 Niagara campaign and left a fine memoir of his experiences. (Portrait by Thomas Philips, reproduced by permission of the Duke of Northumberland)

of the division in place of Major-General Phineas Riall, who had been captured at Lundy's Lane, and Drummond was particularly glad to see this veteran of thirty-three years service who would relieve him of a considerable burden. Also welcome was news of the approach of De Watteville's Regiment, a Swiss mercenary unit in British service with a strength of more than a thousand all ranks.[33]

Drummond decided it was now time for a general advance. First, he reorganized the Right Division into four smaller formations: an advance demi-brigade of light infantry under Lieutenant-Colonel William Drummond of the 104th Foot, the 1st Brigade under Colonel Hercules Scott of the 103rd Foot, the 2nd Brigade under Lieutenant-Colonel Viktor Fischer of De Watteville's Regiment and a reserve under Colonel John Tucker of the 41st Foot. The artillery, under the command of Major Henry Phillot, RA, consisted of eight pieces of ordnance and a Royal Marine Artillery rocket detachment.

This step completed, Drummond issued a general order containing precise instructions on how the Right Division was to behave in battle. He admonished the division against "firing without orders," which was "the greatest proof of indiscipline Troops can be guilty of"; insisted it avoid "a profound expenditure" of ammunition; and cautioned that "there be no Noise or inattention to the Word of Command." Drummond stressed that any charge "will not only be Executed with perfect regularity, but also with profound Silence" avoiding "Screams and Shouts" as British "discipline and intrepidity do not require such paltry aid."[34] He concluded with the exhortation that "Coolness on the part of the Officers, Steadiness and regularity in the formation, movements and firings on the part of the Troops – Precision on the part of the Artillery – are the qualities which the Lieut. General Confidently Expects to be displayed."[35] With this sermon ringing in their ears, on 1 August 1814 the Right Division, now about 3,500 strong, moved to Palmer's house, six miles north of Fort Erie.,

Drummond had been receiving regular reports from Norton, who had scouted the American position, and knew his opponent had constructed an entrenched camp adjoining the stone fort. He decided that if he could destroy the American supply depots at Black Rock and Buffalo, the enemy at Fort Erie would be compelled "either to come out and fight or to surrender."[36] Toward this end, he ordered Colonel John Tucker to take a picked force across the Niagara. He stressed the importance of the mission, which, if successful, would cause the Americans at Fort Erie to not only "be reduced to the necessity of fighting under desperate circumstances or surrendering unconditionally" but might also "lead immediately to the re-establishment of our naval ascendancy on Lake Erie."[37]

It was an assignment that required a competent officer to lead it but unfortunately Colonel John Goulston Price Tucker of the 41st Foot was not that man. A native of Bermuda, the 39-year-old Tucker had seen some action in South Africa and South America early in his career but had only commanded a garrison battalion and had been on half pay for four years before he was appointed to the 41st Foot in 1814. He had gained some attention for his defence of the forts at the mouth of the Niagara in July but his reputation in the Right Division was not very high. Soldier's nicknames for senior officers are often very telling and Tucker was known as "Brigadier Shindy." "Shindy" was a period slang word that had two meanings, either a "dance, party or spree," or a "row, uproar or fight" – neither of which was very flattering as the inference was that Tucker was more than a little flighty (i.e., a "dancing master") and prone to quarrellng about trifles. The division actually possessed two fine light infantry commanders who were well qualified to lead the attack on Buffalo and Black Rock: Colonel Thomas Pearson and Lieutenant-Colonel William Drummond. Both had excellent combat records – indeed Pearson was a veteran of Wellington's army who had fought at Crysler's Farm, Chippawa and Lundy's Lane – but both, unfortunately, were junior to Tucker. Tucker was given the command because he was the most senior officer who could be spared and because half of the force assigned to the operations was from Tucker's own 41st Foot.

Drummond gave Tucker the two flank companies and four battalion companies of that unit,* the flank companies of the 104th, the light companies of the 89th and 100th, and a detachment of the Royal Artillery – a total of about

---

* In 1814, a British infantry battalion usually consisted of ten companies: eight centre or battalion companies and two flank companies. The latter were the light and grenadier companies which were positioned on the left and right flanks, respectively, when the battalion was formed in line. The grenadier company, supposedly consisting of the most experienced and biggest men in the battalion was the shock or assault company. The light company, supposedly consisting of the most intelligent and agile men, constituted the battalion's integral skirmishing capability and usually formed the advance guard when the unit was moving forward and the rear guard when it was withdrawing.

600 men. He ordered him to embark his command under cover of darkness at 10 P.M. on 1 August and cross the river, but to wait on the American side until it was almost daylight before moving toward his objectives.

Lieutenant John Le Couteur of the 104th Foot recalled that his unit only received their orders at the ferry station late in the morning of 2 August. The 104th had spent "a wretched, wet night, rain & thunder" during which a cow "breaking over a fence was construed into Jonathan upon our right flank and the division had to turn out under arms" until 5 A.M.[38] After nightfall, when Le Couteur and his comrades clambered onto a flotilla of small boats near the mouth of Frenchman's Creek, they had hopes "of making lots of prize money, *plunder* etc." They were somewhat puzzled, however, when after landing on the American side just below Squaw Island and a few miles from Black Rock, Tucker halted and did not move. About an hour before daylight, he ordered an advance south toward Black Rock but Le Couteur was again puzzled when the column moved "*without an* advanced guard or any apparent precaution." Somewhat concerned, he raised the matter with his own commanding officer, Lieutenant-Colonel William Drummond, who replied that "it was no business of his" – the Brigadier "might please himself."[39]

Tucker had already lost the element of surprise. American sentries had spotted his force crossing the river. Even worse, waiting for him on the New York side was a very competent soldier – Major Lodowick Morgan of the First United States Rifle Regiment. Known in the regular American army as "Little Morgan" because of his short stature, this Maryland native was a prewar regular who had served as a rifle officer for six years. Morgan had just arrived on the Niagara with a small battalion of riflemen, 240 strong but mostly recruits. Observing the British moving up the Canadian side of the river during the afternoon of 2 August, and suspecting that they might raid the American side, he had moved his command to Conjocta Creek,* about two miles north of Black Rock, and ordered his men to remove the flooring from the bridge and construct a simple breastwork on the south bank of the waterway. Then, he waited.

It was a clear night with no moon but enough starlight for the riflemen to discern motion and around 4.15 A.M. on 2 August Morgan observed a column approaching from the north. It was now that Tucker's decision not to use an advance guard produced a dire result. Morgan waited until Tucker's force "had got within good rifle distance," then blew his whistle and his men "opened

---

* Now known as Scajacuada Creek but in the early 19th century known variously as Conjocta, Conguichity, Conkuighty, Kenjockety, Shogeoquady or the unthinkable Skeutyoghkwati Creek – among other names. I have chosen to use Conjocta ("kon-jock-ta") because it is the easiest to pronounce and because that is what the intrepid Major Lodowick Morgan called it – and he should know since he defended it.

Lieutenant John Couteur (1794-1875). A teenage officer in the 104th Foot, Le Couteur fought in the Niagara in 1814 and left a very entertaining and readable memoir of his experiences. (Portrait, c. 1812, courtesy of the Société Jersiaise, Jersey)

a heavy fire on them, which laid a good number of them on the ground and compelled them to retire."[40] Morgan was using understatement: another American rifle officer remembered that this initial volley, "deliberate and unerring, from every rifle," completely "decapitated" the head of the approaching column."[41] Private Shadrach Byfield of the 41st Foot, who was in that column, remembered it somewhat differently; he recalled that, when they came under fire, his comrades continued to advance, "thinking to charge" only to discover "that the bridge was gone" and "instantly retreated."[42]

In fact, the six companies of the 41st Foot, which were the lead element of Tucker's force, let off a ragged volley of musketry, then broke and ran for the rear. The next few minutes were somewhat chaotic. Le Couteur, whose company of the 104th Foot was immediately behind the 41st, remembered that "the men in our front of another corps began firing in a shameful style and ran past us."[43] To prevent his men being swept away in the panic, Le Couteur ordered them to come "to the charge," to present their bayonets "to keep the others off," and the troops behind him did the same. The fleeing men sought cover in the woods and it took some time for Tucker to get them under control and re-formed. When he did, he deployed his entire command into line and advanced within musket shot of the creek, where he engaged in an exchange of fire with the Americans.

This is the most puzzling aspect of the action. Morgan's men were most likely armed with the 1803 Harper's Ferry rifle, the first rifle to be designed and produced for the United States Army. It was accurate out to a range of 150 yards and, in the hands of an expert marksman, perhaps out to 200 yards. Most of Tucker's troops were armed with the standard India Pattern .75 calibre smoothbore musket, accurate – on a good day – perhaps to 100 yards. The advantage of the rifle was its range and accuracy; the advantage of the musket was its ease of loading and higher rate of fire.

Unfortunately for the men under Tucker's command, he opted to engage in a fire fight with better-armed opponents who enjoyed a clear advantage in weaponry. When his line emerged from the protection of the trees, Morgan's men began to drop their opponents with aimed fire while the British returned it with wildly inaccurate musketry. The result, Le Couteur angrily commented, was that the Americans "shot every Fool that came near the Bridge." One of those hit was Private Byfield who

> received a musket ball, through my left arm, below the elbow. I went into the rear. One of my comrades, seeing that I was badly wounded, cut my [cross] belts from me and let them drop. I walked to the doctor, and desired him to take my arm off. He said it might be cured without it; and ordered me down to a boat, saying, that the wounded men were to cross the river, and they (the doctors) would soon follow.[44]

Although Morgan believed that his opponent was attempting, by forming line, to outflank him and ford the creek upstream, it appears that Tucker never even contemplated such a move. This was unfortunate because, as John Norton commented, the Conjocta was "fordable at less than a Mile above the Bridge" where it was "an ordinary Brook, which the Droughts of Summer had rendered yet more inconsiderable."[45] Unfortunately, Norton was not with Tucker, who continued the costly duel for nearly an hour, before withdrawing to his boats and returning to the Canadian side of the Niagara. The result of this miserable little affair was that "Brigadier Shindy" lost 12 killed, 17 wounded and 4 missing – mercifully few, all things considered – while Morgan lost 2 killed and 8 wounded. Many of the men who had fought that day were bitter about Shindy's wretched handling of the business – John Le Couteur attributed the failure to Tucker's "total want of military command."[46]

In attempting to rationalize his defeat, Tucker resorted to the last refuge of the incompetent commander – he blamed it on his men. He reported to Drummond that

> it becomes a painful but very necessary duty to apprise you that the men displayed an unpardonable degree of unsteadiness, without possessing one solitary excuse to justify this want of discipline. The officers were perfectly unaware of the sudden impulse of panic which threw their men into a tremendous confusion; their exertions and spirit, however, succeeded in re-forming our column, and I am happy to express my approbation of their conduct.[47]

Tucker did not elaborate on what caused "the sudden impulse of panic," which was concentrated, aimed rifle fire, and indeed there is no evidence that Tucker even realized the type of enemy force he had fought.

Drummond was furious about the defeat. On 5 August he issued a strongly-worded general order blaming the defeat at Conjocta Creek on "the misbehaviour of the troops employed" and, although he did not specify the unit, there is no doubt that he meant the 41st Foot, which had broken during the action. He reminded the officers of that regiment that it was their duty "to punish with death on the spot any man who may be found guilty of misbehavior before the enemy."[48] Furthermore, Drummond warned that "Crouching, ducking, or laying down when advancing under fire are bad habits, and must be corrected."

This very severe (and rather unfair) order resulted from Drummond's anger over the failure of an operation which he had hoped would spare him the effort of having to mount a formal attack on the American position at Fort Erie. Now, as he complained to Prevost,the "enemy having been put on his guard" by the raid, any future move against the American side of the Niagara would have "to be made in considerable force."[49] Not only was that true but – although Drummond could not have been aware of it – his opponents took the precaution of removing the supplies from Black Rock and Buffalo to a point farther west along the shore of Lake Erie, where they could be transferred by boat across to Fort Erie.[50] A few days later, Drummond sent Tucker and his miscreant 41st Foot back to Fort George, retaining only the unit's two elite flank companies with the division.

Following the setback at Conjocta, Drummond wasted no time in assessing just what he faced at Fort Erie. After two nearly sleepless nights, Le Couteur and his comrades in the advance demi-brigade were surprised when, instead of being given a rest after returning from Tucker's expedition in the afternoon of

Conjocta Creek. Unfortunately the site of the battle has become a post-industrial wasteland. (Author's photo)

Lieutenant-General George Prevost (1767-1816). A skilled administrator and a professional soldier, Prevost had the unenviable appointment of governor-general and commander-in-chief during the War of 1812. He held the line with minimal forces for two years but was ordered to go on the offensive when reinforcements finally arrived from Europe. (Courtesy, Château Ramezay Museum, Montreal)

3 August, they were "pushed on, at 4 o'clock, to within a thousand yards" of the American position so that Drummond could make a detailed examination of the defences. The Americans "complimented" the brigade with "some rounds of shot & grape to make us take care of ourselves in a reconnaissance lasting about an hour."[51]

The British commander did not like what he saw. Using the week-long respite they had been granted, his opponents had been very busy. The stone fort had been visibly strengthened and entrenchments had been constructed from it, both to the lake and to the Snake Hill battery. Part of this line was protected by abattis and the entire position, which was about 30 acres in extent, was surrounded by an open area that had been cleared of vegetation out to a distance of some 300–400 yards. Eighteen pieces of artillery were positioned along the defences while the best possible British artillery sites were enfiladed by batteries across the river at Black Rock and by three USN schooners anchored in Lake Erie. Secure behind their entrenchments, the Americans held all the cards. They could easily be supplied and reinforced by water from Buffalo while Drummond's supply line stretched back forty miles to the mouth of the Niagara and thence across Lake Ontario to Kingston. To assault any part of the perimeter except the northern end, the British faced a long and tedious approach march through woods and swamps, while the defenders could easily reinforce any threatened sector.

Having examined it closely, Lieutenant John Le Couteur of the 104th summed up the American position at Fort Erie as "an ugly Customer."[52]

Riflemen, United States Army, full dress. This illustration depicts regular American riflemen in their regulation green uniforms, although they were actually more likely to wear linen frocks. The rifle regiments of the U.S. Army were among its best units. (Painting by H. C. McBarron, courtesy of the Company of Military Historians)

CHAPTER TWO

"Steady my lads, not a shot till I tell you to fire"

FORT ERIE, 3–13 AUGUST 1814

"Who'll serve the King? cried the sergeant aloud.
Roll went the drum and the fife played sweetly.
"Here, master sergeant," said I from the crowd,
"Is a lad who will answer your purpose completely.
My father was a corporal and well he knew his trade,
Of women, wine and gunpowder he never was afraid,
He'd march, fight, left, right,
Front rank, centre rank,
Storm the trenches, court the wenches,
Love the rattle of a battle,
Dies with glory, lives in story.
He always said a soldier's life, if taken smooth or rough
Is a very merry, hey down derry sort of life enough,
Is a very merry, hey down derry sort of life enough."[1]

The military operation conducted by the British Right Division against the American Left Division at Fort Erie in August and September 1814 is commonly but incorrectly called a "siege." In the early 19th century, the term "siege" was generally taken to mean an undertaking in which an army invested a fortified place, isolated it from outside assistance, and then gradually weakened its defences by bombardment or other means to a point where it could make a successful assault without suffering undue losses. "A siege," noted a British engineer officer who participated in several of them, "is one of the most arduous undertakings on which troops can be employed," an operation "in which fatigue, hardships, and personal risk" are great and "in which the prize can only be gained by complete victory, and where failure is usually attended with severe loss or dire disaster."[2] A successful besieger usually needed between two and three times the manpower of the defender, a superiority in artillery and ammunition, and a useful inventory of specialized tools and implements.

This was not the case at Fort Erie in 1814. Lieutenant-General Gordon Drummond was unable to invest and isolate the defenders – indeed the best he could do was deploy on the northern end of the American position and try to cover the remainder with patrols and pickets. The Right Division possessed no great superiority in numbers over its opponent, was actually inferior in artillery, particularly heavy artillery, and lacked many of the basic tools needed to successfully carry out positional warfare. Finally, it was operating at the end of a lengthy supply line while its American opponent was able to receive supplies and reinforcements with comparative ease from across the Niagara River. The so-called "siege" of Fort Erie was actually an attempt to reduce an entrenched bridgehead and, since withdrawal was out of the question, Drummond's only option was to bring up artillery and bombard the enemy in the hopes of compelling him "to surrender, or attempt a sortie which can only terminate in his defeat."[3]

Up to this time the British army had never been particularly successful at siege warfare. Unlike European nations which used fortresses to defend their land borders and devoted much time, energy and finances to constructing them, the first line of defence for the island nation of Britain was always her superb navy. The British army therefore had much less experience with siege warfare than its European counterparts and, indeed, had only undertaken three large formal sieges during the 18th century: Louisbourg in 1758, Belle Isle in 1759 and Havana in 1762. Possessing the means to transport heavy ordnance and ammunition by sea, Britain often preferred to force the surrender of a fortified place or city by bombardment. This was the case at Copenhagen in 1807, where the Royal Artillery used 72 guns, howitzers and mortars to carry out a three-day bombardment which killed 2,000 civilians and nearly destroyed the city, and at Fort Desaix in Martinique in 1809, which surrendered after British gunners, manning 42 pieces of artillery, nearly levelled it with 14,000 roundshot and shells.[4]

Another weakness of the British army was that the Royal Engineers consisted only of officers and there were no units of specialized soldiers trained for siege warfare. Although they were paid extra for this very hazardous work, British soldiers disliked being used in this capacity as they regarded the heavy and dirty physical labour as demeaning. There was a corps of Royal Military Artificers but it was mainly concerned with the construction and repair of fortifications and military buildings. In 1811 a step was made in the right direction when this corps was renamed the Royal Sappers and Miners, and several companies were organized for field service, with the express purpose of siege work.

But there were never enough engineers or sappers and the sieges conducted by Wellington in Portugal and Spain did not constitute the brightest chapter in the record of the Peninsular army. Only too often, raw courage had to take the place of missing expertise and equipment. William Napier, not only a veteran of the Peninsular campaign but also one of its historians, summed up a lamentable situation:

When the first serious siege was undertaken by the British army, to the discredit of the English government, no army was ever so ill-provided with the means of promoting such an enterprise. The engineer officers were zealous; and many of them were well versed in the theory of their business. But the ablest trembled when reflecting on their utter destitution of all that belonged to real service. Without a corps of sappers and miners to carry on an approach under fire, they were compelled to attack fortresses defended by the most warlike, practised and scientific troops of the age. The best officers and private soldiers were obliged to sacrifice themselves, in a lamentable manner, to compensate for the negligence and incapacity of a government always ready to plunge the nation into war, without the slightest care of what was necessary to obtain success. The sieges carried on by the British in Spain were a succession of butcheries; because the commonest materials, and the means necessary to their art, were denied the engineers.[5]

A case very much in point is the April 1812 assault on Badajoz, a strongly-fortified Spanish city which had already successfully withstood two previous British sieges. Wellington finally took it by assault during the night of 6 April at the cost of 3,600 killed and wounded, but was saddened by the heavy casualties. "The capture of Badajoz," he commented in a lengthy letter to Lord Liverpool, the British prime minister,

affords as strong an instance of the gallantry of our troops as has ever been displayed. But I anxiously hope that I shall never again be the instrument of putting them to such a test as that to which they were put last night. I assure your lordship that it is quite impossible to carry fortified places by "*vive force*" [raw force] without incurring great loss, and being exposed to the chance of failure, unless the army should be provided with a sufficient trained corps of sappers and miners. ...... These great losses could be avoided, and, in my opinion, time gained in every siege, if we had properly trained people to carry it on.[6]

Unfortunately matters had not improved much when Drummond arrived before Fort Erie in August 1814. While the greater war in Europe was still in progress, North America was not high on the priority list for anything, including personnel, and one officer complained that it "got the rubbish of every department in the army" because any man whom Wellington "deemed unfit for the Peninsula was considered as quite good enough for the Canadian market, and in nothing was this more conspicuous than in our Engineer Department."[7] In fact, the engineering component of the Right Division consisted of just two officers, Captain Samuel Romilly and Lieutenant George Philpotts, RE, and an acting corporal and five privates of the Royal Sappers and Miners, equipped with a total of 120 entrenching tools, twenty felling axes and 200 sand bags. "This was everything we had," Philpotts recorded in August 1814, "to enable us to commence our operations, so that during the whole of the attack, we were constantly in want of entrenching tools and felling axes."[8] Nonetheless, the two officers got down to business quickly, choosing a site for an artillery battery on 3 August and then supervising the manufacture of fascines – bundles of tightly-wrapped branches between 6 and 12 feet long – which would be used to shore up the earthen walls of the battery to protect the guns from the defenders' fire.

The chosen battery site was in the woods about 1,100 yards to the north of the stone fort, and to provide cover the trees between it and its target were left uncut until it was finished. This site was conveniently close to a ravine running into the Niagara, which was transformed into a trench for the infantry who would protect the fatigue parties labouring on the battery. The preliminary work was completed by the night of 5 August and the two engineers next supervised the building of the embrasures, or openings for the guns, which were the most vulnerable part of a battery and had to be carefully and strongly constructed. This step took two days to finish, and Romilly and Philpotts then commenced working on an epaulement* to protect the guns from the American battery at Black Rock and also extending the infantry entrenchment to the right of the battery. A shortage of tools limited the size of the working parties, who were detailed from the infantry units, and this slowed progress although work went on night and day. It was not long before the noise of the construction alerted the defenders to what was happening and they began to fire into the wood, albeit blindly, from the stone fort, Black Rock and the three naval schooners on the lake.

Romilly and Philpotts got some additional help when Lieutenant John Le Couteur of the 104th Foot was temporarily assigned to them as an engineer. Le Couteur was a graduate of the Royal Military College at Marlow – a rare thing in the British army – and had studied field fortification at that institution. Always energetic, the 19-year-old went to work with gusto as he recorded in his journal:

---

* An epaulement is a temporary defence work erected to cover infantry or artillery positions. It was usually about chest high and constructed of earth or sandbags.

4 August [1814]

Appointed an Acting Engineer till some Engineer Sub[altern] comes up. ...... Col[onel]. Harvey gave me carte blanche as to the numbers of men [to be put to work] ...... – thus I had a Gun mounted in the day behind a half-moon battery.

6 August

Constructed the front of a two-gun battery within one thousand yards of Fort Erie last night as the first breaching battery – a mortar, one 18 and one 24-Pdr. [gun] [to be] mounted. ......

The enemy got our range and the shot came plunking into our battery pretty hotly.

7 August

Sunday. Up till ten last night, hard at work making fascines a mile off and taking them to the battery. At work again before daylight – it rained so hard that we were wet through nearly all night. Completed two embrasures of the battery by 12 o'clock. Several shots from the Schooners fell about us, but without effect.

8 August

Philpotts kept me at work. From 6 till 3 in the morning hard at it. Came to camp thoroughly fagged & slept till ½ past seven. Down at the battery from nine till five. The Schooners fired at us the whole day long.[9]

Le Couteur's temporary duty as an engineer came to end on 8 August when, without consulting either Philpotts or Romilly, he constructed an epaulement to guard the working parties from the fire of the American artillery at Black Rock across the river. As he tells the story, when Philpotts

saw what had been done, He got into a violent passion and wanted me to take it down again, which I declared I would not certainly do as He chose to be absent all day and the Field Officer of the day could testify how many lives it must have saved. I had made it about seven feet high and eighteen feet thick, a secure work which covered the very rear of the Battery. We had such high words that I said I would no longer serve under his orders and the next day I rejoined [my] company [of the 104th Foot].

After he cooled down, the young Jerseyman – who was perpetually short of money – regretted his hasty decision as his temporary assignment had brought him "Ten shillings a day extra, two horses and a Guinea a week lodging money ...... £400 a year lost!" Drummond replaced him with another junior officer but informed Le Couteur that he was displeased with his conduct because a young officer "may be blamed unjustly and must bear it."[10] Such is life in the service.

While working parties, protected by pickets, laboured on the battery and entrenchments, the remainder of the army camped about a mile and a half to the
northwest, almost on the site of the present Fort Erie racetrack. As there were
no tents available, the soldiers built huts for shelter. According to Surgeon William Dunlop of the 89th Foot, the best shelters were constructed by the men of
the Canadian units, experienced woodsmen who "erected shanties, far superior,
in warmth, tightness and comfort, to any canvas tent." The only unit that could
equal them was De Watteville's Regiment, which was recruited from

> all the nations of Europe, but all of them had served in the armies of Napo-
> leon, and all of them had there learned how to make the best of a bad bar-
> gain. These, though they had not the skill in the axe inherent in their breth-
> ren of the Militia, took down hemlock boughs (a species of the pine, "*pinus
> canadensis*,") and cutting off the tails of them, made thatched wigwams, per-
> fectly weatherproof; and though they could not equal the Canadian Militia
> in *woodcraft*, they greatly excelled them in gastronomic lore; and thus, while
> our fellows had no better shift than to frizzle [fry] their rations of salt pro-
> visions on the ends of their ramrods, these being practical botanists, sent
> out one soldier from each mess, who gathered a haversack full of wild pot
> herbs, with which and a little flour their ration was converted into a capital
> kettle of soup.[11]

Huts – even leaky huts – were needed as between 31 July and 15 August 1814 it
rained on no fewer than six days.*

A couple of miles away, the officers and men of the American Left Division were also working day and night. Like their British counterparts they
were discovering that aching muscles, fatigue, sweat and thirst play a greater
part in a soldier's life than do fear, anger and fighting. They were more fortunate, however, as they had tents to protect them from the rain and received
regular rations from provision boats, which crossed over from Buffalo at night.

On 4 August there was much relief in the division when Brigadier-General
Edmund Gaines arrived and assumed command.[12] A native of Virginia, the
37-year-old Gaines had first been commissioned in 1799 and had spent much
of his prewar service on the western frontier. He had taken a leave of absence
to practise law in 1811 but had returned to the army the following year. Gaines
had campaigned in the northwest and then served in Major-General James

* See Appendix G for data on the weather at Fort Erie

Brigadier-General E. P. Gaines (1777-1849). A tough if somewhat bombastic officer, Gaines assumed command at Fort Erie on Brown's orders, replacing the ineffectual Ripley. He lifted the morale of the Left Division and efficiently prepared his position for a British attack. (From Benson Lossing, *Pictorial Field-Book of the War of 1812*)

Wilkinson's army, where he had commanded the Twenty-Fifth Infantry at the battle of Crysler's Farm in November 1813. Promoted brigadier-general in March 1814, Gaines had raised some eyebrows when he told a congressional inquiry that the army's rations should be improved as bad food was killing more men than enemy action. Perhaps because of his legal background, Gaines tended to write bombastic orders in orotund prose and this was evident in the first order he issued to the Left Division when he directed that the firing of an artillery piece would be

> the signal of every man to be at his post, ready for action. No man is to fire until he receives the order of his Commanding Officer – when he will be careful to make his shot tell and the General persuades himself that the gallant Corps he has the honor to command will make the enemy recollect the *Scenes* of Chippawa and the *falls* of *Niagara*, where this army has covered itself, with imperishable Glory, and secured the approbation of the Grateful Country.[13]

But Gaines was also a tough and seasoned professional with an excellent combat record.[14] Although he reported the Left Division to be "in good spirits and more healthy than I could have expected," he was concerned about the situation at Fort Erie. As he put it, "there seemed to exist no reasonable prospect of effecting any thing beyond mere self preservation, and even this required a combination of the skill, vigilance and valor of every officer and man."[15] Nonetheless, Gaines moved quickly to take the reins of command. He tightened discipline and insisted on proper camp police (or sanitation precautions). When New York militia units in Buffalo complained about having to labour on fortifications, he was quick to point out that they were required to do so under the articles of war and threatened to court martial any miscreants. His command style differed completely from that of the rather diffident Ripley and it should come as no surprise that the first thing Ripley did after Gaines's arrival was to request a furlough for two months. Gaines passed the request along to Brown, who refused it.[16]

Buffalo from Fort Erie. This photograph, taken by the author from the site of the stone fort, shows the proximity of the modern city. The defenders drew their supplies from Buffalo, just across the lake, while the attackers were forced to use a long, tortuous and threatened supply line 250 miles long.

For his part, Brown's opinion of Ripley had steadily grown worse. When Secretary of War John Armstrong commented that Ripley would probably demand a court of inquiry because of the criticism levelled at him in Brown's official report on the battle of Lundy's Lane, Brown's reply was blunt. If Ripley did that, Brown stated, he "will be ruined" and added that he "had been greatly embarrassed by the movements of this Officer upon more than one occasion" and Ripley was "one of the few men in whom I have been disappointed."[17]

Brown was much happier with Brigadier Peter B. Porter, an officer he regarded as "brave and efficient" and who, in the "midst of the greatest danger I have found his mind cool and collected, and his judgement to be relied upon."[18] Brown was anxious that Porter's volunteer brigade be reinforced and, now that Gaines had arrived, he planned to tour the western counties of New York to raise volunteers from the state militia to fight in Canada. As he explained to Governor Daniel D. Tompkins, the people of New York must not "attempt to shrink from the war in which they are engaged," because "if they do not arm and exert themselves at a distance from their farms they will soon find the war brought to their firesides."[19]

The arrival of Gaines was not the only piece of good news for Brown – on 4 August he learned of the long overdue appearance of Commodore Isaac Chauncey's squadron off the mouth of the Niagara River. He had expected Chauncey three weeks before, but when the naval officer did not show up, Brown had withdrawn south to Chippawa, setting off the train of events that had eventually culminated in the battle of Lundy's Lane. Chauncey had not sailed from his base at Sackets Harbor because he was ill and refused to let one of his subordinates take command of the Lake Ontario squadron. He did

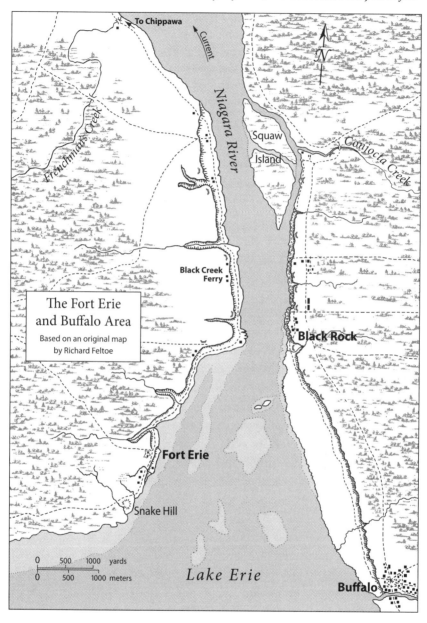

The Fort Erie
and Buffalo Area

Based on an original map
by Richard Feltoe

To Chippawa

Current

Niagara River

Squaw
Island

Conjocta Creek

Frenchman's Creek

Black Creek
Ferry

Black Rock

N

Fort Erie

Snake Hill

0   500   1000   yards
0   500   1000   meters

Lake Erie

Buffalo

not explain this decision, either to his subordinates, to Brown or to Secretary of the Navy William Jones. "I am not able to ascertain certainly why it has not sailed before," an army officer stationed at Sackets Harbor commented about the squadron, and there seemed to "be some mystery about it" although Chauncey's own officers "have, some of them, spoken freely on the subject."[20] Secretary Jones, becoming exasperated, ordered Commodore Stephen Decatur

Commodore Isaac Chauncey, USN, (1779-1840). Yeo's counterpart on Lake Ontario, Chauncey also felt that gaining naval superiority was the main object of the war, not assisting the army in taking objectives set down by the government. He was nearly removed from his command by the secretary of the navy in 1814. (Toronto Reference Library, T-15206)

to proceed to Sackets Harbor to replace Chauncey but later changed his mind. Having just commissioned a new large warship, the 58-gun frigate USS *Superior*, Chauncey's squadron was now more powerful than that of his British rival, Commodore James Lucas Yeo, who tactfully withdrew into his base at Kingston until he could commission a larger ship.

Chauncey's arrival set off a testy exchange of letters with Brown, who hinted to the naval officer that the commodore had disobeyed his orders by not cooperating with the army. This drew the retort from Chauncey that his squadron had been created to fight the British squadron on Lake Ontario and he would not be "diverted in my efforts to effectuate it by any Sinister attempt to render us subordinate to or an appendage of the Army."[21] Brown's response was equally curt – he pointed out that the squadron was not Chauncey's "private property" but that "of the Nation, subject to the orders of the Government," and the government had ordered Chauncey to support the army.[22]

For Lieutenant-General Gordon Drummond, however, the appearance of Chauncey was a disaster. In July Yeo had assigned Commander Alexander Dobbs, RN, and five small ships to assist in supplying and reinforcing British forces in the Niagara, and Drummond had acknowledged that Dobbs's little flotilla had rendered him "great assistance" and "valuable aid," but with Chauncey on the lake this support ceased.[23] In very short order, Chauncey drove one of Dobbs's vessels, the schooner *Magnet*, aground, where its captain destroyed it, and blockaded the remainder under the protective guns of Forts George and Niagara. Drummond's supply line now stretched back 250 miles to Kingston over very bad roads and, even if the units just arrived from Europe reached him, it would be difficult to feed them. Within ten days of Chauncey's arrival, he reported to Prevost that "the diminution of stores and provisions is beginning to be felt."[24]

Drummond suffered another blow when he was deprived of the services of Major-General Henry Conran. A man who "had gained the esteem and confidence of every officer and man in the army," Conran was forced to leave the division after he fell from his horse and suffered a compound fracture of his leg. Drummond replaced him with Colonel Archibald Stewart of the 1st Foot, but when that officer arrived, he proved to be "so ill as to be unable to leave his bed."[25] Matters were not improved when Colonel Hercules Scott of the 103rd Foot, who commanded one of the small brigades that made up the division, asked for permission "to resign the command of the brigade to which he had been appointed and to serve in command of his regiment, under a *junior* officer."[26] Scott, a twenty-year-veteran who had fought under Wellington in India, was not impressed with Drummond, who he suspected "got his command, like many others, from the interest of friends, not from his own merit."[27] As Drummond "could derive no assistance" from Scott, he requested Prevost to send another general officer to the Niagara as soon as possible.

As if he did not have problems enough, the wound Drummond suffered at Lundy's Lane continued to bother him. His physical state was clear to the men under his command. Lieutenant Joseph Mermet of De Watteville's Regiment noted, that despite the fact that he was "suffering from his wound," Drummond was "always at the advanced posts and visits the batteries, giving orders which one is pleased to execute."[28] John Norton agreed that, although "suffering much from the effects of a severe wound," the British commander "was indefatigable."[29] Those officers closest to Drummond were not as optimistic – on 6 August Drummond's chief of staff, Lieutenant-Colonel John Harvey, informed Major-General Edward Baynes, the adjutant-general of the British army in North America, that his superior's physical condition was not good and his responsibilities were "evidently hurting his constitution & health."[30] But for now, because there was no other choice, Drummond continued in command and very nearly lost the services of Harvey when that officer was wounded in the face by splinters from one of the rounds fired by the schooners on the lake.[31]

The first days of August 1814 witnessed more than the construction of fieldworks and the occasional artillery round sent in the opponent's direction – there was almost daily skirmishing in the "no man's land" between the two armies. Drummond did not have enough strength to completely invest the American position and there were ravines leading from it that provided a convenient hidden way to cross the cleared area between the lines. Gaines's object was to hamper the working parties at the battery site; Drummond's object was to prevent that happening. The result was that, in the first two weeks of August, skirmishing took place almost every other day.[32] On the American side, the troops that carried out this bush warfare were usually detachments from the First and Fourth Rifle Regiments, under the command of Major Lodowick Morgan, who had been brought over the river after their action at Conjocta

Creek. On the British side it was undertaken by the light infantry companies of the line regiments – usually under the command of Lieutenant-Colonel William Drummond of the 104th Foot – the Canadian Glengarry Light Infantry and Incorporated Militia, and the various groups of aboriginal warriors, often led by Norton. Few of those involved in these daily skirmishes liked them because they exacted a constant toll of casualties for seemingly little gain.* As one British officer put it: "though the numbers lost in each of these affairs may seem but trifling, yet the aggregate of men put *hors de combat* in a force so small as ours became very serious in the long run."[33] His complaint was echoed by Lieutenant Jonathan Kearsley of the Fourth United States Rifle Regiment who felt that many "valuable soldiers were killed or wounded" in "this severe and wasting, yet fruitless warfare" and "their loss was the greater and more irreparable" because they were all trained men."[34] As the American riflemen were usually the aggressors, Kearsley blamed Gaines for ordering these actions, which he believed was done to enable Gaines to "issue a daily order on morning parade, which order no doubt reached the newspapers, if not the War Department, setting forth the gallantry of his troops" and demonstrating that he was "not only defending the place but engaged offensively against the enemy."[35]

Surgeon Dunlop recalled that these actions followed a pattern and "generally commenced with some accidental" meeting of sentries and the firing "brought out the piquet, then the brigade on duty, and then, not infrequently, the brigade next for duty" and "on a fair average," the British and Canadians enjoyed "this amusement about three times a week."[36] On the afternoon of 6 August, Morgan's riflemen appeared for the first time and their dress initially confused their opponents. As John Norton remembered:

> I perceived through the foliage of the Woods a number of men in light coloured frocks† coming towards me. At first sight I supposed them to be our Men from the Camp, moving on to our assistance, – and only discovered my Mistake, when the foremost of them pointed their rifles to me, calling out "Stop!" I paid no regard to them, – they fired: – I found the few soldiers stationed hereabouts much confused at being assailed from a different quarter but I soon saw my gallant Friend Lt. Col. Drummond encouraging them to rally. Many of our Warriors came running to our assistance, & we compelled

---

* See Appendix G for data on the rate of skirmishing at Fort Erie.

† A frock was a garment very popular at this time in North America and often worn by American militia and regular units. It was a loose and comfortable jacket, usually made of linen, that buttoned up the front and descended below the waist. It normally had one or more "capes" or additional layers over the shoulders and was often decorated with fringes. Regular riflemen of the U.S. Army frequently died their frocks green.

Surgeon William Dunlop (1792-1848). An army surgeon who preferred to be a combat officer, Dunlop of the 89th Foot fought throughout the siege and left a frank and funny memoir of his experiences. (Archives of Ontario, S. 17142)

them to retire with some Loss; on our side we had a few killed & wounded.[37]

Le Couteur, who participated in this action, remembered it as a "sharp skirmish" in which the riflemen tried to "turn our right but our picquets were well placed" and the enemy "were driven off soon" but with a loss of twenty killed and wounded.[38]

Dunlop was impressed with the warriors serving with the army at Fort Erie, particularly the Sacs from the Northwest, under their war chief, Matauss (or Metoss). The Sacs "were very fine men," he wrote, "few of them under six feet high, and their symmetry perfectly faultless." Matauss himself had such a strong resemblance to King George III that even his men "called the head on the half penny Matauss, and he certainly might have passed for a bronze statue of that worthy and estimable Monarch."[39] There was no doubt that the warriors – particularly those from the Northwest who had good reason to hate Americans – were ferocious. Drummond reported that on 10 August they "surprised, took, and scalped every man of one of the enemy's picquets."[40] Matauss had particular reason to hate the Americans as, during the siege of Fort Meigs in July 1813, his young son who was with him, intrigued by a shell which landed nearby, approached it while its fuze was still burning. Just as he was about to touch it, it exploded, disembowelling him, and he died shortly thereafter.[41]

Drummond also thought highly of the Glengarry Light Infantry and Incorporated Militia. He praised these Canadian units which had "constantly been in close contact with the enemy's outposts and riflemen," during which "their steadiness and gallantry as well as their superiority as light troops have on every occasion been conspicuous."[42] William Dunlop particularly admired the Glengarries, who had a reputation as good marksmen, and the literate Scotsman has left a charming word portrait of the skirmish warfare around Fort Erie in the summer of 1814:

Excepting only a melée of cavalry, a bush skirmish is the only aspect in which modern warfare appears in anything picturesque. Look at all attempts at painting a modern battle, and unless the painter takes such a distance as to render everything distinct, you have nothing but a series of stiff, hard, regular, straight lines, that might represent a mathematical diagram in uniform.

Not so with light infantry in a wood. There a man ceases to be merely a part of a machine, or a point in a long line. Both his personal safety and his efficiency depend on his own knowledge and tact. To stand straight upright and be shot at is no part of his duty; his great object is to annoy the enemy, and keep himself safe ……

Perhaps there can be no military scene more fit for the pencil than a body of light infantry awaiting an attack. The variety of attitude necessary to obtain cover – the breathless silence – the men attentive by eye and ear – every glance (furtively lowered) directed to the point – some kneeling, some lying down, and some standing straight behind a tree – the officer with his silver whistle in his hand, ready to give the signal to commence firing, and the bugle boy looking earnestly in his officer's face waiting for the next order. That is worth painting …. [43]

A large scrap took place on 12 August when Gaines ordered Morgan to send a detachment of eighty riflemen under Captain Benjamin Birdsall to ascertain whether the British were working on a second battery site closer to the fort. Birdsall accomplished his mission but on his return was attacked by a larger British force, and Morgan went to his rescue. Le Couteur, who was on outpost duty that day, has provided a detailed account, not only of the action, but also the accuracy of Morgan's riflemen:

It was about 1 o'clock in the day when [Lieutenant Michael] Considine & I had gone to [Captain George] Shore's picquet to eat, or snatch, our dinners with Him. We heard the drums beat to arms, or the volunteer drums as we called them, in Fort Erie – an ominous sound of preparation for attack. Shore desired us to return to our picquets and place our men in readiness.

The picquet in my charge was placed behind a stout breastwork with a heavy abattis in its front about thirty yards off, it would be a difficult matter to pull it aside, or cut it down under the fire of forty or fifty men. The woods in which we were posted were part of an endless forest marching to the North pole, for ought we knew, some of the trees of the growth of centuries, with their heads in the Clouds.

Some time about three, I heard "bang, bang" far on the right – the well-known sharp ring of the American rifle. I instantly placed my men under cover all along the breastwork and made them place their caps on it away from themselves. I then heard two more shots – then the music began to gather like a girl playing preludes, now it came on, all along the right towards the Captain's picquet. Just then, I saw my poor brother Sub., Considine, supported by a soldier passing by the rear of my picquet badly wounded. "What's the matter my boy?", I ran up. "I got it here, and it came out there", pointing to a wound received over one hip and emerging over the other. "God bless you!" I thought it was all over with him and ran back to my men.

The fire was ragged and closing on me fast past the center, a rifle ball just grazed my whisker as I came up. One of the men said "Mr LC [illegible] yourself or you will be hit." "Steady my lads, not a shot till I tell you to fire – level every man at a rifleman and wait till we see lots of them close to the attack – now my boys!" and a steady roll brought down a lot of them. The riflemen knocked the men's caps over nicely – which greatly amused my men. The enemy made a desperate attempt to turn our flank but after an hour's hard fighting they were driven back with serious loss, leaving many of their dead and rifles along our front.

I did not lose a man. When the men who were on the right advance [illegible], were examined they were found to have met instant death – though both on the alert and in the act of levelling. One was shot over the left arm and in the left eye, the other near the waist and shot through the heart, both their firelocks were cocked and neither trigger pulled. Death had been instantaneous in both cases. Considine went to see what was coming and got the third shot, the fourth missed his Corporal. We lost several men in the other two picquets – my having concealed my men saved them all while our own fire was deadly – they never passed me to get towards that battery – and I got praised. I was glad nevertheless to have got out of the Scrape alive.[44]

Lieutenant Kearsley remembered this particular action as being a costly one, as "Little" Morgan, the victor of Conjocta Creek, was killed. Kearsley was with Morgan and both officers were in advance of a line of riflemen "who were extended and acting independently, that is, each man loading and fir-

Lieutenant Jonathan Kearsley (1786-1859). An officer in the Fourth Rifle Regiment, Kearsley fought at Conjocta Creek and Fort Erie and left a memoir of his wartime experiences. He did not like the constant skirmishing around the fort and was eventually badly wounded in one such action. (Burton Historical Collection, Detroit Public Library)

ing when prepared and upon his object selected."[45] Morgan had just warned Kearsley not "to expose yourself, the enemy have marked us individually and are firing at us," when he was shot in the head and died instantly. Kearsley ordered four men to take Morgan's body back to the American lines but three were wounded and one killed by accurate fire. He then assisted a fifth man to get away the bodies of both Morgan and the dead rifleman, as well as the latter's weapon and those of the three wounded. The riflemen made a practice of taking both their fatal and wounded casualties back to their position so that they were not left to the British warriors, who they believed would mutilate them. Kearsley was particularly annoyed that on 12 August, while the riflemen were engaged against superior numbers, Gaines did not send regular infantry out to support them. Gaines did, however, report Morgan's death in action "after a display of gallantry worthy of the [rifle] corps and meriting the gratitude of his country."[46]

Throughout all this, Romilly and Philpotts, the two Right Division engineers, continued to supervise the construction of the battery. Its completion was delayed by a shortage of tools and the need to construct a protective works to shelter the battery from the fire of the American schooners on the lake and the battery at Black Rock. Major Henry Phillot, RA, Drummond's artillery commander, sited a 24-pdr. gun at a point north of the battery site to deal with these annoyances. His fire was returned by the schooners and Lieutenant Douglass, whose battery between the stone fort and the lake had just been completed.[47] By 11 August Philpotts recorded that the battery

being now nearly completed, the platform laid and the magazine finished, the guns were brought into it. During the night an order was given that it should not open [fire] till the morning of the 13th so that the clearing of the wood in front of it was postponed till the 12th.

The battery was armed with a long 24 Pr. [gun], two brass 24 Prs [guns]. a 24 Pr carronade and 8 inch mortar.[48]

In all, it had taken the engineers nearly nine days to finish the battery and Drummond was not happy. He reported to Prevost his concern that the "enemy has unavoidably had so much time for preparation, and has in his position so considerably a number of heavy guns, that I much fear that we shall find the fire of our battery unable to effect much."[49] Furthermore, he did not approve of the battery site Romilly had chosen and, having "had reason in other respect to be so little satisfied with that officer in the field," sent Romilly away from the division. Philpotts took over as command engineer and was assisted by another Royal Engineer officer, Lieutenant Joseph Portlock, as well as Captain William Barney of the 89th Foot and a Lieutenant Stevens of the Royal Marine Artillery.

There was a constant two-way traffic in deserters. The British recorded seventy from the Left Division during the period from 25 July to 27 August, and American records show that thirty-one British or Canadian soldiers deserted during August 1814, more than half being from the Glengarry Light Infantry. On 8 August Drummond reported that three British soldiers, who had earlier deserted from their units, had now returned to the fold after serving in an American rifle regiment. They were fortunate that Drummond decided to pardon them, as otherwise they would have been executed, because death was the standard British army penalty for traitors who joined the ranks of the enemy.[50]

On 11 August a deserter from De Watteville's Regiment swam the Niagara and brought the interesting information that the British were transporting boats by land around the American position at Fort Erie, for the purpose of capturing the three schooners in the lake. Colonel George McFeely, the commander at Black Rock, immediately sent this intelligence to Gaines. That same day McFeely met Lieutenant Augustus Conckling, USN, captain of the USS *Ohio*, one of the schooners, on the street in Buffalo and warned him of the possibility of a surprise attack. Conckling, McFeely remembered, "scarcely condescended to listen, turned on his heel and said he would desire no better fun than to see twenty or thirty boats coming to take him."[51]

The deserter's information was dead accurate. When Commander Alexander Dobbs's ships were blockaded in the Niagara, he looked around for some useful work for his sailors. An officer who had joined the RN as a midshipman at the age of thirteen and seen service in the Mediterranean and Atlantic before coming to North America, the 30-year-old Dobbs had been promoted commander in February 1814. That same month he married Mary Cartwright, the only daughter of Richard Cartwright of Kingston, one of most prominent mercantile and political figures in Upper Canada. Wedlock did nothing, however, to temper Dobbs's natural aggressiveness and he conceived the idea of "cutting out" or capturing the three American schooners on Lake Erie, whose fire was a constant annoyance. Assembling a small force of seventy seamen and marines, Dobbs took the captain's gig from his flagship, HMS *Charwell*, and his men carried it from Queenston along the Portage Road around the falls of Niagara to Chippawa, where it was refloated and brought upstream to Frenchman's Creek. At this point Dobbs took five boats out of the river, loaded them on wagons and, with his men still carrying the gig, made a tortuous two-day journey eight miles around the American position at Fort Erie, being forced at points to cut a road through the forest.

By the evening of 12 August all was ready and, embarking his little force of seamen and marines, Dobbs set off on a very dark night to "cut out" the schooners by boarding. As the British boats neared the American vessels, they were spotted and hailed by a sentry on one of the schooners, but replied "Provision boats," which, one American officer reported, "deceived the Officer of the Deck, as our Army boats had been in the habit of passing, and repassing throughout the night."[52] In a few minutes Dobbs's men had grappled and boarded both the *Ohio* and the *Somers*, and Lieutenant Conckling of the *Ohio*, the same officer who had ignored McFeely's warning, reported that

> Instantaneously they were along side of me and notwithstanding my exertions aided by Mr. McCally Act[ing] S[ailing] Master (who was soon disabled) I was unable to repulse them but for a moment, I maintained the Quarter Deck until my sword fell in consequence of a Shot in the shoulder and nearly all on deck either wounded or surrounded by bayonets, as their force was an overwealming one. I thought farther resistance vain & gave up the vessel with the satisfaction of having performed my duty and defended my vessel to the last.[53]

The noise of the fighting on board the *Ohio* and *Somers* alerted the crew of the third schooner, the USS *Porcupine*, who cut its cable and escaped. Dobbs then brought his two prizes down the Niagara to a safe anchorage. It had been a very gallant and professional little operation which, at the cost of only two killed and two wounded, had reduced the harassment of the British position from the water.

Both armies had listened to the night-time battle on the lake. Lieutenant Mermet of De Watteville's Regiment recalled that at around midnight,

> eight pistol shots were heard, and an hour later we saw approaching our shore the eight [sic] victorious boats and the two armed *Schooners* of the enemy which protected Fort Erie and communicated with the peninsula (Black Rock and Buffalo). Our prize is a long 18-pounder gun – two long 12-pounder guns – munitions, two pretty *Schooners*, five naval officers and seventy-five sailors.[54]

Colonel George McFeely was not entirely displeased when he learned that the arrogant Conckling had lost his command and been taken prisoner before "he got on his clothes."[55]

The noise of the naval action provided a very convenient distraction for the British working parties, who cleared away the trees in front of the completed battery. Shortly after dawn on 13 August, the British gunners opened fire at Fort

Dobbs cuts out the schooners, 12 August 1814. The successful British night attack on the three USN schooners reduced an irritant for the besiegers. (Drawing by Owen Staples, Toronto Reference Library, T-15221)

Erie, waking Le Couteur out of a deep sleep to listen to the sound of artillery fire echoing through the "ancient forests."[56]

During the night, the defenders of Fort Erie had heard the noise of chopping as the British working parties cleared the battery's field of fire. The Left Division was just assembling for morning parade when the British gunners let fly. Douglass recalled that

> the troops were paraded, with colors, as for a grand field-day; the national standard was displayed at every flag-staff; as soon as the first volley from the enemy was received, the Regimental Bands of the entire army commenced playing the most animating national airs, and, in the midst of it, a salvo of artillery was fired from every piece which could be brought to bear upon the hostile position.[57]

From that time on, he added, "the cannonade became severe and unremitting, on both sides."

Commander Alexander Dobbs, RN (1784-1827). Just twenty years old, Dobbs had been in the navy since the age of ten and had served with Yeo prior to being sent to the Great Lakes. He was an innovative and aggressive officer who not only captured the two schooners but who also took part in the assault on Fort Erie. (Ontario Archives, ACC 6988, S-12772)

"That went as swift as any goose egg!" A close call at Fort
Erie as depicted by George Balbar. (Drawing by George Balbar,
reproduced from *Soldiers of 1814*)

CHAPTER THREE

"That went as swift as any goose egg!"

FORT ERIE, 13–14 AUGUST 1814

Enemies beware, keep a proper distance,
Else we'll make you stare at our firm resistance;
Let alone the lads who are freedom tasting,
Don't forget our dads gave you once a basting.
To protect our rights 'gainst your flint and triggers
See on yonder heights our patriotic diggers.
Men of ev'ry age, color, rank, profession,
Ardently engaged, labor in succession.
    Pick-axe, shovel, spade, crow-bar, hoe and barrow
    Better not invade, Yankees have the marrow.

Scholars leave their schools with patriotic teachers
Farmers seize their tools, headed by their preachers,
How they break the soil – brewers, butchers, bakers –
Here the doctors toil, there the undertakers.
Bright Apollo's sons leave their pipe and tabor,
Mid the roar of guns join the martial labor,
Round the embattled plain in sweet concord rally,
And in freedom's strain sing the finale.
    Pick-axe, shovel, etc.[1]

Once started, the British artillery fired throughout 13 August, ceasing only at nightfall. "The enemy," Philpotts recorded, returned the fire "very briskly but not skilfully most of their shot going very much over us."[2] The American batteries at Black Rock and the remaining schooner, USS *Porcupine*, "annoyed us a little," he added, "tho they did no injury of any consequence." The engineer extemporized a hot shot furnace to fire at the schooner from the separate one-gun battery and soon drove it off. Hour after hour, the bombardment continued and the men of the Right Division were interested spectators. For the most part, they were disappointed. Le Couteur felt that the bombardment, instead of creating a breach or gap through the earthen walls of the old fort "seemed to me and others to ram the earth harder."[3] Dunlop doubted whether "one shot in ten reached the rampart at all, and the fortunate exceptions that struck the stone building at which they were aimed, rebounded from its sides as innocuous as tennis balls."[4]

Almost everyone believed that the battery was too far from the stone fort. The normal range for a breaching battery was between 500 and 600 yards from its target but the battery at Fort Erie was nearly double that distance. In actual fact, what most of the onlookers did not realize was that the task of Major Henry Phillot, Drummond's artillery commander, was not to breach the walls of the American entrenchment but to harass the defenders until, in Drummond's words, the enemy was compelled "to surrender, or attempt a sortie which can only terminate in his defeat."[5] Unfortunately, Phillot's gunners were poorly equipped to carry out even that lesser task. The evidence varies, but the consensus is that, during the bombardment, Phillot used two brass 24-pdr. guns, an iron 24-pdr. carronade and an iron 8-inch mortar. A fifth piece of ordnance, either an 18 or 24-pdr. iron gun, was mounted in the separate battery that fired at Black Rock or the USS *Porcupine*.[6]

With the exception of the mortar, which lobbed explosive shells at a high trajectory, none of these weapons were particularly useful for the task at hand. The brass 24-pdr. guns were experimental weapons, originally sent to North America during the Revolutionary War as part of the artillery armament for General John Burgoyne's army. He rejected them and they went into the ordnance stores but had been put back into service in 1812 as field pieces. They had not been much use in that role as the weight of their carriages and ammunition required a greater number of horses to draw them and thus more forage – a scarce commodity in Upper Canada. There was also the consideration that a 24-pdr. round shot did not inflict wounds that were appreciably more serious than one fired by the more nimble 6-pdr. gun, the standard British field piece. On the other hand, the brass 24-pdrs. were inadequate as siege pieces as their short 5-foot barrels provided less muzzle and impact velocity than the standard iron 24-pdr. siege gun, which had a 9-foot barrel. Finally, there was the problem that the rate of fire for brass siege guns had to be kept low – no more than five rounds per hour – as their barrels became overheated to the point where a cartridge might "cook off" and ignite while the piece was being loaded, a happening gunners found very distressing. The carronade, primarily a naval weapon, was a light, short piece with a large bore but a limited range, usually within 500 yards, and was basically a large shotgun.[7]

Given the limitations of these weapons, Phillot probably fired shrapnel shells from the carronade – explosive projectiles packed with small lead bullets –

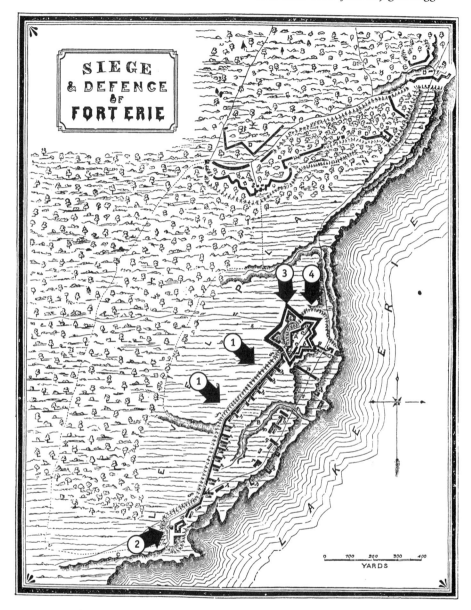

Drummond's assault plan, 15 August 1814

This plan shows the defences at a later stage, not as they were on 15 August.

1. Demonstrations by warriors and pickets
2. Snake Hill assault force (De Watteville's Regiment, 8th Foot and attachments) commanded by Lt. Col. Viktor Fisher, De Watteville's Regiment
3. Fort Erie assault force (104th Foot, light infantry attachments, Royal Marines and Royal Navy sailors) commanded by Lt. Col. William Drummond, 104th Foot
4. Northern assault force (103rd Foot) commanded by Col. Hercules Scott, 103rd Foot

18-pdr. gun. The 18-pdr., which had range, accuracy and hitting power, was favoured for siege work but Drummond never had enough of these useful weapons. (Author's photograph)

which the Royal Artillery officially designated "spherical case shot" but which their American opponents called "tarnation spiritual split shot."[8] Owing to their limited velocity, the brass 24-pdr. guns were used either in a direct fire role against the American artillery on the defence works or in the indirect role for ricochet fire – firing at maximum elevation with a minimum charge in the hope that the shot would bounce several times on touching down. If skilfully practised, ricochet fire could hit areas normally protected by the defences and could thus prove unnerving to the defenders, who were never entirely sure they were safe. Normally, a ricochet battery was sited not more than 600 yards from its target but the American encampment at Fort Erie was so large – some 30 acres in extent – it was impossible to miss. In a similar vein, the 8-inch mortar could also reach behind the defences with explosive shells.

The British gunners loaded and fired, loaded and fired throughout Saturday, 13 August. They stopped at nightfall but resumed work at daylight on 14 August. Along with many others, Dunlop watched them, "admiring our abortive attempts to do any mischief, while a gun of the enemy was practising with the most admirable precision on us."[9] Another spectator, a warrant officer or NCO of the Glengarry Light Infantry, whom Dunlop identifies only as "Mr. K." but who was actually Ensign John McKay, got into an argument with Philpotts over the distance between the battery and the stone fort. McKay offered to settle the dispute

> by either cutting a fuse or laying a gun for the supposed distance. To this it was replied that both the powder and the fuses were bad, and no faith could be had in them.
>
> Mr. K. then asked leave to lay the 24-pounder; and the Engineer, with a sneer, looking at his green [Glengarry] jacket, observed, that there was some difference between a rifle and a 24-pounder; however, Mr. K. then [placed]

himself on the trail of the gun, brought out the coign [or elevating device] further than it had been before, and from the orders he gave to the artillery men even, showed, at least, that he knew the words of command in working a gun. The presiding Engineer, seeing the elevation he was taking, asked him if he was aiming at the truck [pole] of the flagstaff of the Fort. He replied, no – the site of the embrasure would be high enough for him.

The gun was fired, and the ball entered the sand bags about a foot below the mark. He then asked leave to try a second shot. He laid the gun with great care, and took a long while to do it, – at last he gave the word "fire," away went the ball, and driving the sand up from the site of the embrasure, took the enemy's gun on the transom, and capsized [dismounted] it. "Pray, sir," said the Engineer, "where might you have learned to lay guns?" "At Woolwich [the RA depot outside London]," was the reply, "where I was three years Sergeant Major of Artillery."[10]

The British gunners' efforts may have seemed humorous to Dunlop and his comrades but they were not funny to their targets. After the first few hours of bombardment, the defenders devised a system whereby a sentry watching the British battery yelled "shot or shell," as the case might be, when ordnance was fired from it. If a shot, "every soldier hid himself in a moment behind the embankment, if he was not there already; if a shell, all eyes were turned upward, to ascertain where it was to fall."[11]

The 8-inch mortar shells, with their higher trajectory and smoking fuzes, were usually easier to track during their flight and thus easier to avoid. One of these projectiles hit the wooden floor of the gun platform of the northeast demi-bastion in the stone fort and broke through it to land in the expense magazine below. The American gunners in the bastion froze, certain that "the instant the bomb exploded would be the last moment they had to live," but after "a few moments of awful delay," some brave soul looked

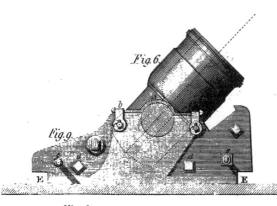

Fig.6.

Fig.9.

Fig.16.

10-inch mortar. Firing explosive shells at a very high trajectory, the mortar became one of the weapons most feared by the defenders. It was a mortar shell that seriously wounded Brigadier-General E. P. Gaines. (From Louis Tousard, *American Artillerist's Companion*, 1813)

into the magazine and announced that the fuze of the shell had gone out. On examination, "it was found that in passing through the triple oak platform … the fuse had been providentially cut off even with the external surface of the bomb before the fire had reached the same point."[12] If any shell proved, like this one, to be a dud, it was fitted with a new fuze and fired back at its former owners. Sometimes, as the shells rolled along the ground, hissing and sputtering, the boys of the army would chase them, throwing stones at them as though they were hornets' nests, a very dangerous game. Lieutenant John Weeks of the Eleventh Infantry recalled that three of his fellow officers were in a tent when a shell crashed through the canvas and penetrated nearly two feet into the ground "and exploded without anyone in the tent being hurt, but a fragment killed a man several feet away."[13]

The roundshot were more dangerous because they were unpredictable. Douglass, who took a keen professional interest in the effectiveness of the bombardment, noted that

> as the shot of the enemy passed lengthwise [through the position], it became necessary to dispose the tents in small groups along the line of the entrenchment, and to [begin to] erect massive embankments, (called traverses) transversely for their protection. The most secluded [i.e. safest] spaces were selected for the horses and spare carriages of the [artillery] Park, for the tents of the Hospital department, and for the parade and inspection of the guards. Yet, notwithstanding all these precautions, scarcely a day passed without considerable loss; and the annoyance were incessant. Shots fired with very small charges and great elevations … were made to fall into the area between the traverses, and, sometimes, to knock over a whole range of tents, at a single stroke. Others, glancing against accidental obstacles, were thrown off into oblique and transverse directions, producing the same effect. No spot was entirely safe.[14]

To protect against the ricochet fire, as Douglass noted, the defenders began the immediate construction of traverses, earth banks running at right angles to the direction of fire, to stop rounds bouncing through the camp.

The defenders learned quickly that roundshot rolling along the ground still retained great velocity after a man attempted to field one like a ground ball, only to lose his hand. Two particular incidents of the bombardment were noted in the letters and memoirs of many American veterans of the siege. The first concerned Private Robert White, who was just lifting a pot onto a cook fire when a 24-pdr. shot came booming over the ramparts and struck off both my arms above my elbows! The blow struck me so numb that at first I did not know what had happened, and the dust and the ashes raised by the force of the ball so filled my face that I could not see. My left arm, as I was subsequently informed, was carried from my body some two rods, and struck a man in the back with such force as nearly brought him to the ground. This same shot took off the right arm of another soldier standing not far from me, and passing on to the other side of the encampment, killed three men! It was the most destructive shot of any that the enemy sent into our works.[15]

The second incident concerned Corporal Reed and Sergeant Waits of the Eleventh Infantry. Reed was shaving Waits in what they thought was a safe place when a shot, deflected by striking something solid, "took off the Corporal's right hand, and the Sergeant's head; throwing blood, brains, hair, fragments of flesh and bones upon a tent near them, and upon the clothing of several spectators of the horrible scene."[16]

Shortly after the bombardment started, one soldier who had been narrowly missed by a roundshot exclaimed "that went as swift as any goose egg!"[17] The phrase became instantly popular and was repeated hundreds of times by anyone who experienced a close call.

The Right Division included a small Royal Marine Artillery detachment armed with Congreve rockets. On 14 August it fired several rockets into the American position but Philpotts thought they "appeared to have no effect."[18] Douglass did not think highly of the

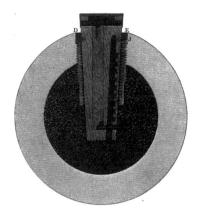

Shells and fuzes. Shells were hollow iron spheres filled with powder. Fuzes were wooden cylinders with a hollow core filled with combustible matter and marked as to the duration of burning before explosion. Gunners cut the fuze to the desire length, inserted it into a hole in the shell casing and loaded it into the bore of howitzer or mortar with the fuze resting against the propellant charge. When the gun was fired, the propellant charge ignited the fuze which (hopefully) burned to the desired length of time before exploding the shell. (Author's collection)

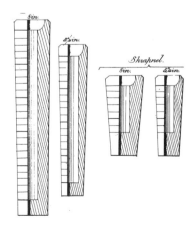

Congreve rockets. Britain's "secret weapon" of the Napoleonic war, they were impressive in flight but rarely hit what they were aimed at. The photograph at right shows reproduction rockets at Fort Erie, and the illustration below is of land rockets being fired from William Congreve, *The Rocket System,* 1814.

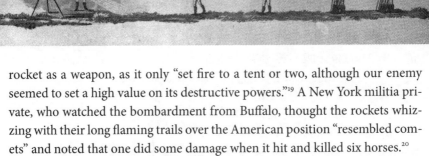

rocket as a weapon, as it only "set fire to a tent or two, although our enemy seemed to set a high value on its destructive powers."[19] A New York militia private, who watched the bombardment from Buffalo, thought the rockets whizzing with their long flaming trails over the American position "resembled comets" and noted that one did some damage when it hit and killed six horses.[20]

The hospitals, magazines and animals – there were sixteen oxen and more than 200 horses in the American position – were vulnerable but one place was usually safe. This was the western side of the Snake Hill battery and Towson recalled that "the invalids of the camp generally repaired to it: not being certain that, if they lay down in their own tents, they would rise with their heads on their shoulders."[21] This area was a popular meeting place "and many a good story was told, many a jovial song sung, and not a little whiskey drunk under its protection; which, but for it, had never been enjoyed."

The besiegers also had a place near their camp, "an old thorn, up which a wild vine had climbed, and then descended in long branches to the ground, forming a natural bower impervious to the rays of the sun."[22] Here, officers would gather to discuss the events of the day and exchange stories and jokes. The most popular topic of conversation was the date an assault would be made against the fort as

> it was known in the camp, from the General to the drum-boy, that it was in contemplation. A worthy old officer of De Watteville's used to salute his friends every morning with – "Well, gentlemans! this would be one very fine day for *de grand object.*" As the intelligence was so universal in our camp, it is not well supposable that it should be unknown in that of the enemy, and accordingly they had a full week to prepare for our attack.[23]

Speculation rose to fever pitch on 13 August after the bombardment began and Drummond issued a general order praising Captain Dobbs and his men for their "brilliant achievement" of cutting out the two schooners and informing the division that he had "a similar service for them to execute, and he invites corps and individuals desirous of volunteering" to contact his principal staff officer, Lieutenant Colonel John Harvey.[24] Almost every unit in the division volunteered except the 1st Foot, the senior regiment of the line, whose commanding officer, Lieutenant-Colonel John Gordon, stated that the Royal Scots were "ready for any service that they might be wanted for, and, therefore, their volunteering was useless."[25] Gordon's words were, apparently, "not very well received at head-quarters."

The speculators under the thorn tree did not have much longer to wait. At about 4 P.M. on 14 August, after about twenty-two hours of bombardment, which had killed or wounded thirty-seven men of the Left Division, an 8-inch mortar shell hit and blew up a small magazine in the stone fort. As Gaines reported, it was almost empty and the explosion was "more awful in its appearance than injurious in its effects."[26] The British, remembered Douglass, greeted the explosion with "three hearty cheers," to which the Left Division

> not to be outdone, in anything, immediately responded in three equally hearty. One of their shots, also, a few minutes after, cut away the halyards of one of our flag-staffs and lowered the flag. It was instantly restored; but the omen was thought too good a one to pass unnoticed; and three cheers were again given [by the British] and responded to, in like manner, as before.[27]

Convinced that this event "would lead the enemy to assault," Gaines made his "arrangements accordingly."[28]

Gunner and sergeant of the Royal Artillery, 1814. After the engineers, the most technical corps in the army, the artillery has always contributed a professional element to what would otherwise be a dreadfully vulgar brawl. Drummond's problem was that he did not have enough gunners or guns. (C. Hamilton Smith, *Costume of the Army,* 1812)

He was right to do so. Drummond had been observing the results of the bombardment and, feeling that the nearest mess building in the stone fort was "much injured" and "the general outline of parapet and embrasures very much altered," decided it was time to attack.[29] Philpotts disagreed, recording in his journal that the effect of the bombardment had been "very trifling," some of the fraises or palisades had been destroyed "and a few holes made in the gable end of the stone building nearest to us, but no injury of any consequence appears to have been done to it."[30] Drummond, however, only saw what he wanted to see and in the early evening of 14 August issued orders for an assault to be made that night.

His plan was a complex one that involved the movement at night of five different elements, three of which would actually attack. Shortly before 2 A.M. the British pickets posted along Buck's road west of the fort, assisted by parties of warriors, would make a demonstration against the American line between the stone fort and Snake Hill, in the hope of drawing the defenders' attention and forces to that area. At 2 A.M., a strong column under Lieutenant-Colonel Viktor Fischer of De Watteville's Regiment would attack between Snake Hill and the lake, to seize the southern end of the defences. As soon as Fischer had penetrated the perimeter, a force under Colonel Hercules Scott of the 103rd Foot would attempt to seize the entrenchment between the stone fort and the lake while another, under Lieutenant-Colonel William Drummond of the 104th, would attack the stone fort itself. The reserve, commanded by Lieutenant-Colonel John Gordon of the 1st Foot and consisting of the remaining infantry units in the Right Division, would move forward to occupy the positions of the forward pickets and thus be ready to exploit any successes.

Drummond regarded the attack on the right, in the area of Snake Hill, as the most crucial part of the operation. For the past week, he had "carefully refrained from making any demonstration" in that area and was convinced that "the whole of the enemy's attention has been drawn to the left" or northern end of the American position.[31] The attack on the right, he cautioned, "considering the strength of the enemy's position and the number of men and guns by which it is defended, must certainly be considered as one of great hazard." For this reason, Drummond assigned Fischer two regiments as well as two additional light companies, about 1,800 men, nearly half his strength.*

It is interesting to speculate why Drummond chose De Watteville's Regiment to make the assault on the right. This unit had been raised for the British army in 1801 by Colonel Frédéric de Watteville from a number of Swiss mercenary units that had been in Austrian service. For the next decade it served in the Mediterranean, participating in the important battle of Maida in 1806, one of the first major British victories against French troops in the Napoleonic period. Because Switzerland had been occupied by France in 1798, the unit had trouble finding Swiss replacements and began to enlist other nationalities, many being deserters from Bonaparte's legions. By the time the regiment arrived in North America in June 1813, its strength was 1,455 all ranks but only the officers and a small cadre of NCOs and enlisted men were Swiss, the remainder being a heterogeneous mixture of French, Germans, Hungarians, Italians, Poles, Spaniards and other nationalities.[32]

The other major unit in Fischer's command was the 8th Foot, a solid regiment that had rendered good service during the campaigns of 1813 and, more recently, had fought at Chippawa and Lundy's Lane. Those two actions had cost the 8th more than one hundred casualties and it had also lost two companies serving as the garrison of Fort Erie when one of its officers, Major Thomas Buck, surrendered the post to the Left Division in early July. By the middle of August the 8th Foot would have mustered about 670 all ranks. Drummond might have used Lieutenant-Colonel John Gordon's 1st Foot to bolster De

---

* See Appendix B for organization and strength of opposing forces on 15 August.

Watteville's Regiment but it had suffered heavily at Chippawa and Lundy's Lane and could only parade about 500 all ranks. Drummond may have chosen the 8th in preference to the 1st Foot as De Watteville's, a strong regiment, might need less assistance. Whatever the reasons for Drummond's selection of units, he had actually made it six days before he issued Fischer orders for the assault.[33]

Those orders contained very precise and detailed instructions on how Fischer was to conduct both his movement and his attack and it is clear from their contents that Drummond did not entirely trust Fischer's regiment, which had suffered a high rate of desertion since arriving in the Niagara. The orders – which must have been issued late in the afternoon of 14 May, if not earlier – directed Fischer "to march immediately in order to enable you to pass through the woods before dark." He was to move by way of Buck's road around the American position to the lakeshore road, where he was to halt

> using every precaution which your experience and prudence can suggest, aided by the necessary personal vigilance of the officers of every rank under your command, to prevent *desertion* and the consequent discovery of your situation and intentions to the enemy. No fire must be lighted, nor any loud chatting by your sentries or patroles permitted. Frequent (hourly) roll-calls must take place, and no officer allowed to quit his company, section, or subdivision for a single moment except while employed in performing duty on visiting videttes or patroles, and which duties officers of every rank must be required to perform. The surprize of the enemy and perhaps the success of the attack may depend upon on this.[34]

This stress on security indicates Drummond's lack of confidence in De Watteville's Regiment and again raises the question as to why he chose it to undertake the most important part of the assault.

Drummond instructed Fischer to attack precisely at 2 A.M. Fischer's objective was to be the American line between Snake Hill and Lake Erie but Fischer was given discretion to alter this objective if he thought it right to do so. To get through the abattis or make an escalade on the Snake Hill battery, Drummond provided his troops with short ladders and hay-bags, as well as axes and picks.

In what was later to become a subject of some controversy, Drummond recommended that Fischer remove the flints from his men's muskets. In December 1813 Drummond had organized a nighttime bayonet assault at Fort Niagara and was convinced that it had succeeded because no accidental firing had given away the element of surprise. "In order to *ensure secrecy*," Drummond strongly recommends that the flints are taken out of the firelocks with the exception of a reserve of select and steady men who may be permitted to retain their flints, (if you think necessary or advisable,) not exceeding one-third of your force. ......

The advantages which will arise from taking out the flints are obvious. Combined with darkness and silence it will effectually conceal the situation and number of our troops, and those of the enemy being exposed by his fire and his white trousers, which are very conspicuous marks to our view, it will enable them to use the bayonet with effect which that valuable weapon has been ever found to possess in the hands of British soldiers.[35]

Although he professed to leave much to Fischer's "judgment and discretion," Drummond actually left very little to chance. He provided Fischer with directions about how to handle surrender negotiation, rendezvous positions in case the attack failed, his own location and the American strength, which he estimated at about "1,500 fit for duty." On the subject of prisoners, he advised that "Clemency to prisoners it is unnecessary to recommend to you, but in removing them to the rear must be careful not to detach too many men."[36] Such a statement might be accepted at face value or it might be construed to mean that, as guarding prisoners was a bothersome task, it might be best not to take too many.

Drummond did not issue similar detailed orders to the commanders of the other two assault columns but did give them with a copy of Fischer's orders "for their guidance" and "most strongly" recommended "a free use of the bayonet."[37] William Drummond discussed the matter of removing the flints with the officers of his own 104th Foot and they were vehemently opposed to the idea because, as Le Couteur commented, "such a proceeding must ensure defeat, if troops could not be trusted with their flints they had better leave their arms behind them."[38] William Drummond agreed and his men kept their flints. Fischer, however, removed the flints from all his units except the light companies of the 8th and 89th Foot, which constituted his reserve of "select and steady men."

Such obedience is no surprise as the 48-year-old Fischer had served as a mercenary since the age of sixteen and was a European officer who would regard a lieutenant-general's "recommendation" as a direct order. Colonel Hercules Scott and Lieutenant-Colonel William Drummond were British officers and, as such, could afford to treat a recommendation – even a strong one – as nothing more than that. They were also more fortunate in the composition of their columns. Scott had his own 103rd Foot and the flank companies of the 1st Foot, about 850 bayonets. William Drummond had a small but elite force consisting

Lieutenant-Colonel William Drummond, 104th Regiment of Foot. An artist's conception of the charismatic commander of the 104th Foot, based on period descriptions. Admired and respected by all who served with him, Drummond managed to penetrate farther into the American defences than any other British attacker. (Digital painting by Sharif Tarabay, courtesy of the artist)

of the flank companies of the 41st and 104th Foot and a detachment of sailors and Royal Marines under the intrepid Commander Alexander Dobbs, RN, a total of about 340 bayonets.

Both Hercules Scott and William Drummond had reservations about the forthcoming assault. In a letter to his brother James, completed on 14 August just before he received his orders for the attack and which contained instructions for the disposal of his estate should he be killed, Scott noted that he expected to be ordered "to storm" the American position. "I have little hope of success from the manoeuvre," he added, but promised his brother to write more, "that is, if I get over this present business."[39]

William Drummond's premonition was much stronger. On the morning of Sunday, 14 August 1814, as the artillery of both sides resumed firing, "something whispered" to the 35-year-old Scotsman "that this would be his last day."[40] William Drummond (no relation to the commanding general) was one of the most admired British officers in North America and the affection with which he was regarded is evident in the recollections of the men who served with him. Le Couteur worshipped his commanding officer, whom he described as "a splendid looking man, the personification of Rhoderic Dhu," one of Walter Scott's heroes.*[41] To Dunlop, he was "everything that could be required in a soldier; brave, generous, open-hearted and good natured" and "a first-rate tactician."[42] A Canadian officer remembered this "brave and excellent officer" as being "above the medium in height" with "a dignified appearance, regular and clear-cut features and a charming expression"[43] The aboriginal warriors particularly admired him – to Norton, he was "my Gallant friend" – and they presented him with several strings of beads which he wore around his neck in uniform.[44]

---

* Roderick Dhu was a character in Walter Scott's *Lady of the Lake*. He was an adventurous outlaw and bandit chief but a man of strict honour.

Drummond was wearing those beads when he breakfasted that morning with a group of officers. Among them was Dunlop, who remembered Drummond as being "in high spirits" and

> We sat apparently by common consent long after breakfast was over. Drummond told some capital stories, which kept us in such a roar that we seemed more like an after dinner than an after breakfast party. At last the bugles sounded the turn-out, and we rose to depart for our stations; Drummond called us back, and his face assuming an unwonted solemnity, he said, "Now boys! we never will all meet together here again; at least I will never again meet you. I feel it and am certain of it; let us all shake hands, and then every man to his duty, and I know you all too well to suppose for a moment that any of you will flinch it." We shook hands accordingly, all round, and with a feeling very different from what we had experienced for the last two hours, fell into our places.[45]

Thankfully, the weather was clear. During the afternoon, however, as the opposing gunners continued to duel with each other and the carpenters constructed scaling ladders, it "became dark and cloudy and a thick drizzle of rain began, which towards evening, increased to a heavy shower."[46] At about 7 P.M., Fischer's column moved off under a steely curtain of rain. As evening came on, William Drummond said goodbye to the officers of his own 104th Foot with the words, "Remember the honor of the Regiment, dear Boys, God Bless You!" With tears in his eyes, Le Couteur urged Drummond to remember his "many escapes" in previous actions and "to look cheerfully upon this attack" but Drummond's response was to ask the young Jerseyman to send his papers and trinkets to his wife. He then "stowed himself away in a rocket case" (which bore a marked and unfortunate resemblance to a coffin) and fell fast asleep to the steady patter of rain on its lid.[47]

He awoke at around midnight, just about the time the British gunners ceased firing and the rain slackened to a low drizzle and then stopped. Drummond ordered his column to fall in quietly, ready to move. Dunlop, who, although a medical non-combatant, was forever trying to get into action, accompanied the column when it moved forward. He was close to William Drummond, who suddenly stopped about 200 yards from the stone fort, unbuckled his sword belt and gave the weapon to Dunlop, who, thinking "that he had no great faith in it," offered the colonel his own sword, "which was a Ferrara of admirable temper and edge."*[48] Drummond replied that he would get "a boarding pike from the sailors whom he was going to join" and told Dunlop to remain where he was to

---

* A blade forged in the Italian city of Ferrara, famed for its sword-making.

treat the casualties "and not expose myself" before disappearing into the night.

For his part, Hercules Scott's spirits seemed to improve as the day wore on. In the evening he spent the time waiting with Surgeon Colin Young of the 103rd "under a piece of canvas suspended from a branch of a tree, but not sufficient to protect us from the inclemency of a dreadfully rainy night."[49] The surgeon asked Scott's opinion of the forthcoming assault and remembered that "he spoke unfavourably of it, yet tho' drenched with rain he was in high spirits, and his last words to me" before moving off with the 103rd Foot column, were, "We shall breakfast together in the fort in the morning."

Although the two column commanders may have been pessimistic about the outcome of the assault, this was not the case with their men. They were fed up with the weather and did not want to endure the labour and tedium of a lengthy siege, if there was a chance they could take the fort by storm and get the thing finished. Dunlop recalled that, when the orders for the attack were issued, the officers and men of the Right Division were pleased as

> we were tired of our busy idleness! which, though fatal to many of our comrades, had as yet produced no military result; and we knew that whatever they might be at a distance, the enemy had no chance with us at a hand-to-hand fight, and therefore we hailed the prospect of an assault as a relief from trouble – a glorious termination to a fatiguing and harassing campaign, where, if we had got some credit by the Battle of the Falls [Lundy's Lane], accounts from that date to the present had been pretty evenly balanced.[50]

Many of those in the assault columns – like their commanding general – fully expected the defenders to surrender if seriously attacked.[51] After all, Lieutenant-General Drummond had assured William Drummond, Fischer, and Scott that Gaines's command did "not exceed 1500 fit for duty and those are represented as much dispirited."*[52]

In actual fact, Brigadier-General Edmund Gaines had about 2,800 men fit for duty on 14 August and they were far from being dispirited. After the explosion of the magazine and the mutual cheering session late in the afternoon, Gaines had guessed that his opponent might try an assault, and when the British artillery continued to fire after darkness had fallen, this suspicion became a certainty. He therefore made the rounds of his entire line, warning all officers "to be watchful and vigilant."[53] Major William McRee, the chief engineer, and other staff members undertook similar tours and Douglass remembered that, when McRee reached Douglass's position, he warned the young Yale graduate

---

* See Appendix B for organization and strength of opposing forces on 15 August.

to be "prompt and energetic" in all his actions "for you may be assured that, whatever else they may do, *this* will be one of their points of attack."[54]

The Left Division was therefore in a high state of alert and ready for an assault. Apart from the guards and pickets, one third of each unit was assembled behind its own section of entrenchment, while the remaining two thirds were permitted to sleep – in their clothes and with their weapons close by – although, with the British bombardment continuing into the night, it is doubtful whether they got much rest. Each infantryman had 60 rounds in his cartridge box and there was an immediate reserve available of 65 rounds per man. At his Snake Hill battery, Captain Nathan Towson ordered his gunners to lie down near the position each man "was to occupy in battle" so that no time would be lost coming into action and double-shotted his guns so that, at any time, he could open fire with every weapon "ten seconds after the alarm was given."[55] Douglass had a similar arrangement with his gunners and reloaded his gun every evening with "round-shot, grape, or canister, either, or all together, as the case might require," and placed lanterns and implements ready to hand. In addition, the young engineer officer had manufactured his own anti-personnel rounds by quilting "bags of musket balls in the fragments of an old tent" which were sized to fit the bore of his 18-pdr. gun.[56]

Just after midnight, when the rain had stopped, the humid conditions created a thick mist. Otherwise, remembered Douglass, the night was so "undisturbed and calm" that the defenders began to doubt an attack would be made and this being the case, the young officer, "wearied with long watching and strong emotion," gradually fell asleep.[57] Shortly before 2 A.M. Captain Benjamin Ropes of the Twenty-First Infantry, stationed to the rear of Towson's battery on Snake Hill, heard a dog barking in the direction of Picket No. 4, located on the shore of Lake Erie about 300–400 yards from Snake Hill, and decided – for some reason best known to himself – that it was a British dog.[58]

Lieutenant William Belknap of the Twenty-Third Infantry, a 19-year-old native of Newburgh, New York, commanded Picket No. 4. Strongly cautioned about a possible attack, he had earlier sent out a patrol, "which after an absence of one or two hours returned, & the corporal of which reported no sign of the enemy."[59] A few minutes later, however, the sentry nearest the lake reported the sound of boats being rowed on the water. With Dobbs's successful venture of two days before in mind, Belknap shifted the main body of his picket to the shore to counter a possible British move. He then heard the sound of a musket firing, and then another – followed by a "hurried volley of eight or ten similar reports."[60] And so it began.

Colour Party, 1814. The junior officer carries the Regimental Colour and is protected by a colour sergeant armed with a halbard. (Painting by Charles Hamilton Smith, from *Costume of the British Army*)

PART TWO

Night Assault on Fort Erie

15 AUGUST 1814

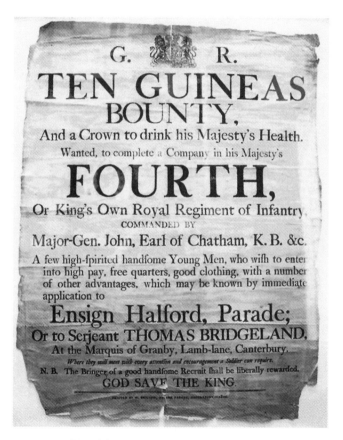

Recruiting poster, 4th Regiment of Foot.

British Grenadier, 1814. This soldier wears the older, stovepipe shako, which was gradually replaced by the "Belgic" shako after 1812, and the loose, grey trousers which had replaced the white pants and black gaiters of previous forms of dress. The units in North America, being far from the source of supply, often wore older uniforms, equipment and weapons. (Painting by Peter Rindlisbacher, courtesy of the artist)

CHAPTER FOUR

"Bravery, coolness, ingenuity and perseverance were useless"

FISCHER'S ATTACK, 2 A.M.–5 A.M., 15 AUGUST 1814

Thus, my lads, we soldiers live:
We live a life like man and wife,
Now making love, now in a row;
A noble glorious trade we drive;
From morn to night, we love and fight,
And follow the noisy rowdydowdydow
Now courting honour in some trench,
And now some willing comely wench;
To victory leading now the way
Now leading at some ball that they;
To the fair now kneeling for some boon –
Now at the head of a platoon;
Ever equally delighting,
Now in love, and now in fighting.

But when the trumpet sounds afar,
And we let slip the dogs of war,
Then to see the dead and dying,
Hear bullets whistle as they're flying;
Oh! what delights, so sweet, so glorious,
That proudly cover the victorious!
Hacking, hewing, cutting, slashing,
Killing, wounding, mincing, mashing;
While drums and fifes and cannons loud
Upon the astonish'd senses crowd,
And strike the ears with hideous yell,
As if it were the yawn of hell,
Of the dying to sound out the knell.[1]

As a picket commander, Lieutenant Belknap's duty was to delay the oncoming British long enough for the remainder of the Left Division to fully man its defences. He accomplished this task admirably. After his outlying sentries had fired and fallen back on the main body of his picket, Belknap placed his men in a two-rank line across the shore road to Point Abino, held his fire until his opponents were within 10 to 15 yards, and then hit them with a concentrated volley. This, he recalled, "checked their progress, and thereby gave me an opportunity of retiring" to a position closer to the main defences.[2] The British, formed in close column, staggered, then recovered their stride and came on again as Belknap fell back. In the American camp, meanwhile, all was frantic activity as, alerted by shouts of "To arms, to arms!", officers and men ran to their posts.

Captain Nathan Towson found himself with a problem. Thanks to his precautions, his gunners had their double-shotted 6-pdr. guns in the battery atop Snake Hill ready for action within minutes. If Towson opened up, however, he ran the risk of hitting Belknap's picket, which was falling back toward him. The previous evening Towson had watched Belknap's detachment march out to relieve Picket No. 4 and had been struck with anxiety at the "apparent youth" of its 19-year-old commander – he now faced the hard choice of firing and possibly killing or wounding Belknap and some of his men, or not firing and letting the British hit the main American line before it was completely manned. As Towson later commented, it was

> the most perplexing moment of my military life. Every minute's delay in firing jeopardized the whole army. On other hand, it was next to an impossibility for the [picket] guard to have performed, in such gallant style, the duty assigned to it, and have gotten out of the way in the time agreed upon. The inevitable consequence of an immediate discharge from my battery, under such circumstances, would be the destruction of the gallant troops that had so faithfully performed their duty. There was, however, no time to deliberate.[3]

Making his decision Towson opened fire with the three 6-pdr. guns that could bear on the lakeshore road. Fortunately, given the height of the battery, some twenty feet higher than Belknap's picket, most of his rounds went over their heads and only one American was killed and a few wounded. "Thus," Belknap later recalled, as his men "disputed every ounce of ground" they were "between the fire of friends, & the bayonet of the enemy."[4] As the picket neared the main defences, Belknap was challenged for the password, which was "Defend." He shouted it but the sentries guarding the gap through the abattis, which was used as a gate on this side of the camp, thought he had replied "Friend," so there was some delay until the confusion was sorted out. Belknap was the last man through the gap and the British were so close behind him that he was stabbed in an embarrassing part of his anatomy by a pursuer's bayonet. Dragging Belknap to safety, the men on the gap hastily closed it with an obstacle and opened fire.

Lieutenant-Colonel Viktor Fischer of De Watteville's Regiment had opted to move along the lakeshore or Point Abino road because it presented a useful approach route. Fischer had organized his column into three distinct elements. The first element, under the command of Major Thomas Evans of the 8th Foot, consisted, in order of march, of half the light company of the 8th Foot, the light company of De Watteville's Regiment, the light company of the 100th

American infantry, Left Division, 1814. A shortage of regulation blue uniforms resulted in some of the First Brigade of the division being issued grey jackets. They made this humble garment famous at the battle of Chippawa, 5 July 1814. (Drawing by Robert Marrion, author's collection)

Foot, the remaining half of the 8th Foot light company, the grenadier company of De Watteville's and the light company of the 89th Foot. It appears that only the light companies of the 8th and 89th Foot under Lieutenant Charles Barstow and Captain James Basden, respectively, were permitted to retain their flints. Fischer's second element consisted of the remainder of De Watteville's Regiment and the third element was the rest of the 8th Foot.[5]

The defences between Snake Hill and the lake were the weakest part of the perimeter. Not as much effort had been paid to this sector as it was the part of the camp farthest from the British and, as noted above, Drummond had deliberately refrained from making any movements in the area, in an effort to try to keep American attention focused on the opposite flank. There were no ramparts or ditches and the only defensive work was an abattis, not all that thick, which ran from Snake Hill down to the lake and then curled back along the shore. Near the lake, this abattis was not fixed very firmly as the shore was flat rock and the best that could be done was to weigh it down with logs.[6]

The defence of this sector was the responsibility of Ripley's Second Brigade and Ripley had assigned the abattis to the Twenty-First Infantry, recruited in Massachussetts and New Hampshire, and one of the best units in the Left Division. Ripley had been this unit's first commanding officer and he had turned it into a well-trained and disciplined regiment. When Ripley was promoted brigadier-general in early 1814, Colonel James Miller had assumed command of the Twenty-First and, under Miller, it had earned laurels at Lundy's Lane, when it captured the British artillery by a bayonet charge.* This feat gained Miller promotion to brigadier-general and, as the most senior unwounded of-

---

* When Brown ordered Miller to attack the hill and take the British artillery at Lundy's Lane, Miller's modest response was "I'll try, Sir." That famous phrase is now the motto of the Fifth Infantry Regiment, United States Army, the descendant of the wartime Twenty-First Infantry.

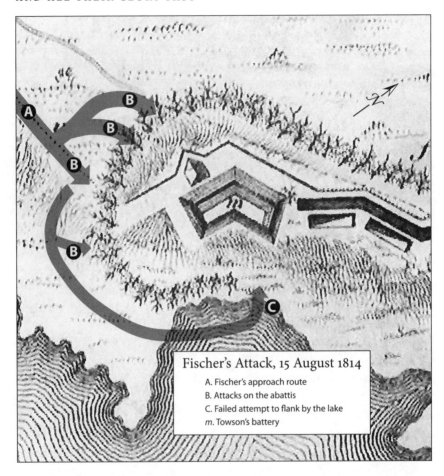

Fischer's Attack, 15 August 1814

A. Fischer's approach route
B. Attacks on the abattis
C. Failed attempt to flank by the lake
m. Towson's battery

ficer present with the unit after Lundy's Lane was only a captain, Gaines had appointed the competent Major Eleazar Wood of the engineer corps as a temporary commanding officer.

When the alarm was given, Wood quickly moved his men to their assigned posts. Three of his companies, under the command of Captain Morrill Marston, took position behind the abattis from Snake Hill to the lake, a fourth took post to the right of Towson's battery as a reserve, while a fifth company under Captain Benjamin Ropes was also placed in reserve behind Snake Hill.[7]

Once they had commenced, Towson's gunners kept up a continual fire of canister on the British – although much of it went over the attackers' heads. From the "sheet of fire rolling from Towson's battery," Gaines, who had rushed to his left flank as soon as the first rounds were fired, was able to see "the enemy's column of about 1,500 men approaching on that point" and it "was not checked until it approached within ten feet of our infantry; a line of loose brush representing an abattis only intervened; a column of the enemy attempted to pass round the abattis through the water, where it was nearly breast deep."[8]

After Towson opened up, Marston could see from the muzzle flash that

> the enemy were quite up to the works. I gave orders for my command to commence firing, which was kept up for about 10 minutes. I discovered that some of the enemy in the centre, were getting over the abbatis and at the same time charging with their bayonetts [sic]. At the same time I also discovered a large body of the enemy in the water and I judged from there being no firing on the part of the enemy, and from the words "charge" and "give the damned yankees no quarter" being very often repeated along of the line of the enemy, that they depended upon their bayonetts.[9]

Wood ordered Ropes to bring his company and the other reserve company into action on his left flank where some of the attackers had almost got around the part of the abattis that curved back along the shore. Always a creative speller, Ropes later wrote that "we oppened on thim with About one hundred & fifty or Sixty Men together with Capt. Towsons Artillery from the battery they brok fell back to from wich they did & made a second attack with Great furey comming so near that we bayoneted them in the Abbetus."[10] The two companies took up a position where they could fire at the British in the lake, who, wading in water up to their chests, could not return it because they had no flints and, even if they had, it is extremely difficult, if not impossible, to load and fire a musket while standing nearly chest deep in water. Those few who managed to get around the abattis and into the interior of the American position were quickly surrounded and forced to surrender.

All this time, part of the attacking force continued to penetrate the abattis, some attempting to chop through it with axes, others to pull it apart with picks and bayonets. Most American witnesses state that the British made a series of bayonet "charges" at this point but disagree about the number: Marston thought it was three, Ripley and Wood thought it was five. It is likely that these movements were not really charges as such but "surges" as an officer or noncommissioned officer gathered some men around him and made an attempt at getting through the abattis. It is unclear from the eyewitness accounts but apparently a second attempt was made to wade out into the lake around the abattis but it met no better success than the first. What all American participants agree on is that after a combat that lasted between 15 and 30 minutes, the British fell back, "apparently in great disorder," according to Marston.[11]

To Lieutenant David Douglass, at his position on the north end of the position, the fighting around Snake Hill was both visible and audible because it was

Defensive fire. While wading through the lake to flank the American position, British attackers came under vollies from the defenders as depicted in this photograph of American re-enactors. Most of the attackers who were not killed were forced to surrender. (Courtesy, Niagara Parks Commision)

marked by an illumination of exquisite brilliancy, shining far up in the dark, cloudy atmosphere which hung over us; while the battery, on its right [Snake Hill], elevated some twenty feet above the level, was lighted up with a blaze of artillery fires, which gained for it, after that night, the appellation of " Towson's lighthouse." To the ear, the reports of musketry and artillery were blended together, in one continuous roar, somewhat like the close double drag of a drum, on a grand scale.[12]

Reconstructing this action from the British side is a much more difficult task. No soldier in Fischer's column really had a clear picture of what happened and Fischer himself was badly wounded in the attack. He did manage to submit a brief report and Lieutenant-General Drummond certainly questioned some of the surviving officers as he provided additional details in his report to his superior, Sir George Prevost. From the scant evidence available it appears that the lead element of Fischer's column, consisting of the light companies of the 8th, 89th and 100th Foot and the flank companies of De Watteville's Regiment, were arrested at the abattis. The light companies of the 8th and De Watteville's Regiment, moved to the right and it was men from these sub-units, under the command of Major Charles de Vilatte of De Watteville's and Lieutenant Brooke Young of the 8th, who attempted to wade around the abattis. The remainder of the lead element tried to cut their way through the abattis and suffered from the heavy fire of Marston's three companies of the Twenty-First Infantry which were defending it. It appears that the grenadier company of De Watteville's attempted to assault the Snake Hill battery but, finding their ladders too short, took shelter below it where American artillery fire could not reach them. They were spotted there by Towson's gunners, who began to pot at them with muskets, but the grenadiers, having no flints, were unable to return this fire. They milled about in some confusion until the defenders, "finding only cheers to oppose them, got on top of the parapet" and shot them down "like so many sheep."[13] At this, the grenadiers broke and ran, taking the other part of the lead element with them, except for Captain James Basden's light company of the 89th Foot, which, "not withstanding they were nearly overwealmed," managed "to preserve its order and remained firm on the ground."[14]

The remainder of De Watteville's Regiment and the 8th Foot had left the road when they came under fire from Towson's battery and tried to move along the shore itself. Unfortunately, as Fischer reported, they soon became

> entangled between the rocks and the water, and by the retreat of the flank companies, were thrown into such confusion as to render it impossible to give them any kind of formation during the darkness of the night, at which time they were exposed to a most galling fire from the enemy's battery and the numerous parties in the *abbatis*, and I am perfectly convinced that the great number of missing are men killed or severely wounded at that time when it was impossible to give them any assistance.[15]

When the men from the flank companies came running back from the abattis and tried to push through them, the De Wattevilles, in turn, "became utterly terror-stricken and ran over, beat down, or swept before them" the 8th Foot coming behind.[16] In a letter written only a few hours after the assault, Lieutenant Joseph Mermet of De Watteville's, an aspiring poet who was with the main part of the Swiss regiment, used near stream-of-consciousness form to describe his comrades' experience: "Six hours of marching brought us to the enemy's abbatis," he recalled, "and there, without a path, without a guide, water up to our waistbelts, with canister, musketry, the order had been not to fire, those who drowned ... a little murmuring ... confusion ... vain efforts ... We fell back, and dawn lit up our defeat." Mermet believed the attack failed because "the obstacles were insurmountable" and "bravery, coolness, ingenuity and perseverance were useless" in the face of them.[17]

After Fischer's column had fallen back – no doubt hoping for better things in the future – and the firing died away, the only sounds to be heard were the moans and cries of the wounded. A few hours later when it started to grow light, Marston could see British soldiers moving in the bushes and presumed they were stragglers. One of Ripley's staff ordered him to send a detachment out to investigate so Marston dispatched a sergeant and a dozen men, who soon returned with nearly thirty prisoners, many still carrying their muskets but who did not seem disposed "to make any resistance."[18] Marston examined their weapons and noted that the flints were missing. Throughout the next few hours, detachments from the Twenty-First Infantry collected the British wounded and recovered weapons, ladders, axes and picks dropped by their opponents. Wood reported taking 120 prisoners and, in all, Fischer's casualties were listed as 212 killed, wounded and missing with the light company of the 8th Foot suffering the loss of 48 men or just over 25 per cent of the column's total losses.[19] The assault on the right had been a total failure.

It was not the only part of Drummond's plan that went wrong. His orders called for the British pickets on duty to mount demonstrations or feint attacks against the American line between the stone fort and Snake Hill to distract the defenders. These demonstrations were supposed to be undertaken before Fischer's assault commenced but were either never made or made late. The reason is unclear but a hint may be gathered from the experience of John Norton, the Mohawk war chief. Late in the afternoon of 14 August, Norton and a small party of warriors, along with a detachment of the Glengarry Light Infantry, had escorted the engineers to reconnoitre for the best site for a second battery that would be closer to the American position. Returning to camp in the early evening Norton learned that an assault was to be made that night and encouraged his warriors to participate in it because, although they had "no Directions to join the Attack, I could not consent to lie inactive, whilst our friends the Red Coats were going to undertake an arduous contest."[20]

His warriors unanimously agreed to join the assault. Shortly thereafter, however, Norton learned that the Indian Department officers who were attached to the warriors from the Northwest had received orders to move to a position from which they could mount a demonstration against the middle of the American line. There was never any love lost between the independent-minded Norton and the white officers of the department but he decided to join them with his small but select band of warriors. The entire force moved along Buck's road but Norton, "apprehending that the Rout[e] mentioned might eloign [align] those who followed it too far from the Scene of the Action to allow them to give timely assistance to the troops engaged," decided to go his own way and join William Drummond's column in an attack on the stone fort.[21] Progress was difficult, however, as the so-called "cleared area" west of the American position was obstructed with fallen trees, logs, stumps and brush. As Norton's warriors wended their way through this obstacle course,

> we heard the firing commence at Snake Hill. Hastening forward, – through the Darkness of the night & closeness of the Woods, we separated from a numerous Division of our Men, which constrained us to check our speed at a point of Rendezvous previously appointed, until they had joined us. We were within half a Mile of Fort Erie, – when we heard the Cracking of Musketry & the Roar of Cannon announce the attack upon it, – We then ran forward as fast as the woods and darkness would permit, stumbling over Logs and fallen Trees.[22]

Norton was mistaken. What he had heard was not the attack on the stone fort but one of the long-delayed demonstrations.

This is confirmed by Lieutenant David Douglass, who had been woken by the sound of Belknap's picket firing at Fischer's column and, along with the rest of the Left Division, had stood to his arms. He recalls that the sound of battle around Snake Hill "blended together in one continuous roar, somewhat like the close double drag of a drum, on a grand scale."[23] Suddenly, Douglass heard "a volley of small-arms, followed by a rapid running fire and occasional discharges of artillery" coming from that part of the line immediately to the south of the stone fort. This was the delayed demonstration and apparently it was the only one mounted, as the other parties appear to have done nothing. As quickly as it flared up, the firing died away when the demonstration ended but the British pickets continued to hover about for the next hour. Brigadier-General Peter B. Porter recalled that, opposite his brigade's position in the centre of the line, two or three British officers "approached to reconnoitre us in that direction, and every appearance indicated an immediate advance of a column on our centre."[24] The threat of an attack on this part of the American line, however, was strong enough to keep the units manning it from sending reinforcements to those areas that were attacked.

At about the same time the demonstration ended, Douglass remembered that the sounds of fighting around Snake Hill also began to fade. But, he commented, all "remained quiet in front of us" – meaning the northern flank of the American position.

In the stone fort itself, Captain Alexander Williams of the artillery, the commandant, had earlier welcomed a detachment of the Nineteenth Infantry, almost all raw recruits, under the command of Major William Trimble. The Nineteenth was a western regiment, which had only joined the Left Division the previous day. Trimble, a 28-year-old prewar lawyer from southern Ohio, had served as an officer in a volunteer unit that had surrendered with Hull at Detroit in 1812 and, after being exchanged, had received a commission in the regular army. With this reinforcement, the garrison of the stone fort was about 200 men, and Trimble and Williams toured the post by lantern light, deciding where best to post the new arrivals. It was clear to both officers that the northeast demi-bastion, Williams's post in action and that part of the defences closest to the British lines, was almost certain to be a point of attack. Trimble offered some of his infantry to Williams to reinforce the gunners but the artillery officer declined. The two men finally decided to position most of the infantry on the V-shaped curtain wall that connected the two demi-bastions, and when this was done, Trimble told his officers to let their men lie down but not let them go to sleep. He advised them, in case of attack, to caution the men "to be very deliberate and careful and to fire low and also that there was no need of Exposing unnecessarily while in the act of loading and to step up when firing so as to be able to fire over the parapet."[25]

Having assisted Trimble, Williams returned to the northeast demi-bastion. This was a crucial part of the defences as it could bring fire not only north against the most likely British approach but also along the line of defences down to the Douglass battery. For this reason, it was heavily armed with a 24-

pdr. gun, two 12-pdr. guns and a 6-pdr. gun – manned by about 30 gunners. The bastion was very small in area – not more than 200 square feet – and thus very cramped. It was probably for this reason that Williams had turned down Trimble's offer of infantrymen because he had no place to put them. On the outside of the stone fort, between the two demi-bastions, a start had been made on building

Mohawk warrior. Drummond had a sizeable force of aboriginal warriors under his command and they proved useful for scouting and skirmishing, although they always fought in their own style, not that of the regulars. (Painting by Ron Volstad, courtesy Department of National Defence)

two outlying bastions, but this work was in its early stages and these new defences were as yet large mounds of earth.[26]

The three officers in the bastion were Williams, Lieutenant Patrick McDonough and Lieutenant John G. Watmough, all prewar residents of Philadelphia. Williams was the son of Colonel Jonathan Williams, the former chief of the corps of engineers. An 1811 graduate of the military academy at West Point, the 24-year-old Williams had joined the Left Division in July but had not seen action at either Chippawa or Lundy's Lane. McDonough, aged twenty-eight, had been commissioned in the Second Regiment of Artillery, commanded by Winfield Scott, in the spring of 1812 and had served under Scott for more than a year. John Watmough, aged twenty, was a recent graduate of Princeton who had also attended the University of Pennsylvania before being commissioned in the artillery the previous September. Watmough had been slightly wounded by a shell fragment during the bombardment of the previous two days but had insisted on remaining on duty. None of the three young officers had seen much action and Watmough later remembered that they congratulated themselves on being stationed at an important post where they were sure to win "honour and promotion" should the British attack – and nobody doubted that they would.[27]

By now, the defenders of the northern flank, running from the stone fort to the lake, were very much on the alert. Captain Eben Childs of the Ninth Infantry, which was positioned between the fort and Douglass's battery, was tired as he had only slept two or three hours during the last two days. He had about a hundred men who were securely protected by an earthwork nearly 18 feet thick and about 6–7 feet high but he was concerned about the 20-foot gap that had been left between it and the stone fort to permit access to the interior of the camp and the lakeshore road that ran through it. Childs was sure that the British would head for this gap, which was protected only by a "slender" abattis. As the moments ticked by with no sign of the enemy, he sent a corporal and a dozen men outside his line, with orders to put their ears to the ground and listen for the sound of running feet.[28]

A few yards away, on the lime kiln that he had converted into a battery, Douglass's gunners, "familiarized, by daily use and constant vigilance," were in their places, and the priming number of his detachment "had already done their work, and were holding their hands over the priming to protect it from dampness; while the firemen, opening their dark lanterns, were in the act of lighting their slow matches." Douglass kept thinking about McRee's words spoken a few hours earlier that "Whatsoever else they do," his battery was sure to be one of the enemy's "points of attack." In his mind, "without the shadow of a doubt," that assurance would soon "be realized."[29]

U.S. gun detachment. Towson's company were manning 6-pdr. guns like that shown here. As their firing position was fairly high, there was "dead ground" in front of the battery which they could not reach with their guns. The attackers sheltered here and Towson's men were reduced to using muskets to pick them off. (Painting by H. C. McBarron, Courtesy of the Company of Military Historians)

To the right of Douglass, Captain Cornelius Broughton commanded a company of eighty dismounted New York volunteer dragoons who held the line down to the lake, a distance of only about twenty yards. There were no defence works in this gap; it was covered by Douglass's 18-pdr. gun and also the brass 6-pdr. field gun captured from the British at Lundy's Lane.[30]

Everyone peered as intently as he could into the night but there was no sign of the attackers. The "suspense began to be painful," Douglass remembered,

and the inquiry was impatiently made, "Why don't the lazy rascals make haste!" That they would fail to come, no one, for a moment, entertained the thought. We had seen the signal rockets thrown up, from their right column, at the even of its approach, and answered from the edge of the woods, in our front; and we knew, as well as they did, what was the meaning of it.

...... Yet the intensity of the fire had begun to abate, on the left, and still nothing was heard or seen, in front of us. Hundreds of eyes were gazing intently through the darkness, towards the well-known position of the picket guard, some four hundred yards in advance. Ears were laid to the ground, to catch the first impression of a footfall; but the darkness and the stillness of the night were, as yet, in *our* front, unbroken.[31]

Suddenly, "without the previous notice of a single shot, the trampling of feet, and the sound of voices were heard nearly under the muzzles of their guns."[32] The challenge, "who goes there?" rang out, only to be met with the rather timid response, "the picket guard." It seems that the commander of Picket No. 1, which was posted outside the northern flank of the American position, had only joined the Left Division a few days before and had misunderstood his orders. As Watmough explained, the picket commander's instructions were

> to hold on firmly until the attack commenced, and then retreat slowly within our lines. He entirely mistook their object, and upon the report of the first gun from the American left, he commenced his own retreat, without waiting to be attacked, and in spite of the entreaties of his brave veterans. The error sprang from ignorance, not from want of patriotism or courage.[33]

A "terrible volley of imprecations" fell on the heads of the wretched picket, who were told: "Go back to your post, you infamous cowardly poltroons! Go back this instant, or we'll fire upon you!"[34] To that, Alexander Williams added the additional advice that the miscreants should return and "die upon your post."[35] The shame-faced pickets disappeared into the dark.

A few minutes later, several musket shots were heard and then, by listening carefully, the defenders could discern "the measured tread" of a large number of men approaching from the north. Shortly thereafter, they could make out hushed voices giving words of command and caution: "Close up" – "Steady! men" – "Steady! men" ... and other like words."[36]

Within seconds, every American artillery piece and musket that could be brought to bear opened fire into the darkness.

Assault on the northeast bastion. Painted in the 1830s, this imaginative artist's conception of the attack on the bastion shows Drummond waving on his men while Lieutenants McDonough and Watmough fend off the assault and Captain Williams lies, mortally wounded, in the foreground. (Photograph by Rene Chartrand of painting by "ECW" in the *United States Military Magazine*, March 1841)

CHAPTER FIVE

"Give the damned Yankees no quarter!"

THE NORTHERN COLUMNS ATTACK,
2.45 A.M–5 A.M., 15 AUGUST 1814

Ye Parliament of England,
You Lords and commons, too,
Consider well, what you're about
And what you're going to do.
You're now to fight the Yankees,
I'm sure you'll rue the day,
You roused the Sons of Liberty
In North Amerikay

Lament, ye sons of Britain,
Far distant is the day
When you'll regain by British force
What you've lost in Amerikay;
Go tell your King and parliament,
By all the world 'tis known,
That British force, by sea and land,
By Yankees is o'erthrown.[1]

The American artillery fire was too high and much of it missed the advancing British columns. Le Couteur of the 104th Foot recalled that this opening salvo was fired when his column was about 200 yards from the fort, but as the attackers neared the defences and became more visible, the American gunners adjusted their aim and their fire became more accurate. For speed, William Drummond and Hercules Scott had moved their columns along the lakeshore road until they neared the defences when Scott's 103rd Foot shifted to the water's edge while Drummond's force of seamen, marines and soldiers headed directly for the fort.

Scott had probably opted to form his regiment in a column of subdivisions or half-companies. This meant that the 103rd Foot was moving in a formation of 40 ranks, one behind the other, with each rank being 15-16 men wide.

British 6-pdr. gun, Fort McNair. Captured at Lundy's Lane, this weapon was used to good effect by its new owners at the assault on Fort Erie. This weapon has killed many American, British and Canadian soldiers. (Photograph courtesy the U.S. Army Center for Military History, Washington)

This was the most useful formation for an infantry battalion to assume when it needed to cover ground quickly but the massing of the ranks made them extremely vulnerable to artillery fire. When the leading ranks were able to see the defence works, Scott would have ordered the 103rd to move at the "quick step" of 108 paces (270 feet) per minute, which would permit it to get to grips with the defenders quickly and lessen his men's exposure to the American artillery.[2]

Unfortunately for the 103rd Foot, it was advancing almost directly into the muzzles of Douglass's 18-pdr. gun and the captured 6-pdr. gun – which had now been taken under command by no less than Major William McRee, the Left Division's senior engineer – and approximately 180 muskets. Douglass had loaded his gun "for short quarters" with roundshot, grape, canister and bags of musket balls until he "could touch the last wad, with my hand, in the muzzle of the piece." Translated, what this means is that his 18-pdr. was double-charged with two cartridges, on top of which his gunners rammed down two roundshot, two rounds of canister, one round of grape and as many canvas bags of musket balls as possible. Even at a conservative estimate this would mean that each discharge from this weapon would propel two solid iron shot weighing 18 pounds each, 10 lead grape bullets, each weighing 8 ounces, 110 canister bullets, each weighing 1.5 ounces, and possibly as many as 300 musket balls each weighing just under an ounce, at the 103rd Regiment of Foot. Having a smaller weapon with a smaller bore, McRee could not match this deadly combination but he would have, at the least, loaded two rounds of canister, which would add another 110 canister shot of 1.5 ounces weight each.[3]

The head of Scott's column was within 150 feet of the defenders when it was struck by this deadly iron hail. An eyewitness later testified that the 103rd Foot "recoiled" and came to a dead halt.[4] This is probably an understatement as even if half of the 500 projectiles, weighing approximately 78 pounds in total, hit the leading company, it would have been immediately transformed from a military sub-unit into a charnel house as men were smashed into a bloody pulp, lost heads or limbs, were disembowelled, or simply knocked over when a man in front was hit and thrown backward. The leading company, almost certainly the elite grenadier company, simply melted away. The following companies came to a complete stop and then moved backward into the darkness, followed by shouting officers and NCOs who struggled to reform the men and get them again going forward.

Drummond's column was more fortunate. As it moved toward the stone fort it took shelter behind the mounds of earth that constituted the early stages of the two new outlying bastions. Although Williams's four guns in the northeast battery and the 18-pdr. on the curtain wall kept up a constant fire, they inflicted far fewer casualties than those that fired on Scott's column. Drummond's "forlorn hope" or lead element in his column – the most dangerous position in an assault of this type – consisted of sailors, many of whom were carrying ladders. It was guided by Captain William Barney of the 89th Foot and commanded by Colour Sergeant Richard Smith of the 104th Foot, who, as was traditional, had been promised an officer's commission if he survived the assault. The forlorn hope waited behind the earth mounds until the remainder of the column had caught up and an American officer heard someone, probably Colour Sergeant Smith or William Drummond himself, shouting in the darkness, "Stand my boys here under their guns they can't hurt you."[5] When the remainder of the column had caught up, the forlorn hope jumped down into the ditch in front of the V-shaped curtain wall. It suffered some casualties doing so, but it was now in "dead ground" where only one 6-pdr. gun in the northeast bastion could reach it and any American infantry that tried to fire from the curtain wall would expose themselves.[6]

This done, the forlorn hope threw up its ladders, which thankfully were long enough, and climbed to the top of the curtain wall. Coming behind, Le Couteur of the 104th remembered that

> We still marched at a rapid but steady pace, in a few minutes the head of the column, or rather the forlorn hope, got to the ditch, jumped in, reared the Scaling ladders and cheered us as they mounted. We increased our pace and cheered loudly, defying the fire of the enemy. I jumped with our Company into the ditch. It was slow work to get up the ladders – of which there was not one quarter enough – there were palisades to be cut away, while a galling flank fire from a Gun and musquetry annoyed us sadly.[7]

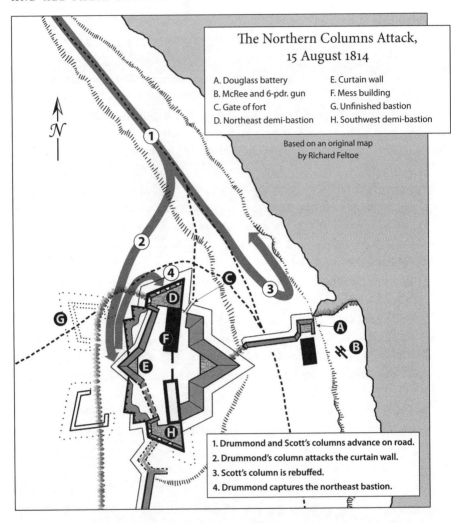

The Northern Columns Attack,
15 August 1814

A. Douglass battery
B. McRee and 6-pdr. gun
C. Gate of fort
D. Northeast demi-bastion
E. Curtain wall
F. Mess building
G. Unfinished bastion
H. Southwest demi-bastion

Based on an original map
by Richard Feltoe

1. Drummond and Scott's columns advance on road.
2. Drummond's column attacks the curtain wall.
3. Scott's column is rebuffed.
4. Drummond captures the northeast bastion.

Crouched down, so as not to expose themselves, on the earth bank behind the curtain wall, the men of the Nineteenth Infantry were waiting. Trimble had ordered them "not to fire until they could fire with effect"[8] and they did not open up until the heads and shoulders of Drummond's men appeared above the palisades. They then let loose with a volley that dropped many of the British into the ditch. This being done, Trimble's men moved up to the wall itself, elevated their musket butts and fired blind down into the milling mass of sailors, marines and soldiers below before pulling back to reload. The night was pierced by tongues of flame as the muskets clattered in a frenzy. Lieutenant Charles Cessna of the Nineteenth Infantry, commanding one section of the curtain wall, remembered that the British placed their ladders and ascended them. We met them on the inside. The first charge was but a small space of time. After firing, on them, we charged [stabbed] with the bayonet and beat them down. In a few minutes the enemy rallied and came to the second charge. It lasted … longer than the first and was more serious, in its consequences.[9]

This time, shouting "No quarter!" according to eyewitnesses, more of the attackers were able get over the wall and proved much harder to evict. A vicious struggle took place on the small gun platform, only twelve feet square, located at the point of the V-shaped curtain wall. Cessna recalled that, in a melee waged with bayonets, boarding pikes, cutlasses and musket butts, "we lost two or three men and had a good many wounded."[10] In hand to hand fighting like this, the attackers armed with long boarding pikes had an advantage over those armed with shorter weapons but they were also marked targets for those Americans firing with their muskets. Trimble moved constantly behind his men and encouraged them. He later recalled that "the bayonet was used with good effect" as the combat on the wall see-sawed back and forth. Finally, the British were again pushed back into the ditch and the struggle subsided for a few moments.[11]

But Drummond's men came back a third time. Cessna thought that, compared to the second charge, the third was not as resolute and it is likely that many attackers, realizing that the curtain wall was stoutly defended, were either reluctant to risk going up the ladders or had moved away, looking for a more vulnerable part of the defences. Although casualties were taken on both sides, including Cessna, who was shot through the stomach, this charge did not last as long and the attackers were repulsed and withdrew into the darkness. This time they did not return.[12]

While Drummond was tackling the curtain wall, Scott had not been idle. He had managed to rally and re-form the 103rd Foot and get them moving again toward the gap between Douglass's battery and the lake. Scott's objective was evident to the defenders for, as Douglass commented, the enemy's aim was clearly "to pass our breast-works, with scaling ladders, or to penetrate [into] the open spaces [of the

Major William A. Trimble (1786-1821). Shown here in a postwar portrait, Trimble was the infantry commander in the stone fort and ably defended it. Dissatisfied with Gaines's official report, which he did not feel did either him or his command justice, Trimble later brought charges against Gaines. (Print after portrait, author's collection)

camp]."[13] For a second time, the 103rd Foot was repulsed by heavy musketry and artillery fire and, again, faded into the darkness. A few minutes later they were back but, as Broughton of the dragoons remembered, "this effort to charge our line was very feeble" and after a third rebuff, Scott's column did not return.[14]

It seemed to the Americans that the British attacks had been decisively repulsed and the business was finished. Although they could hear voices and commands in the darkness, it was assumed that these were concerned with organizing a withdrawal. By this time the frequent discharges of artillery and muskets had resulted in dense clouds of powder smoke that, combined with the mist resulting from warm temperatures and heavy rain earlier in the evening, had created a thick cloud that hovered over the entire northern flank of the American position. Although the defenders tried to remain alert, there was a palpable relaxation of tension all along the line of defences.

It was at about this time that Surgeon William Dunlop began to feel nervous. He had been ordered by William Drummond to remain in the rear to attend the wounded but as the minutes ticked by he began

> to feel my situation most particularly unpleasant. A man must possess more courage than I can pretend to, who can stand perfectly cool, while having nothing to do, he is shot at like a target. Accordingly, I determined to advance at all hazards, and at least have the pleasure of seeing what was doing for my risk of being shot.[15]

Dunlop had only moved a short distance when he stumbled over the body of an officer who "was wounded in the arm" and had "fallen in attempting to get to the rear." Dunlop fixed a "field tourniquet on his arm, and throwing him over my shoulder like a sack, carried him to a ravine in rear, and delivered him to the care of a Naval Surgeon I met with there."[16] The man turned out to be Captain James Rowan of the 1st Foot, who, as Dunlop commented, "but for my lucky stumble, would most probably have given promotion" to the officer next senior in that regiment. His mission of mercy completed, Dunlop gave up all pretence of being a non-combatant and hurried forward to join his comrades, armed with two swords – his own Ferrara blade and William Drummond's weapon, which its owner had earlier given to Dunlop for safe keeping.

When they retreated from the curtain wall, most of Drummond's men had filtered east along the ditch in front of the fort. Here they encountered remnants of Scott's 103rd which had moved west along the ditch from the lake – the two columns joined and Drummond was able to establish some control. He was now immediately below the northeast bastion in what appears to have been a blind spot in the defences and his men were hidden by the cloud of smoke that hung over the stone fort. Certainly the American gunners in the bastion about twenty feet above were not aware of them and were still peering in the direction of the earlier attack, ready to resume firing. William Drummond made the decision, the order was given, the ladders were placed and the men climbed up, with Drummond going first.

Inside the bastion were Williams, McDonough and Watmough, and about thirty gunners manning four pieces. They were taken totally by surprise – Watmough was directing the return of a gun to its firing position when, to his amazement – and probable horror – "a British officer followed by several seamen and Five or six soldiers jumped into the Bastion on to one of the 12-pounders."[17] There was enough light for Watmough to recognize Drummond, whom he had previously seen when the British officer came to the fort under a flag of truce. Drummond lunged at Watmough with his boarding pike but the young officer dodged. Before the startled gunners could grab their muskets leaning against the wall of the bastion, more attackers boiled over into the bastion from different sides and went at them with swords, boarding pikes, bayonets and musket butts. The Americans fought back with whatever came to hand – Watmough grabbed a rammer from an artillery piece and frantically fended off bayonet and pike thrusts.[18]

The British were in no mood to be merciful. Watmough remembered that they called us "dam'd Yankees" and "rascals" and repeatedly cried "no quarter," meaning "no prisoners." Watmough and his comrades were learning a hard lesson in the laws of war as they were observed in the early 19th century. The rule of thumb was that an army that mounted an assault over the wall of a fortified position – an "escalade" as it was technically known and a very dangerous operation – was not expected to take prisoners under the "Laws of War" as they were understood at that time.* In any case, Drummond's men, having suffered heavy casualties during the repulse at the curtain wall, were in a state of red rage and well beyond legal niceties. Drummond himself is reported to have shouted "give the damned Yankees no quarter!" and his men obeyed this command and threw themselves at the defenders. Watmough received a blow on the head with a musket butt that knocked him unconscious off the far side of the bastion. He was lucky. His fellow officers, Williams and McDonough, fought desperately but both were cut down without mercy, as were two gunners, Privates Eben Edwards and John Shute. As more and more British climbed into the bastion, the remaining defenders fled into the interior of the fort.[19]

The bastion had fallen so fast that the other American units on the northern

---

* See Appendix C below for a discussion of this subject.

The northeast bastion (below) and curtain wall at Fort Erie. The northeast demi-bastion, seen here with the stone mess building behind, was the part of the defences closest to the British lines and the scene of heavy fighting. The first British attacks went in against the palisaded curtain wall but were beaten off. (Author's photographs)

flank were unsure of what had happened. Captain Alexander Hill of the Nineteenth Infantry, whose men were manning the right face of the V-shaped curtain wall, remembered that as soon as he heard shouts and cheers from the bastion, he turned toward it to see men running out of it. At first he thought they were British but when they identified themselves, Hill quickly deployed his men into a line blocking the exit from the bastion. Douglass's men were firing their 18-pdr. gun "when a mysterious and confused sound of tumult, in the salient bastion of the fort, just above us, was followed by the cessation of the artillery-fire, at that point."[20] Douglass was confused but Captain Childs of the Ninth Infantry grasped what had happened and immediately brought the bastion under musket fire but ceased when he heard shouts that he was firing on Americans.[21] Douglass also distinctly heard a command, "in a loud voice and tone of authority," to "Cease firing! You're firing upon your own men." As he recalled, however,

The foreignness of the accent … betrayed the person and purpose of the speaker. The firing did, indeed, slacken, for a moment, … but the reaction was short. Another voice was presently heard above the tumult, commanding, in a different strain, and with no foreign accent "Go to H[ell]— . Fire away there, why don't you?" and so we did, with more animation than ever.[22]

The British were now in possession of a vital part of the defences but it did them little good. The only way out of the bastion into the interior of the fort was a narrow gorge or passageway, about seven feet wide, between the bastion and a stone mess building. Trimble reacted quickly to the threat and reinforced Hill's men blocking this exit with Lieutenant John McIlwain's command of the Nineteenth Infantry. Drummond led an attempt to break into the interior of the stone fort but, as McIlwain reported, by "heavy fire and by some charges we drove them back."[23] The evidence is contradictory but Drummond apparently tried several times to gain the interior, recklessly exposing himself because he was an officer who believed in leading from the front. The result was inevitable. During one of the British charges, Trimble pointed out to McIlwain an enemy officer "advanced as far as the Door of the mess house" and "gave us orders to kill him – we shot him down and his party gave back at his fall."[24] At first McIlwain could not distinguish Drummond from his men but Trimble, "directing us where he was" and seeing the British officer "giving his men command," ordered his own men to concentrate their fire on Drummond and they killed him."[25] Drummond's premonition had come true.

Trimble realized that the mess building adjoining the fallen bastion was the key to the defence of the fort because from its upper storey fire could be brought down on the attackers in the northeast demi-bastion. He ordered Hill to take fifty men of the Nineteenth Infantry into the building and hold it "to the last extremity."[26] Lieutenant Charles Cass took half of Hill's men and occupied the second floor at the north end, which overlooked the bastion. The mess building was loop-holed but none of the firing ports permitted Cass's men to fire into the bastion. They could reach it, however, from two windows, approximately two feet wide and five feet high, as well as a chimney hole in the roof. Cass assigned men to each of these apertures and, in turn, they opened a "brisk fire" into the bastion, which was crowded with British troops, with more pouring in every minute. Once a man had fired, he stepped back to load and was replaced by another man, so that an almost continuous hail of musketry was kept up. The opponents tossed taunts back and forth like grenades. Cass's men in the mess house shouted insults at the British in the bastion: "Come over you rascals, we're British deserters and Irish rebels."[27] While Hill's men occupied the mess building, the remainder of the Nineteenth Infantry under the command of McIlwain took position, either on the interior of the curtain wall or behind the end of the mess building.

Cass's men barely had to aim as the bastion was crowded with men from both Drummond and Scott's columns. After Drummond had been killed, Captain Joseph Glew, commanding the light company of the 41st Foot, assumed command but he was almost immediately wounded and replaced by Captain Richard Bullock, commander of the 41st grenadier company. Like Trimble, Bullock realized that the mess building was the key to the defence and he was familiar with it as he had been stationed in the fort prior to the war. He ordered Lieutenant Harris Hailes, a young Canadian officer serving in the 41st, to "collect what men you can of the light company, join me, and attempt to get possession of the barracks," or mess building. The two officers ordered their men to break down the door nearest the bastion and managed to enter, only to find that the Americans had drawn up the ladders leading to the upper storey. The defenders opened such a heavy fire from the upper level that, as Hailes later remarked, although his men had "succeeded in getting into the lower part of the building," they "met with such a violent resistance that we were quickly driven out." Bullock was hit in the head and had to be taken to the rear and a few minutes later Hailes himself was wounded. At this point, Hercules Scott arrived and assumed command – only to be shot in the head and carried away. The situation of the leaderless men in the crowded bastion was becoming desperate and many crouched or even lay down to avoid the fire of Cass's men.[28]

Trimble now began to receive reinforcements as several small detachments were ordered to the fort to assist him. The first to arrive was a party of twenty-five men of the Twenty-Second Infantry commanded by Lieutenant John Brady. Brady found that most of the Nineteenth Infantry were either in the mess building under Trimble's direct command with only McIlwain's small party sheltering behind the far end of that building. Brady positioned half his men along the curtain wall and the other half with McIlwain. He was shortly followed by Captain William Foster of the Eleventh Infantry with about sixty men of that unit. Foster assumed command and, after much shouting back and forth, got Trimble to order his men to cease firing from the mess building while he made an attempt to retake the bastion by rushing the passageway. He made two attempts and both were decisively rebuffed by the British in the bastion. Foster then took post with McIlwain and Brady and positioned his men to bring the bastion under musket fire.[29]

Next to arrive was a detachment of 150 men of the Fourth Rifle Regiment under the command of Captain Benjamin Birdsall. Birdsall had been ordered to the support of the Ninth Infantry outside the stone fort but when he arrived at that unit's position, he found that the Ninth was holding its own and decided to enter the fort. As he led his men toward the gate, Birdsall observed a large body of troops outside the northeast bastion. The rifle officer recalled that

> I could not tell whether they were British or American Troops. I hailed and was answered the 103rd. Being cautious to make no mistakes, I was a second time answered the 103rd after hailing a second time. I then immediately ordered my command to fire. [30]

Birdsall took his men into the fort, where he was joined by Major Nathaniel Hall, the assistant inspector general of the Left Division. Determined to retake the bastion, Hall and Birdsall mounted two charges against the passageway and were twice repulsed. Trimble shouted to them from the mess building that it "was useless to charge" as the enemy were not going anywhere. Birdsall could see the British in the bastion ducking down to seek cover from Cass's men in the upper storey of the mess building. The Americans thought that the British, estimated at about 250, appeared to be in considerable confusion. [31]

It was a stalemate: the attackers could not get out of the bastion and the defenders could not get into it. But time favoured the Americans as the sky was beginning to lighten in the east and the attackers' situation could only get worse. Although wounded, Hailes was convinced that the deadlock could be broken with fresh troops. As he passed some staff officers on his way rearward to get medical attention for his wound, he urged them, "For God's sake push on the reserve ... and the fort is yours." [32] Drummond did order the 1st Foot to advance to a ravine about midway to the fort but that was all. Incredibly, even at this point, some men were still trying to get up the ladders into the bastion, although others, seeing the hopelessness of the situation, "were sneaking out by one, two or three from the ditch" for the cover of the British lines. [33] William Drummond's assault column had included a subaltern of the Royal Artillery and a small detachment of gunners for the purposes of using any guns captured against their former owners. Lieutenant George Charlton, RA, commanded the artillery party with Drummond's column and, after considerable effort, he and his men managed to swing the 24-pdr. gun in the bastion around and fire two rounds: one at the American positions to the east and a second "thro' the mess house." [34]

For his part, Gaines tried to reinforce the defenders of the fort but, given his strength and the length of the defence works, he found it difficult to find men. He ordered Captain Thomas Biddle to move a howitzer from his battery on the west wall and position it to fire into the bastion and Biddle immediately complied. In the interior of the fort, meanwhile, Hall and Birdsall, convinced that they could retake the bastion, began to form their men for a third assault on it. [35]

The interior of the stone fort. These photographs by the author show the gorge which was the only exit from the northeast bastion, seen behind, and the stone mess building. The soldier stands approximately where William Drummond was killed. The interior shot from the second floor of the mess building shows the clear field of fire into the bastion. Below left is the interior gate of the fort, which is in the stone curtain wall that connects the two mess buildings.

Suddenly, Douglass remembered,

> every sound was hushed by the sense of an unnatural tremor, beneath our feet, like the first heave of an earthquake; and, almost at the same instant, the centre of the bastion burst up, with a terrific explosion; and a jet of flame, mingled with fragments of timber, earth, stone, and bodies of men, rose, to the height of one or two hundred feet, in the air, and fell, in a shower of ruins, to a great distance, all around.[36]

The demi-bastion had exploded. The conflagration was caused by the detonation of the expense magazine beneath the firing platform of the captured bastion.* The stone walls of the structure channelled the force of the explosion upwards, tossing artillery pieces and carriages, the timbers of the gun platform – and men – into the air. More than a half century later, one witness could still

---

* For a discussion on the causes of this explosion, see Appendix C below.

clearly see in his mind's eye the "forms of human beings" flying through the air with "their cartridge boxes filled with fixed ammunition ignited and spangled out in every direction."[37] Most of the debris and the dead and living fell into the ditch on the east side of bastion, which was crowded with men from both assault columns, but some of it was scattered a great distance. Private Michael Carroll, one of Douglas's gunners, was killed when a chunk of the bastion hit him at his post 300 feet away.[38]

Le Couteur had been about to step off a ladder into the bastion when the explosion took place. Before he lost consciousness, he remembered seeing "a black volume rise from the earth," and when he regained his senses, the young officer found himself

> lying in the ditch fifteen or twenty feet down where I had been thrown by a tremendous explosion of gunpowder which cleared the Fort of three hundred men in an Instant. The platform had been blown over and a great beam had jammed me to the earth but it was resting on the Scarp. I got from under it with ease, bruised but otherwise unhurt. ......
>
> On getting upon my legs, I trod on poor Lt. Horrens broke leg of the 103rd, which made me shudder to my marrow. In placing my hand on Captain [George] Shore's back to steady myself from treading on some other poor mangled person, for the ditch was so crowded with bodies it was almost unavoidable, I found my hand in a mass of blood and brains – it was sickening.[39]

Surgeon Dunlop, who was also in the ditch, was determined to escape:

> All was now confusion, and – d[evi]l take the hindmost! How I got across the ditch, I cannot, nor never could call to my memory; but I found myself scouring along the road at the top of my speed, with a running accompaniment of grape, canister and musketry whistling about my ears, and tearing the ground at my feet.
>
> When about half way between the ditch and the ravine, I heard a voice calling on me for help. I found it was a wounded officer; so, calling a drum-boy of the Royals, who had a stretcher, we laid him into it, and carried him after the manner of a hand-barrow; he entreated us to get into the wood, as, on the road, we were likely to be cut to pieces with the shot.
>
> Accordingly we turned for that purpose; but just as we were entering, a round shot cut a large bough just above our heads, and down it came on top of the three of us. I crawled backwards and the drum-boy forwards; and there we were staring at each other; however, there was no time to express our surprise. I ordered him in again, and I crawled in at the other side; and by our

joint exertions we got the poor fellow out of his uncomfortable situation, and once in the wood we were safe for the rest of our journey. I handed him over to some medical men in the battery, and went in search of my own men.[40]

It took some time for the defenders to recover from the shock of the explosion, but when they did, they made efforts to bring fire to bear on the ditch. Biddle brought up his howitzer and commenced firing and, as the smoke began to clear, Hall and Birdsall led parties into the ruined bastion and began to fire down on the men in the ditch. As the "Yankees yelled, fired and cheered," Le Couteur made himself as "pancake as possible" against the wall of the ditch but, determined not to be taken prisoner, he too started out for the safety of the British lines:

> I dashed across the Plain under such a roar of voices, Musquetry & Artillery as I never desire to run from again. Just as I had cleared half the distance, L[ieutenan]t. [John] Fallon of the 103rd Grenadiers was close before me, staggering, his sling belt caught [in] a stump. "Oh" he exclaimed, "I am caught at last." "No, Jack, my boy", I said, "you're not caught, its a tree." "Oh Johnny, I'm so dreadfully wounded in two places, I can't get on, I'm so weak." As we spoke, a grist of grape shot scattered at our feet. We escaped, as all of us have seen a Sparrow escape from a charge of No. 4 [buck shot]. "Never fear, place your arm over my Neck and I'll take your waist, I'll run you in and not desert you – hurrah!" And we got to our batteries safely.[41]

As he neared the British lines, Le Couteur saw four soldiers carrying a wounded officer on an extemporized stretcher and asked them who he was – the reply was: "Col. Scott, sir, shot through the head."[42] Le Couteur was followed by other survivors of the explosion who made their way, under fire, across the cleared area north of the stone fort to their own line.

Birdsall's riflemen had repossessed the wreckage of the bastion and he ordered them to cheer to indicate that it was back in American hands. The response was so enthusiastic that he ordered a second cheer. Birdsall should perhaps have left well enough alone because, as he recalled, while "in the act of cheering the second time," he was hit by a musket ball that "entered near the mouth and fracturing very severely the underjaw and teeth … came out behind and near the point of the jawbone."[43] It would be quite some time before Captain Birdsall again cheered.

The defenders sent a number of small detachments out beyond their defences to harass the retreating British but no attempt was made to mount a serious pursuit, although McRee urged that this be done. The Left Division's victory, "decisive as it was," commented Major Roger Jones, one of Gaines's staff officers, "was considered as much as the troops at the moment were capable of atchieving [sic]" and "we were all contented with the results."[44]

John Norton arrived at the northern flank of the American position shortly after the explosion, which "blew the broken fragments of buildings & works in all directions." As the sky lightened, he and his warriors

> met the Troops retiring from the Fort which they had gallantly entered. – We saw none advancing, – our own number nothing when compared to the host of foes which opposed us. After hesitating a little while, we retired with others to the Ravine, on the Summit of which we waited, until the whole of our Troops had retired. The Enemy did not come out of his works, but continued firing round Shot, Grape Shells, and Musketry. We left them there and followed our friends, – enraged at their misfortune.[45]

As it grew light and visibility increased, the British artillery commenced firing, both to cover the retreat of the survivors of the assault and to let the Americans know that they were ready to repel any attempt by the defenders to mount a sortie. The area between the fort and battery became dotted with men moving singly or in clumps, looking for their officers and units like frightened children seeking their parents to make it right. Dunlop remembered that when he arrived back at the British lines,

> there was a scene of sad confusion. Sir Gordon Drummond was with great coolness forming the men as they came in, and I, with others, set to work to assist him. Without regard to what corps they belonged, we stuck them behind the breast-work, anticipating an attack. Sir Gordon asked me what officers were killed; I told him all that I knew of ….[46]

Drummond also questioned Le Couteur when he came back from the fort:

> The General called me to Him. "Do you know anything about Y[ou]r Colonel [William Drummond]?" I could not articulate for grief. "Killed, Sir." "Col[onel]. Scott?" "Shot thro' the head, Sir, Your Grenadiers are bringing Him in, Major Leonard & Maclauchlan wounded & Capt[ain]. Shore a prisoner." The General felt for me and said "Never mind, Cheer up. You are wanted here. Fall in any men of any regiment as they come up, to line our batteries for fear of an attack.[47]

Once 19-year-old Le Couteur realized he was safe, he was overcome by the horror he had just experienced and, "regardless of who was by, in a fit of sorrow," threw his sword on the ground and sobbed: "This is a disgraceful day for Old England!"[48]

After the battle. When it was all over, the medical personnel laboured to try to save lives and relieve suffering. (Drawing by George Balbar reproduced with permission from Robert Foley, *The War of 1812*.)

CHAPTER SIX

"Oh God! what a scene!"

THE AFTERMATH

Ah! the moment was sad when my love and I parted,
Savourneen deelish Eileen oge!
As I kissed off her tears I was nigh broken-hearted,
Savourneen deelish Eileen oge!
Wan was her che'ek which hung on my shoulder,
Damp was her hand, no marble was colder,
I felt that again I should never behold her.
Savourneen deelish Eileen oge!

When the word of command put our men into motion,
Savourneen deelish Eileen oge!
I buckled my knapsack to cross the wide ocean,
Savourneen deelish Eileen oge!
Brisk were our troops, all roaring like thunder,
Pleased with the voyage, impatient for plunder,
My bosom with grief was almost torn asunder.
Savourneen deelish Eileen oge![1]

The dawn of 15 August not only brought the resumption of British artillery fire but also a heavy downpour of rain. For most of the night, the residents of Buffalo and Black Rock had listened to the sounds of the battle being fought a mile or so across the Niagara and – as they had no idea of its outcome – feared the worst. It was only when a boat arrived from the Canadian shore that they learned the welcome news that the result was an American victory.[2]

With the coming of day, the defenders saw for the first time, the carnage they had wrought a few hours before. Buoyed by their victory the men of the Left Division began to examine the area of the heaviest fighting, which was covered with the detritus of war, abandoned weapons, scraps of paper and bodies – many bodies – either whole or in part, and some still writhing. "Oh God! what a scene!" was Douglass's reaction because

At every point where the battle had raged, were strewed the melancholy vestiges of the recent terrible conflict. There is the ruined bastion, the scene of such desperate strife, smoking with the recent explosion, and, all around it, the ground covered with the bodies of the dead and wounded – the former in every stage and state of mutilation. ...... In front of our fires, between the bastion and the water, the ground was literally piled with dead. ......

I was called upon to re-lay the platform of the ruined bastion. The whole bastion and its immediate neighborhood were heaped with dead and desperately wounded; while bodies and fragments of bodies were scattered on the ground, in every direction. More than a hundred bodies were removed from the ruin, before I could proceed with the work ......

Several hours were employed in carefully disengaging the wounded and burnt from the ruins: those who were yet alive were sent to the care of the Army Surgeons; while the dead bodies were passed over the embankment. While the repairs were in progress, the parties detailed for the purpose excavated large graves, a little distance without the fortification, and gathered the dead, who were buried, forty and fifty together, side by side, with the honors of War.[3]

Lieutenant Jonathan Kearsley of the Fourth Rifle Regiment described the area around the ruins of the bastion as being an "appalling scene" with men scattered about "some dying, others groaning under their wounds and dead bodies heaped upon them, others burnt and blind, many crying for water to slake their burning thirst, in short, every form of human suffering."[4] Teenager Jarvis Hanks, hardened by military service, was morbidly fascinated by the human wreckage:

During the forenoon, I inspected the awful scene. I counted 196 bodies lying in the ditch and about the fort, most of them dead, some dying. Their faces and hands were burned black, many of them horribly mutilated. Here and there were legs, arms and heads, lying, in confusion, separated, by the concussion, from the trunks to which they had long been attached. One trunk, I observed, deprived of all its limbs and head.[5]

Hanks noted that his comrades looted the British casualties and "even picked the pockets of those who were dead and dying in the ditch." One of Douglass's men presented him with a sword marked to the 103rd Foot, which

evidently had been cut away from the body of the owner, who could not be found and probably had been carried off the field. Of his rank, therefore, we could but conjecture; though the peculiarity of its shape and workmanship has since led me to suppose that it might have belonged to the leader of the One hundred and third Regiment, Colonel Scott, who was killed at the head of the enemy's left column.[6]

William Drummond's body, which lay in front of the stone mess building, was identified. He had penetrated farther into the American position than any other British soldier in the assault columns – and he had paid the price. His corpse, stripped to its shirt, was exhibited during the day underneath a cart, where it was seen by Jarvis Hanks, who remembered that one of the officers of the Eleventh Infantry purchased Drummond's engraved gold watch when it was offered for sale in the camp.[7] In an inside pocket of his coat, the Americans discovered Drummond's memorandum book and the order for the assault, which were immediately sent to Gaines. On close examination of the body, it was discovered that Drummond had not only been shot in the chest but that someone had made sure of him with a bayonet. Ironically, the point of the weapon had passed through the order for the assault, tearing the paper immediately above the sentence: "The Lieutenant General recommends a free use of the bayonet."[8]

William Drummond was buried, along with the other British dead from the northern columns, in a mass grave in the ditch of the fort.[9] Most of the dead from the explosion were lying in a heap to the east of the bastion but it was difficult to accurately count them as "they were very much torn to pieces."[10] Lieutenant John McIlwain was able to identify many of the bodies, from the engraving on their crossbelt plates and the badges on their cartridge boxes, as being men of the 103rd Foot. During the afternoon working parties dug a series of shallow mass graves in the ditch and dragged the corpses to them. The Left Division buried nearly 200 bodies near the stone fort as well as many in the vicinity of Snake Hill.[11]

Fatal words. A copy of the order by General Drummond strongly recommending a "free use of the bayonet" was found on William Drummond's corpse. A bayonet had penetrated the order just above these words. (From Benson Lossing, *Pictorial Field-Book of the War of 1812*)

The British artillery kept firing throughout this labour and the defenders, believing this fire to be deliberate, characterized it as "an act as contrary to the dictates of policy as to the principles of humanity."[12] It is more likely that the British gunners, unable to discern exactly what was happening in the ditch, decided that the defenders were repairing and improving their defences and so brought them under fire. Late in the afternoon, the British guns did cease fire briefly when Lieutenant-General Gordon Drummond sent an officer to the fort under a flag of truce, to inquire about the fate of three missing British officers. Word soon went round the American camp that Gaines had informed the emissary that he would "receive no Communication" from the British commander unless it was "an unconditional Surrender of all his Majesty's forces in Upper Canada."[13] This makes a good tale for the telling but it is highly unlikely that Gaines ever spoke these words.

And then there were the wounded. When writing about combat, historians must keep a tight grip on their emotions if they are to successfully convey the true nature of war – basically a process of hot and cold-blooded killing – without degenerating into bloodthirsty dramatics or maudlin sentimentality. On the other hand, historians can, and many do, restrain their feelings to the point where combat becomes a mathematical abstract and the beings they write about become so devoid of human characteristics that they resemble toy soldiers capable of moving and firing, but little else. War is by no means a glorious activity and the best testament to the veracity of that statement is provided by the medical personnel who dealt with the aftermath of the British assault.

Surgeon William Dunlop of the 89th Foot, a man more inclined to be warrior than healer, once remarked that there is "hardly on the face of the earth a less enviable situation than that of an Army Surgeon after a battle" because he is "surrounded by suffering, pain and misery, much of which he knows it is not in his power to heal or even to assuage." When the battle is on, the horrors of war "pass unnoticed" but when it is ended, the afflicted "come before the medical man ... in all their sorrow and horror, stripped of all the excitement of the 'heady fight.'"[14] This sentiment was echoed by Surgeon William Horner of the American Left Division, who, writing a medical memoir of the Niagara campaign in later years, noted that "the military man sees in such events the steps of his glory," but the military surgeon knows "the woes of war" as "he hears only the groans of the wounded, sees the horrid mutilation of their bodies, their want of comfortable accommodations and provisions, and the imperfect attendance" by overworked medical personnel.[15]

American surgeons tended most of the wounded of both armies. Through-

In all their sorrow and horror. Drawings made from life by Surgeon Charles Bell of the British army in 1815 show the effect of round shot on a man's arm and facial wounds inflicted by smaller projectiles. (Courtesy, Parks Canada)

out 15 August, those casualties still alive were gradually retrieved and taken to the interior of the camp. "In removing the wounded," Kearsley recalled, Aesop's fable about the blind man carrying the lame man was "fearfully realized" as men "who had a fractured leg were mounted upon the shoulders of others, whose eyes were burnt to a temporary if not lasting blindness," and "both removed to a place of safety."[16] There were far too many for the regimental surgeons to cope with, so the most serious cases were taken across the lake to Buffalo. Eber Howe, who was serving as a hospital attendant at that place, recalled that the boats unloaded many

> poor, miserable, mangled specimens of humanity into our immediate presence and care on the day following. Many were yet insensible, and unable

to move a muscle, although nothing was visible to indicate their wounds. But the worst cases were those who had been burnt by the explosion of the powder magazine. Some of their faces and hands were so crisped that the skin peeled off like a baked pig. ...... One poor fellow, with a marine dress [uniform], lay in a bunk near by, totally insensible to all his surroundings, and only able to move one leg, which he continued to draw up and down constantly for about three days when he expired. He was a fine specimen of physical manhood, and had the mark of a musket-ball, which had just penetrated the skull.[17]

The more seriously wounded were sent on to the general hospital at Williamsville, about seven miles northeast of Buffalo, where they were treated by Surgeon William Horner and his colleagues. Like Howe, Horner was struck by the terrible condition of many of the British wounded – he noted that some were "blackened over the whole face with the explosion of the powder, and their heads swollen to two sizes; some with eyes burned out; in others, limbs mangled and perforated by musket balls, with their clothes torn from their scarified backs."[18] Many were cared for by a Kentucky woman named Betsey, who was remarkable not only "for her height, muscular figure, and the loss of one eye" but also "for her volubility in oaths and queer modes of execration when jeered or incensed."[19] Betsey from Kentucky had actually fought as a combatant at the battle of Chippawa before being ordered to leave the fighting ranks. Despite her rough-hewn personality and profanity, Horner remembered Betsey as "one of the most faithful and kind of nurses, notwithstanding her recklessness of conduct in other respects."

There was very little medical personnel could do for serious head or torso wounds. Generally, those so afflicted were made as comfortable as possible and were then left for nature to take its course. They usually died. For serious limb wounds, amputation was the most common medical procedure and was generally used for all compound fractures of the long bones by musket or artillery projectiles, all wounds to joints and any limb wound that resulted in a major loss of tissue. During the Napoleonic period there was a great debate among military medical personnel as to whether amputation should be carried out as soon as possible or delayed for some time. The leading surgeons of the British and French armies, George Guthrie and Dominique Larrey, respectively, urged that it should be done as quickly as possible and produced statistics to back up that statement.[20] American medical personnel tended to agree – Surgeon Amasa Trowbridge of the Twenty-First Infantry expressed his opposition to any delay of the procedure:

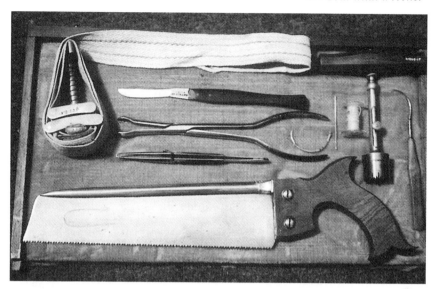

Tools of the trade. A surgeon's amputation kit from the Napoleonic period. Amputation was one of the most effective means of treating serious or complicated limb wounds and military surgeons were very skilled at carrying it out. (Courtesy, Canadian Museum of Health and Medicine at The Toronto Hospital)

It is urged against immediate amputation, that the patient is much agitated, and his system depressed and uninured to diseased action, at the time of receiving the injury; and that amputation ought to be delayed until reaction takes place and the suppurative process is tried and then amputate if the limb cannot be spared.

This shock to the system, when balls pass through the extremities, is not experienced so often as some writers imagine. In cases where the ball passes through large muscles, and thick portions of a limb, the patient may not, at first, be sensible of pain, or even that he has received a wound. His garments being stained with blood is the first intimation he has of the accident. Even if the bone is fractured, he is first made acquainted with it by inability to use the limb. Large wounds of the kind give but little disturbance to the general system, till some time after they are received.

I had much opportunity to witness this phenomenon, in many instances, during the late war.[21]

In his memoir of the campaign, Horner revealed just how inadequate were the means by which he and colleagues tried to ease pain and save lives. He was critical of the instruments provided by the army and, in particular, he disliked the issue bullet forceps used to extract musket balls from wounds, which he regarded as much too large. When he "attempted to introduce them into the wound," Horner was seldom successful "for two reasons; the first was, because it was impossible to do so, without dilating the wound with a scalpel; and the second because few patients will allow the aggravation of pain which their unwieldy size occasions."[22] Horner opted to use common dressing forceps, which had not only smaller but also rounded jaws making this implement easier to use, even though the removal of an imbedded ball required it to be passed along the wound's channel "till the point reaches the ball, it will then be necessary to stretch the wound to twice its diameter before the blades of the forceps can be passed over the ball, and include it in their grips," and then "the whole length of the wound" had "to be stretched in the same manner, in extracting the ball, and that to the very great misery of the patient."[23]

"Great misery" is the operative phrase as the pain created by such a procedure must have been horrendous. Furthermore, as Horner rarely makes any mention of using opium, laudanum or alcohol during such operations, the reader is reluctantly forced to conclude that, for such procedures to be successfully completed, it required burly assistants and the provision of something for the patient to bite on – so as to reduce his screams of agony.

Another problem Horner and his colleagues faced was the appearance of maggots in his patients' wounds, a feature of military hospitals, particularly in the summer. Horner regarded maggots "as a most serious evil" that "frequently involved the life of the patient from the irritation produced." Although their presence might be "attributed to negligence," it was found that "even the most diligent attention from nurses could not prevent it." What Horner did not know was that maggots generally consume only necrotic or dead tissue and therefore might actually have a beneficial effect – indeed the use of maggots has become a somewhat controversial modern medical treatment. An observant man, Horner was amazed "how deeply these animalcules would work their way into wounds, producing, in some instances, as complete a dissection of the muscles, as if it had been performed by the knife."[24] One of his patients informed Horner that elderberry juice, sprinkled on bed clothes and bandages, would keep the flies away" and Horner found that it worked.

While the surgeons were occupied with the wounded, the commanders of both armies wrote their official reports for higher authority. Lieutenant-General Gordon Drummond clearly had a much more difficult task than his counterpart, Brigadier-General Edmund Gaines. Drummond's casualty figures were truly awful. The official account listed 57 killed, 309 wounded and 539 missing, for a total loss of 905 officers and men. This was over a quarter of his strength and the second highest loss the British army suffered in a single engagement during the War of 1812.* [25]

Some regiments had been decimated. The 103rd Foot had not only lost their commanding officer, Colonel Hercules Scott, but also their second-in-command and 531 other casualties, about 76 per cent of the unit's strength. When Scott was buried during the evening of 15 August, only the regimental surgeon and three other officers from the 103rd were in attendance as they were all that "remained untouched after the attack."[26] Of the eight officers of the 41st Foot who participated in the assault, four were wounded, two killed and one captured, while, of the enlisted men, 110 of 160 had become casualties. The two companies of the 104th Foot lost 54 killed, wounded and missing and John Le Couteur remembered that when the roll was called in that unit on the evening of 15 August and only "myself and twenty-three of us" who remained "out of seventy-seven" who had gone into the assault, the survivors "all burst into tears together."[27]

In his official report, completed only a few hours after the assault had ended, Drummond attributed the failure to "circumstances which may be considered as almost justifying the momentary panic which they produced, and which introduced a degree of confusion into the columns which in the darkness of the night the utmost exertions of the officers were ineffectual in removing" although the officers "appear invariably to have behaved with the most perfect coolness and bravery."[28]

This was for public consumption. In a private letter to Prevost, Drummond laid the blame for the failure squarely on De Watteville's Regiment. Confessing that the "agony of mind" he suffered "from the disgraceful and unfortunate conduct of the troops committed to my superintendence" wounded him "to the soul," Drummond complained that "by the misconduct of this Foreign Corps has the opportunity been totally lost for the present of striking such a blow at the Enemy's force in this neighbourhood as would altogether prevent his appearing again in any force on the Niagara Frontier at least during the present campaign."[29]

---

* During the War of 1812, the highest British losses in a single day were suffered at the battle of New Orleans, fought 8 January 1815, when 1,941 men were killed or wounded – see Chapter 16 below. A myth has taken root that the losses from the assault on Fort Erie – a total of 984 in both armies – were the highest ever suffered in a military action fought on what is now Canadian soil but this is not true. As far as can be established, the highest losses in a single battle on what is now Canadian soil were the 2,112 killed and wounded suffered by the British and French armies at the often overlooked battle of Ste. Foy or Sillery, which took place just outside Quebec City on 28 April 1760.

  If the total casualties incurred during the entire length of the siege of Fort Erie, which are about 2,500, are taken into account, however, then the siege was the bloodiest military operation of the War of 1812.

In both his reports, Drummond made no mention of the removal of the flints nor of the tardy movements of the troops who were to mount demonstrations and distract the defenders. Nor did he see fit to comment on the fact that, although two of his assault columns were in possession of a vital part of the fort for more than half an hour, he had not supported them with the three battalions he held in reserve only a few hundred yards away.

To his credit, Prevost did not entirely accept his subordinate's attempt to place responsibility for the defeat on the Swiss unit. He felt that too much "was required from De Watteville's Regiment so situated and deprived, as I am told, of their flints," which had "proved a costly experiment." Night attacks, he cautioned Drummond

> are very objectionable, principally because chance and not skill too frequently decide the contest, and that at night difficulties and dangers are ever magnified, particularly when they present themselves unexpectedly, and in the latter case the best disciplined troops are placed only on a level with raw and unformed soldiers.
>
> It is to be inferred from Lieut.-Colonel Fischer's report and your statement that the Right Column was not sufficiently prepared for the obstacles it had to surmount in attaining the point of attack, otherwise neither hesitation nor consternation would have presented themselves.[30]

In conclusion, Prevost expressed his concern that Drummond had succumbed to "the eagerness of the Right Division to increase its fame, before you were sufficiently prepared for the enterprise."[31]

De Watteville's Regiment, the culprits in the minds of Drummond and many others, naturally disliked being blamed for the defeat. "What a catastrophe!" wrote Lieutenant Joseph Mermet of that unit:

> What a misfortune to be a foreigner! Poor foreigners! Unfortunately they are always wrong.
>
> Say to those who will tell you the worst story of the *Thousand and one nights*: "These people were not sorcerers! Without a flint, can a soldier fire? Can one change night into day? Is it possible to leave a labyrinth without a guide?" If one is knocked down on you, how will you behave in order so as not to be knocked down on others?[32]

The prevailing belief among the British and Canadians was that the major contributing factor to the failure was the order to remove the men's flints. "Alas!" Hailes of the 41st Foot complained, "if this absurd order had not been issued I have no sort of doubt that we should have carried the fortress."[33] Le

Couteur agreed. remarking that the removal of the flints betrayed "a scandalous want of confidence in the brave men who formed the assaulting party."

The other reason advanced was the fact that too many senior officers had been in the forward elements of the assault columns and, as a result, suffered disproportionate casualties – indeed two of the three column commanders were killed and the third severely wounded. As Le Couteur put it:

> Our men behaved admirably, two mistakes leading to the failure. The two Col[onel]s, Scott & Drummond, went in with the forlorn hopes, or leading men, and were both killed – hence all direction ceased. Then the Blockhouse was impregnable to us – the doors below had been removed, the staircases or ladders also – so that when our men got in with a view to assault the garrison, they were shot through the loop-holed floors. It should have been destroyed by hot shot before the assault.[34]

In stark contrast to the British casualty figures, Gaines reported 17 killed, 52 wounded and 10 missing for a total loss of 79 men.[35] Gaines was elated – as well he might be – about his victory. "My heart is gladdened with gratitude to heaven and joy to my country," he wrote in a short note to Secretary of War Armstrong dated 15 August, "to have it in my power to inform you that the gallant army under my command has this morning beaten the enemy."[36] His official report, completed eight days later, is a fairly detailed and factual account of a battle, "which terminated in a signal victory in favour of the United States."[37] Gaines, however, made much of the British refusal to grant quarter and singled out Lieutenant-Colonel William Drummond for particular damnation:

> Lieut. McDonough being severely wounded, demanded quarter; it was refused by Col. Drummond. The lieutenant then seized a handspike and nobly defended himself until he was shot down with a pistol by the monster who had refused him quarter, who often reiterated the order, "give the damned Yankees no quarter." This officer [William Drummond], whose bravery if it had been seasoned with virtue would have entitled him to the admiration of every soldier – this hardened murderer – soon met his fate.[38]

This accusation, which was repeated by American historians throughout much of the 19th century, has unfortunately tarnished the reputation of a very brave man and fine soldier, and it has only been recently that historians have redressed the subject of William Drummond's actions during the assault.*

---

* On this subject, see Appendix C below.

If the result of the failed assault was "mortifying" to the British and Canadians, Lieutenant David Douglass believed "it was gratifying and encouraging" to the Left Division, which had been "somewhat dispirited" but was now

> immediately restored to cheerfulness and confidence; nor were these feelings again subdued, during all the labors and privations of the subsequent siege.
>
> The sensation produced in the neighboring Counties, on our side of the line [the border], was no less remarkable. The inhabitants had been disheartened, as well as ourselves ... [but] after the result of this battle was fully known, ... they began to venture over, in boats, from Buffalo; and, thus familiarized, an intercourse was afterwards kept up, which enabled us to obtain occasional supplies of fresh provisions, of which we were greatly in need.[39]

Captain Benjamin Ropes of the Twenty-First Infantry remembered that the forenoon of 15 August "was a proud Morning for us" as he was convinced that the enemy "would never attempt our works again."[40] He also noted that nearly 1,300 stand of arms thrown away by the attackers were collected by salvage details.*

Despite the victory, senior American commanders remained concerned about the overall situation. They were aware that large British reinforcements had arrived from Europe and inevitably Drummond's strength would be augmented with veteran troops. They also knew that Yeo was constructing a ship at Kingston that was far superior to any warship Chauncey had in commission or under construction. As soon as this vessel emerged onto Lake Ontario, the situation would be reversed and the British would be able to use the lake to move both supplies and troops, while the United States would be limited to land transport.

While recovering from the wound he had suffered at Lundy's Lane, Major-General Jacob Brown had busied himself during his convalescence in trying to obtain reinforcements for the Left Division. In effect, although he was not with the formation, Brown remained in command of it and was regularly consulted by its senior officers. There were few regular troops to be had, however, and a request for a thousand volunteers from the New York militia had resulted in only three hundred actually turning out. In a *cri de coeur* to Governor Daniel Tompkins of New York, Brown professed himself

> very anxious for the ultimate fate of this army. If the Enemy deems it an object of the first importance to destroy this force that has given them so much trouble and cost them so much, the Reinforcements arriving from

* A stand of arms consists of a musket; bayonet, scabbard and belt; and cartridge box and belt.

Europe will, I fear, give them the means. I doubt very much if a parallel can be found for the state of things existing upon the frontier. A gallant little Army struggling with the Enemies of their Country and devoting itself for its Honor and safety, left by that Country, to struggle alone within sight & within hearing.[41]

The Left Division, Brown emphasized, "has so far done its duty and been blessed with the smiles of Providence" but, unless it received immediate reinforcement, "there was cause to be concerned about its ultimate safety."

REMEMBER LAWRENCE!!!

Don't give up the Ship.

WANTED

FOR THE

U. S. NAVY,

SEAMEN,

ORDINARY SEAMEN,

AND GREEN HANDS,

For seagoing Ship Pennsylvania and all others, such as 74's, frigates and Sloops of war.

Good Wages

FOR

GOOD MEN.

APPLY TO

JOHN C. RIGHTER,

Shipping Master of the U. S. Navy, No. 162 South Front St.

"Remember Lawrence" and "Don't Give up the Ship." These potent phrases from the *Shannon/Chesapeake* engagement of 1813 are included in this postwar recruiting poster. The War of 1812 demonstrated to the American government that a powerful fleet was necessary to defend the coasts of the republic. In 1816, authority was given for the construction of a number of large warships, including the USS *Pennsylvania*, designed to mount 140 guns and one of the largest sailing warships ever built. Unfortunately, by the time she was commissioned in the 1830s, the vessel was obsolescent and never entered active service. (Reproduction poster from the National Archives, Washington)

PART THREE

Washington and Lake Champlain

JUNE–SEPTEMBER 1814

A sailor of either the British or American navy with a naval gun.

Final stand at Bladensburg, 24 August 1814. Some of the best fighting at the battle of Bladensburg was done by the officers and men of the United States Navy and Marine Corps. In this painting by Charles Waterhouse, marines man field artillery against the advancing British. (Courtesy, USMC collection)

CHAPTER SEVEN

Entr'acte (1): "No peace
with James Madison!"

THE REPUBLIC'S LONG AND PERILOUS SUMMER, 1814

James Madison my Joe, Jim, 'twas when you first began,
The world did say, and well might they, that you was not the man;
You was a dupe of France, Jim, and Jefferson also:
With gun-boat fleet you'd Britons beat, James Madison my Joe.

Our Capital you lost, Jim; much wealth with it likewise;
Your fame is fled, your honor's dead; your minions we despise:
In wisdom you're deficient, Jim, and energy also;
Most manfully you ran away, James Madison my Joe.

James Madison my Joe, Jim, you've wing'd your flight with speed;
With courage rare, you knew not where you drove your lank old steed,
While British troops were feasting, Jim, on wine and ale you know,
You weary fled, to seek a bed, James Madison my Joe.[1]

Unfortunately for Brown and the Left Division the attention of American leaders was fixed on other matters in the late summer of 1814. This was because the war was not going at all well for the United States. The republic had commenced hostilities against Britain for four major reasons. The first was to prevent the forcible impressment of American seamen into the Royal Navy. The second was to force Britain to repeal the Orders-in-Council, the maritime decrees which forbade all neutral, including American, ships to trade with Napoleonic France or its allies, on pain of seizure. The third reason, connected with the first two, was annoyance with intrusions by British warships into American territorial waters. Finally, Madison's government and many Americans believed that Britain was behind the hostility of the aboriginal nations of the Northwest (the state of Ohio and the Illinois, Indiana and Michigan Territories). There was also the consideration – although never officially stated by

James Madison (1751-1836). A well respected man of principle, Madison did not prove a very effective war leader and was not well served by his subordinates, particularly Secretary of War John Armstrong. By the summer of 1814 Madison was taking more interest in the war because it was not going at all well for the United States. (Print after portrait by Gilbert Stuart)

the government – that, whether the conquest of British North America was an object of war or not, it was the only place that a war could be fought against Great Britain, given the overwhelming superiority of the Royal Navy. This being the case, military success might result in a territorial expansion of the United States.[2]

After two years of fighting, however, eight major American invasions or attacks against Canada had been repulsed and a ninth was currently being disputed at Fort Erie.* The only successful offensive had been Major-General William H. Harrison's drive into western Upper Canada in October 1813, which resulted in a victory at the battle of the Thames, the death of the aboriginal leader, Tecumseh, and the dissolution of his aboriginal confederacy. But most of Harrison's army had been disbanded and Harrison himself had resigned his commission following disagreements with Secretary of War John Armstrong. The United States did hold Amherstburg in Upper Canada and the area immediately around it but Britain retained possession of the strategically-located Mackinac Island, which had been lost in 1812 and which was the focal point of aboriginal resistance. In August 1814 a major American military and naval expedition launched to recover this important post failed miserably.

As for the other grounds for war, Britain herself had repealed the Orders-in-Council just five days after Washington's declaration of hostilities in the misplaced hope of preventing a conflict between the two nations. But Britain had not, however, changed its policy on boarding neutral ships and impressing men it considered British subjects, although it was true that fewer American citizens were being impressed because fewer American ships were at sea. Far from stopping the intrusions of Royal Navy warships into American waters, the

---

* The failed major attacks or invasions were those launched in 1812 by Hull across the Detroit River and Van Rennselaer and Smyth across the Niagara River and Dearborn against Lower Canada; by Dearborn in the Niagara and by Wilkinson and Hampton against Montreal in 1813; and, finally, Wilkinson's attack on Lacolle in 1814.

war had led to a progressive British blockade of the Atlantic seaboard, which by the summer of 1814 was complete from Massachusetts to the border with Spanish Florida. Like the coils of a python, this blockade threatened to crush the republic through economic pressure.

And there was little the United States could do to prevent it. The small but professional American navy – good ships manned by good seamen – had won a notable series of single-ship victories in the first year of the war, but as the conflict entered its third year, most American warships were penned up in ports by superior British blockading squadrons. American privateers were having increasingly poor luck. Late in 1814, Britain admitted that American warships and privateers had captured 1,613 British merchant ships since June 1812. Nearly 30 per cent, however, were recaptured before they reached a friendly port, and in any case these losses represented only 7.5 per cent of the British merchant fleet, which actually increased by 812 hulls between 1812 and 1814. In contrast, the Royal Navy had taken 1,407 American merchant ships – nearly half the U.S. merchant fleet – as well as thirty-four warships and 278 privateers, manned by about 20,000 seamen who now languished in British prisons. And, since privateering is a two-edged sword, some forty Canadian privateers operating from New Brunswick and Nova Scotia cheerfully brought just over two hundred American ships into the Admiralty prize court at Halifax between 1812 and 1814. Worse still, with the end of the war in Europe, the Royal Navy was now free to exert its superior strength in American waters and to establish advanced bases on American soil, notably Tangier Island in Chesapeake Bay and Eastport (and later Castine, Bangor and Machias) in Massachusetts, from which to mount operations.* [3]

The British blockade was catastrophic for the United States. Nearly 90 per cent of the nation's income came from customs revenue, which suffered a precipitate decline from $13,331,467 in 1812 to $4,694,318 in 1814. In two years of war the American national debt rose from $48,000,000 to $63,545,831 and the deficit from $10.6 million to $17.3 million. As waterborne transportation was the cheapest way to move large quantities of goods to market, the depredations of British warships and Canadian privateers had an adverse effect on the economy because producers had to utilize expensive and cumbersome land transport and, of course, passed on the increased costs to their customers. The consumer price index rose 40 per cent between 1812 and 1814 and inflation led to unemployment as commercial activity began to grind to a halt. The government had tried to finance the war by borrowing, not taxation – by 1815 it would

---

* Note that Maine did not become a state until 1820.

The Glorious First of June, 1813. The American navy's notable succession of single-ship victories came to an end on 1 June 1813 when the British frigate HMS *Shannon* captured the American frigate USS *Chesapeake*. (Painting by Peter Rindlisbacher, courtesy of the artist)

owe $90 million to banks and individuals, and as early as June 1814 it was showing signs of defaulting on its debts. Very reluctantly, Madison's cabinet increased taxation to get the funds needed just to carry on the basic operations of government, let alone finance the war. This caused much hardship – former President Thomas Jefferson posed the rhetorical question of how farmers "who cannot get 50 cents a bushel for their wheat, while they pay $12 a bushel for their salt," would be able to "pay five times the amount of taxes they ever paid before."[4]

Nearly as bad as the economic news was the fact that the defeat of Napoleon had released British land forces for deployment in North America. American newspapers reported the arrival of British troops at Quebec and predicted that they would be used for offensive operations. In Britain the attitude toward the United States, stoked by harshly worded editorials in the major newspapers, was vengeful. "Let us have no cant of moderation," shrieked the London *Times*, because there "is no public feeling in the country stronger than that of indignation against the Americans," and just as the watchword for a decade had been "No peace with Bonaparte! so we must maintain the doctrine of, no Peace with James Madison!"[5]

The mood of the republic was sombre and fearful. A resident of Washington, who was clearly no admirer of Madison and the Republican party, wrote that

> the administration are now convinced they cannot attain their objects by War; and must try something else. A great change is taking place in the minds of men all over the U.S. The downfall of Napoleon has opened their eyes and they now perceive the abyss to which they have been led. But it is evident both here and in that crater of democracy, Baltimore, the Warfolk, once so hot, are now very reluctant to buckle on the harness since they find that "playing soldiers" is attended with some danger ...[6]

By the early summer of 1814, it was clear to President Madison and his cabinet that the republic was in mortal peril and the only option was to seek a negotiated end to the conflict.

The republic had actually been involved in a number of attempts to negotiate peace with Britain, including an initiative made by Secretary of State James Monroe on the very day war was declared in 1812. This was refused by the British government because it believed that once Washington learned of the repeal of the detested Orders-in-Council, it would end the conflict, but this optimism was misplaced as Madison elected to continue the war. A second attempt came in March 1813 when Czar Alexander of Russia offered to mediate between the two nations and, by now having suffered several major defeats, Madison was more amenable to discussion and accepted the Czar's offer. His instructions to the American commissioners who travelled to St. Petersburg to meet with their British counterparts, however, directed them to insist on American terms regarding impressment and blockade and also to press for the cession of large portions of Canadian territory. Not surprisingly, Britain rejected the Czar's offer in July 1813. A few months later, however, London underwent a change of heart. The war against Bonaparte had entered a critical stage as the allied armies invaded France, and Britain, wishing to terminate a minor war it had never wanted, proposed that the two nations negotiate directly. Madison was quick to accept and by the end of July 1814 a five-man American commission was awaiting their British counterparts in the Dutch city of Ghent.[7]

The irony is that both Britain and the United States were actually prepared to settle the conflict on the basis of *status quo ante bellum*. A British cabinet document explained that this meant that a peace treaty would be concluded, "without involving in such a Treaty any decision on the points in dispute at the commencement of hostilities."[8] Britain was weary of the financial burden of paying for two decades of war against France – as one British newspaper noted: "We fight with the National Debt at our backs" and while Britons "may escape our enemies … we may perish by the weight of our armour."[9] For the United States, a settlement on the basis of the *status quo ante bellum* meant that she would have to abandon maritime issues such as boarding and impressment – two of the causes of the war. The problem was that neither nation was willing to inform the other of this basis for a settlement and the result was that negotiations were to drag out much longer than expected – nearly five months in all. In the meantime the war would continue.[10]

To John Armstrong, that war was in the north, from Lake Champlain to Buffalo, and the greater part of the United States regular army was deployed in this theatre. A return of the army dated 30 June 1814 reveals that, of a total aggregate strength of 31,503 men, no fewer than 22,482, just over two-thirds, were either serving in the northern theatre or marching toward it. From the time he had assumed office in January 1813, the northern theatre had occupied Secretary of War Armstrong's energy and attention to the detriment of all other matters, something that annoyed many of his fellow cabinet members, for Armstrong was not a popular man in Washington. A New Yorker, his abrupt manner irritated a cabinet dominated by more courteous southerners and he made little attempt to hide his presidential ambitions or disguise his contempt for Madison as a war leader. The result was that he had many powerful enemies, including Secretary of the Navy William Jones and Secretary of State James Monroe. A perpetual schemer who was utterly convinced of his own genius in the field of military strategy, Armstrong was sceptical of the views of others, including his president. Madison, to his credit, had always defended his difficult subordinate against his enemies but the failure of the secretary's grandiose offensive against British North America in late 1813 had damaged Armstrong's credibility as a strategist and weakened his position within the government. By the summer of 1814, even the easy-going Madison had become irritated by his arrogant secretary of war and was taking a much greater interest in the activi-

John Armstrong (1758-1843). A veteran of the Revolutionary War, Secretary of War John Armstrong had an undeserved reputation as a strategist. His obsession with the northern theatre of war led him to neglect a growing British naval threat closer to home. (Portrait by Daniel Huntington, U.S. National Archives, 111-SC-94151)

ties of the War Department and a more active role in military planning.[11]

In contrast to previous years, the president followed events in the northern theatre more closely. Having witnessed the failure of the 1813 offensive against Montreal, which was partially the result of lack of communication between the two senior American commanders, Major Generals James Wilkinson and Wade Hampton, Madison did not want this error to be repeated.* He urged Armstrong to ensure that both Major-General Jacob Brown, commanding on the Niagara, and Major-General George Izard, commanding in the Lake Champlain area, maintain regular communication between their two commands, some 300 airline-miles apart, so that they had a "mutual understanding."[12] Armstrong, who was more concerned with trying to get the navy, in particular Commodore Isaac Chauncey, to cooperate with the army in the north, was irked by this unwanted counsel although he did his best to comply with Madison's wishes.[13]

Armstrong got along well with Brown, a fellow New Yorker, but his relationship with Izard was somewhat more stiff. Izard came from a privileged background and had received more professional military education than Armstrong, who prided himself on being the foremost military expert in the republic. The son of a wealthy South Carolinian congressman, Izard had earned a BA degree from the College of Philadelphia (now the University of Pennsylvania) before attending military schools in England and Germany and spending a year at the prestigious *École du Génie*, the French army's training centre for military engineering. Receiving a commission in the U.S. engineer corps in 1797, Izard had resigned in 1803 because of frustration with promotion opportunities and devoted himself to literary pursuits until 1812, when he was commissioned a colonel and given command of the newly-authorized Second Artillery Regi-

---

* The background and course of this offensive and a detailed account of the two battles that ended it – Chateauguay fought in October and Crysler's Farm fought in November 1813 – can be found in my book *Field of Glory*, the first volume of the "Forgotten Soldiers" trilogy.

Major-General George Izard (1776-1828).
Izard had more formal military education than any other senior officer in the regular army but he was a general who preferred the theory of war to the reality. He was an industrious correspondent and his wartime letters provide much insight into the higher direction of the 1814 campaign. (Courtesy Arkansas History Commission)

ment. Promoted a brigadier-general in 1813 Izard served under Hampton during the ill-fated Montreal offensive and in January 1814 was made a major-general and in April appointed commander of the Right Division, with headquarters at Plattsburgh on Lake Champlain. Being longer than Brown in grade, Izard now became the senior general in the northern army.[14]

On 1 May 1814 he arrived at Plattsburgh to find that his new command was in very poor shape because it had not fully recovered from its participation in Wilkinson's abortive attack on Lacolle in March. To Armstrong, Izard reported on the state of his formation:

> I have been engaged for three days in examining the troops, and am sorry to say that I am greatly disappointed, both in their number and quality. With very few exceptions (and those confined to companies) they are deficient in all the requisites of regular soldiers. Their clothing and equipment are in a wretched state, – their proficiency in field manoeuvres, and even the rudiments of exercise, is lamentably small, – and an undue proportion of them are on the sick list. Of those who appear under arms, a very great number are unfit to take the field, in consequence of indispositions contracted in the last movement to the Lacole [sic]. Whole battalions are composed of one year's men, who in a few days will be entitled to their discharge from the service. In short, I cannot, on this side of Lake Champlain, produce an aggregate force of more than two thousand effectives, and these raw, ill-clad and worse disciplined.[15]

In attempting to correct these defects, Izard encountered a problem that bedevilled all senior American commanders during the war – the lack of an authorized manual to train their troops. In the spring of 1812, shortly before the war had begun, a new manual, Alexander Smyth's *Rules and Regulations for the*

Field Exercise, Manoeuvres and Conduct of the Infantry of the United States, had replaced the manual compiled by Steuben in 1778, commonly called the "Blue Book," which had been the standard training source for regular and militia infantry since that time. In early 1813, however, the newly-appointed Secretary of War John Armstrong had replaced Smyth with a new manual, *Handbook for Infantry*, compiled by William Duane, the editor of the Philadelphia *Aurora* and well connected in the governing Republican party. Few unit commanders liked the *Handbook*, which was inadequate for training above the company level, so they either ignored the order authorizing it and continued to use Smyth, reverted to Steuben or – in one case – compiled their own manual. When he assumed command on the northern frontier in August 1813, Major-General James Wilkinson had stipulated that the army was to use only Duane but Wilkinson was now gone and chaos reigned concerning the subject of tactical doctrine. Brigadier-General Winfield Scott, who trained Brown's Left Division in the spring of 1814, used Smyth to do so, but when Izard assumed command of the Right Division, he found confusion abounded in that formation. "Different systems of instruction," he reported to Armstrong, "have been adopted by the officers of this division" and proposed a solution to the problem:

> As uniformity is indispensable in this particular, I am about to authorize the former practice, agreeably to Baron Steuben's regulations – without, however, giving to the latter the formality of a general order until the first of June, when, unless I receive instructions to the contrary, I shall adopt them as regulations for the troops under my command.[16]

Only in November 1814 did the War Department begin to address the problem of a uniform doctrine but until it did, Izard's division and Brown's division, having trained on quite different manuals, would have difficulty manoeuvring together.[17]

Nonetheless, Izard energetically set to work to transform the collection of dispirited and disorganized units under his command into an effective military formation. Training was increased, food and clothing improved, absent officers were rounded up and returned to their units, discipline was tightened and desertion curtailed. Private Charles Fairbanks of the Forty-Fifth Infantry attested to the "tightening up" when he recalled the day that the division was ordered to form a hollow square to witness the execution of two men, who were forced to kneel beside their coffins. The command was given, the firing squad did its duty but one of the condemned "moved after he fell; the sergeant had orders to walk up to him, put the muzzle of his gun to the top of the prisoner's head and discharge it."[18] Fairbanks saw another man arrested for desertion "branded with a

D upon the forehead" because he "had deserted several times, and had enlisted in other places, this was done that he might deceive them no more." Fairbanks himself was detailed as a prisoner guard for fifty miscreants "that were the most filthy looking objects I ever saw; it was enough to give a person the plague to keep guard over them."[19] One problem Izard could do little about was his men's pay, which was long overdue, and his letters to the War Department contain frequent mention of this matter, which worsened as the summer wore on.

In all other aspects, however, he was successful and by 30 June, his division was a fairly efficient formation with an effective strength of just under 5,000 men consisting of nine regiments of infantry organized in three brigades as well as two companies of regular light dragoons, the regiment of light artillery serving as infantry, and companies of the corps of artillery. While he finalized plans for a summer campaign with Armstrong, Izard employed most of his troops in constructing defensive works along the border and at Vergennes, Vermont, and Plattsburgh, New York, the two bases of the American Lake Champlain squadron.[20] By mid-July, Izard felt that his division was adequate to "defend this frontier against a greater force" but "entirely inadequate to the conquest of any important part" of British territory "with the intention of retaining it."[21]

Izard suggested to Armstrong that he move his army to the St. Lawrence "and threaten the rear of Kingston" as the British were fully occupied in the Niagara.[22] In the meantime he shifted the greater part of the division north to the border, deploying it around the town of Champlain, New York. Shortly thereafter, as he began to receive intelligence of large British troop reinforcements and a build-up of enemy forces near the border, Izard concluded that, far from moving his division to the west, it would be needed to defend the Lake Champlain area.

For this reason, he was disagreeably surprised on 11 August when he received a an order from Armstrong to move most of the division to Ogdensburg on the St. Lawrence "without delay" and prepare to attack Kingston to relieve the pressure on the defenders of Fort Erie.[23] Although he himself had proposed a similar move a few weeks earlier, the situation had changed and it now appeared that, far from invading British territory, Izard might have to fight hard to defend American. He informed Armstrong that he would "make the movement" but only "with the apprehension of risking the forces under my command" and "with the certainty that every thing in this vicinity, but the lately erected works at Plattsburgh and Cumberland Head, will, in less than three days after my departure, be in possession of the enemy."[24] The enemy, Izard continued, "is in force superior to mine in my front, he daily threatens to attack my position at Champlain; we are in hourly expectation of a serious conflict." That the British had not yet attacked, Izard attributed "to caution on his part, from exaggerated reports of our numbers, and from his expectation of reinforcements." Izard promised, however, that he would execute "any project, which the government I have the honour to serve think proper to direct" and assured Armstrong that his "little army will do its duty."

Having issued this stricture Izard prepared to move west. He was making his final preparations when a further change of orders arrived from Armstrong. The secretary now wanted Izard to march, not to Ogdensburg but to Sackets Harbor, there to embark part of his force on Chauncey's squadron and join the Left Division in the Niagara, where he would "be able to reduce fort George and Niagara, and what is of even more importance, capture the whole of Drummond's force on the Niagara."[25] Very reluctantly – because he was by now fully aware of growing British forces just across the border – Izard changed his plans. He issued Armstrong, however, a clear warning that he would "not be responsible for the consequences of abandoning my present strong position" but would "obey orders and execute them as well as I know how."[26]

On 29 August, after turning over command at Plattsburgh to Brigadier-General Alexander Macomb, Izard left for Sackets Harbor. This movement was incomprehensible to the officers and men of the American Right Division, for as one remarked:

> Every individual from the General to the Drummer, saw the absurdity of this order; but it must be obeyed. It was obvious that as soon as the British knew we were beyond striking distance, they would attack Plattsburgh: and before we could march 400 miles, the army at Erie would either have been defeated, or would have beaten the enemy.[27]

Modern commentators have been no kinder to Armstrong's strategic vision – one historian has commented that it was "a dangerous, even reckless, decision" on the secretary's part to order Izard to move west "where nothing decisive could be achieved" while leaving the Lake Champlain area "under threat of an overwhelming invasion."[28]

U nfortunately, Armstrong's preoccupation with the northern theatre had caused him to overlook a more serious threat closer to Washington. In the summer of 1813 British naval and land forces had carried out a series of raids in the Chesapeake before withdrawing for the winter. This was a clear warning that the Atlantic coast was vulnerable and many Americans were concerned that Britain would send a major expedition to attack that coast. The favoured objectives were Baltimore, Norfolk or Philadelphia, although a growing number, including President Madison, feared that Washington itself might be

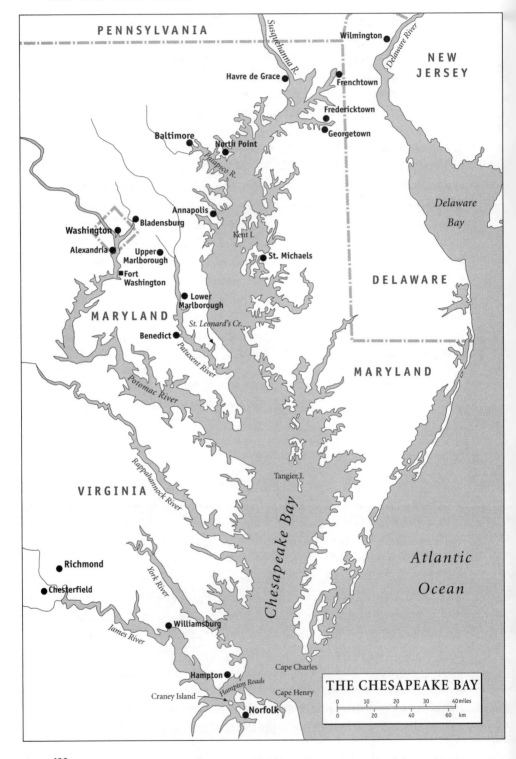

THE CHESAPEAKE BAY

| 0 | 10 | 20 | 30 | 40 miles |
| 0 | 20 | | 40 | 60 km |

at risk. Armstrong, however, was unconvinced and in mid-June 1814 blithely dispatched north nearly a quarter of the regular troops in the vicinity of the capital. By the end of that month, Madison had been seriously alarmed about the security of Washington and ordered the creation of Military District No. 10, consisting of the District of Columbia, Maryland and Virginia north of the Rappahanock, with the primary mission of defending the capital. Brigadier-General William Winder, who had fought the previous year on the northern frontier – and had the infernal bad luck to be captured at the battle of Stoney Creek in June 1813 – was appointed to command and energetically began to organize the defence of the district. He got very little assistance from Armstrong, who remained convinced that if the enemy attacked, their objective would not be the capital, which was too far inland. By early August reports of British troop reinforcements destined for the Chesapeake and an increasing tempo of raiding in the bay area convinced Madison that Washington was in danger and he urged both Armstrong and Winder to pay attention to its defences. It was too late: on 17 August lookouts stationed at the mouth of the Patuxent River reported a large British fleet numbering nearly fifty vessels anchoring off Drum Point.[29]

This fleet was under the command of Vice-Admiral Alexander Cochrane, the Royal Navy's North American commander-in-chief. Cochrane, who had lost a brother at Yorktown in 1783, despised Americans and, as has been noted above, hoped "to give them a complete drubbing before peace is made."[30] He was transporting a force under the command of Major-General Robert Ross, a 48-year-old veteran of Wellington's army who had orders "to effect a diversion on the Coast of the United States of America in favour of the Army employed in the Defence of Upper and Lower Canada."[31] After disembarking at Grace Point, across the Patuxent from Benedict, Maryland, on 18 August, Ross moved north by land, accompanied on the water by a naval force in boats under the command of Rear-Admiral George Cockburn, an officer with much experience raiding in the Chesapeake area. Cockburn's objective was an American gunboat flotilla commanded by Commodore Joshua Barney, which had given British raiders much trouble during the previous months. This flotilla was anchored off Pig Point, but when Cockburn's boats approached it on 22 August, Barney's men destroyed their vessels to prevent capture. Cockburn then landed most of his men and joined Ross's troops, who had reached Upper Marlborough, having encountered very little resistance in their march north.[32]

The two officers discussed their next move. Their position at Upper Marlborough was advantageous as it permitted them to move equally against Annapolis, Baltimore or Washington. Ross sent a naval officer to Cochrane to get his views on the next step and then assessed the situation. His army's current position was sound as it could procure cattle for food and horses for transportation while intelligence was obtained from slaves anxious to join the British force. Moreover, the country was level and communications by land and water were good while the enemy appeared to be in a state of panic and their inexperienced leaders were new to command. Ross decided to attack Washington and Cockburn not only agreed but volunteered to join the force to command the marines and seamen. At almost the same time, the officer sent to Cochrane returned with a communication "recommending in strenuous terms, an immediate retreat," which Ross, "with the entire concurrence" of Cockburn, decided to disregard.[33]

At 6 A.M. on 24 August, Ross set out for the capital of the United States with an effective strength of about 4,500 soldiers, marines, seamen and a few small artillery pieces. There was little resistance beyond sniping and some skirmishing and by noon his advance guard was approaching Bladensburg when it discovered a strong American force posted on high ground west of the village.[34]

This force, under the command of Winder, consisted of nearly 6,000 men, mainly Maryland and District of Columbia militia, but also 450 regular infantry and cavalry, 600 marines and sailors, and more than 20 pieces of artillery. Winder had positioned them in three lines but his attempts at deployment were hampered by confused communications and the interference of senior members of the government. On the morning of 24 August he was visited by the president and the secretaries of the army, navy, state and treasury, who rode out from the capital, just four miles away, to offer unsolicited advice and all assistance short of actual aid. As one observer noted, these newcomers possessed "many and varied characteristics" but little or no "military perceptions."[35] Secretary of State James Monroe was the most active and offered to assist Winder to place his troops, an offer that was accepted. Secretary of War John Armstrong, on the other hand – although he perhaps had the greatest stake in the matter – seemed disinterested. When Madison asked whether he had any advice for

Brigadier-General William H. Winder (1775-1824). Winder's basic problem was that he was unlucky as a general. Captured in 1813, he was paroled, returned to active service and was appointed commander of Military District 10 and charged with the defence of Washington. He suffered from constant interference from politicians and was never really able to organize an effective defence. (Engraving of miniature by St.-Menin, Library of Congress)

Winder, Armstrong replied that he did not and, since the battle would primarily be "between Militia and regular troops, the former would be beaten."[36] This was not particularly helpful and Winder later lamented to a subordinate that he was "only a nominal commander" and feared "for the success of the day."[37] It was actually a recipe for disaster and the presence of Madison's cabinet on the field of Bladensburg must be writ very large in the annals of military incompetence. Around noon, when the outposts reported the approach of the British, the discussions broke off and the politicians departed.[38]

Given the command confusion, it is not surprising that the battle of Bladensburg, fought on 24 August 1814, was brisk but short. Armstrong was right: poorly trained militia were no match for the British regulars, who, in two and a half hours of fighting, managed to push through two of Winder's defence lines, after which the third collapsed and his troops then dispersed in all directions. Due to command confusion the American regular infantry and cavalry never got into action, much to the anger of their commanding officer, and the best fighting done for the United States that day was the work of Commodore Joshua Barney's sailors and marines, who staged a stubborn rearguard action until nearly overwhelmed by Ross's infantry, at which point they too departed. American losses were about 100 killed and wounded but the British losses were higher, Ross reporting a total of 249, including 64 killed and 185 wounded. Poor leadership was not restricted to the American force; there had been very little superior direction or tactical skill displayed by the British. Captain Harry Smith of Ross's staff later remarked, "Suffice it to say we licked the Yankees and took all their guns, with a loss upwards of 300 men," but his old Peninsular commander "would have done the same thing with a loss of 40 or 50."[39] Ross spent several hours cleaning up the battlefield, tending to the wounded and burying the dead, and then, about 6 P.M., marched for Washington.[40]

The British found the capital undefended as Madison and his cabinet, as well as the regular and militia forces, had abandoned the city. Ross expected to find some official with whom he could negotiate a surrender but was disappointed in this expectation. He moved one of his three brigades into the city and then commenced to systematically destroy public buildings, a legitimate act of war in the early 19th century.* The British set fire to the Capitol, the White House,†

---

* A discussion of the "laws of war" as they were observed during the 1812 conflict and the justification for destroying non-military public buildings will be found in my article, "Why the White House Was Burned: An Investigation into the British Destruction of Public Buildings at Washington in August 1814," *Journal of Military History*, 76 (October 2012), 1095-1127.

† Contrary to popular myth, the president's residence was actually referred to as the "White House" prior to the War of 1812. See Donald R. Hickey, *Don't Give Up the Ship! Myths of the War of 1812* (Toronto, 2006), 81-82.

Major-General Robert Ross (1766-1814). A veteran soldier who had performed very well in the Peninsula under Wellington, Ross was sent to North America to create a diversion in favour of the British defenders of Canada. He succeeded beyond anyone's expectations, and captured the capital of the United States. (Print from portrait, author's collection)

the Treasury, State and War Departments and three bridges over the Potomac, and completed the destruction of the navy yard which had been begun by their opponents. Captain Smith had "no objection to burn" military and naval buildings, barracks and storehouses but being "fresh from the Duke's humane warfare in the South of France," where Wellington had protected both public and private property, he and his comrades "were horrified at the order to burn the elegant Houses of Parliament [the Capitol] and the President's house."[41] The invaders behaved very well, and although there were instances of looting, they were committed by civilians one American newspaper called "*knavish* rogues about the town, who profited by the *general distress*."[42] Major Norman Pringle of the 21st Foot, who commanded the provost guard during the occupation, recorded that his men preserved the peace in the city but admitted that they did consume the "ample repast" set out in the White House and toasted James Madison "in his own best claret, for being so good a fellow to leave us such a capital supper."[43]

His task completed, Ross marched out of Washington at 9 P.M. on 25 August and, five days later, having met with absolutely no harassment from American forces, re-embarked on Cochrane's fleet. To London, Ross reported that the successful attack on the American capital had been made in compliance with his orders "to attract the attention of the Government of the United States and to cause a Diversion in favour of the Army in Canada."[44] In his report, Cockburn listed the various public buildings destroyed and stressed that not "a Vestige of Public Property or a Store of any kind which could be converted to the use of the Government, escaped Destruction."[45] Ross's operation against Washington, in which his little army had conducted a 100-mile return trip from its landing place, won a battle and occupied the capital of the United States, had been a masterful operation resulting from a combination of professionalism, calculated risk, a confused and incompetent opponent – and a considerable dash of luck. In essence it was a prime example of amphibious warfare, which has been defined as "the ability to project force from sea onto land, into a hostile or potentially hostile environment, in a tactical posture, without any reliance on ports."[46] It was also a clarion signal to Madison's government that declaring war was one thing, fighting it quite another, particularly against an opponent with two decades of recent military experience and total command of the sea.

A scapegoat had to be found for the debacle and John Armstrong – who bore no small responsibility for it – was a prime candidate. So high was feeling against the secretary that many of the militia of Military District No. 10 refused to obey any orders issued by him and he was generally excoriated in the press, the drawing room and the tavern for his half-hearted efforts to defend the capital. After he returned to Washington on 27 August, Madison met with the secretary and informed him of his dissatisfaction with Armstrong's performance. When Armstrong suggested that he might take a brief leave of absence to visit his home in New York until the tempest blew over, Madison quickly agreed. The secretary departed on 30 August but resigned six days later after he realized the depth of public feeling against him. There was many a dry eye in Washington when John Armstrong left the cabinet and Madison replaced him with Secretary of State James Monroe, who had long coveted the War Department.[47]

In the wake of the disaster, the president attempted to rouse the patriotism of the republic. On 1 September 1814 he issued a proclamation condemning Britain for wantonly destroying "public edifices having no relation in their structure to operations of war" and for exhibiting "a deliberate disregard of the principles of humanity."[48] The enemy's recent acts, Madison continued, gave "to the existing war, a character of extended devastation and barbarism, at the very moment of negociations [sic] for peace." The president called on all Americans to display a "manful and universal determination to chastise and expel the invader" and "to unite their hands and hearts in giving effect to the ample means possessed for that purpose."

It was well that President James Madison urged his fellow citizens to unite and resist invasion because on the same day that his proclamation was issued, some of the finest soldiers Britain ever sent to North America crossed the border at Champlain, New York, to commence that nation's major offensive of the War of 1812.

British infantry, 1814. On the left a fusilier of the 23rd Foot and on the right a soldier of the 6th Foot. The 23rd served in Nova Scotia from 1808 to 1810 and the 6th Foot arrived as part of the reinforcements sent across the Atlantic in the summer of 1814. (Painting by Charles Hamilton Smith, from *Costume of the British Army*)

CHAPTER EIGHT

"O how high the pulse of hope beat at that moment"

LOWER CANADA, SUMMER 1814

Come, all you British heroes, I pray you lend your ears,
Draw up your reg'lar forces, and then our volunteers;
We're going to fight the Yankees, boys, by water and by land,
And we never will return, until we conquer, sword in hand.
 We're the noble lads of Canada, come to arms, boys, come.

O now the time has come, my boys, to cross the Yankee's line,
We remember they were rebels once, and conquer'd John Burgoyne.
We'll subdue those mighty Democrats, and pull their dwellings down,
And we'll have the states inhabited with subjects to the crown.
 We're the noble lads, &c.

We've as choice a British army as ever crossed the seas,
We'll burn both town and city, and with smoke becloud the skies,
We'll subdue the old green mountain boys, their Washington is gone,
And we'll play them Yankee Doodle, as the Yankees did Burgoyne.
 We're the noble lads, &c.[1]

The British invasion of the Lake Champlain area in September 1814 was the result of high-level decisions taken earlier that year in London. In February, Lord Bathurst, the colonial secretary who was responsible for the conduct of overseas military operations, had consulted the Duke of Wellington, Britain's foremost soldier, for advice on how to conduct the war in North America. The duke went right to the point, telling Bathurst "that the defence of Canada, and the co-operation of the Indians, depends upon the navigation of the lakes" and, therefore, any "offensive operation founded upon Canada must be preceded by the establishment of a naval superiority on the lakes."[2] That superiority could be obtained not only by outbuilding the enemy but also by destroying his naval bases. In early June, when Bathurst informed Lieutenant-General Sir George Prevost, the commander-in-chief in North America, about the additional forces being sent to him, he stressed these reinforcements would ensure that Canada "will not only be protected for the time against any attack which the enemy may have means of making," but would also enable Prevost "to commence offensive operations on the Enemy's Frontier before the close of this [the 1814] Campaign [season]."[3] Bathurst cautioned Prevost, however, that he did not wish to "encourage such forward movement into the Interior of the American Territory" as might jeopardize "the safety of the Force placed under your command." Instead, the object of offensive operations would be "first, to give immediate protection; secondly, to obtain if possible ultimate security to His Majesty's Possessions in America."[4] The colonial secretary then got down to specifics:

> The entire destruction of Sackets harbour and the Naval Establishments on Lake Erie and Lake Champlain come under the first description.
>
> The maintenance of Fort Niagara and so much of the adjacent Territory as may be deemed necessary; and the occupation of Detroit and the Michigan Country came under the second.[5]

This optimistic list of objectives, most of which were separated by hundreds of miles, was the product of calculations by a government which simply did not appreciate the vast distances of North America.[6]

It was early July before Prevost received these orders and they must have caused him no little consternation. A competent and veteran soldier who had seen much active service in the West Indies, Prevost had established a positive record as a colonial governor in Dominica and Nova Scotia before being appointed governor-general and commander-in-chief of British North America in December 1811. Essentially a defensive-minded general, he had held the line for two years, with minimal reinforcement or instruction from a government that was preoccupied with the greater war in Europe. He was now being ordered to carry out a major offensive.[7]

It was well into August before the last of the reinforcements arrived from Europe. Given the need to form them into an offensive force and the necessity of obtaining "complete naval ascendancy," Prevost advised London that the naval squadrons on Lakes Champlain and Ontario "cannot attain sufficient strength" to co-operate with the army for an attack on either Plattsburgh or Sackets Harbor before the middle of September and "without their Aid and protection, nothing could be undertaken affording a reasonable hope of substantial advantage."[8] Since this implied that it would be the following year before Prevost would be able to accomplish the objectives outlined in Bathurst's instructions, the colonial secretary was not happy and wrote a letter that did not reach Prevost until after the Plattsburgh campaign had ended. Expressing his surprise at Prevost's attitude, Bathurst felt "bound in fairness to apprize you that if you shall allow the present Campaign [season] to close without having undertaken offensive measures against the Enemy, you will very seriously disappoint the Expectations of the Prince Regent and of the Country."[9] As if that was not pressure enough, the Duke of York, the commander-in-chief of the British army, cautioned Prevost that, although he must resist "vain and ignorant clamour," given the size and quality of the force under his command,

> the Hopes and expectations of the government and the country would be much disappointed in the non-attainment of signal Success against the enemy opposed to you, and this disappointment would be aggravated if the occasional ascendancy on the Lakes, ... should paralyze the Exertions of an Army, so Infinitely His Superior.[10]

It was clear that an offensive there must be and, therefore, an offensive there would be.

Lake Champlain was the only theatre where Prevost could quickly mount such an operation. Commander James Yeo refused to take his squadron onto Lake Ontario until his ship of the line, HMS *St. Lawrence*, was in commission and this ruled out an immediate attack on Sackets Harbor. Prevost decided to move on the New York side of Lake Champlain as he did not want to push troops up the Vermont side since that state had shown "a decided opposition to the War" as well as providing "the whole of the Cattle required for the use of the Troops," particularly the new arrivals from Europe.[11] As he expressed it to Drummond, Prevost's plan was to "establish" his army at Plattsburgh and "to detach from thence a Brigade for the destruction of Vergennes [Vermont] and its Naval establishment."[12] It is evident that Prevost was not greatly enthusiastic about the forthcoming operation. Two years of defensive warfare had left its mark on him as a commander and he disliked taking undue risks that might result in heavy casualties that could not easily be replaced. An inveterate reader of American newspapers, he was also aware that many Americans, particularly in New England, did not approve of "Mister Madison's war," as they called it, but a major British invasion of U.S. soil would increase support for the government.[13]

Throughout the summer of 1814, as the reinforcements, some 13,000 in total, arrived at Quebec, Prevost pushed them on to Montreal, where they were organized into four brigades. One brigade, under Major-General James Kempt, was shifted farther west to Kingston with a view to it eventually being used for the attack against Sackets Harbor. The other brigades, under Major-Generals Thomas Brisbane, Manley Power and Frederick P. Robinson, were made

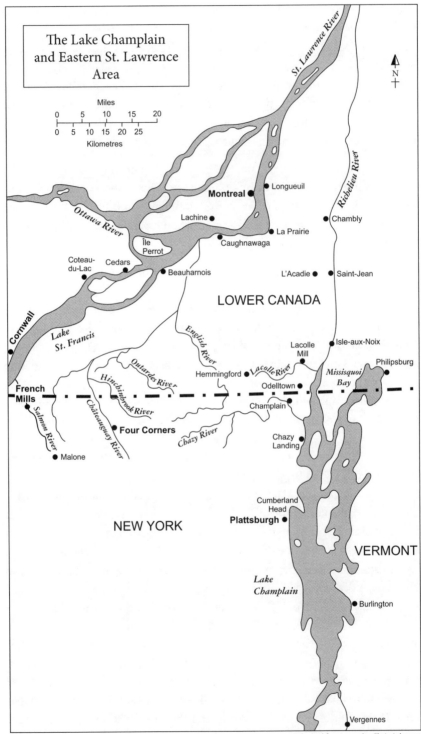

The Lake Champlain and Eastern St. Lawrence Area

Adapted from map by Chris Johnson

Major-General Thomas Brisbane (1773-1860). The veteran Brisbane, who had fought in Holland, the West Indies and the Peninsula, arrived in North America with his brigade staff in the summer of 1814. He was given command of the 2nd Brigade of the British Left Division. (Print after portrait, author's collection)

part of the Left Division of the British army in North America* and Prevost selected Major-General Francis De Rottenburg to command this formation. A former mercenary officer, the German-Polish De Rottenburg had seen much active service in Europe and had created the first rifle battalion in the British army. At age 57, however, he was past his prime and had not performed that well in 1813 when he had served as commander in Upper Canada. Although respected as a soldier, De Rottenburg was also something of a figure of fun to younger officers, who, although they admired his beautiful wife, Juliana, thirty years his junior, referred to him as General "God-for-Damn" after his favourite oath, *"Gottverdammt."*[14] Prevost, however, had no choice but to appoint De Rottenburg to command the division as he was the senior major general in North America and would have had grounds for a protest if he had been passed over. Prevost kept a careful eye on him, however, and during the coming campaign De Rottenburg would be conspicuous by his seeming absence.[15]

The three brigade commanders, all veterans of the Peninsular army, were younger men. A Scot, the 41-year-old Thomas Brisbane had been educated at the University of Edinburgh and commissioned in the army at the age of 16. He had served in Holland and the West Indies before commanding a brigade in Spain, where he had distinguished himself in the recent battles along the Spanish-French border. Manley Power, also 41, had, like Brisbane, been commissioned at an early age and served in Holland, Minorca and Egypt. Wellington had appointed him to command a brigade in the Portuguese army,† which he had led successfully for the last three years. The odd man out was Frederick

---

* Lest the reader get confused at this point, I should reiterate that on the Niagara frontier a British Right Division was opposed to an American Left Division, while in the Lake Champlain area a British Left Division was opposed to an American Right Division. Remember that if life was simpler, it would not be nearly so interesting.

† During the Peninsular War of 1808-1814, Britain assumed the task of reorganizing the Portuguese army and many British officers were seconded to serve in its higher appointments. A combination of their professional expertise and the patriotic enthusiasm of the soldiers combined to create a force that was almost equal to the British army as a fighting service.

Major-General Francis De Rottenburg (1757-1832). A veteran European officer who had commanded the first rifle battalion in the British army, De Rottenburg was a professional soldier but at 57 somewhat past his prime by 1814. (*Journal of the Society of Army Historical Research*, 1931)

Robinson, who at 51 was not only older but the American-born scion of a prominent New York family from the Hudson highlands. The Robinsons were Loyalists and in 1777 Frederick had joined his father's unit, the Loyal American Regiment, and fought with them before obtaining a commission in the British army in 1778. He had remained in service and had fought in the West Indies in the early 1790s before being invalided back to Britain. Much of his subsequent career had been spent in administrative appointments but in early 1813, somewhat surprisingly, he was given a brigade in the Peninsular army, where he had performed very well at the siege of San Sebastian in the late summer and early autumn of that year.[16]

Of the 13½ infantry battalions in the British Left Division, only six were veterans of Wellington's army. The Peninsular units were placed in Robinson's 1st Brigade, which received the 3/27th, 1/39th, 76th and 1/88th Regiments of Foot. Manley Power's 3rd Brigade was allotted two Peninsular units, the 1/3rd and 1/5th Foot, and two units, the 1/27th and 1/58th Foot, from another British army in Spain. Brisbane's 2nd Brigade comprised three units which had seen varying amounts of service in North America, the 2/8th, 13th and 49th Foot, as well as De Meuron's Swiss mercenary regiment, and two Canadian units, the Canadian Voltigeurs and Canadian Chasseurs. Each infantry brigade was allotted an artillery company (or battery) consisting of five 6-pdr. guns and one 5.5-in howitzer.* In addition, there was a reserve of artillery consisting of two 24-pdr. brass field guns, an 8-inch brass howitzer, three 24-pdr. naval carronades mounted on field carriages and a Royal Marine Artillery rocket detachment. Two squadrons of the 19th Light Dragoons completed the division which, by the last days of August, had reached a total strength of about 11,500 officers and men.[17]

As the third wartime summer wore on and the new units arrived from Europe, the province of Lower Canada became an armed camp. Alicia Cockburn,

---

* In 1814 the Royal Artillery was organized in companies commanded by captains. No distinction was made between garrison and field artillery; companies served in either role as required. If designated for field service, however, the company would normally form a brigade (a battery in modern military parlance) which usually consisted of six pieces of ordnance.

Major-General Manley Power (1773-1826). Another veteran brigade commander transferred to North America, Power took over the 3rd Brigade of the British Left Division. (Print after portrait, author's collection)

wife of Lieutenant-Colonel Francis Cockburn of the Canadian Fencibles and sister-in-law of Rear-Admiral George Cockburn of Chesapeake fame, captured the mood of many in the province when she wrote from Montreal to her cousin in Britain that

> All is bustle in the neighbouring Camp – Guns – Drums – Bugles – Horse
> – Foot – Brigadiers – Grenadiers – & Fuzileers – Right – Left – here – there
> – march – halt – wheel – double quick – tumble down – tumble up – fire
> away – thus they "keep moving" and a most moving scene it is, but I think if
> I commanded, I would move it *a little nearer the enemy.*[18]

That movement was not long in coming. In the last half of August the three brigades took up advance positions, the 1st Brigade at Chambly, the 2nd at L'Acadie and the 3rd at La Prairie. All of these places were within twenty-five miles of the border.

The 88th Foot – that jovial collection of fighting Hibernian reprobates – went to Chambly, passing through Montreal on their way. The Ranger officers were sad not to stay longer in that city because in their opinion (and that of most other British soldiers) it contained the most beautiful and fashionable young women in Canada – a statement that remains true to this day.[19] As they marched toward their new station, the Rangers chuckled over the recent experience of Sergeant Patrick Anthony, who had managed to smuggle his fiancée, Sally Grimes, on board a troopship in Europe with the intention of marrying her when they arrived in North America. After they landed, however, Sally perceived a cooling of Pat's feelings toward her and had promptly decamped to places unknown. A few days later, she wrote Anthony a letter:

Major-General Frederick Robinson (1763-1852). Born in New York state, Robinson fought in his father's Loyalist regiment during the Revolutionary War. More familiar with campaigning in North America than many of his colleagues, Robinson trained his 1st Brigade in skirmish warfare. (Print after portrait by George Berthon, author's collection)

Dear Pat

I write these few lines hopping [sic] i will find you in good health, as I am at present.

Och! Pat, God may forgive you as I do, but if you brake [sic] all the promises you made me, don't you think God Almighty will shoot [shut] you out of heaven.

Yours, till death.

Sally[20]

Sergeant Anthony, upset at the sentiments expressed in the letter, consulted his company commander, who advised him to track the girl down and marry her as the regiment had been warned to be ready to march. Anthony did so and the couple were "churched" by a French-Canadian curate whose mispronunciation of the service ("those who *Cot* hat *shined* together") caused much stifled hilarity on the part of those Rangers who attended.[21]

The officers of the 88th Foot, and those of the other units from Wellington's army, lost much of their good humour on 23 August when Prevost issued a general order concerning their appearance. Stating that having "observed in the Dress of several officers of Corps and Departments, lately added to this army, from that of the Duke of Wellington, a fanciful variety inconsistent with the Rules of the Service," he was taking steps to rectify the matter. From now on, general officers would "only permit such deviations from the regulations … as may be justified by particular causes of Service, and climate, and even then uniformity is to be retained."[22] Sir George Prevost was within his right to issue such an order but the action betrays a certain "garrison" mentality on his part, a preoccupation with *minutiae* when he had more important things to concern him. The Peninsular veterans – who naturally compared his attitude with that of their former commander – resented it, but grudgingly packed away their outlandish campaign costumes and resumed "the old red rag."

The order concerning dress was not the newcomers' major grievance. They disliked many of the senior officers in the North America, who, in their opinion, did not compare well with their counterparts in Europe. They did not want De Rottenburg as a divisional commander because, although a respected soldier in his earlier days, he had never commanded anything larger than a brigade and that only for a short period. They thought that Major-General Thomas Beckwith, the quartermaster-general responsible for routes, quarters, rations and intelligence – and a man described by one subordinate as a "very clever" fellow but "rather an odd fish." – was not equal to the demands of his office.[23] The newcomers, however, particularly disdained Major-General Edward Baynes, Prevost's adjutant-general or chief of staff in modern terms. Baynes had

Major-General Edward Baynes (1768-1829). Prevost's chief of staff, Baynes had been in North America a long time and many believed he had too much influence on his superior. Baynes was the complete staff officer and generally detested by the veteran commanders from Wellington's army. (From John Richardson's *War of 1812*, 1902)

not seen active service for more than a decade and had spent much of his career in staff appointments. As expressed by one officer's wife, it was the opinion of many that Baynes "possesses not one qualification to form either a Statesman or a Soldier" but "by the lowest cunning & the dirtiest offices" had made himself indispensable to Prevost.[24] Major James Campbell, one of Brisbane's staff officers, summed up the feelings of the Peninsular veterans about the North American staff in the division:

> we had far too many commanders, for they were actually in each other's way. Here was Sir George Prevost himself, Baron De Rottenburg and his staff, a brilliant headquarter staff, consisting of Adjutant and Quarter-master-general, assistants to both; Military Secretary, Aides-de-camp, Chiefs of Engineers, Artillery, &c. &c., in short, enough to have caused confusion in an army three times our numbers, and much more so amongst the three brigades, whose experienced generals and staff wanted no help.[25]

The new arrivals also found that the staff departments in North America, unused to administering to the needs of such a large body of troops, too often got into a muddle. Robinson thought his 1st Brigade consisted of units "as fit for any service as it was possible for regiments to be" but was exasperated by the local staff. He had to expend much effort to correct "abuses in the different departments and urging them to common activity." "I had no idea," he recorded, "that such confusion existed in any part of the British service, as I found to be the case at this post." Robinson, however, found "great relief from these vexations" in preparing his brigade

> for the service they were soon to likely encounter, and which from early experience I knew to be totally different from the open, manly warfare they had been accustomed to, under the Duke of Wellington.
>
> ......Every morning from six to eight o'clock the regiments alternately fired ball and [after] a short time premiums [prizes] were given for the best shots. The Light Companies were also practised in skirmishing in woods, after the American fashion.[26]

Brisbane and Power, experienced commanders, did the same with their brigades.

With veteran troops and generals, the army could fairly quickly be made ready for the forthcoming offensive but this was not the case with the navy. Unlike previous North American conflicts, where it had been the scene of major operations, Lake Champlain had not been a very active theatre during the present war. In 1812 both nations had small gunboats in service on it and these naval forces were steadily built up over the next year both by new construction and the conversion of merchant vessels. The loss of two of the largest American warships, the sloops *Eagle* and *Growler*, which were captured after unwisely venturing too far down the Richelieu River in June 1813, tipped the naval balance in favour of Britain. The result was that the RN commander on Lake Champlain, Commander Daniel Pring, raided Plattsburgh in late July and captured several merchant vessels. Both Pring and his American counterpart, Master Commandant Thomas Macdonough, continued for the next year to work hard to increase their respective squadrons.[27]

By the late summer of 1814 the British squadron based at Isle-aux-Noix on the Richelieu consisted of a brig, two sloops and eleven gunboats mounting 53 guns. Macdonough's squadron, based at either Plattsburgh or Vergennes, was superior in weight of metal, comprising a small frigate, a brig, a sloop, a schooner, six galleys and four gunboats mounting 88 guns. Pring, however, had laid down the keel of a frigate, the *Confiance*, to mount 37 guns, which would dominate the lake when she was ready for service in late August. In the interim, Captain Peter Fisher assumed command at Isle-aux-Noix, retaining Pring as his second in command. In the last days of August the carpenters worked desperately to finish the new frigate as the forthcoming operation depended on Fisher being able to secure naval supremacy on the lake. The *Confiance* was launched on 25 August but still needed considerable work to be fitted out. Six days later the British squadron was thrown into confusion when Yeo unexpectedly replaced Fisher with Captain George Downie. According to Yeo, Fisher's temper was too "violent to entrust him with a separate command" and his "very intemperate comments" had annoyed too many people.[28] In reality it was more likely that Yeo felt Fisher's constant demands for personnel verged on impertinence.[29]

Downie only arrived at Isle-aux-Noix on 1 September, the day before the first British troops crossed the border. A veteran of nearly twenty years of service, the 36-year-old Downie had not been in North America long and, on taking up his new appointment, he reported a shortage of equipment, particularly gun locks (firing devices), for the new frigate. "In a few days," he informed Prevost, "she will be before the enemy and the want of locks may be seriously injurious in action."[30] Like his predecessor, he also complained about a shortage of manpower, especially trained seamen in his squadron. Most of the *Confiance*'s com-

Anne Elinor Prevost. The teenage daughter of the British commander-in-chief was an astute observer of her times and the people around her father, recording what she saw in her diary and a postwar memoir. (Portrait by Thomas Philips, courtesy of Sir Christopher Prevost)

pany had not yet joined the ship when Downie officially took command of her on 3 September and they continued to arrive in driblets over the next week. Prevost did what he could and ordered a reinforcement of seamen to Lake Champlain but they were not to arrive in time.[31]

The basic problem was that Yeo had starved the squadron at Isle-aux-Noix of weapons, equipment and manpower to complete the *St. Lawrence*. As Prevost put it, the provision of "armament & equipment of the large Ship" was an objective, to which "all others have hitherto given way."[32] This included manpower – Yeo had recently received a reinforcement of almost 900 seamen but very few were sent to the Lake Champlain squadron. The result was that the ship's company of the *Confiance* consisted of drafts from several warships, soldiers, militiamen and assorted odd bodies. In the words of the frigate's first lieutenant, *Confiance* would go into action unprepared because her ship's company was "unacquainted with each other, and with the Officers."[33]

Yet, for all these problems there was confidence in both the army and navy that they would beat the Jonathans on land and water. This attitude was expressed by Prevost's 19-year-old daughter, Anne Elinor, who cooked breakfast for her father and his staff on 30 August before they left Montreal for the frontier. She was

> most sanguine that something very brilliant would be achieved. I had often thought with regret that my Father had never yet been engaged in any bright affair – he had considered it necessary to conduct the defence of the Canadas with much caution, – a defence, not conquest was necessarily his object. But now I thought the time had arrived when all murmurs would be silenced – I was delighted to think my Father was commanding some thousands of Wellington's Soldiers! ...... O how high the pulse of Hope beat at that moment. I do not recollect that I had any sort of fear as to the result of the Expedition. I looked forward to certain Victory.[34]

That same day, Prevost issued orders to his three brigade commanders to march to the border.

On the other side of that boundary, meanwhile, Major-General George Izard, hoping that Armstrong would rescind his order to move west to Lake Ontario, tarried as long as he dared in the Lake Champlain area. It was only on 29 August that he left Plattsburgh with the rear guard of his division, informing Secretary of War Armstrong that his troops "devoutly prayed" for a British attack that would end the movement.[35] Taking the advice of his senior officers, Izard decided to proceed by way of Schenectady, an indirect and lengthier route to Sackets Harbor. He turned over command at Plattsburgh to Brigadier-General Alexander Macomb, leaving that officer with about 1,500 effectives and 930 men on the sick list. It was a polyglot force; Macomb's own "fine brigade" having been broken up, he now commanded a collection of detachments, recruits and convalescents.[36] As Macomb later commented, everything at Plattsburgh was "in a state of disorganization – works unfinished and a garrison of a few efficient men and a sick list of one thousand," but whatever happened, he assured Washington, "you may rely on the garrison to do its utmost."[37]

Alexander Macomb was born in 1782, which made him thirty-two years old when he assumed command at Plattsburgh. He had joined the army in 1799 and after brief service in the Quasi-War with France, he was sent to the military academy at West Point as an officer in the engineer corps. After three years at the academy, he spent seven years supervising the construction of fortifications in the southern states and in his spare time wrote what was to become the standard treatise on courts martial. In 1812 Macomb was a lieutenant-colonel when he was made adjutant-general of the army and at the outbreak of war was promoted colonel and given command of the new Third Artillery Regiment. He had served on the northern frontier, participating in the Niagara and St. Lawrence campaigns of 1813, and had been made brigadier-general in early 1814 and given a brigade in the Right Division.[38]

When he first assumed command on Lake Champlain, Macomb apparently did not think that Plattsburgh was in any immediate danger. This was despite accurate intelligence brought to him by Eleazar Williams, a 26-year-old aboriginal lay preacher and Superintendent General of the Northern Indian Department, who had organized a corps of "rangers" or scouts that provided useful information to American commanders in the Lake Champlain area. Williams's rangers were not only able to furnish accurate estimates of the strength of the British land forces but also the exact size and armament of the new British vessel building at Isle-aux-Noix. In one of his first interviews with Macomb, Williams recalled that the new commander believed that when the British "shall be informed of General Izard's march for the west, and if they had any troops to

Brigadier-General Alexander Macomb (1782-1841). The young American army commander at Plattsburgh proved to be a competent and level-headed leader despite the serious odds against him. (Print after portrait by Thomas Sully)

spare from Montreal, they will send them up to oppose him on the Niagara frontier."[39] On the contrary, Williams informed Macomb that the enemy were massing just north of the border. On 26 August Macomb held a council of war and Williams's rangers were called to give intelligence on British strength and intentions. Following some discussion, the council decided that the British were "gradually advancing towards the lines, that his intentions were to invade the State of New York and that Plattsburg was his object."[40] The council also suggested that the state militia should be called into service and that a request be made to the governor of Vermont to send militia units from that state as reinforcements.[41]

The citizens of Clinton County, of which Plattsburgh was the county seat, had no doubt that the British were coming and many decided to remove themselves to safer pastures. Williams remembered that there was a general alarm

> among the citizens of the place, and the inhabitants in the vicinity, of the expected invasion of the enemy. Some have already began to leave the village [Plattsburgh], taking their effects with them. It is not only melancholy, but distressing, to see the poor taking their all upon their backs, and flying from their peaceful abodes, and seeking an asylum in places where they are unknown.[42]

Not all commentators were as generous and there were those who suspected the loyalty of some locals. Surgeon William Beaumont of the Sixth Infantry acidly wrote that

> The people are all frighten'd nearly out – out, did I say? rather into their *wits* – if they have any – moving everything off – under the expectation that all will be burnt or destroyed – poor souls, many of them, love & uphold the British – censure and condemn our own Government – complaining they have no protection – neither will they take up arms to defend themselves – indeed I pity their depravity – but don't care much for their losses – if they should maintain any.[43]

By the last days of August 1814, Williams remembered, although the inhabitants were "flying from their homes," preparations for the defence of Plattsburgh

Master Commandant Thomas Macdonough, USN, (1783-1825). Like his army counterpart, Macdonough proved to be an outstanding commander in combat, winning a total victory on Lake Champlain, although it was not an easy battle and he lost many casualties. (Print after portrait by Gilbert Stuart)

were well advanced. Working night and day, Macomb's troops had nearly finished three redoubts on the peninsula formed by the Saranac River and the lake. These large earthworks, mounting heavy guns and protected by abattis, were dubbed Forts Brown, Moreau and Scott.* Two smaller blockhouses had been constructed, one about a thousand feet south of the bridge that connected the two parts of the town, the other near the lake. Every healthy officer and man under Macomb's command was employed on these defences and Eleazar Williams, reporting to Macomb on 27 August, was surprised to find the commanding general hard at work "with his men, with a heavy pine stick [log] on his shoulders, which had painted him with its black coat, so that I could scarcely know him."[44] Macomb sent the sick of the division, about 800 men, to Crab Island just offshore and a draft of 250 men to Macdonough's squadron on the lake. Not counting militia, this left him with some 2,600 effectives to defend Plattsburgh. His infantry consisted of a company of the Fifteenth Infantry and a large detachment of the Thirteenth, as well as the Sixth, Twenty-Ninth, Thirtieth, Thirty-First, Thirty-Third and Thirty-Fouth Infantry Regiments. The Sixth and Thirteenth were sound regiments, raised in New York, and had a good record. The remaining infantry units had been raised in early 1813 as one-year units and, when that term had concluded, had been re-raised to serve during the duration of the war. Many of their men had not agreed to extend their enlistments so these regiments were fairly green in the late summer of 1814. Macomb also had Major Daniel

---

* Major-General Jacob Brown and Brigadier-General Winfield Scott of the United States Army need no further introduction. Jean-Victor-Marie Moreau (1763-1813) was a French general who had risen to prominence in the revolutionary wars but was forced to flee France in 1804 after being involved in a failed plot against Bonaparte. He spent his exile in the United States, where he occasionally advised the government on military matters. At the outbreak of the war, Madison offered him the command of the American army and Moreau accepted, only to change his mind after he learned of Napoleon's invasion of Russia. In 1813 Moreau entered service as a military advisor to the Czar but was mortally wounded at the battle of Dresden in August of that year.

Appling's detachment of the First Rifle Regiment as well as a company of the Light Artillery Regiment and two veteran companies of the Corps of Artillery.[45] Macomb assigned the Sixth and Twenty-Ninth Infantry to Fort Moreau, the Thirtieth and Thirty-First Infantry to Fort Brown and the Thirty-Third and Thirty-Fourth Regiments to Fort Scott. A detachment of regular riflemen and some convalescents from the Fourth Infantry, healthy enough to fight, were assigned to the blockhouse near the bridge while Lieutenant Abraham Fowler manned the blockhouse on the point with part of a company of regular artillery. The remainder of the riflemen, a large detachment of the Thirteenth Infantry and Leonard's company of the Light Artillery Regiment, were kept as a mobile reserve.* On 31 August, Brigadier-General Benjamin Mooers, the local state commander, called out the militia of Clinton and Essex Counties.[46]

The following day Macdonough brought his squadron into Plattsburgh Bay. Just 30 years old, Thomas Macdonough was a fourteen-year veteran of the navy who had distinguished himself for gallantry during the war with the Barbary pirates. In October 1812 he had been appointed to Lake Champlain and had proven himself a very effective commander in a theatre which was often overlooked by Washington. A witness who visited the squadron in August 1814 described Macdonough as having "a fine countenance" and being "a most amiable man, not less loved than esteemed" by his subordinates, who "put the most unbounded confidence in his bravery and prudence."[47] Macdonough was a devout Episcopalian, a fact that pleased Eleazar Williams, the lay preacher and intelligence chief, who characterized him as "the only navy officer, I have found who appears to be pious and attends upon the divine institutions."[48]

By this time, Prevost's Left Division was ready to cross the border. Williams's rangers reported that his force consisted of 14,000 British and Canadian regulars, 200 aboriginal warriors and 36 pieces of ordnance. Williams was also able to furnish accurate information about the British naval squadron, including the number and calibre of its weapons, which pleased Macdonough "as he had been somewhat troubled in not knowing the metal of the enemy's naval guns."[49]

During the first two days of September 1814, the units of Brigadier-General Thomas Brisbane's 2nd Brigade entered the United States and occupied Champlain, New York, about two miles south of the border. As his redcoated infantry tramped over the bridge spanning the Chazy River, which ran through the village, the regimental bands played "Yankee Doodle" and the men in the ranks were in good fettle, convinced that at long last they were going to give Cousin Jonathan the drubbing he so richly deserved.

---

* See Appendix D for information on the opposing forces during the Plattsburgh campaign.

British troops advancing. As Prevost's army crossed the border, their bands played "Yankee Doodle" to annoy the Americans. (Drawing by George Balbar reproduced with permission from Robert Foley, *The War of 1812*)

CHAPTER NINE

"The eyes of America are on us"

THE PLATTSBURGH CAMPAIGN, 2–10 SEPTEMBER 1814

O now the time has come, my boys, to cross the Yankee's line,
We remember they were rebels once, and conquer'd John Burgoyne.
We'll subdue those haughty Democrats, and pull their dwellings down,
And we'll have the states inhabited with subjects to the Crown.
      We're the noble lads of Canada; come, boys, come!

We're as choice a British army as ever cross'd the seas,
We'll burn both town and city, and with smoke becloud the skies;
We'll subdue the old Green Mountain Boys, their Washington is gone,
And we'll play them Yankee Doodle, as the Yankees did Burgoyne.
      We're the noble lads of Canada; come, boys, come!

Now we've reached the Plattsburgh banks, my boys and here we'll make a stand,
Until we take the Yankee fleet, McDonough doth command;
We've the Growler and the Eagle, that from Smith we took away,
And we'll have their noble fleet that lies anchored in the bay.
      We're the noble lads of Canada; come, boys, come![1]

As soon as he entered American territory, Major-General Brisbane distributed a proclamation signed by Prevost assuring the "peaceable and unof-
fending inhabitants" of New York state that they had "no cause for alarm from
this invasion of their country," or

> the safety of themselves and families, or for the security of their property. He
> explicitly assures them, that as long as they continue to demean themselves
> peaceably, they shall be protected in the quiet possession of their homes and
> permitted freely to pursue their usual occupations ……
>
>   The quiet and unoffending inhabitants, not found in arms or otherways
> not aiding in hostilities, shall meet with kind usage and generous treatment;
> and all just complaints against any of his majesty's subjects, offering violence
> to them, to their families, or to their possessions, shall be immediately re-
> dressed.

> The magistrates and other civil authorities, who maintain the faithful discharge of the duties of their respective stations, shall continue to exercise their ordinary jurisdiction, for the punishment and apprehension of crimes, and the support of good order, shall not fail to receive countenance and protection[2]

Brisbane reinforced these sentiments by ordering his unit commanders to "use every exertion to maintain the strictest discipline in the troops under his command."[3] He explained to his men that if the civilians were treated well, they would sell food to the army, as had happened in France the previous spring. Major James Campbell, one of Brisbane's staff, recalled that "the effects of these orders, which were widely circulated," were so evident "that the brigade thought it was "still marching through Canada, and I do not remember that a shot was fired at us until we fell in with some of the United States troops as we approached Plattsburgh."[4] In another wise move, Brisbane did not permit aboriginal warriors to cross the border, as they were greatly feared by the people of northern New York.

Major-General Frederick Robinson's 1st Brigade and Major-General Manley Power's 3rd Brigade followed Brisbane over the border. Robinson recalled that his formation marched over "very bad roads, rendered much worse by the number of artillery and other carriages."[5] As the long columns entered the village of Chazy, about eight miles south of the boundary, 14-year-old Catharine Shute remembered that the gun carriage and wagon wheels "made a noise like distant thunder."[6] She was afraid of the Canadian Voltigeurs, who formed the advance guard, because they were "awful looking creatures" wearing "some kind of leather caps, with cows' tails fastened on to them behind" and "had beards across their faces on a line with their moustaches." By 4 September all three brigades of the Left Division were camped in and around Chazy with the advance guard at Sampson's tavern (now Ingraham, New York), about ten miles from Plattsburgh.[7]

As soon as he heard of the British advance Macomb sent a force to obstruct the State Road (now Route 9), which ran directly from Chazy to Plattsburgh, so as to delay the British advance. It consisted of Major Daniel Appling's detachment of the First Rifle Regiment, about 110 strong, 200 men of the Thirteenth Infantry under Major John Sproull and two field pieces. Sproull set up a defensive position on the south bank of Dead Creek, which emptied into Plattsburgh Bay about two miles north of the town, while Appling took up an advanced position north of the waterway. Both officers had their men fell trees across the State Road. At the same time Macomb ordered Brigadier-General Benjamin Mooers of the New York militia to take the militia units that had responded to the call he had issued on the last day of August, to deploy on the Beekmantown Road (now Route 22),

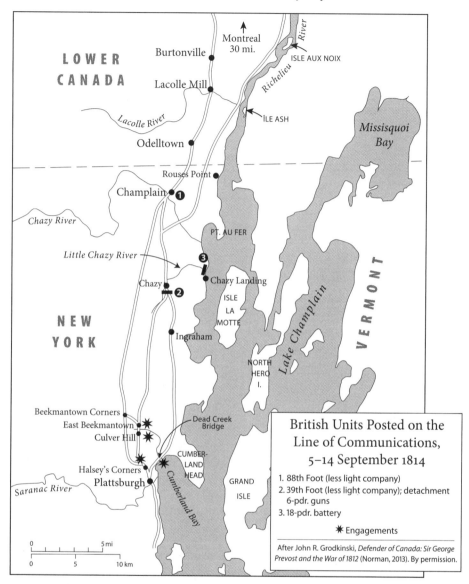

British Units Posted on the
Line of Communications,
5–14 September 1814

1. 88th Foot (less light company)
2. 39th Foot (less light company); detachment
   6-pdr. guns
3. 18-pdr. battery

✳ Engagements

After John R. Grodkinski, *Defender of Canada: Sir George Prevost and the War of 1812* (Norman, 2013). By permission.

which paralleled the State Road to the west. Mooers positioned his force, which included a troop of dragoons under Captain Gilead Sperry who were, ironically, dressed in red uniforms, around the hamlet of East Beekmantown.[8]

Early on 5 September, Brisbane sent the Voltigeurs to reconnoitre south along the State Road. They arrived at the farm of William Mooers, a nephew of the general, and after having drunk "all the milk they wanted," conscripted William's 20-year-old brother Moses and his horse "to show them the way." Moses recalled that, as they moved south down the State Road, they found it filled in with trees and they were mad at me because they thought I had mis-led them, but I hadn't. A lieutenant rode my horse. He was very gentlemanly and gave it back to me, and fifty cents for my trouble. ... I had gone about three miles south with them, and they all came back with me.[9]

The obstruction of the State Road was reported to Prevost at Chazy. Major James Campbell of Brisbane's staff was ordered to take some of the flank companies from the 2nd Brigade and reconnoitre routes west of the State Road. He found them viable for infantry but difficult for artillery. Prevost decided to push Brisbane down the State Road with the greater part of the divisional transport while Power's brigade would move to the area around the hamlet of East Beekmantown. Late in the afternoon of 5 September Power marched west along a country route but did not get far before nightfall and camped to the north of East Beekmantown. Some minor skirmishing took place between a patrol of Mooers's militia and a British picket but it gradually died away.

At about midnight on 5 September, Major John Wool left Plattsburgh with three companies, 250 all ranks, of the Twenty-Ninth Infantry with orders from Macomb to "meet the Enemy and give an Example to the Militia."[10] Wool camped for the night just south of East Beekmantown. The 30-year-old Wool was a very capable officer. At the outbreak of the war, he had given up his legal practice in Troy, New York, to accept a captain's commission in the Thirteenth Infantry. He had performed well at the battle of Queenston Heights in October 1812 and was promoted a major in the Twenty-Ninth Infantry. Wool had served with that regiment throughout Major-General Wade Hampton's 1813 campaign against Montreal and at the battle of Lacolle Mill in the spring of 1814.[11]

At daybreak on 6 September, both Brisbane and Robinson moved their brigades down the State Road. Robinson's formation had been weakened after he was ordered to leave the 39th and 88th Foot at Champlain and Chazy respectively, to secure the line of communications. This would not have been welcomed by either battalion as they were veterans of the Peninsular army and, having come all this way, probably felt they should get a crack at the Yankees. Robinson retained the light companies of both battalions but the strength of his brigade was now reduced to just over 1,200 all ranks. He followed Brisbane down the State Road but then turned west to move along country lanes. He recorded that the roads were the worst he had ever seen, "bad by nature, and rendered extremely dangerous by the breaking of old logs, with which a kind of causeway had been formed many years before."[12] This was a fair description of a corduroy road, much favoured in the frontier areas of North America, but as Robinson recorded, "Scarcely a horse got through without losing a shoe and the artillery stuck fast for three hours." As they trudged along this wretched path, Robinson's men could hear musketry coming from their front and quickened their pace.

This shooting started when Power encountered Wool and Mooers. Power had roused his 3rd Brigade at daybreak and moved south down the Beekmantown Road. The 3rd Foot, or the Buffs, a solid unit of Peninsular veterans, headed the column, which was preceded by the brigade's light companies. Formed in column of march, the brigade had hardly started to move when it met some of Mooers's militia, who let off a volley and then ran away. Without breaking formation, the brigade pushed on to East Beekmantown, where they ran into the main body of the militia and Wool's detachment of the Twenty-Ninth Infantry. A more serious exchange of fire took place here. The militia were shaky, however, and, as Macomb later commented, fired at the British advance guard but then, "except a few brave men, fell back most precipitately in the greatest disorder, notwithstanding the British troops did not deign to fire on them, except by their flankers and advanced patroles."[13]

In their flight the militiamen encountered Captain Azariah Flagg's company of riflemen. Recruited from Plattsburgh schoolboy volunteers, who were too young for militia duty, it had been mustered into service a few days before and had just received rifles from Macomb's quartermaster. The company had been marching north along the Beekmantown Road when, as 16-year-old Henry Averill remembered, the teenagers saw the frightened militiamen streaming towards them "in the utmost confusion – some without a hat and others without shoes having thrown them aside as rather cumbersome and unnecessary in flight."[14] When the boys urged the fleeing men to return to their units, they received the retort that "When we had fought as long as they had – we would be glad to retreat too." Undaunted, Flagg's young riflemen pressed on, moving toward the sound of musketry coming from the north in the vicinity of East Beekmantown.[15]

Wool's regulars held their position at East Beekmantown until the British, far superior in numbers, threatened to overwhelm them, and then fell back. Captain Nathaniel Rochester of the Twenty-Ninth – the son of the man who founded the northern New York city – recalled that Wool's three companies "retired in excellent order" and for the next few hours "had every opportunity of lying behind stone fences & secreting in the wood" until the British came within range "when we would fire & retire about half a mile" and take up a new position.[16] Rochester recorded that "in this manner we fought them for six miles when their main force arrived & we were compelled to give up half the town." Although Wool, in Macomb's words, disputed the road with "great obstinacy," the same could not be said for Mooers's militia, who could not be prevailed upon to stand, nothwithstanding the exertions of their general and staff officers; although the fields were divided by strong stone walls, and they were told the enemy could not cut them off. The State dragoons of New York wear red coats and they being on the heights to watch the enemy, gave constant alarm to the militia, who mistook them for the enemy, and feared his getting in their rear.[17]

Wool now took up a new position on Culver Hill, a mile or so south of East Beekmantown and four miles from Plattsburgh. Here he was joined by Mooers, who had managed to re-form about 200 militiamen. As the British approached in column, preceded by a cloud of skirmishers, the American regulars and militia opened a heavy fire that killed Lieutenant-Colonel James Willington, commanding officer of the 3rd Foot, who was on horseback at the front of the column, and a junior officer.* The Buffs did not hesitate, however, but went straight up the hill with bayonets fixed and Wool fell back to an intersection called Halsey's Corners, about two miles north of Plattsburgh.[18]

Captain Luther Leonard of the Regiment of Light Artillery now arrived with two 6-pdr. guns. Leonard had been ordered to march to support Wool before dawn but had not done so, causing Macomb to note in his official report that he "was not well pleased" with the artillery officer. Late or not, Leonard's gunners soon got down to work.[19] As the British column came within range, he fired roundshot from both his weapons into the massed ranks and followed it with two rounds of canister. For a moment it looked like Power's advance would be halted but his brigade soon regained its stride and again moved forward. By this time, Wool had become aware that another British force moving down a secondary road to the east of the Beekmantown Road was threatening to flank him – this was Robinson's brigade, which had finally caught up with Brisbane and Power.

Wool decided to fall back to Plattsburgh. At the outskirts of the village he met with Appling and Sproull's troops. Appling had skirmished with Brisbane's ad-

---

* Lieutenant-Colonel James Willington and Ensign John Chapman were buried by local civilians at the foot of Culver Hill. Willington was wearing a particularly fine pair of boots and during the night someone excavated the lower half of his grave and made off with them. It was always suspected that the culprit was David Phelps, a local blacksmith who helped to bury Willington. See Allan S. Everest, *Recollections of Clinton County and the Battle of Plattsburgh, 1800-1840* (Plattsburgh, 1964), 52.

  Willington was later re-buried in the Plattsburgh Cemetery. Contrary to popular myth he was no relation to the Duke of Wellington. There is some confusion over Willington's name as some sources have it as Wellington, including the *Army List*, but I have decided to go with Willington as more sources give it than the other. Many people do not realize that the duke was born Arthur Wesley and progressively changed his name to Wellesley and finally to Wellington.

vance guard, probably the Canadian Voltigeurs, before falling back to Sproull's position at Dead Creek. Macomb, realizing that the British were advancing on almost every road into Plattsburgh, sent his aide, Lieutenant Chester Root, to order Appling and Sproull to withdraw to the town and they did so just in time. In Macomb's words, "every road was full of [British] troops crowding in on us from all sides" so he "ordered the field pieces to retire across the bridge and form a battery for its protection and to cover the retreat of the infantry." This was done, and the commands of Appling and Wool, as well as that of Sproull," moved back alternately, keeping up a brisk fire until they got under cover of the works." It had been a neatly-fought delaying action but, as Macomb noted, so "undaunted was the enemy" that "he never deployed in his whole march, always pressing on in columns." But then, to the veteran units in Prevost's army, the fighting that took place that day was a picnic compared to what they had seen in Europe.[20]

Brisbane's 2nd Brigade waded Dead Creek but, once across, came under fire from American gunboats out in the bay. Campbell recalled that Brisbane was anxious to turn his field artillery against these nuisances but "a senior general" (whose name Campbell does not provide) forbade it as "it would only attract the enemy's fire towards a point upon which it was already directed with right good will."[21]* As soon as the anonymous general officer had ridden off, however, Brisbane ordered the Royal Marine rocket detachment to open up at the gunboats and,

> a rocket well laid by the officer commanding it, having, I believe, the very first discharge, struck one gun-boat, and as we heard afterwards wounded the officer commanding on board, and as it in its continued flight went close over most of the others, the whole took to their oars in an instant, and we were no more molested by them.[22]

In fact, the rocket hit Lieutenant Silas Duncan of the USS *Saratoga*, whom Macdonough had sent to assume command of the gunboats and extricate them from what might be a very dangerous situation. Duncan was terribly wounded: "the whole of his right shoulder, including the joint and all the bones and muscles about the shoulder, were carried away, and his shoulder blade and his collarbone were also fractured, besides extensive contusions."[23] The wound was clearly mortal, and after Duncan was removed to the hospital on Crab Island, it was lightly dressed and the young officer was made as comfortable as possible and laid aside to die.

---

* The anonymous "senior general" could only have been Prevost or Major-General Francis De Rottenburg as Brisbane was senior in rank to Baynes and Beckwith, the highest-ranking staff officers of the division, and Robinson and Power were not near this spot.

Canadian Voltigeurs skirmishing. The Canadian Voltigeurs, among the best light infantry units in the forces defending Canada, provided the advanced guard for Prevost's army. (Watercolour by Eugene Leliepvre, courtesy Parks Canada)

It was now early afternoon and British troops were streaming into Plattsburgh. William Apess, a member of the Pequot people serving in the regular artillery, never forgot the sight. With dramatic language he described the "very imposing aspect" the invaders showed with "their red uniforms and instruments of death, which they bore in their hands, glittered in the sunbeams of heaven like so many sparkling diamonds."[24] Wool ordered the floor planks of the lower bridge to be taken up but the detachment that did this work came under fire from British skirmishers, who mortally wounded one officer. Among the last Americans to cross the Saranac to safety was Flagg's little company of teenagers, which, unable to get over on the lower bridge in time, waded the river upstream. They then took up a position in an old mill near the lower bridge from which they exchanged fire with the British snipers infesting houses on the opposite bank of the Saranac.

Prevost's troops had now occupied the northern part of Plattsburgh and it only remained to take the southern part and Macomb's defence works. The senior staff decided to make an immediate assault – a few minutes after he arrived at the outskirts of Plattsburgh, Robinson was asked by the divisional quartermaster, Major-General Thomas S. Beckwith, if his brigade would be able to undertake that attack. Robinson pointed out that he had heard that "there was a river between us and the enemy's works which was fordable in several places," and inquired whether Beckwith's staff were "acquainted" with these crossing places. Beckwith replied that they were not. Robinson became justifiably annoyed that his brigade should be committed to action by Beckwith, who had no information to assist him, when it was Beckwith's duty to provide that very information. This was bad staff work and certainly not the way business had been conducted under the Duke of Willington. It did not bode well.[25]

Prevost now rode up and repeated the request to make an immediate attack. Robinson asked how his brigade was to do so, and was told that "there were fords to cross over the Saranac." "Upon enquiry," however, Robinson found "that no one of the Staff knew the Fords, the country on the other side, or the distance from the Redoubts, *nor had they any Guides of any kind.*" As his men had been marching since 5 A.M. and had not eaten the entire day – and "taking into account the total ignorance that pervaded" – Robinson tactfully suggested that the attack should be postponed until daybreak "and that the intermediate time should be employed in obtaining every necessary information, and in procuring Guides *at any price.*" Prevost agreed and ordered Robinson to have his brigade ready to march "an hour before day break to lead the attack, but not to move without further orders."[26]

During the remaining daylight hours, the Left Division took position in and around Plattsburgh. The senior officers chose billets in houses while their brigades camped nearby in sites that were out of range of the American artillery south of the Saranac River. After selecting a camp site for his brigade, Robinson sought a billet for himself and his staff. One of his young aides spotted the house of 73-year-old Nathaniel Platt, brother of the man who had founded Plattsburgh and a patriot veteran of the Revolutionary War. Platt was sitting on his porch when the aide rode up and accosted him: "Well, old man, who are you?" Platt, somewhat infirm but annoyed by the impudence of this arrogant young puppy in a scarlet coat, rose slowly but with dignity from his chair and gave the Britisher both barrels: "Young man, I'm Captain Platt and be damned to you." Robinson, coming behind, heard the exchange and admonished the aide: "You are well answered and you ought to be more respectful in addressing an old gentleman."[27]

With the coming of night, the shooting across the Saranac gradually tailed off and the invaders, about 8,300 all ranks strong, settled down in the northern part of Plattsburgh. It was a pretty little place, with some seventy-eight dwellings, mostly wood-frame and with fine views of the adjoining bay. It boasted four taverns, thirteen stores, eleven shops, a tannery, two saw mills, a grist mill and a fulling mill. Its residents were kept informed by two newspapers and, being the seat of Clinton County, it had the county court house. Prior to

Looking north down Culver Hill. The high ground at Culver Hill made an ideal delaying position and Wool fell back to it on 6 September 1814. (Author's photo)

the war Plattsburgh had been the centre of a thriving lumber trade and it had not suffered all that much during the conflict, despite the fact that it had been raided by the British in the summer of 1813. Now it was a battleground.[28]

At 4.30 A.M. on Wednesday, 7 September, the drums rolled in the camp of Robinson's 1st Brigade and shouting NCOs roused sleeping men. An hour later, when the sun had appeared, Robinson was ready to march but no orders came until 6 A.M. when aides brought a request for him to attend a meeting of senior officers at Prevost's headquarters. Almost immediately a second order arrived, putting off the meeting until 9 A.M. At 8 A.M. a third message arrived with a request for Robinson to come immediately and, once there, the commanding general asked for Robinson's assessment of the situation. He replied by first putting two questions to Prevost: "whether he intended establishing a post at Plattsburgh in case of success, and whether the enemy had a large depot in the place."[29] Prevost replied to both questions in the negative and Robinson told him that "there would be no use in attacking the works without co-operation upon the Lake."[30]

This was clearly the answer Prevost wanted and he showed Robinson a letter he had just written to Captain George Downie, commanding the Lake Champlain squadron, "urging him to make every exertion as a *golden* opportunity presented itself for totally annihilating the Enemy's Flotilla and gaining the superiority of the Lake for the war."[31] This letter was dated at 7 A.M., that day, 7 September. After giving details of the American squadron anchored in the bay, Prevost assured Downie that

> If you feel that the Vessels under your Command are equal to a contest with those I have described, you will find the present moment offers many advantages which may not again occur.
>
> As my ulterior movements depend on your decision, you will have the goodness to favor me with it, with all possible promptitude.[32]

Prevost had decided to wait for the Royal Navy before launching an attack. As he later explained to his superiors, "no Offensive Operations could be carried on within the Enemy's Territory for the destruction of his Naval Establishments without Naval Support" and since he was confidently "relying upon the successful exertions of the Squadron," he "made his arrangements for the assault of the Enemy's Works, the moment it should appear."[33]

Prevost's letter reached Downie that same day. Since assuming command on Lake Champlain four days before, Downie had faced seemingly endless problems. His flagship, the 37-gun frigate HMS *Confiance*, had only been launched on 25 August and was far from complete, as much work had to be done on her decks, gun carriages, pumps and rigging. The frigate was so incomplete that when she moved along the Richelieu River to the lake, most of her powder and cartridges had to be towed in boats behind her as workers were still trying to finish her magazine. Only about two-thirds of the frigate's company was on board and they were strangers to each other. Downie sent the rest of the squadron ahead to Chazy while his sailors and shipyard carpenters worked frantically to finish the vessel. Worse still, as he took the frigate out of the naval base at Isle-aux-Noix, she ran aground, causing yet more delay.[34]

When Downie received Prevost's letter, he was off Ash Island, in the Richelieu River, just north of the border. He replied immediately saying that, as soon as he could "put this Ship into a State for Action," he would meet the enemy but warned Prevost that

> The *Confiance* is at this moment in such a state as to require at least a day or two to make her efficient before the Enemy; but with all the exertion I can make it will probably be that time at least, before I can get her up to Chazy, where I shall be happy to receive any further communications from Your Excellency.[35]

It being clear to Prevost that it would be some days before he could expect the squadron to appear, he gave orders for batteries to be constructed on the north bank of the Saranac.

That same morning, Macomb, annoyed by the British snipers' use of residences on the north bank of the river, ordered them destroyed by hotshot. As they gradually took fire, Captain James Wood of the Royal Artillery recalled that the British sent a flag of truce over the river, with a request for a cease fire while they extinguished the blaze but the Americans "declined, and kept up their fire, warmer than before."[36]

It turned out that the engineering department of the British Left Division was no better prepared than that of the Right Division on the Niagara. Robinson, who had participated in the bloody two-month siege of the Spanish fortress city of San Sebastian the previous summer, was scathing in his comments:

> Directions were now given for constructing Batteries against the Enemy's Works but Fascines were not thought of, nor were there tools for making them until all the Old worn out Billhooks* of the Peninsular Regiments were now collected.

---

* A billhook is an agricultural cutting implement, resembling a long knife with a curved blade, about 10–12 inches in length, used to cut small branches and shrubs. They were very popular in the Peninsular army for gathering firewood and forage.

The Engineers demanded a Working Party of *500* and a Covering Party of *One Thousand* Men – which, with the Pickets and the Support, amounted to more than the whole of the American Force under B[rigadier] Gen[era]l Macomb.

Owing to some mistake, nothing was done towards erecting Batteries that night [of 8 September] and the next morning the Chief Engineers, Colonel [Philip] Hughes, was directed to return to Montreal.[37]

Captain J. H. Wood, RA, confirms that Hughes was dismissed on 9 September because no progress had been made on constructing the batteries during the previous two days and an angry Prevost also fired his artillery commander, Lieutenant-Colonel Edward Pritchard, RA. Majors John Sinclair and William Payne took over as the divisional artillery and engineer commanders respectively and, with the change in management, progress was better, but the shortage of tools forced Payne to use sandbags instead of the more normal gabions.[38]*

Construction was also delayed because work could only be done at night. The Americans were very observant and quick to fire at any target they deemed worthwhile on the north bank of the Saranac – and they seemed to have plenty of ammunition. "Whenever they observe an individual," Wood complained, "they direct a volley; if more than one or two, a cannon shot."[39] During daylight hours the exchange of fire was unending and occasionally it rose to high tempo. Apess, himself a gunner, recalled that "rockets, bombshells, and cannonballs poured upon us like a hailstorm" and "for six days and nights we did not leave our guns, and during that time the work of death paused not, as every day some shot took effect."[40] British probes at the two bridges and a ford upriver were met with determined firing by the defenders. What made the situation more disagreeable for the British was that they were outgunned by the defenders, the largest weapons on the north bank being two light brass 24-pdr. field guns, the same as those being used by British gunners at Fort Erie, and no match for the 18- and 24-pdr. guns served by Macomb's gunners. As a result, Prevost ordered two 8-inch mortars and two 12-pdr. guns to be brought from the defences of Isle-aux-Noix.[41]

Finally, at nightfall on Friday, 9 September, Sinclair gave orders for the guns to be placed in the batteries. Unfortunately for him, that was the night that Captain George McGlassin of the Fifteenth Infantry rose from his sick bed and volunteered to take a fifty-man party over the Saranac and attack one of the batteries. Guided by John Williams, the brother of Eleazar, they waded the river, divided into two groups and attacked from opposite sides just as Sinclair's

---

* A gabion is a wickerwork basket made out of interwoven branches and filled with sand, earth or stone. It was used to construct defence works against enemy fire.

gunners were hauling their pieces into position. Captain Wood, who was present, remembered that

> We accordingly, at midnight, moved down and were proceeding to the batteries, when a heavy fire of musketry was thrown in upon the working parties, and shameful to relate, the covering party ran off, scarcely returning a shot, the whole running in upon our guns like a flock of sheep. It was at that moment supposed the enemy had discovered the work and made a sortie to destroy it.[42]

Brisbane, whose brigade had provided the infantry covering party, was furious and issued a "very severe order" criticizing the behaviour of the troops who had participated. Sinclair, however, inspected the batteries the following day and judged them to not be "in a fit state to receive the guns" and, thus, Wood commented, "had three days and nights elapsed and nothing effectually done." His conclusion was there was "a great deficiency of arrangement and decision" in the division and "timidity and indecision appear to prevail, where energy and vigor ought to exist."[43]

There was no shortage of energy south of the Saranac, particularly around Alexander Macomb. Eleazar Williams recalled that, when the American commander watched the British columns enter Plattsburgh, he was "silent and thoughtful – he saw too much, no doubt, of his dangerous position" but the defences of Plattsburgh "were committed to him for safe keeping, and he would defend them to the last extremity or be buried under them."[44] This was certainly the spirit of the general order Macomb issued to his troops on 5 September. Making reference to the American Left Division fighting on the Niagara, he urged that

> Let it not be said that Erie was better defended than Plattsburgh. It was there that the American Soldiers bested and defeated the heroes of Spain, France and Portugal,* and their example must be followed or our reputation is lost. The eyes of America are on us and fortune always favours the brave.[45]

As Captain Jonathan Rochester of the Twenty-Ninth Infantry put it, he and his comrades would have to "either *distinguish* or *extinguish* themselves."[46] Brigadier-General Mooers of the New York militia chastised his men for their conduct on 6 September, informing them that, to his regret, some were "lost to patriotism and to honor" and "fled at the first approach of the enemy, and

---

* Macomb was mistaken as no veteran Peninsula units were involved in Drummond's 15 August assault on Fort Erie.

Brigadier-General Benjamin Mooers (1758-1838). The local state commander, Mooers was able to assemble a large number of New York militia, but most of them were unable to stand up to British regulars in a pitched battle. (From Benson Lossing, *Pictorial Field-Book of the War of 1812*)

afterwards basely disbanded themselves and returned home; thereby disgracing themselves, and furnishing to their fellow-soldiers an example of all that brave men detest and abhor."[47]

Macomb had no doubts that Prevost would cross the river and attack. He issued detailed instructions on how the redoubts were to be defended and bluntly warned his officers "to put to instant death any man who leaves his Post."[48] Both officers and men laboured to improve the defences and each night Macomb burned some of the buildings around them, to provide light for the defenders and reduce cover for the enemy, should he attempt a night assault. He made a point of marching troops in front of these fires, to give the impression that they were newly arrived reinforcements and also turned out a considerable number of his regular troops at guard mountings to give British observers the idea that the garrison was larger than they thought. He built and armed a battery of two guns on Crab Island to assist Macdonough's flotilla in the bay and constructed primitive Congreve rockets both as signals and weapons. Suspecting that the main British attack would cross the Saranac at a ford upstream, he took efforts to camouflage the roads and laneways near it on the south bank. Work parties disguised the existing roads and paths with leaves and hastily-embedded pine trees. Macomb did his best to encourage the militia who were assembling in great numbers but was wise enough not to place too much faith in their ability to fight British regulars in the open.[49]

The New York militia were coming forward in great numbers – Mooers now had about 700 men from Clinton and Essex counties while units from Montgomery, Saratoga and Scoharie counties were on their way. On 8 September, they began to be joined by comrades from Vermont. Macomb had appealed to Governor Martin Chittenden of that state to do everything in his power "to throw a detachment over the lake."[50] Chittenden had refused to call out the Vermont militia because he believed that he had no constitutional authority "to order the Militia out of the state" but, feeling that "every aid, constitutionally in our power," should be afforded to Macomb, he did authorize Brigadier-General Samuel Strong of Vermont to call for volunteers to cross the lake and defend Plattsburgh. The call went out on 6 September and the response was enthusiastic as men hastily formed themselves into units, chose officers and embarked on any craft they could find to cross over to Plattsburgh. Herman Green of St. Albans, remembered that

> a drummer & fifer were engaged by the leading men of the town, and beat up for volunteers, and something like sixty embodied and about thirty of the number staid at Daniel Dutcher's house, … others returned home for clothing, provisions and teams of convey their baggage to Milton, to the ford called the sand bar opposite. ……
>
> We collected on the west side of Sand Island and there organized a company, and made choice of Samuel Farnsworth for our Capt. and Daniel Dutcher Lieut. and a Roll was made of the men then present. Toward eight Wednesday [7 September 1814] a boat came from over from Plattsburgh and carried our company with many others across on the York shore.[51]

In all, about 2,500 Vermonters would join Macomb although one man had sober second thoughts when he heard gunfire coming from across the water. He made an abrupt about face, explaining to his comrades that "he had on his best Sunday shoes" and since his wife "would feel *dreadfully*" if he spoiled them, he was going home to change footwear but would shortly return.[52] Needless to say, he never did.

Jonathan Stevens of Panton, Vermont, volunteered, as did his four sons. Stevens crossed the lake on 8 September and arrived in Macomb's position with several hundred Vermont men on the next day, where they received ammunition and "such as had no Arms drew them." Stevens recalled that the regulars were glad to see the Vermont men but his comrades were less happy when they found they "had to shift as we could for lodging & this night was very cold." The Vermonters were trying to sleep when

> about 3 or 4 Oclock at night we heard a smart firing from the river. immediately 2 sky rockets Assended [sic] from the fort. I was standing by the fire with our General [Strong] who had no better Quarters than the soldiers. he said that was the token of an Alarm and gave Orders to stand to our Arms. some confusion Ensued but we were at length paraded. in A short time news came the Attack was not from the Enemy but that one of our Capt[ains] with fifty men had Crossed over & had Attacked thrice his number and had routed them from where they were entrenching 300 yds of our fort Directly Across the river.[53]

Stevens, of course, was describing McGlassin's attack on the British battery north of the river.

There were Americans north of the Saranac who found themselves occupied by a foreign army. Generally, relations between invaders and invaded were good – there was the occasional theft but discipline was strict in Prevost's command and punishment swift and severe. At first many civilians were fearful of their uninvited guests. Gideon Rugar of Plattsburgh was eight years old when British troops approached the town on 6 September. He recalled that his anxious parents wanted "to go away to a place of safety" and "took an oxcart with a haystack on it, loaded [it] with furniture" and left their home. Just as the Rugar family were exiting Plattsburgh, they encountered

> two British commissioned officers on horseback. These officers had on red uniforms and side arms. They asked us where we were going. We told them we were going to get away from the trouble. They said we might as well go back because we couldn't cross the river at Morrisonville. The bridge was torn up. We went home and were not molested.[54]

Mary Sheldon, who lived near East Beekmantown, was also eight in 1814. She remembered hearing the sounds of musketry and

> saw British soldiers frequently. They were all redcoats. Some of the women with the British army stopped on the State Road where it turned to the [Dead?] Creek and did their washing. They came up to our house and borrowed an iron kettle of us, which they never returned. ...... The British kept some mules in our log barn. Two women brought two large mules and kept them in our barn one night at least.[55]

Although occupied, the people of Clinton Country were not conquered, and some teased or taunted their unwelcome guests. At Chazy, local folk visited a British camp and got into a conversation with some British officers, who expressed a wish to see real Yankee fighting men, whom they believed to be small people. Someone went and fetched Philip Honsigner,

> a local boy standing six feet seven inches and weighing 260 pounds; his bearing was in keeping with his dimensions: portly and dignified, and his speech staid and weighty. Astonished, the British looked at him in amazement; he gazed down on them in all his gravity and tranquillity. Instinctively receding, the British were overheard to say, "If the Yankees are all like him, Lord deliver us from fighting them."[56]

Mollie Hamilton, a Plattsburgh housewife, went a bit farther. When she heard British infantry marching by on the street outside her house, singing loudly, she stuck her head out an attic window and yelled at them: "You are marching to the tune of 'God Save the King' now" but "you'll come back to the tune of 'Yankee Doodle.'" An angry redcoat shouted a retort: "Stick your damn long neck back or I'll shoot it off."[57]

Captain Nathaniel Platt, of course, was not a man to put up with any non-sense from redcoats. Platt remained in his home because, as he later remarked, "he had never turned his back to the British and he never would."[58] The captain liked to taunt Robinson's young staff officers who were billeted in his house by chiding them: "Why don't you take those Yankee forts and not wait for your fleet?" "Well, Captain Platt," they would reply (by now having reason to treat the old veteran with respect) "we are in no hurry about it. We will take them all at the same time when the fleet comes in."

The whereabouts of that fleet was the question on the mind of just about everyone in both armies. On 8 August Prevost again wrote to Downie, reminding him that the army "only wait for your arrival to proceed against General McCombe's last position on the South bank of the Saranac."[59] He sent this letter by the hand of Major Foster Coore, his principal aide, and Coore found Downie in his flagship, anchored with the squadron about three miles north of Chazy. After reading it, Coore recalled, Downie said with "some warmth" that he was surprised that Prevost "should think it necessary to urge me upon this subject" as "I am as desirous of proceeding to active operations" but "I am responsible for the Squadron I command and no man shall make me lead it into action before I consider it in fit condition."[60]

Downie's reply betrayed a certain impatience with Prevost's lack of understanding of the naval situation:

In the letter I did myself the Honor to address to you yesterday, I stated to you that this Ship was not ready. She is not ready now, and, until she is ready, it is my duty not to hazard the Squadron before the Enemy who will be superior in Force.

I purpose anchoring at Chazy until I am enabled to move, which I trust will be very shortly, it depending on my guns being ready.[61]

Downie's reference to guns was relevant. Downie had no locks – devices or implements required to ensure smooth and quick firing – for the 24-pdr. main armament of the *Confiance*. An urgent appeal to a warship captain at Quebec had brought a supply of carronade locks, not the proper equipment but better than nothing. The flagship's gunner and his mates were busy fitting these to her guns as well completing their carriages. Lieutenant James Robertson, the first lieutenant of the frigate, recorded the activities of her ship's company on 8 and 9 September:

Quartr'd [assigned duties to] the Ships Company. Employed clearing the Decks. Artificers employed fitting Cheeks, Beds, and Coins [quoins] for the Guns, and Magazine passages.

On the 9th remained at anchor, Employed setting up the Rigging, scraping the Decks. ... Exercised the Great Guns, Artificers fitting Beds, Coins [quoins] belaying pins &c.[62]

The gun drill revealed that the weapons "worked heavy" because the gun deck was not finished, being only "rough scraped" with "a quantity of Pitch on them."[63] There had not been enough time to plane or smooth the rough planks of green wood on the deck, which meant that the guns did not recoil smoothly, thus putting additional strain on their mountings and making it more laborious for the gun crews to run them back up to firing position. This would not only reduce the rate of fire; it would create more stress on the gun crews.

On 9 September the frigate received the final drafts of men. Robertson later recalled that the *Confiance*'s company consisted of men "collected together from time to time, between the 24th of August and the Night of the 9th of September" and "were not, nor could they be expected to be" known "to their Officers or to each other."[64] A later investigation revealed that the frigate received drafts of men from no fewer than twelve different warships as well as transports. The largest number came from HM Ships *Leopard* and *Ceylon* and were described as being sent to the lake service "against their inclination." Two drafts that came from HM Ships *Warspite* and *Ajax* were described as "men who were in disgrace" – that is, had bad conduct records. Eleven gunners came from the Royal Artillery and Royal Marine Artillery while ten men came from the 39th Foot. Finally, just to round out the complement, seven men were impressed or drafted from prison volunteers. It was not a promising situation and Downie would have little time to transform these people into an efficient organization.[65]

Prevost, meanwhile, was growing impatient. On 9 September, he addressed another letter to Downie informing him that, in view of the naval officer's letter of the previous day, he had postponed attacking Macomb until the squadron was "in a state of preparation to co-operate with the division of the Army."[66] Prevost added that he "need not dwell with you on the Evils resulting to both Services from delay" but was "convinced you have done everything that was in your Power" to make the squadron ready. Downie's reply was that he intended to sail at midnight and expected to round Cumberland Head into Plattsburgh Bay about dawn to commence an attack on Macdonough's squadron "if they should be Anchored in a position that will offer chance of success."[67] The naval officer stressed that he would "rely on any assistance you can afford the Squadron." This letter did not come into Prevost's hands until some time after 9 P.M. and he immediately alerted his brigade commanders to be ready to move at 6 A.M. on the following day.[68]

But there was no sign of the squadron when dawn came on 10 September. Downie had indeed weighed anchor at midnight but the wind was so unfavourable that the squadron could not proceed up the lake. At 7 A.M. the squadron tried again but came to anchor at 11 A.M. "having made little or no progress."[69] It was not long before Major Coore arrived with another letter from Prevost that informed Downie that the army had been ready "to storm the Enemy's works at nearly the same moment as the Naval Action should commence in the Bay."[70] But this latest missive had a sting in it – Prevost ascribed the disappointment he felt "to the unfortunate change of wind, & shall rejoice to learn that my reasonable expectations have been frustrated by no other cause." These words must have been bitter gall to Downie, an officer relatively junior in his rank and exercising his first important independent command – a command that was clearly unready for action. He discussed the matter with Coore, and they agreed that, if the squadron could attack the following day, it would signal its approach by scaling its guns, or firing blank charges, to alert the army that it was on its way.

By now Downie was becoming annoyed by Prevost's frequent letters. After Coore had left with his reply, he remarked to Commander Daniel Pring of HMS *Linnet*, who was present, that Prevost's most recent message did not really deserve an answer and that he would not write any more letters to the land commander. Instead, he would convince Prevost "that the naval Force will not be backward in their share of the attack."[71]

Prevost perhaps would have been better advised to ride the fifteen miles to Downie's anchorage off Chazy Landing and meet with him in person. Downie was now under an understandable but mistaken impression that Prevost wished him to attack the American squadron at anchor in Plattsburgh Bay and that, when he did so, the army would attack Macomb's defences south of the Saranac. The scaling of the guns, in the words of Pring, Downie's second in command, would "be the signal by which the Land forces should be informed of the approach of the Naval Squadron, in order that they might know, when their co-operation was wanted."[72] Downie, Pring and the other officers of the squadron believed that the attack on Plattsburgh was to be a joint operation with both services attacking at the same time, with the army supporting on land the navy's attack on water. This was not how Prevost understood it – although the rather vague wording in some of his letters may have given the naval commander a reasonable expectation that this was the case. What Prevost wanted was for Downie, when he was ready, to attack the American squadron in the bay or anywhere

Nathaniel Platt's house, Plattsburgh. The old gentlemen, a veteran of the Revolutionary War, was sitting on his porch when one of Robinson's young aides failed to treat him with due respect. Platt, however, got the last laugh. (Author's photograph)

else on water because Prevost never specified where or how a naval attack was to take place. As soon as the squadron appeared, Prevost planned to commence a separate operation on land, with the object, not of supporting the squadron, but of taking the American defences and rendering Plattsburgh useless as a naval base in obedience to his instructions from London. It was a natural misunderstanding but one that was to have serious consequences in the future.[73]

For both opponents, Saturday, 10 September, was a busy day. Captain Aiken's teenage riflemen had resumed their usual position in the old sawmill that overlooked the lower bridge and woe betide any redcoat foolish enough to come within in range of these sharp-eyed young men. In between shots, the boys no doubt shouted rude things and made impudent gestures at their enemy. The little company had become favourites in Macomb's command and Eleazar Williams thought that no unit "was more useful or watchful."[74] Despite his religious convictions Williams himself had decided to take up the "carnal weapon" and joined as a volunteer at one of the artillery pieces. The regulars continued to labour on their fortifications while Mooers and Strong's militia, which Macomb had deployed to cover the upper reaches of the Saranac, spent the day resting. Out in Plattsburgh Bay, Macdonough was making his final preparations. He had fully briefed his captains on what he had expected of them and how he wished a battle to be fought and he had worked his gun crews hard to improve both their accuracy and rate of fire. Macdonough, however, continued to worry about a shortage of manpower and sent an officer to Macomb to ask for more assistance from the army. The land commander could not spare any of his men but he did give Macdonough's officer permission to take forty-six prisoners who were under guard for various offences, some of them in chains. The officer freed the men and took them to the brig USS *Eagle*, where they were washed, fed and given new clothing.[75]

In the British squadron, the ship's company of the *Confiance* spent much of the day "Exercising the Great Guns" and "shortening the breechings [of the guns] fore and aft" while the artificers were busy "making Shot lockers, altering Beds and Coins [quoins] and driving in belaying pins &c."[76] At Plattsburgh, Major John Sinclair's gunners were trying to complete the batteries in the face of determined American fire. It was planned that the heavy ordnance – the two 12-pdr. guns and the two 8-inch mortars – would be moved into the batteries after dark.

That Saturday Prevost called Robinson to his headquarters to inform him that he intended to attack in the morning and that Robinson would command that attack. Robinson was to cross at a ford over the Saranac upstream from the town and would have, in addition to his own reduced 1st Brigade, Power's 3rd Brigade, two squadrons of the 19th Light Dragoons and an artillery detachment with two 6-pdr. guns. This was a powerful force, numbering about 4,300 men, just over half of Prevost's strength, and Robinson was to have it "in readiness at a moment's notice" to march when ordered in the morning.[77] Robinson requested that Prevost issue a movement order early enough for him to have his troops "at the Fords by day break" because he was "master of the ground, and would be answerable for the success of the crossing."[78] Prevost promised to do so.

Later in the day, Robinson had a pleasant surprise when his brother, William, the commissary-general of the British army in North America, arrived in Plattsburgh. William had come forward because he wished to see for himself how the division's logistical system was working, some twenty-five miles from the border and thirty-five miles from the nearest supply depot. He became concerned when he saw that much of the division's transport – most of it being a mixed collection of two-wheeled farm carts impressed in Lower Canada – had broken down during the march southward. His subordinates, however, had managed to stockpile five days' worth of provisions at Plattsburgh and he found "the troops were amply provided for." Each day his staff were, by regulation, issuing 12,000 lb. of flour or biscuit, 8,000 lb. of salt or fresh beef or 5,000 lb. of salt pork, 7,000 lb. of cheese as well as smaller amounts of salt, oatmeal and vinegar to the two-legged members of the division. The four-legged members received 8,000 lb. of oats or 14,000 lb. of bran, 18,000 lb. of hay and 3,000 lb. of straw – unless, of course, they gathered their own rations in a nearby field.[79]

His official duties completed, Commissary Robinson engaged in a little sight-seeing, inspecting the American defences from a distance. He decided they were "rather too strong" and that many "a valuable Life must be lost before we conquer" but he had no doubt that the outcome would be a victory for the Crown as the British Left Division had "good officers and good Troops."[80]

The battle of Plattsburgh Bay, 11 September 1814. This painting shows the last stages of the action. HMS *Confiance*, at right, having failed to alter her position, has ended up bow-on to the American line, which can rake the British flagship's complete length. (Painting by Peter Rindlisbacher, courtesy of the artist)

CHAPTER TEN

"A signal victory on Lake Champlain"

THE BATTLES OF PLATTSBURGH, 11 SEPTEMBER 1814

Now the battle's growing hot, my boys, I don't know how 'twill turn,
Macdonough's guns, on swivels hung, continually do burn;
Shall we fight like men of courage, and do the best we can,
When we know they'll flog us, ten to one? I think we'd better run.
    We've got too far from Canada; run, boys, run!

O Prevost sighed aloud and to his officers did say,
The Yankee troops are hove in sight and hell will be to pay;
I'd rather fight a thousand troops, good as ever crossed the seas,
Than fifty of these Yankee boys behind the stumps and trees.
    We've got too far from Canada; run, boys, run!

Behind the hedges and the ditches, the hills and every stump,
You can see the sons of bitches, and the cursed Yankees jump,
The troops of France and England can't stand before them well,
For I believe they'd lick the devil and drive him back to hell.
    We've got too far from Canada; run, boys, run![1]

In the early hours of Sunday, 11 September, the wind shifted and started "blowing a smart breeze up" Lake Champlain.[2] This was exactly what Downie needed to bring his squadron to Plattsburgh and, just before daylight, he apparently sent a message to Prevost that he was going to move, and then ordered his squadron to weigh anchor and steer south.[3]

As it sailed for Plattsburgh Bay, the British squadron "cleared for action." On HMS *Confiance* this process was supervised by James Robertson, the first lieutenant. Under his stern eye, work parties took down the wood and canvas partitions that formed the rows of officers' cabins at the stern of the gun deck and cleared that deck of encumbrances such as furniture and chests, which were placed either in the orlop, or lowest deck, or the hold below it. Other work details brought up extra shot for the guns and piled the folded hammocks of the ship's company in nettings arranged on the bulwarks of the upper deck to pro-

Plattsburgh Bay, from the town. Author's photograph showing Plattsburgh Bay, where the two squadrons engaged. In the distance is Cumberland Head.

vide protection from musketry and splinters. Men wet the gun deck to prevent sparks that might ignite loose powder and placed tubs of water in convenient places to be used as refreshment, swabbing the guns or extinguishing fires.

Each captain of a crew responsible for loading and firing one of the 24-pdr. guns or the two 24-pdr. carronades that were to be manned on the *Confiance*, checked to see that all its implements and accessories – rammer, sponge, worm, wads, shot, and handspikes – were ready for use.* The captain also took care to check his gun's breeching cable, the thick rope that secured the weapon and prevented it from recoiling too far, and the gun-tackles, used to pull the weapon back to its firing position. He then placed the special bucket containing a slow match, which could be used to fire the gun if the lock failed – and since the *Confiance*'s guns had carronade locks mounted, which might not work well in action – all the captains had this secondary means of firing ready to hand.

Although they were generally acknowledged to be the ship's experts in the use of great and small arms, Gunner Robert Elwain and his mates had a special duty in combat. As soon as the order was given to "clear for action," they repaired to the magazine, located below the water line so that, if necessary, it could easily be flooded. Using the dim light shining through a small window from a lantern hanging outside, they prepared to load and handle the cartridges. In action, these flannel bags filled with powder would be passed through holes in the thick curtain that covered the door of the magazine to the powder monkeys, the ships' boys who would take them to the gun crews. When the

---

* The frigate's four 32-pdr. carronades and the remaining four 24-pdr. carronades were not manned during the battle because of a shortage of manpower. See Statement of the British Squadron in Action with the American Squadron on Lake Champlain, 11 September 1814, in William Wood, *Select British Documents of the Canadian War of 1812*, (4 volumes, Toronto, 1920-1928), volume 3, 476.

order was given to "beat to quarters" and the ship's company went to action stations, these curtains would be soaked in water to lessen the danger of sparks. Following regulations, Elwain prepared cartridges filled with 2 lb. of "White L.G." or large grain powder for scaling the 24-pdrs. That done, he and his mates then filled 24-pdr. cartridges with a standard charge of 8 lb. or a reduced charge of 6 lb. of "Red L.G." powder. A standard charge would propel a 24-pdr. iron shot with a diameter of 5.8 inches a distance of nearly a mile with enough velocity to send it crashing through three feet of oak or six feet of a lesser wood.[4]

Boatswain John Davidson, meanwhile, took pains to ensure that every thing "necessary for repairing the rigging is in its proper place; that the men stationed to that service may know where to find immediately whatever may be wanted."[5] Davidson and his mates checked all the frigate's rigging, made sure all blocks were greased and running free, secured the yards with chains so that they would not fall to the deck if hit, lowered the larger ship's boats to be towed astern and placed axes at selected points around the main deck to be used to cut away fallen or damaged rigging.

Carpenter Henry Cox and his mates constituted another specialized unit. They prepared shot plugs, conical pieces of wood of various diameters covered with oakum and tallow that could be hammered into small shot holes. For larger holes, they prepared hides or sheets of lead that could be nailed over them. Cox also rigged tackles so that the ship could be steered if the tiller or wheel were shot away. He was particularly concerned about the breeching bolts of the main armament, the iron loops that secured the breeching rope to the bulwarks and took the strain when the gun was fired. Cox did not feel they were properly secured.[6]

Captain Alexander Anderson mustered his detachment of shipboard marines, sixty-seven all ranks, and posted them along the bulwarks of the frigate. If it came to close action, their musketry would be added to that of the main guns and they would serve either to repel boarders or lead a boarding assault. Anderson's men were probably the most stable element among the flagship's company and most were from one of the two elite battalions of Royal Marines that had been sent to North America in 1813 and recently broken up to serve in shipboard detachments on the Atlantic and Great Lakes. There were a number of young boys under Anderson's command as, given the scarcity of men, in 1804 permission had been granted for the Royal Marines to enlist "stout Boys of a promising appearance, between the ages of thirteen and sixteen Years of age, from five feet to five feet two inches high."[7] The boy marines were paid a lesser rate until they reached seventeen, when they received full pay.

As Anderson's marines clumped along the deck in their heavy boots, Sur-

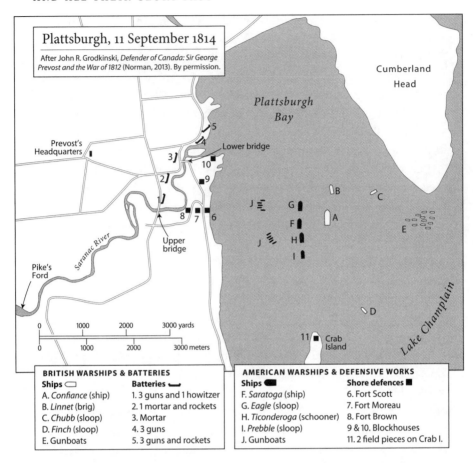

Plattsburgh, 11 September 1814

After John R. Grodkinski, *Defender of Canada: Sir George Prevost and the War of 1812* (Norman, 2013). By permission.

BRITISH WARSHIPS & BATTERIES	
Ships 🖝	Batteries 🖝
A. *Confiance* (ship)	1. 3 guns and 1 howitzer
B. *Linnet* (brig)	2. 1 mortar and rockets
C. *Chubb* (sloop)	3. Mortar
D. *Finch* (sloop)	4. 3 guns
E. Gunboats	5. 3 guns and rockets

AMERICAN WARSHIPS & DEFENSIVE WORKS	
Ships 🖝	Shore defences ■
F. *Saratoga* (ship)	6. Fort Scott
G. *Eagle* (sloop)	7. Fort Moreau
H. *Ticonderoga* (schooner)	8. Fort Brown
I. *Prebble* (sloop)	9 & 10. Blockhouses
J. Gunboats	11. 2 field pieces on Crab I.

geon William Martin and his mate, Charles Todd, descended to the cockpit, the middle section of the orlop deck "where a platform shall be prepared for the reception of the wounded men."[8] In action, the wounded would be laid on this platform until Martin or Todd could attend to them as, to avoid favouritism, there was a firm rule that men were treated in the order that they were brought into the cockpit by the loblolly boys, the ship's medical orderlies. This platform was usually one or more tables or planks laid across coiled cables, and positioned nearby would be other tables on which the two surgeons would operate. Here Martin and Todd laid out the tools of their trade: amputating knives, amputating saw with spare blade, metacarpal saw with spare blade, artery forceps, curved needles, tenaculums, tourniquets, bone nippers, trocars, catheters, scalpels, lancets, scissors, scarificators, probes, scoops, probangs, lancets, splints, syringes and bandages.[9] It was a lengthy list and both surgeons kept a careful eye on their implements as they were not provided by the Crown but paid for out of their own pockets. Surgeon Martin had the additional duty to instruct all those stationed with him, and all others whom the Captain shall appoint, in the use of the tourniquet, many of which when clearing for action shall be distributed to the different quarters, two or three at least being sent into each top to be applied whenever it may be useful, that the Wounded men may suffer as little as possible from loss of blood, while they are waiting until he shall be able to attend to the and to dress their wounds.[10]

Just in case the tourniquets were not effective, another work detail spread sand around the decks so that men would not slip in the puddles of blood that would shortly besmirch them.

Even as this activity was taking place, a party of twenty-five dockyard workmen were frantically trying to complete the *Confiance* because the frigate still lacked many necessary pieces of equipment. Carpenter Cox faced the job of putting the second of her two pumps in order, a task he would not complete until his ship was in action. In Cox's expert opinion, the *Confiance* "was in an unfinished State altogether."[11]

If he had doubts about the readiness of his flagship for action, Captain George Downie, RN, did not reveal them. As the squadron neared the tip of Cumberland Head, he ordered her guns to be "scaled," firing blank charges through the main armament to clean or "scale" their bores of any rust. The gun crews then reloaded with double shot.

Downie and Master Robert Brydon of the *Confiance* now went ahead of the squadron around the tip of Cumberland Head in the frigate's gig to make a reconnaissance. Downie had accurate intelligence about his opponent and knew that the opposing squadrons were almost evenly matched in terms of vessels and number of guns. Downie had a frigate, a brig, two sloops and eleven gunboats armed with 90 guns while Macdonough's command comprised a ship, a

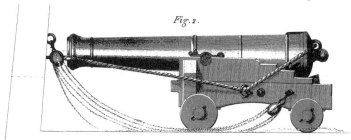

Fig. 2.

24-pdr. naval gun. This weapon fired a round shot, 5.8 inches in diameter and 24 lb. in weight up to a distance of one mile with enough velocity to penetrate nearly 3 feet of oak. Downie possessed 27 of these weapons against Macdonough, who only had eight, giving the British naval commander a significant advantage. (From William Congreve, *A Treatise on the Mounting of Naval Ordnance*)

brig, a sloop, a schooner and ten gunboats armed with 86 guns. But Downie did possess one significant advantage – the *Confiance* mounted 27 long-range 24-pdr. guns, while Macdonough possessed only eight similar weapons, all on the *Saratoga*, his flagship. If he chose, Downie could stay at a distance and pound the American squadron to pieces.

The British naval commander examined the American squadron through a telescope. The four larger vessels were anchored in a line a little over 300 yards long, running approximately southwest to northeast. The brig USS *Eagle*, 20 guns, was at the head, followed by the ship (sometimes called a corvette) USS *Saratoga*, 26. Next came the schooner USS *Ticonderoga*, 17, and the sloop USS *Commodore Prebble*, 7 guns. Macdonough's ten gunboats were placed in elements of two or three at the ends of the line or between the larger vessels and their task would be to prevent the British gunboats from getting close enough to rake them. Each of the large vessels had "springs,"* cables fastened to their anchors that would permit them to be shifted in position to bring their broadsides to bear in different directions. In effect, the *Eagle*, *Saratoga*, *Ticonderoga* and *Prebble* were floating batteries and, since it was intended that they not move during the forthcoming action, most of their ships' companies were available to man their guns.[12]

His reconnaissance completed, Downie returned to the *Confiance* and called a conference of his captains and commanders on board the flagship. In the words of First Lieutenant James Robertson, he "gave them particular directions to what object they were to direct the Fire of their respective Vessels" so as to prevent "as much as possible the necessity of making Signals."[13] For some reason never disclosed, Downie decided not to engage at long range but to take his squadron into the bay and fight a close-range action. Perhaps he felt his raw, untrained ship's company would not be equal to the gunnery required by a long-range battle or he may have just been confident that he could beat the Jonathans – shortly after taking over his new command, Downie had been heard to boast at the mess table that, "with the Confiance alone," he "could lick the whole American squadron."[14] Whatever his reasons, the British naval commander's decision to fight a close battle negated his advantage in range. Downie issued his captains fairly specific instructions as to which American vessel they were to engage. His eleven gunboats, aided by the sloop HMS *Finch*, 11 guns, were to attack the *Ticonderoga* and the *Prebble* at the rear of the Ameri-

---

* A spring is "a cable run out through one of the sternmost ports and carried to a second cable attached to an anchor that has been dropped ahead of the vessel." See Robert Malcomson, *Lords of the Lake: The Naval War on Lake Ontario, 1812-1814* (Toronto, 1998), 351. By hauling in the first cable using the capstan, a ship could be turned to alter its heading without leaving its station.

can line while the brig HMS *Linnet*, 16, and the sloop HMS *Chubb*, 11, were to attack the *Eagle* at the head of the line. Downie with the *Confiance* would sail between the *Eagle* and the *Saratoga* and rake the American flagship. It was an aggressive plan that required tight timing, swift manoeuvring and the right wind but it was very much in keeping with the Royal Navy's tradition of captains laying their ships alongside the enemy.[15]

Downie next dismissed his commanders and mustered his ship's company aft to receive the traditional exhortation before battle. Indicating the masts of Macdonough's squadron, which were visible behind Cumberland Head, he told them that these were "the Enemy's Ships" that the squadron would attack and added that the "our Army" was "to storm the Enemy's works at the moment we engaged, and mind don't let us be behind."[16] The sailors and marines cheered and the squadron then "beat to quarters," the marine drummers commencing the staccato rolls that sent everyone to their action stations.

As most preparations had been made, all that was left was to put a fresh flint in the locks of the guns and light the slow matches in their tubs. On the *Confiance* Lieutenant Robertson, feeling that "a repetition of the same sort of harangue" that Downie had just given "might inspirit so disorganized a Crew that was going into Action under circumstances apparently so disadvantageous" went round the frigate and pointed out to the men that they would have the co-operation of the army.[17] If Royal Navy tradition was upheld – and there is no reason to think that it was not – the marine drummers and fifers marched up and down the main deck of the *Confiance* playing "Hearts of Oak" or "Britons, Strike Home" as, one by one, the British ships approached Cumberland Head and prepared to tack to enter Plattsburgh Bay.

For his part, Master Commandant Thomas Macdonough, USN, preferred a milder and more spiritual form of encouragement. He offered his officers the prayer before battle at sea from the prayer book of the Episcopalian Church, almost unchanged from the 1662 Church of England *Book of Common Prayer* from which the Episcopalian Church derived most of its services. It appealed to the Almighty to take their cause "into thine own hand, and judge between us and our enemies."[18] Macdonough, however, was not beyond a little patriotic encouragement and shortly hoisted a signal from his flagship to inform his officers and sailors that "Impressed seamen call on every man to do his duty."[19]

Shortly after 8 A.M., by Macdonough's watch, anxious lookouts on both land and water spotted the British squadron rounding Cumberland Head.* William

---

* There is a great deal of discrepancy in the times given by various witnesses for the scaling of the guns and just when the two squadrons came into action – in some cases as much as two hours. This can be explained by a combination of faulty memory and the difficulty of establishing time

Apess thought it "a fine thing to see" Downie's warships "moving like things of life upon this mimic sea, with their streamers floating in the wind."[20]

Prevost's troops were patiently waiting for them. Major-General Frederick Robinson had his command ready to march by 6 A.M. but became somewhat puzzled as the minutes passed with no direction to move. During the previous night, Major John Sinclair, RA, the divisional artillery commander, had moved his guns into the battery positions and was ready for an order to open fire. He had not had time to deploy the two 12-pdr. guns or the two 8-inch mortars brought up from Isle-aux-Noix and would have to rely on the lighter field pieces that had accompanied the division from Lower Canada. At about 7 A.M. Sinclair received orders to open fire as soon as the first gun was discharged from the British squadron, which by now everyone knew was on its way. At around 8 A.M., however, Robinson was incredulous when he received an order to have his men cook their breakfast. He gave direction to that effect and just before 9 A.M. was ordered to report to Prevost.[21]

On that Sunday in September there was much evidence of confusion in the higher command element of the division. Prevost told Robinson that he "must be ready to move at a moment's warning," which was actually redundant as Robinson had been ready to do so for nearly three hours.[22] After some discussion, it was decided that Robinson would cross the Saranac at a ford about three miles to the west – which the locals called Pike's Ford – and would be guided to that place by the staff of Major-General Beckwith's quartermaster department. Prevost then countermanded the order that the troops cook their breakfast – by now it was probably just ready to eat but then such is life in the service where there is often no justice for enlisted men. Robinson, growing impatient, "took the liberty of requesting" that the commanding general "name an hour for our advancing" and the reply was 10 A.M.[23]

Sinclair's gunners also received a confusing series of orders. Captain James Wood, RA, recalled that at first they were ordered to open fire when the opposing squadrons engaged; this was soon countermanded and a new order issued to hold their fire until Robinson had attacked the three American redoubts south of the Saranac. "This indecision," Wood commented, "at such a moment was particularly distressing."[24] There is an old (but very true) military maxim that "an order followed by a counter order usually results in disorder" and it

---

in a period when there were no fixed time zones. As naval witnesses tend to state that events took place much earlier than land witnesses, it raises the question whether the British and American armies and navies were working on different times. Macdonough, however, kept careful track of the time by his watch and the times in my account generally follow his record.

appears that Prevost and his senior officers lacked what a later generation of soldiers would call "grip" or firm control of the situation. As it happened, Sinclair was actually ordered to open fire when the opposing squadrons came into action at about 9.30 A.M.

Before he returned to his troops, Robinson paused for a moment to watch the beginning of the naval engagement. He became somewhat concerned when he saw the *Confiance* receiving "the heavy fire of the enemy's fleet, almost all the guns of which bore upon her."[25]

Robinson's assessment of the opening moments of the naval battle was accurate. As the British squadron rounded Cumberland Head in line abreast and tacked to enter the bay, the wind shifted from north-northeast to west-northwest. Downie's ships were now sailing close hauled, with the minimum of breeze in their sails, and they gradually began to lose headway and slow down. The *Confiance*, in the lead, was preparing to carry out her assigned task of hitting the *Eagle* before reaching her anchoring position. As she moved, Robertson recalled, "the whole of the Enemy's line commenced firing on her when within Gun Shot" and the frigate sustained considerable damage.[26] Downie was unable to take up his planned station and was forced to drop anchor a half mile from Macdonough's line. The *Linnet*, coming behind, did reach her assigned position, anchored and engaged the *Eagle*.[27]

The *Chubb*, next in line, came under heavy fire which damaged her rigging and slightly wounded her commander, Lieutenant James McGhie, RN, who left the deck and went below. Matters then became somewhat chaotic on board and the sloop never properly anchored but, apparently out of control, began to drift between the two opposing lines. On the *Linnet* a rather surprised Lieutenant John Drew remembered that the *Chubb* passed "between the Linnet and the Confiance, then between the Confiance and Saratoga apparently in a very disabled State with her Colours struck, this was about a Quarter of an hour after the action commenced, she was drifting not steering."[28] The *Chubb* was in a very bad way. Midshipman John Bodell, who assumed command after McGhie left the deck, later reported that the vessel had all her sails shot away, with the foresail trailing over the side. She had also suffered heavy casualties and many of her company were soldiers of the 39th Foot, who, unnerved by the ferocity of their first naval action, went below to seek shelter. Bodell decided that there was no choice but to lower the sloop's colours and surrender, and this was done. The vessel, however, continued to drift out of control until she eventually ran aground on the mainland.[29]

The *Confiance* and *Linnet* now engaged the *Eagle* and *Saratoga*. The British

The effect of naval gunfire. These photographs, taken from a live fire exercise carried out on a section of reconstructed deck and bulwark, show the effect of roundshot. Not only did the projectile penetrate the side of the target, it created a murderous spray of wooden splinters flung from the interior by the velocity of its impact. (Courtesy, Erie Maritime Museum, Pennsylvania Historical and Museum Commission)

flagship's first broadside – double-shotted and loaded without haste before she came into action – is said to have killed or wounded forty men on the *Saratoga*, about a fifth of the flagship's crew. Among them was her first lieutenant, Peter Gamble, who died instantly when a roundshot hit the carriage of a gun he was aiming and drove part of its quoin into his chest. Another shot smashed a poultry cage on the upper deck, releasing a game cock, a favourite of the crew, who flew up into the rigging and perched on a shroud, where he "clapped his wings and crowed lustily."[30] Macdonough's men regarded this as a good omen and took heart. Given her position, the *Confiance* could only bring two-thirds of her port broadside to bear while the *Saratoga* could use her entire starboard battery against the *Confiance*, and the American flagship returned the British flagship's fire with interest. Fifteen minutes after the action commenced, Downie was mortally wounded when a roundshot dislodged a gun that he was standing near and it struck him. He was carried below but died within minutes. Lieutenant James Robertson now assumed command. His first duty was to inform Commander Daniel Pring of the *Linnet* that Pring was now in command of the squadron, but he could not find the signal book, which had been with Downie, and could not send a message by boat as all the frigate's boats had been damaged or sunk.[31]

At the same time, a separate battle was taking place at the southern end of the American line. Downie had ordered the sloop HMS *Finch*, 11 guns, and all his gunboats to attack and if possible board the schooner USS *Ticonderoga*, 17, and the sloop USS *Commodore Prebble*, 7 guns. Owing to a sailing error on the part of her commander, Lieutenant William Hicks, RN, the *Finch* failed to get to her assigned station. Midshipman Thomas Eyre of the *Finch* described the sloop's part in the action:

> At nine she went round Cumberland Head, about 9 30 she was abreast of the Prebble, I am not positive to the time, about half a Mile distance she brought her Broadside to bear and engaged her [the *Prebble*]. In about forty, fifty or sixty minutes the Prebble ceased firing and stood with her Head in Shore, whether her Colours were up or down, I cannot say, we were then I suppose a Mile and a Quarter from her and drifted to Leeward and in about an hour we took the Ground [i.e., ran aground] on Crab Island ..., we used every ex-ertion to get her off threw four Caronnades overboard, she had then settled having two or three feet of water above the lower Deck.[32]

Before she ran aground, the *Finch* came under fire from the battery at the north end of Crab Island manned by invalids from the military hospital on the island. The invalids opened up and the British sloop replied with grape and canister. To Hicks, *Finch's* fire appeared very accurate and he later reported that his men "had the pleasure of killing or wounding every man at the guns on shore and silence them."[33]

The *Finch* was out of the battle but, with the assistance of the British gun-boats, she had hit the *Prebble* hard. The sloop's captain, Lieutenant Charles Budd, USN, recorded that his ship received two "eighteen pound shot through her hull about a foot" from the sloop's wales* and an "eighteen pound shot lodged in her stern, having carried away the head knees"† and "one 24 pd shot through her quarter bulwarks" as well as "the dents of two 18 pd shot."[34] The *Prebble* drifted helplessly out of the fight and also went aground on the mainland.

With the *Finch* and *Prebble* out of the battle, the British gunboats faced only the *Ticonderoga* and her attendant gunboats, which the Americans termed "gallies." Although Macdonough praised his small craft for obeying orders "with alacrity," they seem to have played little part in the battle.[35] On the other side, the British gunboats were nimble little craft, between 40 and 60 feet long and armed with one or two long guns or carronades. Unfortunately, their crews were a polyglot mixture of sailors, marines, soldiers and Canadian militia and

---

* Wales are defined as a "band of heavy planking between the waterline and the gundeck that strengthened and stiffened the vessel fore and aft," see Robert Malcomson, *Lords of the Lake: The Naval War on Lake Ontario, 1812-1814* (Toronto, 1998), 352.

† "Knees" are wooden right-angles which provide strengthening and support at the points of intersection of a ship's timbers.

they were badly commanded. Of the eleven gunboats in the British squadron, seven never went into action and their commander, Lieutenant John Raynham, RN, later deserted rather than face a court martial for his conduct. The remaining four craft did try to attack and board the *Ticonderoga* but in this they were unsuccessful as the heavy fire from the American ship was too much for their crews. In the gunboat *Murray*, twenty-three of the crew were Canadians, who, at the first broadside, lay down in the bottom of the vessel and refused to row or fire the guns. Lieutenant Christopher Bell, RN, who commanded the *Murray*, was furious with their conduct but continued to fight although he was hit by a grape shot in the foot and then a second shot, which took his right leg "compleatly off." Even then, Bell tried to continue in action but found it impossible.[36]

Meanwhile, the gunnery duel between the *Eagle* and *Saratoga*, and the *Confiance* and *Linnet*, continued without pause. It was murderous work. On all four ships the powder monkeys grabbed cartridges that were thrust at them by the gunner or his mates through holes in the wet curtains covering the magazine doors, put them securely in their leather cylindrical carrying cases and ran with them to the upper decks, where they gave them to the loaders at their assigned gun crew. The guns being run back, the loader inserted the cartridge in the muzzle and a man shoved it down the with a rammer, giving it a few sharp thrusts to seat it properly. It was then followed by a projectile – almost certainly roundshot at the ranges between the ships – and then a wad which was also rammed home to pack tightly the entire combination. The gun crew then grabbed the tackle cable attached to blocks and, at the command "Run out!", hauled the gun forward until it was firm against its port. This was no easy task as a 24-pdr. gun on its carriage weighed nearly three tons and, by now, many gun crews were shorthanded because of casualties and, as well, the decks were slippery with blood. The weapon being run up, the gun captain thrust a brass wire into the vent – a small aperture on top of the breech – several times so it made a hole in the cartridge seated in the bore. He then inserted a quill, a thin hollow tube filled with powder, down the vent so that it was in contact with the cartridge. The gun was now loaded, and if the gun captain had time, he aimed the weapon, elevating or depressing it by means of the wooden quoin or wedge under the breech, or traversing it by means of handspikes and training tackle. At the command "Fire!," the captain pulled the lanyard of the gun lock which sparked the tube, which ignited the cartridge – or he used a slow match to the same purpose. The gun fired with a large boom that put pressure on the ear drums and created a thick cloud of dirty white powder smoke that stung the eyes and obscured vision, and recoiled about six feet until brought up short by its breeching cable. The whole procedure was then repeated.[37]

All this time, of course, the gun crews were under fire from their opponents. Roundshot came battering through the sides of their ships, destroying men and equipment or creating a hail of deadly wooden splinters that killed or inflicted hideous wounds. To keep the decks clear, the dead were thrown overboard without ceremony while the wounded were carried by the loblolly boys down to the cockpit. During a close quarters naval engagement, this dimly-lit compartment was a dreadful place in which the roar and rumble of the guns was pierced by the moans, screams and pleas of the wounded awaiting treatment or undergoing it – and in the few quiet moments, the rhythmic whine of the bone saws. Surgeons Mitchell on the *Linnet* and Martin and Todd on the *Confiance* laboured without pause as did their American counterparts, bandaging, stitching, plastering and, above all, amputating because amputation was their swiftest and most effective procedure. On the British flagship, Martin and Todd were assisted by the purser's wife, but unfortunately she was hit by a large splinter and died shortly thereafter.[38]

Samuel Leech, a British sailor who served as a powder monkey on the frigate HMS *Macedonian*, during her losing battle with the American frigate USS *United States*, has left a glimpse of the particular hell that the men of both squadrons endured on Plattsburgh Bay that Sunday in September:

The roaring of cannon could now be heard from all parts of our trembling ship, and mingling as it did with that of our foes, it made a most hideous noise. By-and-by I heard the shot strike the sides of our ship; the whole scene grew indescribably confused and horrible; it was like some awfully tremendous thunderstorm whose deafening roar is attended by incessant streaks of lightning, carrying death in every flash, and strewing the ground with the victims of the wrath; only, in our case, the scene was rendered more horrible than that by the presence of torrents of blood which dyed our decks. ......

I was busily supplying my gun with powder when I saw blood suddenly fly from the arm of a man stationed at our gun. I saw nothing strike him, the effect alone was visible; in an instant the Third lieutenant tied his handkerchief round the wounded arm, and sent the groaning wretch below to the surgeon.

The cries of the wounded now rang through all parts of the ship. These were carried to the cockpit as fast as they fell, while those more fortunate men who were killed outright were immediately thrown overboard. ......

A man named Aldrich had one of his hands cut off by a shot, and almost at the same moment received another shot, which tore open his bowels in a terrible manner. As he fell two or three men caught him in their arms and, as he could not live, threw him overboard. ......

One of the officers in my division also fell in my sight. He was a noble-hearted fellow named Nan Kivell. A grape or canister shot struck him near the heart; exclaiming, "Oh! my God!" he fell and was carried below where he shortly died. ......

Our men fought like tigers. Some of them pulled off their jackets others their jackets and vests; while some, still more determined, had taken off their shirts, and, with nothing but a handkerchief tied around the waist-bands of their trousers, fought like heroes. ......

Grape and canister shot were pouring through our port-hole like leaden rain carrying death in their trail. The large shot came against the ship's side like iron hail, shaking her to the very keel, or passing through her timbers and scattering terrific splinters, which did more appalling work than even their own death-giving blows. ......

What then with splinters, cannon balls, grape and canister poured incessantly upon us, the reader may be assured that the work of death went on in a manner which must have been satisfying even to the King of Terror himself.[39]

The opposing armies were interested spectators of the battle on the bay and gunner William Apess recalled "the cloud of smoke, that mantled the heavens, shutting out the light of day, while the continual roar of artillery added to the sublime horrors of the scene."[40] Civilian spectators also watched the engagement and indeed some Canadians actually came up the lake in boats to witness what they confidently expected would be a British victory. Judge Julius Hubbell of Chazy, who observed the battle from Cumberland Head, remembered that the firing "was terrific, fairly shaking the ground, and so rapid that it seemed to be one continuous roar, intermingled with spiteful flashing from the mouths of the guns, and dense clouds of smoke hung over the two fleets."[41] *

After about ninety minutes of pounding, Lieutenant Robert Henley, commanding the USS *Eagle*, found that most of his starboard broadside guns were out of action and that he could not "bring a gun to bear" on either the *Confiance* or the *Linnet*.[42] Henley decided to change his station but, finding that his spring cable had been shot away, ordered his anchor cable cut and cast off. With minimum sail, he was able to come about and, using another anchor, take up a position behind and between the *Saratoga* and *Ticonderoga*. He could now bring his port broadside to bear on both British ships. Macdonough was not happy about this development because he felt that Henley's duty "was to remain in the

---

* There is a local legend in Clinton County that when a British gun crew spotted a crowd watching the engagement from the comfortable environs of a tavern on Cumberland Head, they fired a round at them. It is doubtful, however, that a British gun crew had the time, the ammunition or the inclination to waste a round. See Everest, *Recollections of Clinton County*, 49.

station" assigned to his vessel, "as long as it was possible to maintain it."[43] The result, however, was positive for the American squadron because now, recalled Robertson of the *Confiance*, the *Eagle* "kept up a destructive fire on the Confiance, without being exposed to a shot from that ship or the Linnet."[44]

By this time, the fire of both flagships had begun to slacken. Nearly every gun on the starboard side of the *Saratoga* had been put out of action, while the *Confiance* only had four guns still firing on her port broadside. Macdonough decided to wind his ship and, unlike the *Eagle*, he was able to accomplish this manoeuvre. Under the direction of Sailing Master Philip Brum, the *Saratoga* was rotated 180 degrees to bring her undamaged port side guns to bear on the *Confiance* and *Linnet*.[45]

On the *Confiance* Robertson tried to follow suit. The frigate had been rigged with a spring before it went into action but it had disappeared during the battle. Robertson ordered his ship's company to fix a new spring but, as he later remarked, this "could not be expected to be easily executed, as the surviving Crew now evinced an evident disposition to discontinue the Action."[46] With the help of the surviving officers, Robertson got a spring rigged and actually convinced the crew to pull on it and the frigate began slowly to turn. Unfortunately, a shot from the *Saratoga* went right down the length of the deck, killing or wounding "several of the Men on the Spring, and it was impossible to rally them afterwards."[47] The result was that the *Confiance* was placed in a terrible position with her bow pointing towards the *Saratoga*, which would be able to rake her entire length with a broadside, while she would be almost unable to reply. Robertson summed up the dire condition of his vessel:

> It was now impossible to get a single gun of the Confiance to bear with effect on the Enemy. My much lamented Captain and Relative and many of the best of our Men had fallen, the water was above the Gun Room Deck, the unfortunate wounded below were in extreme danger of being drowned, the Chubb had struck early in the Action, the Finch was aground & our Gun boats were at a distance, the Ship was in a Sinking and Shattered state, the Carnage on board was dreadful and the Co-operation [from the army] which we had been led to expect was not afforded.[48]

Robertson called his surviving officers together and "with their approbation with such distressing prospects before me I gave the painful orders to strike the Colours." Only sixteen days from her launch and, after a short and unhappy career in the Royal Navy, the *Confiance* had become the property of the republic.

Macdonough now directed the fire of his three large vessels against the *Linnet*. Pring reported that "the shattered and disable[d] state" of the brig's rigging and sails "precluded the most distant hope of being able to effect an Escape" by cutting the anchor cable because the result would have been her "drifting alongside the Enemy's Vessels."[49] Pring, however, decided to keep fighting in the hope that the gunboats would come to his rescue. He did manage to get a boat across to the *Confiance* and for the first time learned that Downie had been killed.

When the gunboats did not come to his assistance, Pring knew the end was at hand, because the *Linnet* was in no condition to continue fighting:

> The Water was now nearly a foot above the lower deck and the Wounded were obliged to be put on the Chests and Cables to keep them out of it which was over the Platform placed for receiving them. In this situation we fought nearly a quarter of an hour, when at length I gave up all expectations of retrieving my disasters and came to the resolution of striking my Colours.[50]

Macdonough, who timed the engagement carefully, reported that it had lasted over two hours without interruption, ending around 11.30 A.M. The American naval commander was unable to pursue and attack the British gunboats, which promptly left the bay as "there was not a mast in either squadron that could stand to make sail on; the lower rigging being nearly all shot away, hung down as though it had been placed over the mastheads."[51] He later counted fifty-five shot holes in the *Saratoga*'s hull and the flagship also had serious damage to her rigging. It appears that during the engagement the British gun crews, either from stress or lack of training, had not properly adjusted the elevating quoin on their guns after firing. These devices would gradually start to slip, raising the barrels, with the result that the guns would fire high. There was no problem with the fire of the American gun crews: the *Confiance* had between 250 and 300 roundshot in her hull and "grapeshot without number" while the *Linnet* had 30-50 shot in her hull, the *Chubb* 34 and the *Finch* five, three of which were under water.[52] Still, such was the condition of his own ships that Macdonough was unable to send prize crews to take possession of the British vessels for several hours after the engagement ended. In the meantime, the officers and men of both navies worked hard to keep their badly damaged vessels afloat.

Casualties on both sides had been heavy. Macdonough reported the loss of 52 officers and sailors killed and 58 wounded for a total of 106. The British casualties were 54 dead and 116 wounded, a total of 170, of whom no less than 123 were suffered on the *Confiance*, nearly half her company. The wounded from both squadrons were taken to the hospital on Crab Island for treatment.[53]

When the sun set that Sunday, Master Commandant Thomas Macdonough must have been exhausted. Nonetheless, he took the time to pen a brief note to Secretary of the Navy William Jones to inform him that "The Almighty has been pleased to Grant us a signal victory on Lake Champlain in the capture of one Frigate, one Brig and two sloops of war of the enemy."[54]

It is fairly probable that Lieutenant-General Sir George Prevost did not offer similar thanks to the Almighty that Sunday. Prevost and his staff had watched the naval engagement in the bay and had "the extreme mortification to hear the Shout of Victory from the Enemy's Works in consequence of the British Flag being lowered on board the *Confiance* and *Linnet*, and to see our Gunboats seeking their safety in flight."[55] Thus deprived of naval co-operation, and being a general who was ever reluctant to incur heavy casualties, Prevost decided to end the operation because, as he explained to Bathurst, "the possession of the Enemy's Works offered no advantage to compensate for the loss we must have sustained in acquiring Possession of them." He therefore sent an order to Robinson to withdraw from the south side of Saranac.

After his visit to Prevost, Robinson for his part had returned to his command and ordered his two brigades to march for Pike's Ford, guided by Beckwith's quartermaster officers. At the end of the column were wagons loaded with ladders collected from the local farm houses. Robinson's column was marching through a wooded area, which was in the process of being logged and was cut across by trails used to haul out cut trees but which led nowhere. After half an hour, a halt was called when the quartermaster officers began to argue among themselves whether or not they were on the right road. Robinson was convinced that it was the wrong route and the matter was only resolved when Major Nathaniel Thorn, his own brigade quartermaster – who had previously reconnoitred the route – offered to guide the column. The troops retraced their steps and, eventually, arrived at the ford but, as Robinson noted, "a full hour of precious time had been irretrievably lost."[56] As they neared their objective, the column divined a lessening of the nearly incessant gun fire from the bay and then "cheers from the Plattsburgh side."[57] Robinson believed this celebratory exhortation was due to the success of either Downie or Brisbane – or both – but, just to be sure, dispatched Major William Cochrane, one of his staff officers, to find out what was going on.

At Pike's Ford Robinson faced a tricky situation. At this point both sides of the Saranac were thickly wooded with banks nearly 60–70 feet high. The ford itself was about 2 to 3 feet deep and 60 feet wide but the current was manageable. The opposite side was held by about 300–400 New York militia and

Pike's Ford. There is now a bridge over Pike's Ford at Plattsburgh but the ford itself is still clearly visible. (Author's photograph)

some Vermont volunteers. Crossing it under fire would be a difficult task but Robinson proved equal to the challenge. Deploying the light companies of the 3/27th and 88th Foot in the woods on the north bank to provide covering fire, he sent his remaining six light companies splashing across the water. In Robinson's words, they advanced "under a galling fire from about 400 of the Enemy posted behind Trees and Bushes, and rushed through the Ford with an impetuosity that nothing could check."[58] Under the command of Lieutenant-Colonel Patrick Lindesay of the 39th Foot, all eight light companies of the 1st and 3rd Brigades pursued the retreating militia. They were followed by the 3/27th, an Irish unit, which "forded the river like so many fox hounds, driving the Doodles in all directions."[59] The 76th Foot came next while

> The Light Companies pursued the Enemy until they had reached the ground they [the British] were ordered to occupy. The 76th Regt followed and formed in Column about half a mile on the opposite side of the Ford. The two six pounders were let down the Bank [by means of ropes lowered] by large detachments, the 58th Regt [then] crossed and formed in Column in rear of the 76th.[60]

The scrap at the ford had not taken more than ten minutes and it was now about 12.30 P.M. The American militia had not put up a stiffer fight because they were under orders to fall back toward the bridge over the Salmon River, about three miles southwest of the three redoubts. Vermont volunteer Herman Green recalled that they defended the ford "until ordered to retreat, when our men fell back into the woods and were reinforced, and in turn drove the enemy back to the river."[61] Actually, it was not that simple; as they pulled back from the ford, the militia and volunteers engaged in a running battle with the British light infantry companies who formed the advance element of Robinson's force. The militia were shortly reinforced by Lieutenant William Sumter of the Regiment of Light Artillery with a field piece. Despite being relatively untrained, the New York and Vermont men carried out a credible fighting withdrawal. Captain Martin Lynch, commanding the light company of the 3/27th Foot recalled that, when his company crossed the Saranac, it

> moved in the direction of some hutts, where I found the enemy formed who, on our approach, fired, and continued firing and retiring towards a ravine. When close to it I observe them formed on the other side, and a force on my Right moving in the same direction. I sent a sergt to L[ieutenant] Colonel Lindsay to inform him, and then crossed and pushed on some distance, when I heard a Gun fired to my left which appeared very close, finding no support and my own ammunition nearly expended, I deemed it necessary to halt.[62]

Satisfied with the beginning of his attack, Robinson crossed over to direct the assault on the redoubts, followed by the 1/27th Foot. But all his efforts were to little effect as at that moment Cochrane returned from Prevost's headquarters with an order from the commanding general. Robinson read it with amazement:

> I am directed to inform you that the Confiance and the Brig having struck their Colour in consequence of the Frigate having grounded, it will no longer be prudent to pursue in the Service committed to your charge, and it is therefore the Orders of the Commander of the Forces, that you immediately return with the troops under your Command.[63]

Robinson showed the order to Power of the 3rd Brigade, "who was equally astonished with me at the contents & lamented the cause."[64]

Orders were orders, however, and Robinson pulled his troops back to the north bank.[65] Covered by the two 6-pdr. guns, they withdrew without incident except for the light company of the 76th Foot, commanded by Captain John Purchas. Described as an officer of "great zeal and daring," Purchas was determined to capture Sumter's field piece, which he could see some distance in front of his position. Unfortunately he and about half his company were surrounded by New York militia, who killed Purchas and some of his men and forced the remainder to surrender. As the British withdrew in good order, the New York and Vermont militia advanced but stopped at the ford when they came under fire from the two 6-pdr. guns.

During and after the naval battle, the artillery of both sides exchanged fire across the Saranac. Sinclair had ordered his batteries to open up as soon as the two squadrons had engaged but his later report on the operations of the British gunners is very carefully worded as to the results obtained. He believed that they silenced the American artillery positions near the shore of the bay but also stated that his westernmost battery, which was only 700 yards from the redoubts, came under such heavy fire that Sinclair ordered Captain Frederick Gordon, the battery commander, to "reserve his Fire, until he should perceive our Troops advancing to the Assault."[66] Captain J. H. Wood, who was stationed in that battery, provides some details on what was a very hard day for the Royal Artillery:

> Our battery, No. 1, on the extreme right, and consisting of two light 24-pr. Brass Guns and one 8-inch Howitzer, was so situated that we could not see the shipping, owing to the commanding ground the enemy's works occupied being in the line of view.
>
> The Batteries opened about nine-thirty, and the enemy replied with much spirit and precision. In about two hours not a gun was heard from the fleets; We were aware that the fate of the day had been decided and our anxiety to learn who were the victors was extreme. The melancholy truth at length reached us, that the British Flag had been lowered and the whole flotilla, with the exception of the gun boats, were in the enemies' hands.
>
> In No. 1 the enemy dismounted one of our guns and materially damaged the carriage of another, when we were ordered to withdraw them under cover of the merlons.* We had the light brass 24-pr, charge 3 lbs†, opposed to heavy guns of the same calibre, superior in numbers and having a commanding position. Our casualties were trifling, one killed and five wounded. A round shot stupefied me for some minutes, and an inch or two closer would have made me "shorter by the head."[67]

It appears that Brisbane's brigade was preparing to cross the lower bridge when they were called back by Prevost. As Major James Campbell remembered:

---

* Merlons were the solid parts of the top of a crenellated wall, which were pierced by embrasures for firing. Basically, what Wood is saying is that the battery was being shot to pieces.

† The standard charge for a 24-pdr. iron gun was 8 lb. of powder, probably a little less for a brass 24-pdr. What Wood is saying here is that the Royal Artillery were using half, not full charges. The reason for this is possibly that, if fired with full charge, the brass 24-pdrs would overheat. For this reason they were not fired with full charges and their rate of fire was restricted. The Americans were firing iron 24-pdrs. with full charge, giving them better range and hitting power. On charges for land service guns, see R.W. Adye, *The Bombardier and Pocket Gunner* (London, 1813), 98.

Under the protection of our artillery, the bridge over the Saranac, (the planks only of which the Americans in their retreat had been able to destroy or take up,) was repaired in a few minutes by materials we had ready for the purpose; part of the troops, under Sir Thomas Brisbane were moving down to pass by it to the assault ... when the order from Sir George Prevost to halt arrived, in consequence of our fleet having been discomfited upon the Lake.[68]

On his side, Macomb reported that the British attempted to cross both bridges as well as Pike's Ford. Eleazar Williams, who was serving in one of the artillery batteries on the south side of the river, was quite definite that a serious attempt was made at the lower bridge:

Our position was in range with one of the enemy's batteries, and was placed there to answer it, and to oppose them by cannonading should they attempt to ford the river. As it was expected, they made the attempt more than once, and at first, by two heavy columns, and when they arrived at the brink of the river they were saluted with such a storm of shot and grape form our battery, as to compel them to fall back, and make their way into the houses, shops, barns and ditches. Thence they kept up a heavy fire and contended with our riflemen, who were in two mills near the bridge. While the cannonading went on, we either answered the enemy's fire, or poured shot into every body of their troops, that presented a tolerable mark. Never, perhaps, were skirmishes, if such they deserved to be called, conducted with more bravery on both sides.[69]

The British bombardment, "a constant firing of cannon, shells, bombs & rockets continued all day," and Captain Rochester of the Twenty-Ninth remembered that the men in the redoubts were forced to lie down "except a few artillery who manned our cannons."[70] Seeing that he was seriously outgunned and could achieve little or nothing, Sinclair ordered his gunners to cease fire at about 3 P.M. and this is probably the origin of the belief on the part of many American participants that they silenced the British guns by sheer weight of fire. What is certain is that Macomb's gunners did dominate the duel and kept firing until dusk, when they presented their enemy with "a national salute & three cheers to the tune of Hail Columbia & Yankee Doodle played most elegant by our music."[71]

The twin battles of Plattsburgh were over and they had ended in an unparalleled American triumph. In the pungent words of Jonathan Stevens of the Vermont militia, "Lord Wellington['s] Wonderfull hero[es] of Europe" now "Appear no bigger than men to Yankeys."[72]

In the wake of the naval disaster on the bay, Prevost decided to retreat. He based this decision on the state of his provisions, the concern that American militia might operate in his rear and the poor roads that might hinder his communications. In addition, Prevost was not aware of the extensive damage done to Macdonough's squadron and feared it would be used against his line of supply. Apparently, he never seriously contemplated taking and destroying Macomb's defences before he withdrew. As he explained to his superiors: "I had to determine whether I should consider my own Fame by gratifying the Ardor of the Troops in persevering in the Attack, or consult the more substantial interest of my country by withdrawing the Army which was yet uncrippled" for the security of Canada.[73] To Prevost, it was clear that even the "most ample success on shore after the loss of the Flotilla could not have justified the sacrifice I must have made to obtain it."

Morally, of course, it was the right decision. There was nothing to be gained by attacking Macomb because a British withdrawal was inevitable, given American control of the lake. Although officers such as Campbell of the 2nd Brigade regretted that an attack was not made, "for it would have prevented much boasting, and would have served in some measure to counterbalance the loss of our vessels," it would have changed little and cost lives.[74] Without a doubt the decision to retreat was correct but what is perhaps questionable is Prevost's order to carry out an immediate withdrawal because it appeared very much as though he was running away from an inferior force.

Nonetheless, orders to the division to pull back went out shortly after the British artillery ceased firing. Wood of the Royal Artillery recalled that when they were received, "a murmur of discontent was heard in the ranks, and some difficulty was experienced in restraining the ardor" of some of the units. In Wood's opinion, the worst result was that "it created a feeling of disgust from the General of Brigade to the Drum-boy" and "destroyed all confidence in the Commander-in-chief."[75] Morale was not helped by a torrential downpour of rain that began in the early evening.

The artillery and supply wagons were the first to be put on the roads. Wood remembered that his unit started moving toward Chazy around 11 P.M. There was a shortage of transport and it was not long before overloaded wagons – particularly ammunition wagons which carried the heaviest weight – began to break down as they moved along roads that were soon mires of mud. Sinclair admitted the loss of 50,000 musket cartridges and a number of artillery projectiles, and at least one small vessel carrying provisions and artillery supplies ran aground near Chazy Landing and was abandoned. Sinclair later claimed that every piece of ordnance taken over the border was returned to Lower Canada

The bridge over the Saranac.
This is a modern replacement for the wooden bridge that spanned the Saranac at this point in the town. (Author's photograph)

but other witnesses state that one or more guns were abandoned, probably because of broken carriages. Much had to be left behind at Plattsburgh and the townspeople rejoiced to find stocks of provisions, while two lucky local boys found a box full of jack knives. A thrifty housewife went to an abandoned British battery, sliced open the sand bags of which it was constructed, emptied them and converted them into towels. Macomb reported that his men found quantities of ammunition and provisions "concealed in the ponds and creeks, and buried in the ground," with a "vast quantity carried off by the inhabitants."[76]

Prevost also left behind his seriously wounded and sick under charge of a military surgeon with a note to Macomb "requesting the humane attention of the [American] commanding general."[77] The British had no reason to worry as their wounded were treated very well. Prevost also left his dead, who received a proper burial. The corpses were a subject of much curiosity. Mary Williams, an 18-year-old servant girl, saw the bodies of Captain John Purchas of the 76th and one of his sergeants, which had been taken to a barn:

> The captain was shot behind the ear, but the bullet did not come through his head, it could be felt. The sergeant was shot in the mouth. Blood was oozing from his mouth like beer. A militia man took off the captain's shoes and stockings and put them on his own feet, saying he needed them the most. The captain had on a fine ruffled shirt and one militia man tried to cut off the shirt but was stopped by another one. Some took a button or anything to show that they were from the British. The captain was a little man and said to have been Irish.[78]

The naval battle resulted in considerable human wreckage. Just a few hours after the action, Judge Hubbell of Chazy went on board the *Saratoga* and recorded that

The dead were all packed up in order here, and the decks were cleaned up, but the seams full of blood, and the torn hull, masts and spars told the story of the fearful struggle.

From the *Saratoga* we went on board the British flag-ship, the *Confiance*, and here was a horrible sight. The vessel was absolutely torn to pieces; the decks were strewed with mutilated bodies in all directions, and everything was covered with blood. It was the most fearful sight I ever beheld or ever expect to, and one I shall never forget.[79]

Simeon Doty from Ingraham boarded the *Confiance* with his brother, where they saw Downie "and his *Miss*," a reference to the purser's wife, laid out on the deck covered by the British colours.[80] Doty's brother fainted when "he saw the blood and the dead." Another visitor to the former British flagship, 14-year-old Benajah Phelps, stated that it was "the most awful sight I ever saw" as there was "Blood blood everywhere!" and the decks were "covered with arms and legs and heads and pieces of hands and bodies all torn to pieces! I never seen anything in the world like it! Seemed as if everybody had been killed."[81]

Many of the fatal casualties were interred at the mouth of the Salmon River about four and a half miles south of Plattsburgh.[82] Downie's remains, as well as those of the other British naval, marine and army officers killed during the campaign, were eventually interred in the Plattsburgh village cemetery and rest there to this day.

Most of the naval dead from the battle were buried in mass graves on Crab Island, including some bodies that had to be fished out of the bay. New York militiaman Simeon Doty visited the island immediately after the battle and later gave an account of what he saw to the local newspaper:

many of the bodies were terribly mutilated as they were brought ashore – in some cases only dismembered limbs and other portions having been found, and he recollects well of seeing human entrails and other parts which, as he supposes, had been thrown overboard from the vessels, floating up to the shore at the landing. Inside [the hospital] tents the scene was a terrible one. Shrieks from the wounded soldiers who were undergoing operations at the hands of the surgeons rent the air; others were crying and begging for relief from their sufferings, while men were constantly carrying out the dead on rude biers made of poles to the burial yard south of the hospital tents.[83]

The corpses were buried in shallow trenches and

Some of them were rolled up in blankets and others had only their ordinary clothing on; their heads were placed to the west and their faces downward.

The Americans and British were buried indiscriminately together, probably to the number of at least one hundred, and there they lie today, their graves unmarked, save by a number of long rude mounds indicating the site of the ditches.[84]

Caleb Nichols, the owner of Crab Island, later submitted a bill to the United States government for the damages to his property, which included a request for $150 to compensate him for burying the dead.[85]

After the British artillery and supply wagons had got away, they were followed by the three infantry brigades and the cavalry. Both the Beekmantown and State Roads were used for the retreat, which was a wretched business made "in a most confused and hurried manner" under a steady downpour that showed no sign of letting up and the mud "nearly a foot deep in places."[86] Wood of the artillery recorded that it took him seven hours to cover the fifteen miles to Chazy which, all things considered, was not bad progress. Lieutenant John Lang of the 19th Light Dragoons, which formed the rearguard, left Plattsburgh at 4 A.M. on 12 September and reached Chazy by breakfast after a hard ride over "dreadful" roads blocked by broken down carts, which seemed to be evidence of a "want of arrangement."[87] The Peninsular veterans, many of whom had participated in Wellington's miserable retreat from Spain in late 1812, appeared to be more fit than the men in units that had served for long periods in North America, and they offered to carry the packs and muskets of their weaker comrades. Legend has it that Private Jack Richardson of the 88th Foot took up the musket and pack of a soldier of the 49th but became so exasperated by the wretched man's whining and inability to keep up, that he threw him bodily over his shoulder and trudged on, carrying man, two muskets and two packs.[88]

As the long columns of wagons and gun carriages rolled through Chazy, young Catharine Shute again heard the noise like rolling thunder that she had earlier heard when the British had advanced against Plattsburgh. Inevitably, some soldiers took the opportunity to desert but not nearly as many as has been stated in some of the popular myths that have grown up around the Plattsburgh campaign.* Catharine recalled that

> One of these deserters told us that we were a different people from what they supposed us to be. They had been told they were going to fight the "heathen Yankees." When they got here they found that we talked just as they did. They said we were our own brothers and sisters. One said he had an uncle in Philadelphia.[89]

---

* For a discussion of the British desertion rate at Plattsburgh, see Appendix E.

No longer playing "Yankee Doodle." It was an unhappy British army that retreated back to Canada under a downpour of rain during the night and day following the battle. Officers and men alike knew that they been feebly commanded and were angry with Prevost. (Drawing by George Balbar reproduced with permission from Robert Foley, *The War of 1812*)

For Prevost, the most satisfactory part of these dismal proceedings was that his retreating army was not harassed. It was Campbell's belief that "nothing could be more unhurried or undisturbed than we were in all our movement."[90] Because of the weather and the fact that the Saranac divided the two opponents, Macomb was not even aware that his enemy was gone until the morning of Monday, 12 September. He immediately sent out detachments of militia infantry and cavalry, but they did no harm to the British. Eleazar Williams was one of the pursuers and remembered that his artillery unit moved under a severe rainstorm and the roads were "almost impassable" with mud up to the men's knees "and gun after gun stuck and upset in the quagmires, and the horses were staggering and reeling under their burdens."[91] Williams and his comrades were thankful when the pursuit was called off and they were ordered back to Plattsburgh.

When they had a moment, the senior commanders compiled their losses for the entire campaign, which had lasted twelve days. Prevost reported that his army had lost 37 killed, 151 wounded and 55 missing, for a total of 193 men. Macomb reported 37 killed, 62 wounded and 20 missing for a total of 119.[92] Considering the intensity of the fighting, it was a fairly low casualty rate on both sides.

A retreating army is never particularly enamoured with its commander and the mood in the British Left Division was one of total dissatisfaction. As they tramped north, often under showers of rain, the officers and men of the division were very unhappy and they had reason to be as they had been defeated through no fault of their own. They knew they had been feebly commanded and regretted that they had never been given the chance to truly get to grips with their enemy.[93] Aware of this feeling, Prevost tried to buoy morale by issuing a general order praising

> The high spirit and conduct displayed by His Majesty's troops in surmounting every obstacle to the occupation of Plattsburgh, and in afterwards forcing the Saranac, leaves no doubt in the mind of the Commander of the Forces, that the most complete and brilliant success would have crowned their ulterior operations, had not the existing circumstance imperiously imposed upon him the necessity of restraining their ardor, as without naval co-operation the further prosecution of the service would have been highly inexpedient.[94]

Nobody was fooled – it sounded too much like an excuse and it was. Major James Campbell expressed the feelings of many in the division when he commented that

> what I witnessed during the whole of this unfortunate and miscalculated business, convinced me that the enterprise which embraced, as we understood, many extensive and important objects, no doubt suggested from England, had been begun without almost any fixed plan, carried on in ignorance of the country, and ultimately abandoned, because of an event, the probability of which occurring, from the state of the two fleets, might with good measure, have been calculated upon.[95]

Perhaps the whole wretched business was best summed up by an American bystander who, watching Brisbane's 2nd Brigade marching back across the bridge over the Chazy River at Champlain, shouted in a loud voice: "I guess as how you are not playing Yankee doodle now."[96]

PART FOUR

On the Niagara

16 AUGUST–5 NOVEMBER 1814

Make Ready! This fine painting by H.C. McBarron shows a platoon of American infantry about to take aim at the enemy. They are wearing the authorized late 1813 uniform, which clad some units in 1814. (Courtesy Parks Canada)

Soldier, Glengarry Light Infantry Fencibles. Along with the Canadian Voltigeurs and the Incorporated Militia Battalion, the Glengarry Light Infantry were one of the most effective Canadian units. They were highly trained skirmishers and were issued green uniforms and armed with a light infantry pattern musket that had a back sight. The Glengarries fought throughout the siege of Fort Erie. (Painting by G. A. Embleton, courtesy of Parks Canada)

CHAPTER ELEVEN

Entr'Acte (2): Baltimore, Washington, London, Ghent and the Northern Theatre

AUGUST AND SEPTEMBER 1814

Old Johnny Bull, a vain old man
More vain and proud than witty,
To curb the Yankees formed a plan
'Bout which we sing this ditty,
Said he, one day, to Castlereagh,
"These Yankees are too growing,
They'll gather strength , until at length,
They'll be past all subduing."

On ev'ry shore, on ev'ry sea
We lather'd and we shav'd him;
He was content to treat at Ghent
And this manoeuvre saved him;
But if again he should be vain,
Or dare to be uncivil,
We'll let him know his rebel foe
Can thrash him like the Devil.[1]

When Anne Elinor, Prevost's teenage daughter, learned of her father's decision to retreat from Plattsburgh, it seemed as if a "death's knell" sounded as she was certain it would "bring the greatest odium on my father."[2] She was right – Prevost's somewhat hasty decision to withdraw from Plattsburgh ultimately cost him his appointment as governor-general and captain-general of British North America. During his tenure, which had lasted just over twenty-eight months, Prevost had made many enemies in both the military and civilian worlds, and once they sensed his position was weakening, they were quick to pounce. Prevost had angered the English-speaking population of Lower Canada by bringing personal staff members from Nova Scotia, where he had previously served as lieutenant-governor, instead of appointing them from among their number. They were also annoyed by Prevost's successful attempts to gain the support of the French-speaking majority in Lower Canada – whom they regarded as inferiors – by granting the francophones many of the same privileges they themselves enjoyed. In Upper Canada many blamed Prevost for the loss of the western part of the province and the destruction in the Niagara. Army officers, particularly in the veteran Peninsular units, had come to despise Prevost's senior staff and were disgusted and indignant with his conduct of the Plattsburgh campaign. The Royal Navy believed he was responsible for the capture of the Lake Champlain squadron by forcing Downie into action before he was ready and not supporting him when he did fight. All these enemies now coalesced into a single powerful lobby determined to remove Prevost.[3]

The newspapers were early in play. Less than a week after the battle of Plattsburgh, an anonymous letter appeared in the Montreal *Herald*, one of the most influential English-language newspapers in Canada, which emphasized that if the "scientific, brave Generals, Officers, and soldiers of the Duke of Wellington's army" had not been restrained at Plattsburgh, the American defences "would have fallen into our hands and every American must have fallen or been made prisoner."[4] In a Halifax newspaper, "A Free Thinker" asked whether there had been worse generals than Prevost

> which no impartial person in British North America can be brought to believe. – If incapacity was his only fault, if he has been rewarded with honours and profitable Governments for services which never would have been thought of, but for these unmerited favours, it might have been borne – but what Soldier – what Man of honour can read his pompous and overbearing Gen[eral] Orders in which the Duke of Wellington is mentioned, and not despise the author of it.[5]

The British press was no happier when they learned of the defeat. "It is scarcely possible to conceive the degree of mortification and disappointment," complained the *Annual Register*, "which the intelligence of this defeat created in Great Britain."[6]

Army officers voiced their complaints strongly, if not loudly. Alicia Cockburn, the sister-in-law of Rear-Admiral George Cockburn and the wife of a British officer, moved in the military society of Montreal and knew the Peninsular generals. Alicia Cockburn believed that Prevost, who had "contrived to blind the Ministers at home, is now at his wits' end" because, "convinced that his infamous behaviour can no longer be concealed," he was sending members of his staff – "creatures who are dependant on him" – to Britain to plead his case.[7] She gave "several papers, and documents ... with a plan of the operations"

LIEU.T GEN.L SIR GEORGE PROVOST
GOVERNOR OF CANADA.

Caricature of Sir George Prevost. Prevost's decision to withdraw from Plattsburgh drew immediate scorn from many in British North America and he was harshly criticized. This caricature, which shows him as timid, hesitant general dates from the immediate post-battle period. (Toronto Reference Library, T-p15460)

at Plattsburgh to Captain Arthur Somerset of the 19th Light Dragoons, who was returning to London to join the staff of the Duke of York, the commander of the army. The discontent among the Peninsular veterans eventually reached the ears of the Duke of Wellington. The duke had learned of Prevost's general order concerning dress and confided to Bathurst, the colonial secretary responsible for overseas strategy, that Prevost had "gone to war about trifles with the general officers I sent him, which are certainly the best of their rank in the army" and his "subsequent failure and distresses," Wellington added, "will be aggravated by that circumstance."[8] That being said, the duke did approve of Prevost's decision to retreat, because naval superiority on the lakes was absolutely essential in North America even if Britain's "object be wholly defensive," and once Downie's squadron was lost, the operation was at an end.[9] In private, the duke was more critical, remarking that, although he had sent Prevost the best units of his Peninsular army, at Plattsburgh they had clearly "lacked the iron fist to command them."[10]

But Prevost's most dangerous enemy was Commodore James Lucas Yeo. Yeo had starved the Lake Champlain squadron of men, guns and equipment in order to complete the *St. Lawrence*, the 102-gun ship of the line he was building at Kingston. Still worse, he had changed the naval commanders on Lake Champlain on almost the same day that Prevost's army had crossed the border. To deflect the blame for the loss of the squadron, Yeo mounted an active campaign to shift it onto Prevost's shoulders. Shortly after the battle, both Pring and Robertson, the senior surviving naval officers, had submitted reports that were fairly straightforward accounts of the action. A few days later, however, they wrote additional letters that emphasized the failure of the army to support the squadron. It is not known if Yeo urged the two officers to do so, but he did send the second set of letters to the Admiralty, with a covering note claiming that Downie "was urged and his ship hurried into Action before she was in a fit state to meet the Enemy."[11] When Yeo came into possession of the correspondence between Prevost and Downie, dated 7 through 10 September, he also forwarded it to the Admiralty, alleging that Downie "was urged, even goaded on to his fate" by Prevost, "who appears to have assumed the direction of the naval force."[12] This allegation would have a most serious result.[13]

The United States, naturally, rejoiced over the victory on Lake Champlain. On the day of the battle, the postmaster at Plattsburgh sent a letter to the Albany *Argus,* which ran his report on the action under a masthead reading "Free Trade and Sailor's Rights."[14] In the Chesapeake, however, the celebrations were somewhat muted because another major British operation was in progress in that area. After he had withdrawn from Washington on 25 August, Major-General Robert Ross had re-embarked his army on the fleet. Considerable discussion now ensued about the next objective by which Ross could continue to carry out his orders from London to create a diversion on the Atlantic coast to draw off American strength from the northern theatre.[15] Ross selected Baltimore as his next objective and, after some argument with Vice-Admiral Cochrane, the naval commander on the Atlantic, it was agreed that an operation would be mounted against that port, a city with a population of nearly 50,000 and the third largest in the United States after New York and Philadelphia. Its object would be to "make a demonstration" against Baltimore which might be converted into a real attack, "should the circumstances justify it."[16] At daylight on 12 September, the same day that the British Left Division, cursing and grumbling, retreated from Plattsburgh in the rain, Cochrane disembarked Ross's little army of about 4,000 men at North Point, fourteen miles from Baltimore. Ross's plan was to move on the city while Cochrane tried to keep the fleet abreast of him in the nearby Patapsco River.

Baltimore was ready for the invaders. Major-General Samuel Smith of the Maryland militia, a senator, veteran of the Revolutionary War and opponent of the Madison administration, had been placed in command of the defences. For nearly a year the people of Baltimore had been building batteries and earthworks to defend their city, but now, with the full co-operation of the mayor and the municipal government, and almost every able-bodied man, Baltimore began feverishly to entrench. In a remarkably short period of time, a line of

General Samuel Smith, Maryland (1752-1839). Although an opponent of the Madison administration, Smith was appointed to command the defences of Baltimore and proved to be an effective and able defender of the city. (From Benson Lossing, *Pictorial Field-Book of the War of 1812*)

earth works about a mile long was constructed on the land approaches from North Point. Defended by nearly 11,000 militiamen, regular soldiers, seamen and marines, it mounted a hundred artillery pieces in seven redoubts.[17]

As soon as he learned of the approach of the British fleet, Smith ordered Brigadier-General John Stricker to take his brigade of Maryland militia forward to slow down the enemy advance. With about 3,000 men, including many riflemen, Stricker selected a position at the most narrow part, only a mile wide, of the peninsula formed by the Back and Patapsco Rivers. He positioned his troops behind rail fences at the edge of a wood which had a cleared area in front.

Ross got moving early on 12 September. At about 9 A.M., the British advance guard encountered one of Stricker's outlying pickets and shots were exchanged. As was his habit, Ross was not far behind the point and rode forward to see what was happening. He was shot in the chest by an American rifleman, fell from his horse and was dead within minutes. Colonel Arthur Brooke assumed command and pushed forward, clearing the American pickets from his path until he encountered Stricker's main force, which was placed in two lines 300 yards apart. An artillery duel commenced between the British field artillery and a battery of Maryland militia artillery, but when all his troops had come up, Brooke formed them in line and advanced with fixed bayonets. Some of the Maryland militia stood firm and inflicted heavy casualties on the British but other units

General Samuel Stricker, Maryland (1758-1825). Maryland largely took responsibility for its own defences as it was manifestly clear that the federal government was confused and disorganized. Stricker engaged Ross's British landing force moving on Baltimore and, although driven back, managed to delay it long enough for the city's defences to be completely manned. From Benson Lossing, *Pictorial Field-Book of the War of 1812*)

wobbled, lost cohesion and fell back. Seeing that he could not hold, Stricker ordered his first line to retreat to the second. Brooke, meanwhile, somewhat surprised by the size of the American force and the resistance they had put up, did not renew the attack. It now began to rain heavily and Stricker, considering that his task of delaying the British advance had been accomplished, withdrew closer to Baltimore. The casualties suffered at the battle of North Point had not been insignificant: Brooke reported a total of 339 killed, wounded and missing while Sticker admitted 213 casualties of all types.[18]

The British spent a miserable night on the battlefield under a heavy downfall of rain. Early the next morning, Brooke moved forward and shortly came in sight of the main defence line with its redoubts. He spent much of the day manoeuvring, trying to find a weak spot in the defences, but gradually realized that, with the force under his command, his only chance was a night attack. The British movements took place against a background of noise provided by the fleet, which had begun a heavy bombardment of Fort McHenry. Vice-Admiral Cochrane reasoned that if his fleet could neutralize this very strong defence work, which guarded the entrance to Baltimore harbour, he might be able to turn the flank of Smith's defence line. Cochrane's command included five bomb vessels armed with heavy mortars, as well as HMS *Erebus*, a specialized vessel equipped with Congreve rockets. The fleet commenced firing at 5 A.M. on 13 September and continued throughout the day and into the dark. A British midshipman recalled that during the night "the hissing of rockets and the fiery shells glittered in the air, threatening destruction as they fell, whilst to add solemnity to this scene of devastation, the rain fell in torrents" and "the thunder broke in mighty peals after each succession of lightning."[19]

In the early hours of 14 September, a force of 1,200 sailors and marines embarked in small boats made an attempt to bypass the fort but it was foiled and turned back by alert defenders. The bombardment ended at 7 A.M. when Cochrane gave the signal to cease firing. For his part, Brooke had prepared to make his night attack but, after a receiving a message from Cochrane that Fort McHenry had not been pounded into silence, he withdrew to his landing area at North Point.* [20]

Hundreds of people in Baltimore had observed the bombardment of Fort McHenry from rooftops and upper-storey windows in the city or from the opposite side of the Patapsco. One spectator who had a unique vantage point was

---

* It may not be out of place here to note that Brooke's grand-nephew, General Alan Brooke, later Field Marshal Viscount Alanbrooke, Chief of the Imperial General Staff, 1941-1945, actually flew over the battlefield in 1942 when he accompanied Winston Churchill on a visit to Washington.

a young lawyer, Francis Scott Key, who was on board a British warship to negotiate the release of a doctor who had been taken prisoner after he had tried to arrest British looters. Key watched the bombardment through the night and was greatly relieved on the morning of 14 September to find that Fort McHenry's large American garrison flag was still flying. When he left the British fleet, Key repaired to a hotel in Baltimore, where, on the evening of 16 September, he penned a song which he titled "The Defence of Fort McHenry," intending it to be sung to the tune of a popular drinking song, "To Anacreon in Heaven"* Within days, his creation was in print with a new title, "The Star Spangled Banner," and 117 years later it became the national anthem of the United States.[21]

There was great celebration in Baltimore when the British fleet sailed away. For the second time that September an enemy invasion had been rebuffed but British arms enjoyed better fortune farther north. In July, an amphibious force led by Lieutenant-General Sir John Coape Sherbrooke, who commanded in the maritime provinces of British North America, occupied Eastport on Moose Island. Next, Sherbrooke staged a more ambitious offensive, intended to alter the international boundary between Maine and New Brunswick so as to improve communications between that province and Lower Canada. On 1 September the Royal Navy landed Sherbrooke and a small army of 2,000 regulars at Castine and in the weeks that followed Sherbrooke's troops took every major town in the area. For all intents and purposes, Maine east of the Penobscot River became British territory and most of the inhabitants took an oath to behave peaceably and "not directly or indirectly bear Arms" against the occupying forces.[22] This done, these towns soon renewed their traditional trade with New Brunswick and Nova Scotia, which had been interrupted by a war they had never wanted. The customs revenues generated by this commerce were collected by Sherbrooke and later used to found Dalhousie University in Halifax – a worthy use for the spoils of war.[23]

Despite victories at Plattsburgh and Baltimore, by September 1814 Madison's government was facing an increasing inability to continue the war effort because it was running out of both money and men. The administration had always tried to finance the conflict by means other than taxation but the most recent attempt to obtain a loan of $6 million had fallen short by $3.5 mil-

---

* Anacreon was a 5th century poet who loved wine and song. The song, "Anacreon in Heaven," the words of which were written in the 18th century by Ralph Tomlinson to a tune composed by John Smyth, was sung by the Anacreontic Society of London. It was popular in the United States and the American army during the war, see Donald E. Graves, ed., *First Campaign of an ADC: The War of 1812 Memoir of Lieutenant William Jenkins Worth, United States Army* (Youngstown, 2012), 304.

lion. The capture of Washington had created a financial panic and, outside of New England, most American banks had suspended specie payments. The only way the government could pay its debts was to issue treasury notes, credit notes redeemable in the future with interest. By September the federal treasury was empty and the nation was beginning to default on its loans because, in effect, the United States was bankrupt.[24]

The financial crisis had a negative impact on army recruiting. On the first day of July, the regular army had an aggregate strength of 31,503 all ranks but recruiting lagged during the summer – the army enlisted nearly 7,000 men between March and May 1814 but only 4,477 from July to September, and many of these men would only replace the heavy casualties suffered on the Niagara. Still worse, the secretary of the treasury admitted that he did not have enough funds to pay the bounties for these new entrants. Acting Secretary of War James Monroe blamed the dismal recruiting results on competition from the state militia, which offered higher bounties and shorter terms of service. Whatever the cause, the result was that on 30 September 1814 the army's strength was reported as only 34,029 all ranks, with the figure for those actually present for duty being much lower. The best troops were on the northern frontier: Brown's Left Division, Izard's Right Division and the two independent brigades at Plattsburgh and Sackets Harbor. The declining strength of the army was a serious problem at a time when there were nearly 27,000 British regulars in Canada alone, with more on their way, backed up by the Royal Navy, which posed a threat to every community on the Atlantic coast.[25] The inability of Madison's administration to prosecute the war by solving either its financial or manpower problems was inexorably shifting the balance of power to the state governments, particularly in New England, which had become increasingly dissatisfied with a conflict that was highly unpopular in that region.[26]

For an administration in crisis, the one positive aspect was that on 8 August British and American commissioners met for the first time at Ghent in the Netherlands* to negotiate a peace treaty. The American commissioners were an impressive group that included Albert Gallatin, former secretary of the treasury; John Quincy Adams, the son of a former president and a distinguished diplomat; Henry Clay, a senator from Kentucky and prominent war hawk; James Bayard, a federalist senator from Delaware; and Jonathan Russell, a career diplomat. In contrast the British negotiating team was not nearly as strong, consisting of Henry Goulbourn, undersecretary of state to Bathurst, secretary of the Colonial Office; William Adams, a legal specialist and Vice-

---

* In the summer of 1814, Ghent was located in Dutch territory as the modern nation of Belgium did not exist at this time.

Admiral James Gambier, known in the Royal Navy as "Dismal Jimmy" because of his Bible-thumping ways, who possessed a very mixed service record and no background in diplomacy. The difference between the two parties was striking – the United States had sent its best and brightest while Britain had despatched what was basically its third team. In addition, the British commissioners, unlike the American, did not have much leeway but were really just mouthpieces for Lord Liverpool, the prime minister, Viscount Castlereagh, the secretary of state for foreign affairs, and Bathurst.

If the American commissioners expected to find their counterparts in a receptive mood, they were rudely awakened at the first joint meeting when the British commissioners presented a list of the subjects that London had authorized them to discuss. Among them was a demand that the "Indian allies of Great Britain" were "to be included in the pacification, and a definite boundary to be settled for their territory," which was a *sine qua non* or absolute condition for any treaty.[27] That the British commissioners were aggressive was a logical attitude because in early August 1814 the British government felt no pressure to hasten the process of negotiation. Although it was actually willing to settle on the basis of *status quo ante bellum* – or a return to the conditions as they stood before the outbreak of war – it was hoping to force a treaty on the basis of *uti possidetis*, or military occupation at the time of peace. This meant that, with the territory it had already taken and intended to capture when the planned offensives by Prevost and Sherbrooke had been completed, Great Britain would retain Plattsburgh and the northeastern part of New York state, northern Vermont and New Hampshire, eastern Maine, Fort Niagara and Mackinac Island. Britain wanted to end the war but it wanted to end it on the best possible grounds, and its opening move at Ghent was intended to accomplish that object. After some further discussion, both parties agreed to consult their respective governments.

The British were quick to get a response from London and it came in the form of a note from Castlereagh, the foreign secretary, dated 14 August. Five days later, the two parties met so that the British commissioners could present Castlereagh's points. The Americans listened unhappily as they learned that, for the protection of Canada, the United States would be prohibited from keeping any armed naval force on the Great Lakes, and that territory in northern Maine should be ceded to permit a direct route from Halifax to Lower Canada. As for the aboriginal nations, they were to be given enough land to create "a permanent barrier" between American and British territory and the boundary of that barrier would be that established by the 1795 Treaty of Greenville.[28] That treaty, signed between the United States and a number of aboriginal nations, drew a line between white and aboriginal settlement, a boundary that was soon ignored by the settlers. If it was re-established as the limit of the aboriginal "barrier state," it would mean that the western half of Ohio and the territories of Indiana and Illinois would have to be ceded by the republic. The American commissioners pointed out that this area "would comprehend a great number of American citizens; not less, perhaps, than a hundred thousand; and asked what was the intention of the British Government respecting them, and under whose Government they would fall?"[29] The British reply that "such of the inhabitants as would ultimately be included within the Indian territory must make their own arrangements and provide for themselves" was not very helpful.

The American commissioners flatly refused to even discuss such demands. Five days later, they sent a strongly worded note to their counterparts which rejected most of the British claims because they were

> founded neither on reciprocity, nor on any of the usual bases of negotiation, neither on that of uti possidetis nor of status ante bellum. They are above all dishonorable to the United States in demanding from them to abandon territory and a portion of their citizens; to admit a foreign interference in their domestic concerns, and to cease to exercise their natural rights.[30]

Having said that, the American commissioners concluded that the negotiations were at an end and prepared to leave Ghent.

The war was going to continue.

In the northern theatre it will be recalled that the rearguard of Major-General George Izard's division left Plattsburgh for Sackets Harbor on 29 August. Unwilling to take the shorter route through Chateauguay Four Corners, New York, to Ogdensburg and thence to Sackets Harbor, Izard had opted to go the long way through Utica, which effectively doubled the distance. Considering the miles that it had to cover and the scarcity of draft animals – owing to a shortage of horses, some of its supply wagons were drawn by oxen – the division made reasonably steady progress. Izard did not hurry as he wanted to bring his troops into Sackets Harbor "fresh and ready for immediate service," so he limited the daily march distance to 15 miles.[31] He rested the division for a day at the head of Lake George and then set out on the last leg of 175 miles, through Glen's Falls and Remsen to the Harbor. Private Charles Fairbanks of the Forty-Fifth U.S. Infantry remembered that, when his regiment passed through the village of Greenfield, New York, the patriotic citizens had previously collected bread and cheese, and had it all cut up ready for us. Large tubs of milk sat by the side of the road, and dippers in them for us to drink from. We had had nothing but bread and salt beef for six months. We should have eaten it with a grand relish, but our General would not let us taste of it, or stop at all, although there was no hurry, nor a reason in the world why we should not eat it.

We had evidence of the inhabitants' generosity by the sight of our eyes, but not by satisfying our hunger.[32]

"Such things as that," commented Fairbanks, "embittered the feelings of a soldier towards his general."

On 13 September Izard rode into the Harbor with his staff while the remainder of his division marched in three days later, having covered the 350 miles from Plattsburgh in just under three weeks. He had received no communications en route from the secretary of war and was surprised to find none waiting for him at the Harbor. That same day Izard wrote to Brown, promising that, as soon as he could arrange it with Chauncey, he would transport his division to the Niagara "and place myself in the rear of the British forces in your front" as "the happiest consequence may result from this movement."[33]

Although Brown was happy about the approach of reinforcements, he was not looking forward to the arrival of Izard because what he knew of Izard's "*habits, character*, and *intentions*, is so unsatisfactory, that I hope nothing from him."[34] In this respect Brown and his senior officers were not assuaged when Lieutenant-Colonel Josiah Snelling, one of Izard's senior staff officers, arrived in the Niagara to discuss arrangements about the forthcoming junction of the two divisions. Snelling warned Brown not to place any confidence in Izard, who was averse "to the service given him" and had no intention "to perform it."[35] Izard, said Snelling,

> would not co-operate, as ordered, with my [Brown's] division – that *he disapproved the whole plan* and *had a patron in the Cabinet, who could and would protect him in this act of disobedience* ...... This person and patron, he added was *Mr. Monroe*, the Secretary of State [sic] – whose confidential letters to Gen. Izard he [Snelling] had seen and read.[36]

With this in mind, on 10 September Brown wrote Izard that he had been "expecting with much anxiety to hear from you, and to learn the aid that you can afford this army." "I will not conceal from you," Brown continued

> that I consider the fate of this army [i.e. the Left Division] very doubtful, unless speedy relief is afforded; and my opinion is that the wisest course will be

to effect a junction, by landing below Niagara, marching on the American side of the strait [the Niagara River], and crossing over from Buffalo. Will your force be such as to insure relief to this army if you land on the British side? Our united forces would, I have no doubt, be competent to drive Drummond from the field, and perhaps capture him.[37]

Asking Izard to let him know his plans as soon as possible, Brown acknowledged that Izard was now the senior officer on the northern frontier and his orders "would be received and obeyed with pleasure." The following day Brown sent a second letter in which he suggested that Izard should now consider attacking Kingston as it would "accomplish a much more important object" but again assured him that he would "be happy to receive your orders, and be made acquainted with your plan of operations."[38] It was clear that Brown was feeling under pressure as he added a lengthy postscript in which he suggested yet another objective:

> Forts George and Niagara must be nearly empty. It is not probable that there are many of the enemy's regular troops between this and Kingston. Their militia are worse than ours. They are good for nothing. My private opinion is, that the enemy cannot bring into the field to exceed three thousand regulars between this and Burlington, unless the 90th and 97th have arrived.[*] If you think proper to land north of fort George, and I could know the moment of your landing so as to press upon the enemy, it would perhaps be the shortest cut to your object, the capture of Drummond and his army. He cannot escape, provided you can promptly form a junction with my present command.[39]

What is significant in both these letters is that Brown was strongly suggesting that Izard conduct a separate operation, which meant that Brown would not come under Izard's immediate command.

As he prepared to leave the Harbor, Izard reported to the secretary of war that he was not happy with the defences of the naval base, which he described as "miserable."[40] On that point Private Fairbanks of the Forty-Fifth disagreed because he was impressed by what he saw at the Harbor, by now one of the largest military and naval bases in the United States. It was garrisoned by the Third Artillery Regiment, "the best looking regiment I ever saw," commented Fairbanks, and heavily fortified. Fairbanks, however, was annoyed when the

---

* It should be noted that Brown had such precise knowledge of British troop movements because Chauncey had captured a small British vessel on Lake Ontario which was carrying official dispatches between Prevost and Drummond.

commanding officer of the Forty-Fifth refused his men leave to enter the village to buy food items to supplement their diets but instead forced them to purchase from the camp sutlers, who charged double the price. The commander of Fairbanks's unit was a terrible officer – he was often drunk on duty and liked to beat his men for minor infractions, although this was strictly against regulations. The enlisted men of the Forty-Fifth detested him so much that some "were determined to shoot him if they could get the chance" – a surprisingly modern sentiment.[41]

Izard had hoped to immediately embark on the squadron but, delayed by storms and contrary winds, it was not until 21 September that Chauncey sailed with most of Izard's troops. Izard left the Thirteenth and the Forty-Fifth Infantry Regiments behind to garrison the Harbor, describing these units as "being in good condition, and among the best of my division."[42] While this may have been true of the Thirteenth, a New York regiment that had a distinguished record, it was certainly not true of the Forty-Fifth, a recently recruited unit whose men were looking for an opportunity to murder their drunken commanding officer. Fairbanks believed that his regiment was left behind at the Harbor because, when the regimental commander was absent one day, his second-in-command reported the Forty-Fifth as "unfit for duty" because they had "drawn no clothes for seven months and were in rags."[43] Whether this anecdote is true or not, it is likely that Izard rid himself of the wretched Forty-Fifth when he had the opportunity, as the unit would most likely have proven a liability rather than an asset in the field.

With favourable winds, Chauncey's squadron made good time and on 22 September was able to land Izard's division at the mouth of the Genesee River. Why Izard chose to land here, still some distance from Buffalo, is a mystery, but it may have had to do with suitable anchorages for landing large numbers of troops as these are scarce on the south shore of Lake Ontario. Izard now attempted to "collect a sufficient number of wagons and horses for the transportation of our camp equipage and provisions" but "our appearance being unexpected, and that part of the country so thinly populated," this was difficult and he did not resume his march until 24 September.[44] Moving over "excessively bad roads, and amidst continual and heavy rains," the division entered Batavia, about forty-five miles from Buffalo, two days later. It had been exactly four weeks since Izard had left Plattsburgh with the rearguard of his division. On the following day, 27 September, he received a surprise visit from Brown, who informed him that, since their last communication, there had been heavy fighting at Fort Erie and the situation in the Niagara had radically changed.

Reality versus the dream. Most young officers dreamed that they would use their swords to lead their men to victory. The reality of warfare was otherwise and many ended up like this man, using the weapon as a toasting fork. (Drawing by George Balbar reproduced with permission from Robert Foley, *The War of 1812*)

CHAPTER TWELVE

"I have twenty toads beneath my feet, a hundred grasshoppers on my clothes"

FORT ERIE, 16 AUGUST–27 AUGUST 1814

Sober sadness, we despise.
Bowls and Bottles hither bring,
Hail the Merry Greek and Sing:
Social mirth and wit attends
Welcome them again, my friends

Steer the streams of life with glee,
Pleasant let the passage be,
Wet your whistle, wet your Sails,
Court the Safe propitious Gales.
Sooner or late we shall arrive
Let us live while we're alive.[1]

In the third week of August 1814, Lieutenant-General Gordon Drummond, commanding His Britannic Majesty's Forces in Upper Canada, was not a happy man. On the 15th of that month he had attempted a risky night assault on the entrenched American position at Fort Erie only to be repulsed with heavy losses. Reinforcements were on the way – notably the 6th and 82nd Regiments of Foot from the Peninsular army – but they would only replace his recent losses. To add to his disagreeables, Drummond had just learned that he faced a shortage of artillery ammunition as, by "some extraordinary mistake," Major-General George Glasgow, the commander of the Royal Artillery in Canada, had limited the supply of ammunition in the Niagara to 200 rounds per gun.[2] Drummond's artillery officers had expended almost all their allotment during the heavy bombardment they had carried out before the recent assault, and it was only when they tried to re-ammunition that they learned of the restriction. The British commander took immediate steps to procure more stocks, but in the meantime his gunners would have to limit their fire.

Still worse, Drummond also discovered that he faced a serious shortage of provisions. Earlier he had been informed that there were enough foodstuffs in Upper Canada to last until 1 October but on 18 August his commissary gave him a revised return of available provisions that revealed that there was only enough flour for 33 days, pork for 30 and beef for 12 days. Commissary-General William Robinson, the man responsible for provisioning the army in Canada, undertook an immediate investigation only to find that he had been misinformed as to the quantity of provisions required in the province. Robinson had been advised that rations were required for 9,000 men (soldiers, sailors and aboriginals) and had managed to get a sufficient amount transported to Kingston to feed these people until 1 October. Unfortunately, this estimate was too low and, after checking with his subordinates, Robinson discovered that they were actually issuing 14,000 rations daily with "one-half of these to Indians and their families."[3] The result, as he explained to Prevost, was "that the present state of the magazines" would not permit the division at Fort Erie to be fed – even "with every exertion of the commissariat" – beyond the middle of September. As if this was not bad enough, Robinson added that the supply of flour in Upper Canada was almost exhausted and "the present harvest is not yet available" but estimated it would be only half the size of the 1813 crop, "if the mills had not been destroyed by the enemy." Even if Robinson could get more provisions to Kingston, it would be very difficult to get them to the Niagara as the roads were deplorable and transport vehicles scarce while water transport across Lake Ontario was risky in August 1814 because Commodore Isaac Chauncey's squadron controlled that body of water.

Everyone looked to Chauncey's British counterpart, Commodore James Lucas Yeo, to assist in feeding the troops in the Niagara. Yeo, however, refused to leave Kingston until he had completed and commissioned his new ship, the *St. Lawrence*. The construction of this ship-of-the-line, with her three gun decks bearing 102 guns – the largest warship yet to be built on the Great Lakes – had severely strained the limited capacity of the St. Lawrence River transportation system. As Andrew Cochran, one of Prevost's staff, described that system:

> From Montreal to Kingston the distance is 190 miles. ...... Stores and men go the first nine miles of this distance by land. After that, the only mode of conveyance in summer is by canoes or batteaux. Some of these carry five or six tons. These boats are seldom more than three or four days in coming down to this place [Montreal] and never less than nine going up.[4]

The problem was exacerbated by a perennial shortage of boats. Matters were worse in winter when, with the river frozen, supplies were transported in horse-drawn sleighs or sleds, which could only carry about 1,000 lb. of freight. If conditions were right, it took a horse team five days to travel from Montreal to Kingston on the frozen river and it was reckoned, given the distance and weight, that a horse team could only carry eight or nine loads per winter.[5]

In view of these facts, Commissary General William Robinson's horror was understandable when in April 1814 Yeo decided – without first obtaining permission from the Admiralty in London – to construct a warship "of greater force than any the enemy can launch at Sackett's Harbor of a description to look down all opposition."[6] Robinson noted that the transport of the guns and stores for this vessel,

> with the various other Supplies absolutely necessary to be forwarded from this Province [Lower Canada] for the existence of the Army and Navy in Upper Canada, will engage and occupy the whole of the means of transport by Batteaux, or otherwise, from Montreal to Kingston, which it will be possible to provide for the Summer of 1814.[7]

And that is exactly what happened. Not only did the construction of the new ship prove more difficult and take longer than anticipated; it overburdened the logistical pipeline. This was hardly surprising as the weight of the vessel's main armament – which comprised two 68-pdr. carronades, sixty-eight 32-pdr. guns and thirty-four 24-pdr. guns – alone was nearly 300 tons. A basic allotment of roundshot for these weapons weighed about 22 tons and then there were the iron and copper fittings, rope and cables, glass, canvas, leather, clothing, as well as provisions for her 700-man ship's company.[8] Wood was about the only thing that was in plentiful supply at Kingston naval dockyard and to complete the *St. Lawrence* Yeo scavenged men, guns and equipment from warships at Quebec and Montreal.[9] "I hope to God you will be able to spare me" 32-pdr. guns, he wrote one captain, "otherwise all my exertions will be lost in having built a three Decker."[10] Even Yeo eventually became concerned about the cost and effort needed to complete this leviathan and asked the Admiralty for retroactive

> approval of my conduct in Building so large a Ship without Their previous instructions, which, it was impossible to have received in time. I therefore have acted to the best of my judgement for the good of the Service, and am convinced in my own mind that nothing less would have attained the most important object, that, of the Naval Supremacy on Lake Ontario.
>
> It is impossible to describe the prodigious labour and difficulty we have had in equipping this Ship from having to get all our supplies, from Quebec and Montreal.[11]

The irony is that, given the construction record of the Kingston dockyard, in the six months that it took to construct the *St. Lawrence*, Yeo could have built and commissioned two 50-gun frigates that would have secured him superiority on Lake Ontario throughout the summer of 1814 and possibly the remainder of the year.[12]

Although Prevost and Drummond tried to impress on Yeo that the army in the Niagara depended "almost entirely on his prompt, and vigorous, exertions, for its relief, nay perhaps even for its safety," the naval commander took no positive steps to alleviate the situation.[13] To Yeo, the "most important object" was to gain "Naval Supremacy on Lake Ontario" and anything else, including supplying or transporting the army was secondary.[14] He did not want his squadron to function as an auxiliary transport service for the army – in his mind, its purpose was to engage Chauncey's squadron, and until it was in a position to do so, his two large frigates and three smaller warships rocked gently at anchor in Kingston harbour and, as one naval historian has commented, the "generals were left to fight their own battles."[15]

In the meantime, the best that Drummond and the commissaries could do was to run small boat convoys across the lake – a very risky business – and try to tap all available food sources in Upper Canada. Unfortunately, although the 1814 harvest in the province was good, it was only about half the size of the previous year because of the constant call-out of farmers for militia service. Drummond directed two senior militia officers to tour the Niagara and encourage "the farmers to thresh out their grain earlier than usual, to enable us to hold out until our wants can by relieved by the squadron."[16] He also ordered the commanding officers of the five Lincoln sedentary militia regiments, whose area encompassed most of the Canadian part of the Niagara, to have any of their men who had wheat, "to spare independent of a supply for his own family," to sell from five to twelve bushels to the commissary at the premium price of $2.50 per bushel or $14.00 for flour.[17] Until such measures could take effect and his stock of foodstuffs increase, Drummond would have to make do with what he had but he was thankful that his men remained healthy. Their state of health, he attributed "in a great measure," to an extra daily ration of half a gill* of spirits which he had authorized.[18] He also extended the spirits ration to staff officers, who did not normally receive it. The problem at Fort Erie was not a shortage of drink, it was finding something in which to drink it – a visitor to the British camp that summer reported that Drummond and his staff celebrated the general's wedding anniversary by imbibing whisky from a

---

* A gill is a liquid measure equal to a quarter of a pint or 4 ounces.

"I have twenty toads beneath my feet, a hundred grasshoppers on my clothes"

British officers at leisure. It is a sad fact but many young officers sometimes get a little to the lee of sobriety. Both armies at Fort Erie would have been pleased with a billet as secure as the one illustrated here by caricaturist Thomas Rowlandson. (From *The Adventures of Johnny Newcome,* 1816)

cracked teacup missing its handle, which was passed from man to man.[19]

Despite his problems Drummond was determined to continue with the siege. On 21 August he ordered Lieutenant George Philpotts, RE, his command engineer, to select a site closer to the fort for a new battery. Philpotts had been busy constructing an entrenchment and breastwork to the right of the present battery. He completed this on 24 August and then chose a site for the new battery, in the woods about 300 yards southwest of Battery No. 1 and 700 yards from the stone fort. Work parties began to labour on it that night as well as on an entrenchment to its right. The Americans could hear the noise of the British working parties but were unable to discern their exact location so fired blindly in their general direction. Lieutenant John Le Couteur of the 104th Foot was on a working party on the night of 25 August and recalled that it was a "wretchedly cold" night and that the defenders "fired a great many shells" and "three shells filled with bullets near to us but without their bursting or having *the effect of shrapnels.*"[20] Surgeon William Dunlop of the 89th Foot recalled that throughout the next day the defenders "kept up a constant fire of round shot and shells upon the working parties" but "seemed to have altogether lost their knowledge of elevation, for their shot was uniformly over our heads."[21]

On that same day, Major George Brooke of the Twenty-Third Infantry managed, however, to ascertain the position of the new British battery. He informed Captain Nathan Towson that he could accurately direct the fire of that officer's battery and when the gunner asked him how he proposed to do that, Brooke responded:

> "I will take a dark lantern the first time I go the grand rounds this evening and hang it upon one of the trees on a line between your battery and his, the door of the lantern will be open on the side next you, and you can direct your guns by it." "Capital! capital! said Towson, "but it will be a very perilous undertaking." "I'll do it," said the major, gaily , "it will please ____, naming his lady friend.[22]

That night, Brooke carried a lit lantern covered in a coat out to the tree he had chosen and suspended it. When this was done he pulled a rope attached to the coat and the lantern became visible to Towson's waiting gunners, who immediately opened up in its direction.[23]

Despite such ingenuity, work progressed steadily on Battery No. 2 although Philpotts complained that the infantry only provided small working parties. The battery was completed on 28 August and armed with two 18-pdr. iron guns, a 24-pdr. carronade and an 8-inch iron howitzer. The next night Philpotts cut away the trees in front and, on 30 August Battery No. 2 opened fire. Le Couteur of the 104th was on picket near it and remembered that Lieutenant Edward Sabine of the Royal Artillery commanded the new battery that day "and enjoyed a whole day's practice at the Fort while they repaid the salute in kind," which was not very "amusing to us Frogs in the ditches."[24] The young officer came off duty "with a *thundering* headache."[25]

Philpotts was not impressed with the results of the battery's fire, recording in his journal that it "produced no effect than of annoying the Enemy."[26] The engineer did not give a reason for this poor result but Surgeon Dunlop reported that it was soon discovered that Battery No. 2 had been erected "without taking the levels, and that a rise of ground prevented us even from seeing the Fort," which more or less made it useless.[27] Drummond, on the other hand, thought that the new battery's fire had a "very good effect" but cautioned Major Henry Phillot, his artillery commander, not to waste ammunition but "confine his fire to the annoyance of the enemy, an object in which we have every reason to believe we have hitherto been very successful," as deserters reported that every day between ten and fifteen men were killed in the American lines.[28] For his part, Lieutenant David Douglass of the U.S. Engineers calculated that the Left Division's daily loss rate was 1/16 of its strength. The division did receive some reinforcements in late August when detachments of the Nineteenth and Twenty-First Infantry marched in from outlying posts but the general outlook for the defenders was not encouraging.[29]

"I have twenty toads beneath my feet, a hundred grasshoppers on my clothes"

Major George Brooke (1785-1851). Generally acknowledged as one of the bravest officers in the northern army, Brooke fought throughout the siege and continued on into the postwar army, reaching the rank of major-general by the time of his death in 1851. (Print after portrait by Gilbert Stuart)

Given its poor site, the guns in Battery No. 2 would not have been useful for direct aimed fire but would have been effective for ricochet fire – basically lobbing roundshot somewhere in the American perimeter. By this time, however, the traverses inside Fort Erie – the earthen barriers erected to limit the danger of bouncing shot – were so high that ricochet fire was not as dangerous as it had been earlier in the siege. Battery No. 2, however, was useful for indirect fire from mortars and howitzers using explosive shells and indeed these became the projectiles most feared by the defenders. Young Drummer Jarvis Hanks never forgot a man

> who was killed in an instant while apprehending little or no danger. He was a very large and tall soldier, upwards of six feet. He was reclining on his knapsack, supporting his head with his right hand and elbow, when a 10½ inch shell exploded fifty or sixty feet above our heads. A large piece of it fell upon the center of his body, and cut him in two, as effectually and as instantaneously, as ever the axe of the guillotine severed the head [of] one of its victims. In a few moments, he too was wrapped up in his blanket, carried out and buried.[30]

If he had time, an observer with a trained eye could follow the course of a shell through the air from the trail of smoke left by its burning fuze, and thus could fairly predict where it was going to land. One morning, Majors William McRee and William Trimble were inspecting Douglass's battery with the young officer when "a discharge was observed at the British mortar battery, and an officer in company remarked that the shell was falling precisely in the bastion where we were."[31] All present, however, eluded the explosion by hastily retreating around a row of strong wooden palisades. The battery itself was not damaged. Although he was sparing with his ammunition, Phillot kept his harassing fire up day and night. "The smallest gleam of light," Douglass recalled, drew fire and "it became necessary to prohibit, in Orders, all lights after dark."[32]

The constant night-time alarms annoyed Lieutenant-Colonel Thomas Aspinwall of the Ninth Infantry, who, writing to his father, complained

> that for six weeks I seldom got more than 3 or four hours daily repose, and never undressed or pulled off my boots except to wash myself and change my clothes. My tent was often struck by fragments of shells and by musket balls from their shrapnells, and the tents almost in a range with mine and their batteries often perforated by cannon balls, that I thought myself preserved only by special protection. I had during this period hardly time to write a line to Louisa, [his wife] and, had her health been firm, I would not have done that.[33]

Aspinwall also commented that the defenders were "continually employed in labor," and their work was observed by the besiegers. Drummond, keeping a careful eye on the American defences, reported to Prevost that they had been strengthened by "every means in the power of an active, laborious and ingenious enemy to devise and execute" and "has thrown up such an accumulation of mounds of earth, of batteries and breastworks, as will certainly cost us many men to dislodge him from, and which bid defiance to our shot."[34] By this time, the 82nd Foot had arrived, the 6th Foot was momentarily expected, and the British commander was contemplating another assault. After his disastrous experience on 15 August, Drummond had, not unnaturally, decided that a daylight attack was much preferable to a night attack, for a number of reasons which he summarized for Prevost:

> The enemy, since our last attack, are known to be constantly on their guard by night. By day I think they may be taken very much off their guard. By night it has been found that mistakes may arise that cannot easily happen by day. Moreover, the impression produced on the minds of the enemy by our late attack, and which would be strengthened and confirmed by one made in open day, would be highly favourable to us.[35]

Before he made that assault, however, Drummond wanted to construct a new battery closer to the fort that would be able to "open the rear face and complete the destruction of the stone buildings."[36]

Drummond's observations were correct. Brigadier-General Edmund Gaines, the American commander at Fort Erie, had increased efforts to improve his defences. "The soldiers," recorded Douglass, "since the assault, work with alacrity and the works are making astonishing progress."[37] The two outlying bastions, which had only been started at the time of the 15 August as-

British gunners at work. This drawing by George Balbar illustrates a Royal Artillery detachment firing at the American defences. The garrison of Fort Erie spent thirty-five days under artillery bombardment. (Reproduced with permission from Robert Foley, *The War of 1812*)

sault, were completed and the abattis extended around the entire perimeter and along the shore. It was nearly impenetrable – Douglass recalled that "a deserter from the enemy became somehow entangled in it and remained several hours without the power to extricate himself," and when he "was at last taken out with the assistance of some of our men, his clothes were, for the most part triumphantly retained by the relentless thorns and briars of the abattis."[38] Pikes were manufactured by fitting bayonets on poles "of sufficient length to reach over the parapet, to be used against the enemy, in case he attempted to scale" the wall. There was considerable truth to Douglass's assertion that the defenders' "ability to repel attack became every day more and more apparent." The enemy, somewhat to the young engineer officer's regret, did not test the defences but contented themselves with trying "to cripple or tire us out by the fire of his artillery" as the British bombardment continued.[39]

It was not all one way, however, as the American gunners replied to the British bombardment with interest. Le Couteur remembered the day on picket when

Cap[tain] Alexander McMillan of the Glengarry [Light Infantry] and I were seated on a stump when a round shot from across the river passed between his head and mine, made us both draw back. A man was lying on his back in front of us and the picquet was spread about behind the breastwork. The ball, after passing us, struck the sleeping man's pouch from under Him, exploded the Cartridges and struck the balls among the Men, who jumped in all directions, thinking it to be a shell. I flew to the poor fellow next me, who was unable to rise after a violent jump which He gave on the ball passing under Him. It had not grazed his skin but He was totally paralyzed. We placed Him on a blanket & sent Him to the rear.[40]

The day, however, ended well for the young officer as McMillan invited Le Couteur "to dine with Him after being relieved, and gave me a treat of Port wine which was all expended in the 104th long since."

Although well back from the Niagara River, the British camp was still within range of some American guns. The American gunners could not see the camp but fired the odd round at it – as Le Couteur put it, enemy "shells or roundshot which were very uncomfortable visitors" fell in the camp, "the Yankees sending them occasionally at random to vex us."[41] The besiegers quickly learned to ascertain between the various enemy batteries by the noise they made when firing, as some could hit the camp and others not. The literary Lieutenant Joseph Mermet of De Watteville's Regiment catalogued the different sounds that alerted the British: "Shot from Black Rock – Bang!" "Shot from the Fort – Boom!" "Shot from the Sailor's Battery – Crash!"[42] On 20 August Drummond ordered the camp to be moved farther away from the Niagara River. Although this gave his men peace of mind while they were resting in their bivouacs, it also placed them at a greater distance from their own batteries.

There was constant skirmishing in the "no man's land" between the British and American lines, with a major scrap occurring almost every second day.* Surgeon Dunlop disliked this outpost fighting, "which served no purpose to the parties except to harass one another, and mutually to thin our ranks."[43] Lieutenant Samuel Tappan of the Twenty-Third Infantry, on the other hand, felt that life under a siege was so boring that "skirmishing among picquets and patrols began to be deemed relief, if not diversion."[44]

On 20 August a serious action took place when Gaines attempted to attack the British batteries. Lieutenant Jonathan Kearsley led the large detachment from the First and Fourth Rifle Regiments to make the attack, supported by the Twenty-Third Infantry. Kearsley ran into a small force of Glengarry Light

---

* On the incidence of skirmishing during the siege, see Appendix G below.

Infantry and British regulars who withstood "a short and sharp engagement" before withdrawing.[45] By this time, however, Kearsley had advanced beyond his support and, worse still, a large force of warriors, veterans of this type of warfare, now entered the fray. John Norton remembered that, after his men gave the Americans

> a well directed fire, they attempted to advance, – but seemed checked by the well aimed Bullets, – which brought some to the ground. At this time their Batteries were firing round Shot, Grape, & Spherical Shot upon us – without much effect, & we discovered a party moving obliquely, so as to envelop us, – to baffle this attempt, we divided; – leaving a part of our Warriors to amuse those of the Enemy in front, we hastened to meet the other Division. On the first Encounter the Enemy seemed to hesitate, and in a short time began to retrograde, which move we hastened by closing upon them, both our Divisions answering each other with vigorous Shouts, – We at last drove the Enemy into their Fort.[46]

Unfortunately for the Americans, many of the warriors were from the old Northwest, the most ferocious of all the aboriginal auxiliaries who served with the British army during the war. Drummond reported that they "drove back the whole" of the American riflemen, "supported by some hundreds of his regular troops, without its being necessary for our troops to advance to their support" and, from "the number of scalps that were taken by the Indians and the number of dead seen," he estimated that the American loss was "40 or 50 also a great number of rifles."[47] Le Couteur, who fought in this action, was very pleased to obtain one of the Harper's Ferry rifles picked up by his men. Kearsley was badly wounded in the leg in this action and later lost the limb. He was bitter about Gaines's policy of "feeling out" the enemy with frequent outpost fighting and noted that on 20 August, of the four officers and 133 riflemen of the Fourth Rifle Regiment which crossed the Niagara with him, only one officer and 38 men remained by the time this action was fought, the remainder being dead or wounded.

Five days later another outpost scrap flared up in the late afternoon when Major George Brooke of the Twenty-Third Infantry made an attack on a British picket covering a working party. Brooke drove the picket back but when he advanced on the working party, he was repelled by a detachment of the 82nd Foot, who had just arrived the day before. The officers of that regiment had been cautioned by the veterans of the siege "against exposing themselves rashly to the rifleman's fire" because bush warfare was "not like open warfare as they have been used to against the French."[48] The 82nd officers were amused

Soldier of the Incorporated Militia Battalion. This unit, despite its title, was actually closer to a regular unit, being composed of men enlisted for the duration and trained, armed and equipped as regulars. The Incorporated Militia fought throughout the siege and was involved in many skirmish actions. (Painting by G. A. Embleton, courtesy Parks Canada)

by this advice and did not take it seriously with the result, as Dunlop recalled that, when one of their pickets was attacked on 25 August, the captain commanding it,

> to the utter astonishment of all of us old bush-whackers, gave orders to charge, and the order was executed in a very spirited style. This we thought was consigning our men to inevitable destruction; but no such thing: the riflemen had no more idea of a bayonet being pointed at them than they had of being swallowed up by an earthquake; and when the smoke cleared away, and they saw the 82nd within twenty yards of them, moving on at the "pas de charge,"* it shook their nerves, – they fired, to be sure, but with little effect, and then ran – they were too late, however. The flat-foots got within *their* deadly range, that is, bayonet's length – they *skivered*[49] many of them, and others were shot at two muskets' length, and driven out of the woods to the esplanade of the Fort, where they were treated with a parting volley; and the guns of the Fort immediately opening on us, we took the hint, and withdrew under the cover of the woods.[50]

The 82nd, however, lost two killed and thirteen wounded in this engagement, fairly heavy losses that were incurred because, as Le Couteur remarked, the newcomers were "not yet aware of the value of *treeing*" or taking cover.[51] From that time on the 82nd never went on picket without being accompanied by detachments of the Glengarry Light Infantry or Incorporated Militia,† experienced skirmishers.

---

* The *pas de charge* (charge pace) is the fastest infantry pace, usually about 120 paces per minute.

† Despite its title, this unit was actually closer to a regular than a militia regiment as it was trained, uniformed, armed and equipped as were regular soldiers and commanded by British officers.

A nd so the days passed at Fort Erie for the men of both armies, days filled with labour, danger and, perhaps more common, boredom and fatigue. Shot and shell was not the only things coming from the sky – the latter half of August 1814 was very wet, with rain on five days during the last two weeks of the month. Writing to a friend, Mermet of De Watteville's Regiment complained about the wretched weather:

> It is raining cats and dogs. [Major Charles de] Villatte is sharing my great-coat. Two servants are holding an old blanket in the form of a baldequin* over our heads. "It is only for a moment," we tell them, "have patience." "How honest they are," they answer, "it bothers us very little."
>
> One comes out of hiding with care. "Damned rain!" "Damned wind!" Move the blanket forward, then back "Higher, lower." "The letter is in the rain." "Let's read more quickly." "It's a fiery letter: let's read it." The rain stops, the letter is reread and admired. ......
>
> It is raining, my paper is becoming wet, the humidity communicates itself to the spirit. What the devil can I say? ...... What rain! I have twenty toads beneath my feet, a hundred grasshoppers on my clothes – I believe it is raining them.[52]

The besiegers' camp was a sodden mire. Dunlop tried to make the best of a bad situation. He bunked with a comrade, Tom F ____,[53] who had constructed a very good hut for himself, which was thought safe from the effects of the wet weather. Dunlop recalled that his friend's bed

> being raised on forked sticks, I placed my own under it, so that the rain had to penetrate through his bed clothes and mattress before it could reach me.
>
> This arrangement did admirably for some time, till one night we were visited by the most tremendous thunder storm I ever witnessed in this or any other country, and accompanied with a deluge of rain, that might have done credit to Noah's flood. The hut was very soon swimming, and I was awoke by my bed being overflowed, and started up to get out, but the water that flooded the floor softened the earth in which the forked sticks that supported Tom's bed were driven, and it falling forward jammed me in among the wet bed clothes, where I was nearly drowned, till Tom starting to his feet allowed me to raise the wreck and crawl on all-fours from under it.[54]

Rain was the least of Dunlop's problems. After the much lamented death of Lieutenant-Colonel William Drummond during the night assault of 15 August,

---

* A baldequin is a canopy over an altar or throne.

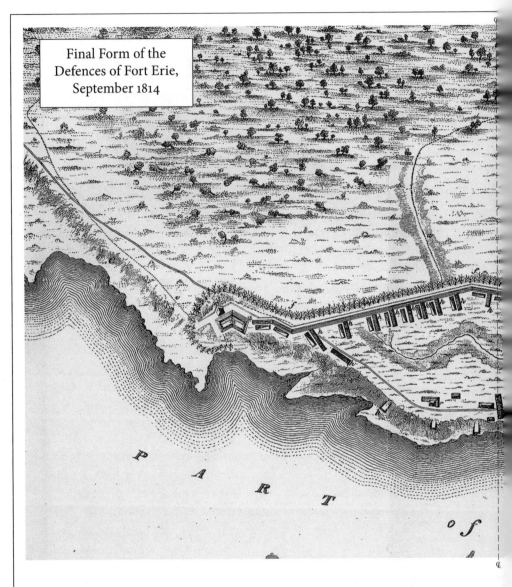

Final Form of the
Defences of Fort Erie,
September 1814

Key

A, old Fort Erie: *a, a,* demi-bastions; *b,* a ravelin, and *c, c,* block-houses built by the Americans during the siege; *e, e,* a redoubt built for the security of the demi-bastions, *a, a.*

B, the American camp, secured on the right by the line *g,* the Douglass Battery, *i,* and Fort Erie; on the left, and in front, by the lines *f, f, f,* and batteries on the extreme right and left of them; *h, h,* etc., camp traverses; *m,* Towson's battery; *n,* main traverse; *o,* magazine traverse, covering also the headquarters of General Gaines; *p,* hospital

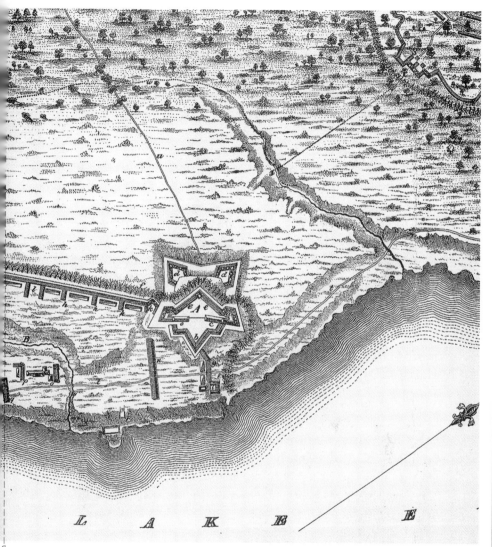

Photograph by René Chartrand of engraving in private collection

traverse; *q*, grand parade and provost-guard traverse; *r*, General Brown's headquarters; *s*, a drain; *t*, road from Chippawa up the lake.

C, the encampment of Volunteers outside of the entrenchments, who joined the army a few days before the sortie.

D, D, the British works. 1, 2, 3, their first, second, and third battery. *v*, the route of Porter, with the left column, to attack the British right flank on the 17th; *x*, the ravine, and route of Miller's command.

the "light demi-brigade," as it was called, received a new commanding officer. This was Lieutenant-Colonel Thomas Pearson, a veteran Royal Welch Fusilier who had seen combat in Egypt, Holland, Denmark, Martinique, Portugal and Spain as well as the battles of Crysler's Farm, Chippawa and Lundy's Lane, and in the May 1814 amphibious assault on Oswego. Pearson was widely regarded as one of the finest combat leaders in British North America but he was also a stern disciplinarian who possessed a ferocious temper, which was not helped by the fact that he was in fairly constant pain from several previous wounds.*
Dunlop thought Pearson "as good a man, and as brave a soldier as ever drew a sword, but too much of a martinet" to be liked by those who served under him.[55] This being the case, everyone in the demi-brigade tiptoed carefully around the new commander. Dunlop, however, perhaps hoping to impress Pearson, let him know that he had discovered a shorter path from the pickets to the camp and offered to show it to him. Unfortunately, by "some fatality" the medical officer "mistook the path, and took a wrong turn," with the result that the two officers blundered into an American picket, which opened up at them but they "were behind trees in a moment, and the next were scampering in different directions at greater or less angles from the enemy."[56]

Dunlop wisely avoided Pearson for a time, but when the brigade commander invited him to breakfast one morning, the surgeon accepted, thinking that Pearson had forgotten the incident. But in this he was mistaken, for, as Dunlop tells the story,

> Lounging about after breakfast, and talking over indifferent matters, a sputtering fire began a little to our left, and the Colonel ordering a look out on the right, proceeded, followed by me, to the scene of the action. We soon saw that this was the point of attack, so he sent me to order up the reserve. This done I rejoined him, and found him standing coolly giving his orders in the middle of a whistling of bullets, far too thick to be pleasant. I stood by his side for some minutes, thankful that none of these missiles had a billet on us,† when on a sudden I felt a severe sharp pain from my brow to the back of my head at the same moment the Colonel exclaimed: "By G_d! you are shot through the head."
>
> I sunk upon one knee, and taking off my forage cap felt along my head for blood, but none was to be found. "It is only a graze," said I. "Colonel, is there any mark?" "Yes," said he, "there is a red mark, but not from a ball, it

---

* The reader who would like to know more about the bad-tempered Thomas Pearson is directed to my biography of the man, *Fix Bayonets! A Royal Welch Fusilier at War* (Toronto, 2006).

† What Dunlop means when he say that no bullet "had a billet on us" is that no rounds hit the two men.

Lieutenant-Colonel Thomas Pearson (1781-1847). One of the toughest defenders of British North America, Pearson was a veteran light infantry officer who had fought on three continents and been wounded three times before being sent to Canada in 1812. He was the only British officer to fight in all of the four major battles in the northern theatre – Crysler's Farm, Chippawa, Lundy's Lane and Fort Erie – and was wounded in two of them. Pearson was a martinet and his subordinates disliked him but they were always glad to see him in a fight as he was a superb combat leader. (Courtesy, Royal Welch Fusiliers Museum)

came from my switch. You gave me a d[evi]l of a fright the other day – now I have given you one, so we are quits."[57]

There was no use complaining about the food or the weather as they were beyond everyone's control. Drummond's officers and men kept their spirits up by organizing swimming parties in the Niagara, listening to concerts put on by the band of the 82nd Foot, relating funny stories and cracking jokes. Le Couteur recalled a night on picket when he and two fellow officers engaged in this entertaining pastime and not only made themselves but also their soldiers "laugh so loud that the Fort fired at us and the Field officer of the night came up" and tore a very wide and deep strip off all three for unnecessarily risking the lives of their men.[58]

Young Le Couteur – whose personal motto was "Merry Hearts Make Light Days" – was a great practical joker. Only a week after the disastrous night assault (which is an indication of how resilient morale was in the Right Division), he played one on Captain George Shore of the 104th. Le Couteur, who was short and wiry, dressed as a young woman "in a couple of night shirts, with a silk Handkerchief for a shawl, and a Cap arranged for the purpose" and sent a messenger to Shore with the information that "a young Lady wished to see him." Shore, probably thinking his fantasies had miraculously come true, quickly emerged from his hut to see this apparition but, as Le Couteur commented, "when He became gallant, I took to my heels with Him following in full chase" through the camp "to the infinite amusement of the wags" who were in on the joke.[59]

On both sides, the high point of the day was the midday meal hour. Drummer Hanks of the Eleventh Infantry remembered that there was "a tacit agreement" on both sides to cease firing around this time, and inside the American position men "would cook and eat their provisions, and expose themselves all over the camp ground, as they would not dare to do" when the British were bombarding.[60] Lieutenant Douglass described meals inside Fort Erie as consisting of "salt pork, raw, and salt pork, fried, served up on barrel-heads and staves, with biscuit and stale bread."[61] If they were in funds, however, the defenders could at least purchase delicacies from the civilian sutlers, whom Gaines permitted to cross the river to do business in the fort. Douglass recorded that the "varieties" available for purchase included "salt butter, at four to six shillings [$1.00 to $1.50] per pound: heavy sour bread, at three shillings [75 cents]: perhaps some onions and potatoes, at two or three dollars per bushel, meagre wine, concocted of logwood and vinegar, with an infusion of gall nuts; and [fresh] *cookery* as we could catch it."[62] When it is considered that the pay of an American enlisted man was between $8 and $10 per month – and many had not been paid for weeks – few could avail themselves of such delicacies. For this reason, there was great celebration when a large shipment of fresh vegetables sent by the patriotic citizens of Batavia, New York, arrived in camp.[63]

Like their British and Canadian opponents, the Americans passed the time telling funny stories and cracking jokes. One story that made the rounds of the Left Division concerned a junior officer in the Eleventh Infantry, a true son of Ireland identified by Douglass only as "Jemmy" or Jimmy, who was renowned for his wild exaggerations. Jemmy belatedly realized that he was acquiring a reputation for being untruthful, so he arranged with a fellow officer that, whenever he "was on the point of committing a rash assertion, the friend should pinch him, or hit him, or touch his foot" to place the Irishman "on guard." It so happened that, seated with his fellow officers one evening , the conversation turned to the subject of barns – which is not surprising as at Fort Erie the weather was generally foul, the wine scarce and the women non-existent – so why not discuss barns? In any case Jemmy let it be known to the assembled that American barns could not hold a candle to those of the Emerald Isle and, despite his friend using his boot to heavily grind the Irishman's toes into the ground, expanded on this assertion by claiming that he had seen a barn in Ireland that "must have been sex [sic] thousand foot long and upwards." There were immediate howls of laughter from those present,

> during which the friend contrived to grind his [Jemmy's] toe with great emphasis. As Jemmy started back, some one called out to know how *wide* the barn was. "How wide!" piteously answered Jemmy who was inspecting his bruised member, "Oh dear! It was six foot." Hereupon the laughter was very loud and long, and Jemmy, losing patience, turned wrathfully on his consid-

erate friend – "See there now – ye've made me a greater fool than ever, for if ye had'nt trod so hard on my toe, I'd have squared the barn."[64]

Another story that went around was that of the trick played by Brooke of the Twenty-Third Infantry on Towson of the artillery. It seems that Towson had an arrangement with a tavern keeper named Goodrich, who operated an establishment west of Buffalo and would send him cooked meals over the river. Goodrich also pastured the horses of many of the officers at Fort Erie, as they were not needed on the Canadian side of the river. Brooke was one of the officers who boarded his mounts with Goodrich and, after sending his soldier servant to see how they were faring, he sent an invitation to Towson requesting "the pleasure of his company at dinner, with a few friends." When the dinner was served, Brooke's guests were curious to know how he had been so lucky to procure the meal but Brooke said he would explain after it had been consumed. As the narrator of this story put it, "None but those who have lived for a long time on camp fare, during a siege, can tell how much Brooke's fare was relished. Chicken-pie reminded his guests of home, and the days of boyhood." When the meal had been consumed, Brooke's soldier servant Tom was called on to explain how he had obtained such fine food and promptly produced a crumpled note which he handed to Brooke. "Why," exclaimed Brooke, "this is not for me – 'tis for Captain Towson" and he handed the note to the artillery officer, who, on reading it, found it contained a list of eatables that Goodrich had dispatched to him by way of Tom. When Towson sternly asked that worthy why he had not delivered the food to the rightful recipient, Tom, "casting a glance" at Brooke "and raising himself erect in the attitude of a soldier," replied that he "obeys orders, sir," meaning that Brooke had waylaid the potables but at least had the courtesy to share them with Towson. The artillery officer took the joke in good humour.[65]

Perhaps the exploits of Irish Jemmy of the Eleventh, the bad temper of Tom Pearson or the practical jokes of Le Couteur and Brooke were not the most amusing of things but at Fort Erie in the summer of 1814 it was always better to laugh at something – in fact anything – because, for soldiers, it is very true that the merrier their hearts, the lighter their days.

U.S. Infantry major, 1814. This fine rendering is representative of the new breed of American officers who had learned their trade the hard way and by 1814 were able to give as good as they received from their British opponents. (Drawing by G. A. Embleton, courtesy of the artist)

CHAPTER THIRTEEN

"As sure as there is a God in heaven, the enemy shall be attacked"

FORT ERIE, 28 AUGUST–21 SEPTEMBER 1814

How happy the soldier who lives on his pay,
And spends half a crown on six pence a day;
He fears neither justices, warrants nor bums,
But pays all his debts with a roll of the drums,
 With a row de dow,
 Row de dow, Row de dow,
 And he pays all his debts with a roll of his drums

He cares not a Marnedy how the world goes;
His King finds his quarters, and money and clothes;
He laughs at all sorrow whenever it comes,
And rattles away with the roll of the drums.
 With a row de dow, etc.

The drum is his glory, his joy and delight,
It leads him to pleasure as well as to fight;
No girl, when she hears it, though ever so glum,
But packs up her tatters and follows the drum.
 With a row de dow, etc.[1]

On Sunday, 28 August 1814, Lieutenant David Douglass of the U.S. Engineers was standing in one of the newly-constructed outlying bastions of Fort Erie when he saw a British shell flying through the air in his direction. Fortunately, it went over him to land somewhere in the interior and he later learned that it hit the small house that Gaines used for his headquarters. The chimney of that house was visible to the British gunners in Battery No. 2 and they used it as a convenient aiming point. When it hit, the shell penetrated the roof and upper floor before bursting on the ground floor where Gaines and his staff were seated at a table eating their dinner. The explosion severely wounded Gaines and that same day he crossed to Buffalo to seek medical attention – he would not return to active service during the war. Brigadier-General Eleazar W. Ripley being absent, command at Fort Erie devolved on Brevet Brigadier-General James Miller and a messenger was sent to find Major-General Jacob Brown and inform him of the change of command.[2]

Brown was at Canandaigua, New York, about ninety-five miles from Buffalo. Since being wounded at the battle of Lundy's Lane just over a month earlier, Brown had been staying with his family at various friends in the northern part of New York State, first at Genesee, then Aurora and finally Canandaigua, to recover from his wounds. These wounds, although not serious, were painful and prevented Brown from riding a horse but he had not been inactive during his convalescence – in fact it might be said that he never really relinquished command of the Left Division. He had tried to procure reinforcements for the formation although the best he had accomplished was to obtain about three hundred New York militia from a call for a thousand men. In the last week of August he met with Brigadier-General Peter B. Porter, commanding the volunteer brigade in the division, who had left Fort Erie to assist in raising the state militia. Porter had issued a somewhat bombastic, but clearly heartfelt, proclamation that was posted throughout the northwestern part of New York. Calling for volunteers, it reminded its readers that

> If the fate of the gallant little army which for six weeks past has been wading through fields of blood for your security, composed in part, too, of your own immediate neighbours and friends, cannot move you to action, I admonish you to recollect that on the support, and immediate and vigorous support of that army depends your own security. That army destroyed and your fruitful fields, your stately edifices, and your fair possessions are laid waste. Your women and children will feel the weight of the tomahawk. Nay, even liberty itself, without which those blessings are of no estimation in a patriot's heart, will forsake a country so unworthy of her protection.[3]

New York Governor Daniel D. Tompkins supported Brown and Porter, and their quest for volunteers was given concrete form on 30 August when Tompkins ordered 4,000 militiamen into service in Cayuga, Genessee, Ontario, Seneca and Steuben Counties. Each man was to bring a "musket or rifle, knapsack, canteen, cartridge box, three flints, a watch coat, and clothing for three months" and to be at Williamsville near Buffalo by 1 September.[4]

As soon as he received word of Gaines being wounded, Brown headed directly for Buffalo, where he arrived on 2 September. Where Brown went, action was sure to follow because the 39-year-old major-general was an aggressive and decisive natural leader. Practical, straightforward and determined, Brown's

Brigadier-General James Miller (1776-1851).
Chosen by Brown to lead the regular force component of the sortie force, Miller had a very good wartime record and had distinguished himself at Lundy's Lane, where his Twenty-First Infantry had captured the British artillery and the hill that was the key to the position. (Courtesy, Essex Institute, Salem, Negative 150222)

major weaknesses were that his determination could turn into obstinacy and his temper, which he tried hard to keep in check, sometimes got the better of him.[5]

At Buffalo, Brown immediately crossed over to Fort Erie "to see the real condition of his command and to determine with prudence the steps to be taken to preserve the remainder of his deeply suffering heroic forces."[6] It was evident to Brown that the Left Division was withering – on 31 July it had mustered 2,222 officers and men, but a month later it had risen only to 2,246 all ranks, despite having received small but constant drafts of reinforcements. Brown issued a series of orders that placed Ripley in command of Fort Erie, reminded the division of its illustrious record and doubled its whisky ration – the latter being well received for, as one wise historian has remarked, those "difficult hours called for drink, lots of it."[7] He then returned to Buffalo to expedite the organization of the militia who by now were flocking into Williamsville, where an officer reported them to be "in high spirits" and "full of fight."[8]

Brown knew that Major-General George Izard was moving west with his division to join him but he had no definite word as to when that officer would arrive. He also had serious doubts whether Izard would act aggressively when he did arrive. By this time Brown had learned of the capture of Washington and realized that he could expect no help from that quarter. He discussed the matter with Major Thomas S. Jesup, the commanding officer of the Twenty-Fifth Infantry, who was on light duties at Buffalo while recovering from wounds he had received at Lundy's Lane. Jesup recalled that Brown was convinced that he would have "to rely on his own resources – that though aid was promised him from other quarters, the daily losses at Fort Erie were such, that it would not reach him in time to save his division."[9] "We must, therefore," Brown concluded, "do the business ourselves."[10]

During the evening of 3 September, Brown was possibly cogitating on that business when he had a visit from Major Eleazar Wood. The engineer told him,

Major Thomas S. Jesup (1788-1860). Another distinguished veteran, Jesup had been wounded four times while leading the Twenty-Fifth Infantry at Lundy's Lane. He was an excellent combat officer, whose opinion was valued by Brown. (Courtesy, Washington National Cathedral)

"as a private friend," that "it was not safe to leave the army with General Ripley," because "no confidence could be reposed in that officer" and "with such a commander the moral efficiency of the army would be lost." If Brown, therefore, "hoped to preserve the honor of his command, he must return to camp and remain with his suffering soldiers in the face of the enemy."[11] Shortly after Wood exited, Major Roger Jones, the assistant adjutant general of the division, entered and Brown questioned him about Ripley. Jones "concurred in sentiment" with Wood and that decided the thing for Brown – he immediately crossed over to Fort Erie and assumed command.

His engineers were certain the British were building a new battery in the woods much closer to the fort. They knew its approximate location and warned that, when it opened fire, it "would rake obliquely our whole encampment."[12] As his men were already "very impatient under the fire" of the British artillery, Brown decided to mount a sortie to eliminate this threat. The enemy's bombardment had slackened in the last few days and on 7 September Brown was able to hold a parade of the entire division in an attempt to improve morale. The next day he called an orders group of his senior officers to discuss a possible sortie. By now almost everyone in Fort Erie knew that Izard was on the way – although the defenders had nicknamed him "Amberzard" for the amount of time he was taking to complete his movement – and the senior officers advised Brown to do nothing until Izard arrived on the Niagara. Brown was disappointed in his subordinates' reaction as he expected them to share his aggressive posture. He still favoured an offensive move and, after the meeting broke up, told Jesup that, while "We must keep our own counsel & the impression must be made that we are done with the affair" of an attack "as sure as there is a God in heaven, the enemy shall be attacked in his works, and shall be beaten too, so soon as all the Volunteers shall have passed over" from Buffalo.[13]

If Brown was frustrated with his senior regular officers, he could take comfort in the fact that the militia were coming forth in great numbers. By the first

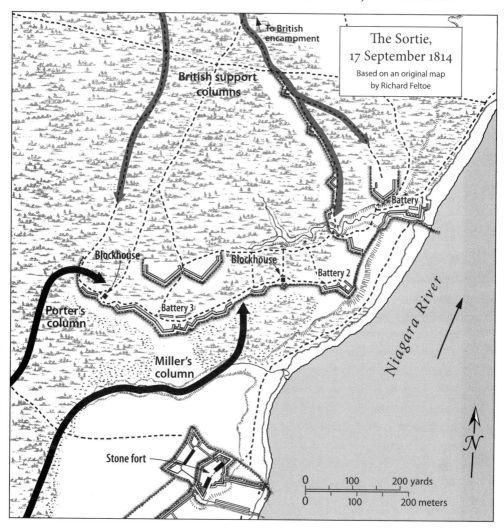

The Sortie,
17 September 1814

Based on an original map
by Richard Feltoe

To British encampment

British support columns

Battery 1

Blockhouse

Blockhouse

Battery 2

Porter's column

Battery 3

Miller's column

Niagara River

Stone fort

N

| 0 | 100 | 200 yards |
| 0 | 100 | 200 meters |

few days of September, nearly 4,000 men had assembled in Buffalo, where they were organized into units and began drilling. This did not necessarily mean that they would cross into Canada because they were not legally obliged to serve outside the United States unless they volunteered to do so. Happily, many showed great enthusiasm to cross the Niagara, and one senior militia officer remarked that "if they do not, the disappointment will be very great indeed."[14] Wisely, Porter did not immediately call for volunteers but concentrated on organizing and drilling the new arrivals to give them a smattering of unit cohesion and pride. On 7 September he held a parade of all the militia to begin the task of separating the wheat from the chaff. According to an eyewitness, after a patriotic address from Porter, the militia were paraded in line and volunteers called for. Several of the most prominent of the officers – among whom was Gen. Peter B. Porter – rode along in the front, making the most urgent appeals to their manhood and love of country to cross the river and rescue those who were in such imminent peril. A line was soon formed on the opposite side by volunteers, which was constantly augmented by those more courageous than their fellows. Then, again, there would be a stand-still till the officers gave a few more lectures in front – and thus the number continued to increase for the best part of a day, until there were only about a hundred left who were unwilling to cross.[15]

Those militiamen reluctant to volunteer were jeered unmercifully by their counterparts – Brown attempted to shame the officers who refused to cross the river by telling them "that if they wished to return home," he would send troops to guard them on the journey "that they might not be hurt."[16] By using a shrewd combination of jeers, cheers, patriotism and bullying, Porter obtained nearly 1,500 reinforcements for the Left Division at Fort Erie while those who stayed behind were assigned to guard duties at Black Rock, Buffalo and Williamsville, releasing regular troops for service in Canada.[17]

Few of the volunteers had uniforms so Porter ordered them to tie red cloth around their necks or arms to identify themselves to their regular comrades. Many were unarmed and the state and federal arsenals were nearly empty because of the attrition of previous wartime campaigns. Quartermasters issued British and French weapons and militia officers scoured their unit areas for arms and equipment issued during previous call-outs, but which had not been returned. Fortunately, weapons were available at Fort Erie because, as Captain Benjamin Ropes of the Twenty-First Infantry recalled, the Left Division had gathered about 1,300 "Stands of arms" after the battle of Chippawa and the assault of 15 August, and they were issued to those who needed them.[18] By now, the regular army quartermaster at Buffalo had amassed a fleet of more than forty boats which operated a regular transport service from the village to the fort and Porter used these to shift his volunteers across the river on the nights of 8, 9 and 10 September. The transfer was done so quietly and quickly, Douglass recalled, that few of the regular troops in the fort were aware of it until they noticed that "a considerable camp of Volunteers was formed on the lake-shore" south of Snake Hill. It was clear to every officer and man in the division that something was brewing. "Everything," Douglass commented, "pointed towards an approaching *coup de main*" or attack "but when, and in what manner, was reserved to the secret councils of the Commander-in-chief," to which few were admitted.[19]

The new British artillery position which so concerned Brown was Battery No. 3. Drummond had ordered Philpotts to construct it when it became clear that Battery No. 2 was not as destructive as he had hoped and it was intended to "open the rear face and complete the destruction" of the stone fort.[20] The engineer placed it about 350 yards nearly due west of Battery No. 2 and about 300 yards from the stone fort, and on 1 September the sappers commenced work. Progress was good, assisted no doubt by the fact that there was no rain in the first few days of September – a rare thing at Fort Erie – and Battery No. 3 was completed in two days and armed with a 24-pdr. iron gun, two 18-pdr. iron guns and an 8-inch iron mortar. It was Philpotts's understanding that Battery No. 3 would commence firing on 6 September, but when that day came, no orders to do so were received and Philpotts's men were actually "allowed to rest a little, our labour having hitherto been very fatiguing."[21] This was no exaggeration as Philpotts's journal reveals that this was the first rest his officers and sappers had enjoyed in nearly five weeks.

Given its position and powerful armament, Battery No. 3 would have had a most destructive effect on the American defences. After consulting with his artillery commander, Major Henry Phillot, however, Drummond decided to delay using it. As he explained to Prevost:

> I determined not to open its fire until the small supply of disposable ammunition which remained at Fort George had been brought up, and until by the arrival of the 97th Regt. I might have it in my power to take advantage of the impression it might produce by an assault on place, should such a measure appear advisable. The ammunition now on its way from the forts leaves them with little more than 200 rounds per gun, and with very little powder, nor is there any prospect of a supply until the arrival of the squadron or of part of the vessels from Kingston. Under these alarming circumstances it becomes absolutely necessary that I should husband every round of my remaining stock of ammunition.[22]

Drummond's caution is understandable because a British artillery manual of the period stipulates that a besieger should have 50 rounds per gun and 30 shells per mortar available for firing *every day*. By this standard, Drummond's gunners only had enough ammunition for about four days of heavy bombardment and it made sense for him to restrict them to one round per hour, day and night, until he had amassed more ammunition or was ready to mount an assault. It was for this reason that Brown could parade the entire Left Division without suffering losses.[23]

There was no doubt, however, that the defenders felt threatened by the new battery. On Sunday, 4 September, they launched one of the biggest outpost actions of the siege. It began in the early afternoon when one of the American pickets under Captain Horace Hale of the Eleventh Infantry started scrapping with its corresponding British picket. Hale was reinforced by a large detachment from Porter's volunteer brigade under the command of Lieutenant-Colonel Joseph Willcocks, a former member of the Legislative Assembly of Upper Canada who had crossed the lines to join the American army. According to his second-in-command, Willcocks launched an attack on the British picket and the volunteers,

> drove them from their position and entered within their outer breastwork in fair view of their battery where we maintained our position for about 15 to 20 minutes, when Col. Willcocks received a mortal wound by a shot through the right breast, when he, together with all those injured, were bore off. Discovering their forces to be vastly superior to ours, and rapidly reinforcing, we gave them two volleys, a cheer for victory, and retired in good order.[24]

In the American camp, a general order was issued praising Willcocks, whose name was now added the list of "gallant heroes who during this unexampled campaign, have gloriously died on the field of honour."[25] In the British camp the reaction to the news of Willcocks's demise was the cause of much rejoicing – particularly in the ranks of the Canadian units – when the "death of that arch-rebel" was announced.[26]

By the first week of September Drummond was starting to have serious doubts about his ability to take Fort Erie and eject the Americans from Canada. This was certainly the opinion of his new second-in-command, Major-General Louis de Watteville, who arrived on 1 September to replace the injured Major-General Henry Conran. The 48-year-old scion of an aristocratic Swiss mercenary family, De Watteville had served in the 1790s with the Dutch and Austrian armies before switching to the British army in 1801 to take command of the regiment created by his uncle. He had seen considerable action in the Mediterranean, including participation in the battle of Maida in 1806, for which he received a field officer's gold medal. De Watteville was also experienced in siege warfare as he spent two years with his regiment defending the Spanish city of Cadiz against the French before being transferred to Canada in 1813. On his arrival, he was promoted to major-general and placed in command of French-speaking *Canadien* units in Lower Canada and had played a significant part in securing the victory at the battle of Chateauguay the previous autumn. Efficient and taciturn, De Watteville was a hard-headed professional who was always prepared to call a spade a shovel (for that is what it is) and to face the truth, no matter how unattractive. After first having made a careful inspection of the British lines on 4 September, De Watteville went straight to Drummond and told him plain that he "should immediately abandon the position at Ft. Erie."[27]

Drummond was not quite prepared to do that but it is clear that he was contemplating a withdrawal. He began to lay the ground work with Prevost for such a move, informing him that

> I shall continue to act according to circumstances, and shall not fail to avail myself of any favourable opportunity which may offer of attacking the enemy. But should no such offer present itself, I feel it incumbent on me to prepare Your Excellency for the possibility of my being compelled by the sickness or suffering of the troops, exposed as they will be to the effects of the wet and unhealthy season which is fast approaching, to withdraw them from their present position to one which may afford them the means of cover.[28]

These words were written on Thursday, 8 September 1814 and that was the day the rains came. The month of August had been unseasonably wet but it was nothing compared to the near monsoon that commenced that day and continued for almost two weeks.* During this time, Philpotts recorded, the weather "was very impossible" and "we had great trouble in keeping the trenches at all dry."[29] The roads quickly became impassable and the constant deluge so weakened a bastion and a large part of the parapet at Fort Niagara that it collapsed and slid into Lake Ontario. Conditions in the British lines, which were never good, now became nearly unbearable. "The Trenches were filled with Water, & the chilling blasts of Autumn began to be felt," John Norton recalled, and the men on duty "were exposed without Shelter to the Storm as well as to the Shot of the Enemy, and those reposing in the Encampment were only out of reach of the fire from the hostile Batteries."[30] Misery abounded and only the most confirmed optimist or the worst fool could have found any solace in the situation.

Throughout the operations at Fort Erie, there had been a steady two-way traffic of deserters. Those arriving in the British lines in early September brought information about the reinforcements that had crossed the river. It was not long before it was general knowledge, as Philpotts noted, that the enemy's strength was increasing and "the number of men in the Fort far exceeded our small army" and that arrangements would have to be made "for resisting a strong attack."[31] The engineers' part in this was to construct two small

---

* For information on the weather during the siege, see Appendix G.

blockhouses, one to the right of Battery No. 3 and the other near Battery No. 2, but a shortage of tools prevented their being completed. "Every preparation," Drummond assured Prevost, "has been made to give the enemy a warm reception."[32] He ordered his senior officers to keep a "most vigilant look out" at all the batteries" and stressed that, if attacked, the brigade on duty was "to defend the Batteries to the last," emphasizing that if the men on duty were "steady and resolute, reserve their fire until the enemy is well within their reach" then "no number of enemy can make any impression on them."[33]

On 14 September Drummond communicated a lengthy list of his woes to Prevost. He complained that the conditions in his lines were "most distressing" as his men "were without tents, and the huts in which they are placed are wholly incapable of affording shelter against such severe weather."[34] He pointed out that his provisions were almost exhausted, that he lacked sufficient draft animals to remove his heavy ordnance and that, because of Chauncey's blockade of the mouth of the Niagara, the 97th Foot had been forced to move by land, delaying their arrival. Drummond added that he expected the defenders to make a sortie, although, in his opinion, such an event might be the best thing to happen "as it will bring us into contact with the enemy at a far cheaper rate than if we were to be the assailants" and might also "bring to a happy crisis a campaign which has been marked by a series of unlucky circumstances, as well as of late severe hardships and privations on the part of the troops."[35] Despite such confident statements, it was evident from his communications that the British commander had more or less decided to withdraw from Fort Erie but remained somewhat reluctant to take the final step.

On 16 September, explaining to Prevost that conditions were so bad that he could no longer "persevere in a vain attempt to maintain a blockade of so vastly a superior and increasing a force of the enemy," Drummond ordered the guns to be withdrawn from the batteries.[36] In his journal for that day Philpotts recorded that

> The 97th Regt not having yet arrived as was expected, and the force of the Enemy being daily augmented by new Regiments and by Militia while ours was diminishing by sickness, in consequence of continued rain: and there not being a tent in the Army the guns were ordered to be withdrawn from the batteries and during this afternoon the brass 24 Prs were removed from [Battery] No. 2 and the 8 In Mortar from No. 3 Battery.[37]

It was heavy, wet, muddy and thoroughly miserable work to pull the heavy guns from their positions, and Philpotts and the other engineer and artillery officers were hard at it on the following afternoon when Brown launched his attack.

Lieutenant Douglass's suspicion that Brown was planning a sortie was entirely accurate. The American commander had not given up on the idea of offensive action despite the lack of support for the idea demonstrated by his senior officers during the council of war held on 8 September. Brown had carefully questioned all the British and Canadian deserters who had crossed into his lines and was aware that Drummond had moved his camp farther from his batteries. He also knew that, at any given time, only one of the three small brigades in the besieging force – about 1,200 to 1,500 men – would be on duty in the British entrenchments. Brown calculated that if he could launch a surprise attack with superior force against this brigade, he could seriously damage or destroy Drummond's heavy artillery before enemy reinforcements arrived. As he later commented, his object was "to storm the batteries, destroy the cannon, and roughly handle the brigade upon duty before those in reserve could be brought into the action."[38]

Brown kept his own counsel while he contemplated the best course of action. He seems to have made the decision to attack during 15 September, as on that day he ordered Lieutenants Donald Frazer and David Riddle of the Fifteenth Infantry to go out on the following day and mark a route from the southern part of the American perimeter toward the right flank of the British lines. The next day the two officers led a fatigue party that carried out this task "with so much caution, that they passed the extreme right of the enemy's line and turned upon the rear of his batteries, without discovery."[39] Brown planned to use this route to get Porter's brigade into a position whereby it could attack Battery No. 3. At the same time a force of regular troops under Brigadier-General James Miller would clandestinely take position in a ravine that was nearly opposite the British centre. As soon as Porter attacked, Miller would seize the British entrenchment between Batteries Nos. 2 and 3 and then assist Porter to take Batteries Nos. 1 and 2. In the meantime, Colonel Hugh Brady, commanding at Buffalo, would take his Twenty-Second Infantry and march in plain view down the American side of the Niagara to give the impression that an attack was planned in the British rear. The sortie was to take place during the afternoon of 17 September but, as a security measure, Brown only communicated it to Porter and Majors McRee and Wood at 9 P.M. on the previous evening.*

In the morning of Saturday, 17 September, Brown, feeling somewhat guilty that he had not informed his second-in-command, Brigadier-General Eleazar

---

* Although he does not mention it in his memorandum of the campaign, Brown must also have informed Brigadier-General James Miller at this time or shortly thereafter of his plans as Miller was tasked with an important role in the attack.

Ripley, of the planned attack, called that officer to his headquarters and briefed him on the operation. Ripley's reaction was completely negative – he stated that he was glad that he had no part in the forthcoming sortie, as he believed it to be a "hopeless one and that he should be well satisfied to escape from the disgrace that in his judgement should fall upon all engaged in it."[40] These were fairly strong words to speak to a superior, particularly a superior who had been consistently disappointed by Ripley's conduct during the campaign. In his behaviour Ripley was actually sailing close to the wind of insubordination and in peril of being charged under the Articles of War, particularly No. 6 ("Any officer … who shall behave himself with contempt or disrespect towards his commanding officer" shall be court martialled) and No. 24 ("No officer … shall use any reproachful or provoking speeches to another" on pain of arrest) or the useful "catch all" Article No. 99, which stipulated that all crimes and disorders not otherwise mentioned in the Articles of War shall "be punished at the discretion" of a general court martial.[41] By this time, however, it seems that Brown had given up trying to make a general out of Ripley and, as he later dryly remarked, was actually "gratified" that Ripley "claimed no situation in the attack, as such a claim at the moment would have been very embarrassing."[42] A few hours later, however, Ripley changed his mind and asked for command of the reserve, which Brown gave him, probably thinking that while holding this appointment, the lawyer-turned-general could do little damage.

The weather on 17 September was very favourable for clandestine movement. Douglass recalled that the "atmosphere was heavily loaded with vapors with, now and then, a slight shower" which not only screened the American advance but also lulled the "enemy's sense of security."[43] Late in the morning the Left Division assembled for the attack. The main assault column consisting of Porter's volunteers, bolstered by regular troops, took up a position south of Snake Hill. It was composed of three elements. Colonel James Gibson commanded the advance element of 200 riflemen from the First and Fourth Rifle Regiments and a few Seneca and Tuscarora warriors. The remainder of the brigade was divided into two columns, which would move through the woods parallel to each other and about thirty yards apart. The column on the right, commanded by Major Eleazar Wood, consisted of 500 New York volunteers and 400 regulars, mainly drawn from the Twenty-Third Infantry. The column on the left was commanded by New York Brigadier-General Daniel Davis and comprised three regiments of volunteers totalling about 500 men. Brigadier-General Miller's force of regulars, consisting of the Ninth and Eleventh Infantry and a detachment of the Nineteenth, moved by small groups as quietly as possible out into the ravine between the opposing lines and deployed in a position about 800 feet from the British entrenchments. The reserve under Ripley, consisting of the Twenty-First Infantry and a detachment of the Seventeenth, took post in the newly constructed outlying bastions of Fort Erie. Finally, Major Thomas Jesup was placed in command of the camp with the Twenty-Fifth Infantry, the artillery and the invalids.[44] All his troops, Brown noted, were "under cover and out of the view of the enemy."[45]

Shortly before noon, the assault columns moved forward. At the same time, Brady's Twenty-Second Infantry marched on the River Road north along the American side of the Niagara River and were observed by British sentries on the Canadian bank, who reported the movement, causing concern that the Americans were, as Surgeon Dunlop remarked, planning "to cross and take us in rear."[46] Despite the undergrowth and the rain, the columns of Gibson, Wood and Davis, guided by Lieutenants Frazer and Riddle, made good time and by about 2.30 P.M. were very close to the British picket guarding the right flank of the British line. At the same time Miller's force moved quietly along the ravine until they were nearly at the treeline behind which was the British entrenchment.

By now, the intermittent showers that had been a feature of the morning had turned into a steady downpour, which served to limit vision and cloak noise. Whether intentional or not, Brown had decided to attack on a day when De Watteville's Regiment was on duty. The men of this foreign regiment were wet and miserable and also annoyed that – unlike European warfare where the outposts and sentries of opposing armies behaved in a courteous manner and did not try to kill each other – the Americans made a thorough nuisance of themselves with their constant skirmishing. De Watteville's Regiment may have been alert when it went on duty but gradually the mist and the steady patter of rain lulled its men into a false sense of security just as Porter's columns approached their right flank and rear. Recruited from the flotsam and jetsam of the Napoleonic wars, including Frenchmen, Germans, Greeks, Hungarians, Italians, Poles and Swiss, the men of this unit were certainly not the elite of the British army and many, having survived fighting for Bonaparte, did not, in Dunlop's words, have any "ardent desire" to die for King George III.[47] For this reason, when Porter's men emerged from the brush with fixed bayonets and wild yells, they immediately crumbled. There was a babble of outrage, cries of fear and a few wild shots but one American remembered that many men from the foreign unit "threw away their arms, and in their attempts to run would fling themselves full length upon the ground, quite anxious and willing to be taken prisoner."[48]

Brown had stationed himself near Miller and, according to his watch, it was 2.40 P.M. when Gibson, Davis and Wood attacked the right flank of the British

New York State militia officer. Although often derided by their regular counterparts, the New York militia provided a strong reinforcement for the Left Division in the latter stages of the campaign when hundreds volunteered to serve in Canada. This officer wears the regulation uniform; not many were so well equipped. (Painting by H. C. McBarron, courtesy Parks Canada)

line. Private Amasiah Ford of the Twenty-Third Infantry recalled that the British picket "opened a brisk fire upon us" and one of his messmates "was shot dead at my right side," inspiring Ford with a thirst for revenge.[49] The three elements of Porter's brigade, about 1,600 men, threw themselves at the enemy picket overwhelming it and then attacked the unfinished blockhouse that had been constructed to guard Battery No. 3. Private Ford remembered that the Twenty-Third "charged upon the blockhouse from which the enemy kept up a brisk fire until they were compelled to surrender" and "took about eighty prisoners while the ground was strewed with the dead bodies of the enemy."[50]

Porter's men next overran Battery No. 3 and set about trying to wreck the 24-pdr. and two 18-pdr. guns that were in the battery. They "spiked" these weapons by driving iron spikes or a bayonet down their vents – the small aperture by which the weapon was fired – and then breaking them off so that the weapon could not be used until this plug had been drilled out, a laborious and time-consuming process. All three guns were mounted on travelling carriages with large wheels and so men chopped the spokes with axes until the weapons collapsed. They then attempted to knock off the trunnions, the short, stubby projections on either side of the barrel by which the gun was fastened to the carriage but had less luck as they lacked both time and the proper tools. There was a small expense magazine with about a thousand cartridges in it and half of these were taken away to be used against their former owners while Riddle of the Fifteenth blew the remainder up using rounds of fixed ammunition. Unfortunately, Riddle either miscalculated the length or the burning rate of his fuze because he "suffered severely by the explosion."[51]

As soon as Miller heard the musketry from Porter's attack, he moved his command forward in open column preceded by an advance guard under Ensign Patrick O'Flyng of the Ninth Infantry. Miller's men entered the woods and seized part of the British line between Batteries No. 2 and 3. This section was defended by the 8th Foot, a more solid unit than De Watteville's Regiment, and it put up a stiff fight. Drummer Jarvis Hanks remembered that when the Eleventh Infantry came upon the enemy "there was quite a little engagement, with their picket guards and several of our officers and men killed," among them Hanks's company commander, Captain Horace Hale.[52] "We had no alternative," Miller reported, "but to fall on them, beat them, and take them" but it was not an easy fight. Lieutenant-Colonel Thomas Aspinwall, commanding the Ninth Infantry, remembered that Miller's brigade

> passed through the wood, driving in their sharp shooters, sentries and guards, until I had arrived within 20 paces of their breastworks, where, as I was passing along the front of the first platoon to give it a concerted direction to the right, I received a musket-shot above the elbow of the left arm, which completely carried away about an inch and a half of the bone. I, of course, had no further part in the active duty of that day.[53]

Aspinwall was not the only officer to fall as Major William Trimble, leading the Nineteenth, was also wounded, as were nine other officers of Miller's brigade.[54]

Once the Americans were in the entrenchments, Hanks recalled, the British "seemed to be thunderstruck" and some "surrendered at pleasure" but the remainder, attacked in front, flank and rear, could do nothing and fell back towards the British camp.[55] Miller quickly consolidated his position. He was then joined by Gibson and his riflemen and the combined force moved on Battery No. 2, but by now British resistance was beginning to stiffen. Sergeant James Commins of the 8th Foot was part of the company defending Battery No. 2 and recalled that his company commander, Lieutenant Charles Barstow (a personal friend of Le Couteur)

> lost his life in rallying some of De Watteville's Regiment who was on duty with him at the battery, but who attempted to leave it on the approach of the enemy and would not stand to their post. A Musket Ball went through his heart. He died instanteously [sic] in a Noble Cause, that of Defending His Country.[56]

Battery No. 2 was eventually taken but the only ordnance in it was a 24-pdr. carronade on a field carriage – it was spiked and the spokes of the carriage wheels cut by axe.[57]

In the British camp, the officers and men off duty had been eating their dinner when the sound of musketry was heard coming from the vicinity of Battery

No. 3. It was first thought that it originated from yet another of the seemingly endless outpost skirmishes. As the firing not only continued but increased in volume, Drummond realized that a major attack was underway and, being a veteran soldier, was quick to react, as was De Watteville. Drummond ordered Lieutenant-Colonel John Gordon to take his 1st Brigade, which consisted of the 1st, 82nd and 89th Foot, and recover the two batteries. Meanwhile, Lieutenant-Colonel Thomas Pearson was ordered to take his light demi-brigade to support Gordon, while the 6th Foot remained in camp as a reserve.*

These orders were swiftly but not completely carried out. Instead of supporting Gordon, Pearson led the Glengarry Light Infantry to a position just to the right of Battery No. 1, where it was soon fiercely engaged with Miller and Gibson, who were moving against that position. Miller reported that his troops came under such heavy fire that they were forced to fall back to regroup, a process that was made difficult by casualties among the officers, including Gibson, who had been mortally wounded, and Lieutenant Lewis Armistead, the brother of the officer who had commanded Fort McHenry during the British bombardment that had taken place four days before.† Miller later noted that he and Colonel Moody Bedel of the Eleventh Infantry were the only officers in his command higher than the rank of lieutenant who were not killed or wounded during the action. On the British side, Pearson, a veteran of war on three continents, suffered the fifth wound of his career when a musket or rifle bullet struck him in the head and he was carried away, deaf and blind.

While the light brigade stopped cold the American advance toward Battery No. 1, Gordon led the 1st Brigade forward to recover the other batteries. He found a remnant of the 8th Foot defending an entrenchment behind the main line and, using this as a springboard, directed the 1st and 89th Foot against the blockhouse to the right of Battery No. 3 while the 82nd, assisted by three companies of the 6th, moved directly against Battery No. 2. At least this is how the British movements were described in the official reports of Drummond and De Watteville but, when writing a report, a general's job is to make sense out of chaos (and also, of course, to put the brightest face on all events, even a disaster). In actual fact, the fighting at Fort Erie on 17 September was not a set-piece affair that was susceptible to orderly narration; it was a confused, swirling, engagement between small groups of men, a soldier's battle that was more like a barroom brawl than a military action. As Porter explained:

---

* See Appendix F for information on the opposing forces on 17 September.

† He was also the uncle of Brigadier-General Lewis A. Armistead, CSA, who would die leading a brigade in Pickett's division during its famous charge at the battle of Gettysburg, 3 July 1863.

The studied intricacy of the enemy's defences, consisting not only of the breastwork connecting their batteries but of successive lines of entrenchments for a hundred yards in the rear, covering the batteries and enfilading each other, and the whole obstructed by *abbatis*, brush, and felled timber, was calculated to produce confusion among the assailants and led to several conflicts at the point of the bayonet. ...... Our success would probably have been more complete but for the rain, which unfortunately set in soon after we commenced our march, which rendered the fire of many muskets useless, and by obscuring the sun led to several unlucky mistakes.[58]

Both attackers and defenders lost cohesion and the fight became a struggle between small groups of men led by relatively junior officers under a continual downpour of rain.

Captain Robert Pattison of the 82nd Foot rushed Battery No. 2 with a couple of companies from his unit. It was crowded with Americans and an incident occurred that is not uncommon in combat when men are crazed by the heat of battle. After the British "poured a volley into the mass of the enemy, who were huddled together into so small a space that they could not return it," Pattison

called out to the American officer in command to surrender, as resistance would only cause loss of life and could do no good. He [the American] did give an order to ground arms, and some of his men were in the act of doing so, when an American soldier raised his rifle and shot Pattison through the heart. In one moment a charge was made by the 82nd into the battery, and every soul in it put to the bayonet, amounting ... to upwards of two hundred men.[59]

The number killed is an exaggeration but Le Couteur, who later talked to officers who were present at the scene, recorded that the recapture of Battery No. 2 "was a very savage affair" as "our Men bayoneted every Soul" and the battery "was full of corpses."[60]

At the same time, Gordon led the 1st and 89th Foot against Battery No. 3. William Dunlop, that fighting surgeon, took part in this attack and recalled that he met

with about twenty of the men of my own Regiment, and took them with me, being guided to where the fire was thickest by the noise. I found myself along with my friend, Mautass, a Soc [Sauk] Chief, and his Indians. I had an opportunity to seeing bush-fighting in the Indian fashion. It seemed to me to be a point with them at every discharge of their rifle to shift their position, and whenever they knocked a fellow over, their yelling was horrible. I was close to Mautass himself, and whenever he performed this feat, after giving the triumphal yell, he jumped behind a tree, and seemed to be engaged in a prayer – perhaps to thank the great Spirit for his success, or as likely to petition him that he might knock over a few more.[61]

Private Ford of the Twenty-Third Infantry, who was defending Battery No. 3, could attest to the volume and accuracy of fire. He had stationed himself with his comrades "behind the enemy's breastworks while they retreated about eight rods [forty-four feet] into the woods behind another breastwork" where the two sides exchanged fire.[62] Ford was "in the act of discharging my piece at a Red Coat when a ball passed through my cap directly under my cockade" so he fired back at his target or mark, "at the same time & never saw my mark again."

The struggle for Battery No. 3 was basically a musketry duel, which continued for some time and both opponents suffered severely. Gordon was killed while Porter lost Davis and Wood, his two column commanders. Porter himself had a very close call after he went out from the blockhouse near Battery No. 3 with a few men to check on some firing he heard in that direction, only to run into a company of British infantry, clearly confused about which direction they should go. Porter, thinking quickly, grabbed a musket from the nearest redcoat and demanded that the remainder surrender. This almost worked but the British soon recovered and, surrounding Porter, demanded that he surrender. Things were not looking bright for the commander of the volunteer brigade but at that moment a company of volunteer riflemen from Cayuga County, New York, happened on the scene and opened fire on the British, which distracted them long enough for Porter to escape with no worse damage than a cut on his hand suffered when an enemy officer tried to slash him with his sword.[63]

It was now clear to Brown that the British had recovered and were pressing on his division from all sides. He therefore ordered Ripley to come forward with his reserve to where Brown was positioned, midway between the lines. True to form, Ripley got it wrong and, as Brown later commented, his order "was either misunderstood or disobeyed" because Ripley "moved his command in a different direction" and it was not until Brown sent him a second order that he arrived where Brown was located.[64] Brown impressed upon Ripley that, as he was now the senior officer, he should establish what the situation was "and to have a care that not more was hazarded than the occasion required" and, if the objectives of the attack had been completed, he should withdraw.[65] Ripley moved off but had gone barely a hundred feet when he was hit by a mus-

British infantry about to open fire. Although initially shaken by the American attack, Drummond's troops quickly recovered and took back the two lost batteries. The sortie of 17 August was a confusing, vicious melee in which both sides suffered heavy casualties. (Courtesy, Friends of Fort George)

ket ball "which penetrated through his neck between the throat and spine" and was carried "from the field, insensible from loss of blood."[66]

As soon as he learned of this event, Brown decided that "the object of the sortie" had been accomplished and ordered a withdrawal to his own lines.[67] As the assault forces fell back to the fort in some confusion, Dunlop remembered, the British warriors

> who had shown so much wariness in the fight, and had talked to me of the folly of my young men exposing themselves, suddenly seemed to lose all their caution, and bounded forward with a horrible yell, threw themselves on the retreating enemy with their tomahawks, and were soon out of our sight; but as we advanced, we saw they left their trace behind them in sundry cleft skulls. They also, when their opponents were from fifteen to twenty yards in advance of them, threw their tomahawks with unerring aim and great force, burying the head of the hatchet up to the eye in the body of their opponents.[68]

The British did not pursue too far because, as soon as they emerged from the woods, Jesup ordered the American artillery to open up to cover the withdrawal of their comrades.

The battle had lasted less than two hours. When it ended, De Watteville commented, "the entrenchments were again occupied, and the line of picquets established as it had been previous to the enemy's attack."[69] Dunlop returned to his medical duties and "traversed the ground with a strong party to look out for the wounded, and finding only a few of the enemy, I ordered them to be carried to the hospital."[70] One of the wounded American officers calmly told the surgeon that his wounds were mortal and to leave him and tend to those who could be saved. Dunlop had this officer carried

> to a hut belonging to an officer of my own Regiment, who undertook to sit by him till my return. After he had been put to bed, I left him, and when I returned during the night from my hospital, he was dead. He proved to be Colonel [Eleazar] Wood of the American Engineers – a man equally admired for his talents and revered for his virtues. His calmness and courage in the hour of death, with his benevolence and kindness to myself and others, who were doing any little they could to render his last moments easy, convinced me that he deserved the high character which all his brother officers that I afterwards met with uniformly gave him.[71]

In his official report on the sortie, Brown characterized Wood as a "brave, generous, and enterprizing" officer who "died as he had lived, without a feeling but for the honor of his country and the glory of her arms."[72] While searching the bodies of the American dead, Norton remembered that someone found "the account of the Naval Victory, which they had gained over our fleet upon Lake Champlain" and for the first time the British Right Division learned of the defeat of its sister formation at Plattsburgh.[73]

Casualties on both sides were heavy. Brown reported losing a total of 511 men: 79 killed, 216 wounded and 216 missing. Drummond admitted to losing 579 men comprising 115 killed, 148 wounded and 316 missing with no fewer than 264 casualties being suffered by De Watteville's Regiment.[74] Most of the British missing were actually prisoners.

Thomas Jesup believed that the sortie from Fort Erie on 17 September was "by far the most splendid achievement" of the 1814 Niagara campaign, "whether we consider the boldness of the conception, the excellence of the plan, or the ability of the execution."[75] It was entirely understandable that, as the Right Division shortly withdrew from Fort Erie, Brown believed his sortie to be the cause of the British retreat, as have most historians who have since written on the subject. It was only very recently, when the journal of Lieutenant George Philpotts was discovered in the British archives, that it was learned that Drummond had definitely decided to withdraw before the sortie took place and his men were actually involved in removing the ordnance from the batteries when the defenders attacked.* Nonetheless, Major-General Jacob Brown could take credit for a well-planned and executed operation, which signalled that, after more than two years of war and numerous defeats, the American army had become a professional fighting force that had to be treated with respect.

In the next four days, as the British gunners and engineers finished removing the guns from the batteries, it rained so heavily that their camp resembled "a lake in the woods."[76] By the evening of 21 September all the guns, stores and *impedimenta* had been sent safely away and only the infantry brigades remained in the British lines, lighting large fires every night to make the Americans think that they were going to remain in position. The sounding of "tattoo," the traditional end of the day call in the British army, on the evening of 21 September was the signal for the Right Division to abandon Fort Erie and march north on the River Road to Frenchman's Creek, four miles from the fort, where it "bivouacked for the night under torrents of rain."[77]

---

* This information first appeared in print in my book *Where Right and Glory Lead: The Battle of Lundy's Lane, 1814*, the second volume in the "Forgotten Soldiers" trilogy, which was originally published in 1993.

American staff and rifle officers. By the third year of the war, American army staffs had learned their trade and become very efficient. The rifle officer wears the new grey rifle uniform introduced in the spring of 1814. The First and Fourth Rifle Regiments played a prominent part in the siege of Fort Erie and paid the price. (Courtesy, U.S. Army Art Collection)

CHAPTER FOURTEEN

"The prettiest little affair any of us had ever seen"

ON THE NIAGARA, 21 SEPTEMBER–5 NOVEMBER 1814

Frae a'lang marches on rainy days,
And frae a' stappages out o' our pays,
And frae the washerwoman's bills, on the damned claise,
  Gude Lord deliver us

Frae mountin' guard whan the snaw rides deep,
And frae standing sentry whan ithers sleep,
And frae barrack beds, whar lice and bugs do creep,
  Gude Lord deliver us.

Frae a' bridewell cages and black holes,
And officers' canes, wi' their halbert poles,
And frae the nine-tailed cat that opposes our souls,
  Gude Lord deliver us.

May a' officers wha make poor men stand,
Tied up to the halbert, foot, thigh and hand,
Die rotten in the pox, and afterwards be damned,
  Gude Lord deliver us.[1]

Following his withdrawal from Fort Erie, Drummond deployed to counter an American advance north from that place or the possibility of a landing in his rear from the American side of the Niagara. Between Fort Erie and Chippawa, from south to north, six creeks flow into the Niagara – Putnam's, Frenchman's, Winterhoot's, Halfway, Black and Street's – at almost regular two- to three-mile intervals and Drummond took advantage of the obstacles they provided. He placed his light troops, the Incorporated Militia Battalion, the Glengarry Light Infantry and the force of western warriors, backed up by a squadron of the 19th Light Dragoons, some light artillery pieces and the 1st and 97th Foot, between Frenchman's Creek and the Chippawa (now the Welland) River. These advance units were under the command of Major-General Louis de Watteville. The 6th Foot was stationed at Chippawa with more artillery while the 82nd took post at Lundy's Lane, where Drummond located his head-quarters, and the 89th and 104th at Queenston. The 103rd, a collection of "use-less mouths" in Drummond's opinion, was sent to Burlington Heights while the remainder of the division was posted in the forts at the river's mouth.[2]

Drummond's greatest concern was the shortage of provisions and the de-plorable state of Fort Niagara, parts of which were disintegrating because of the recent heavy rainfall. Otherwise, he reported that his men were "well accom-modated in barns along the frontier, and are fast recovering from the effects of their late suffering" and would shortly be fit "to undertake any operations which the movements of the enemy may render necessary."[3]

In the days that followed the withdrawal, many units were pressed into the transport service to assist in getting the stores and heavy ordnance north of the Chippawa and beyond immediate American reach. Given the swift current of the Niagara, which became increasingly powerful as it approached the great falls, this could be very dangerous work. Among the units detailed for this ser-vice were the flank companies of the 104th Foot and Le Couteur remembered that at 11 P.M. on 22 September, he was awoken

and sent up with Batteaux for stores [at] Black Creek. Got there 2 in the morning and walked a mile through mud and water to Colonel [Christo-pher] Myers for orders. The Quarter Master General sent me back to take up my quarters in the commissariat store where I laid down in my harness, slept till 6, awoke half frozen and half dry. ......

After sending off the batteaux as they were loaded, and supplied with a good lunch, I started at three with three or four of the last boats of my bri-gade. I ordered them to keep in my wake exactly as I had the river Pilot on board with me. The last boat, instead of obeying My orders, tried to pull past some of the others and got out into the Stream. I shouted, we all shouted to them, but it was too late. She had got into the horrid, rapid Current of the everlasting Falls – We got along perfectly safely.

Saw the men straining every nerve to pull back towards us but, alas, they only made the matter worse by bad steering and the boat was going down broadside on. Some of the men then lost courage to pull, stripped and jumped into the stream to swim for it. One did get to Drake's Island, one got to the shore, the other was hurried over the Falls!! The Corporal, a brave fel-low, left two oars out, pulled first on one Side, then on the other, then some-how steered and shoved his great batteau on Drake's Island so that we soon sent native boatsmen to bring Him and the boat off.

It was a dismal sight, but entirely proceeded from disobedience of orders so I was not at all blamed.[4]

At Kingston, meanwhile, Commodore James Yeo had finally launched the *St. Lawrence* on 10 September. Although there was concern that the massive vessel might not be seaworthy, she went smoothly down the slipway into Navy Bay. The new ship's particulars were impressive: 191 feet on her upper deck, 157 feet on the keel, 52 feet in breadth at her widest point and 2,302 tons in displacement. Each of the three gun decks was pierced with 17 ports a side and she would eventually mount 34 24-pdr. guns on her upper deck, and 34 massive 32-pdr. guns on each of her two lower gundecks. The new ship's broadside weight of 1,496 lb. was equal to nearly half the weight of the American squadron on Lake Ontario, which possessed 3,324 lb. and when added to the 2,837 lb. of broadside in Yeo's other ships, gave him a massive superiority in firepower.[5] The *St. Lawrence* was the largest sailing warship ever constructed on the Great Lakes and was also one of the most powerful warships in the Royal Navy in 1814. A few days after her launch, Yeo moved into her spacious captain's quarters, which, well lit by seven large stern windows and with adjoining sleeping and toilet compartments, were far grander than anything available on shore in Kingston. The process of fitting out the new ship took more than a month, and during that time Yeo's American counterpart, Commodore Isaac Chauncey, occasionally looked into Kingston to see the progress being made. When he saw that the masts of the *St. Lawrence* were up and her rigging was nearing completion, Chauncey widely withdrew his squadron into Sackets Harbor in the first days of October and stayed there for the remainder of the year.[6]

Yeo refused, however, to be hurried in getting the new ship ready for an operational cruise. As September turned to October and the squadron remained at Kingston, Drummond's concern "on the score of provisions" increased "as he had discovered that the agricultural resources of many of the "abundant townships of this frontier have, on a scrutiny, greatly disappointed our expectations."[7] "In short," he complained to Prevost, "nothing but the squadron can relieve us." The commander-in-chief, who had come forward to Kingston, urged Yeo into action and assured Drummond that "every exertion" would be made to resupply him and that the squadron would sail no later than the middle of the month. "Nothing shall be left undone to remove your alarm on the score of provisions," he wrote his subordinate on 11 October and a "few days will decide the extent of the aid the navy will afford for that most desirable purpose."[8] By this time Drummond had been without active naval support for more than two months and he was understandably completely fed up with Commodore James Lucas Yeo and all his works. He told Prevost bluntly that he had ceased

The Chippawa. This modern photograph shows the Chippawa (now the Welland) River near its mouth. It was no mean obstacle and constituted a very good defensive position.

to reckon upon any relief depending on the Squadron. – The troops which may arrive in it may indeed serve to repair my losses, but they cannot now possibly arrive in time to take any Share in the contest which I fear this gallant little Division will shortly have to maintain against [illegible] its numbers. While I feel confident that its gallantry and efforts will be such as to call forth the applause of its King and Country and of every impartial Military Man, (whatever may be the result) I cannot but deeply lament that any circumstances should have placed this portion of the British Army in a situation such I have described.[9]

On 14 October Drummond pounded home the point more strongly by telling Prevost that, "should any disaster happen" to the Right Division, then "His Majesty's naval commander will, in my opinion, have much to answer for."[10]

Since his withdrawal from Fort Erie, however, Drummond had not been harassed by the Americans. Brown had merely pushed his pickets to just south of Black Creek, about six miles above the Chippawa, which was the southernmost limit of the British pickets. In early October, however, Drummond became aware of major movement on the American side of the Niagara River, and when deserters told him this was Major-General George Izard's division approaching at long last, he prepared to meet it. He thinned out his light troops south of the Chippawa and made plans to position his strongest regular infantry units (the 1st, 82nd and 97th Foot) to be able to reinforce the 6th Foot at Chippawa within two hours. He also ordered the defences of Chippawa to be strengthened, including the construction of a *tête du pont** to guard the important bridge

---

* A *tête du pont* is a defensive work constructed on the end of a bridge nearest the enemy with purpose of protecting the bridge being taken by a surprise attack.

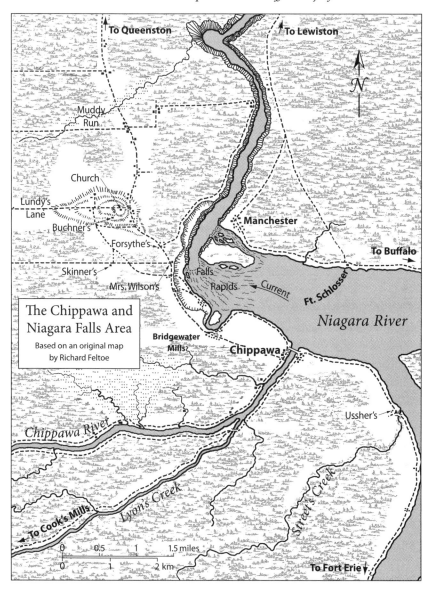

at that point. He formed a mobile brigade at Queenston with the 89th, 100th, flank companies of the 104th Foot, a troop of the 19th Light Dragoons and two field pieces. It was to be responsible for "all the night duties and made the reconnaissances."He gave command of it to Lieutenant-Colonel George Hay, the Marquis of Tweeddale, the commanding officer of the 100th Foot, who was still recovering from a wound suffered the previous July at the battle of Chippawa.[11]

Le Couteur and the other officers of the 104th were very pleased with their new brigade commander. Although an aristocrat, the 27-year-old Tweeddale was a down-to-earth type who had seen considerable action in the Peninsula, having served not only in battle with the Guards but also on Wellington's staff. Still partially lame from his wound, Tweeddale carried two crutches in front of his saddle so that he could walk when he dismounted. Le Couteur regarded Tweeddale as a "fine Gentleman and Soldier," very much in the mould of the 104th's beloved William Drummond, killed in action during the assault on Fort Erie and still sorely missed. Tweeddale was "wonderfully vigilant," joined his men when they were on picket duty at night and "watches by the hour."[12]

The troops posted to Queenston had been enjoying their stay in this scenic little village, which, although much damaged by war, was a pleasant posting after the mud and misery of Fort Erie. While off duty, they hunted birds, fished and picked chestnuts in the verdant foliage on the slopes and summit of the heights that loomed behind the village.[13] This was particularly true of John Le Couteur, who acquired a new friend the first night he was in Queenston. As Le Couteur tells the tale:

> We are in quiet possession of Colonel Dickson's fine large house, with the 89th light bobs [light company], it being the only one with windows left in it. As the big wigs were sure to take the best rooms, I mounted at once to the garret where the Yankees had broken nothing, the doors & other windows being safe & the room snug. At night I turned down, not in, all standing, with my blankets above & bearskin below me.
>
> Just as I was dropping to sleep, I heard a strange cry close by me. I listened, surely no one is being murdered? – another faint plaintive cry! "Hallow, that's no mistake", I grasped my sword, "Who's there?" Another cry! In the very room I could have sworn. "Who's there?" I shouted, determined to be heard. "Say what are You? Where are you?" Another cry like a dying child's! Good God, this is horrid and no answer, no candle and quite dark. I thought it wisest then to grope my way out, find my Servant, and bring a Candle, convinced that some person dying was concealed in the garret.[14]

Fetching a light and searching carefully, the young officer discovered a "beautiful, starved, tortoise-shell kitten – so weak that it could not stir." Although his soldier servant wanted to chuck the thing out the window, Le Couteur patiently nursed the little creature back to health and it was not long before "Queenie," as she was named, was frisking and gambolling about. The problem was that she would not let Le Couteur out of her sight and followed him everywhere, even when he went on duty, eliciting comments from the men of his light infantry company: "Look … see Mr. Le Couteur and his Cat coming to Parade." In the end, Le Couteur gave "Queenie" to the surgeon of the 104th Foot, who dis-

Dickson's House, Queenston. This fine frame building was built by Lieutenant-Colonel Thomas Dickson, merchant and militia officer. It was still standing in September 1814 when Lieutenant John Le Couteur was billeted in one of its upper rooms and found the starving kitten "Queenie," who adopted him. Today Dickson's house is the South Landing Inn. (Author's photograph)

patched her to his wife in New Brunswick, who informed Le Couteur by letter of "her health and progeny long after!"[15]

On 6 October life changed at Queenston when a sentry posted on the heights reported that a "Yankee army is encamped above Lewiston."[16] Later that day, the British observed Izard and his staff "reconnoitring us all along the Banks of the river – lots of 'em about the banks all day" and that night there was "nought but their camp fires to be seen" across the river. A few days later the American force was observed moving up the Niagara and Drummond very shortly began receiving reports of a large number of troops crossing the river at Black Rock. On 13 October the Americans pushed Drummond's pickets over Black Creek and crossed the waterway that night and advanced north on the following day. The Glengarry Light Infantry, which were on outpost duty, retired before the Americans "with the utmost regularity" before forming a picket line just south of the Chippawa.[17] Things were quiet that night but on the morning of 15 October the Americans "advanced to make a reconnaissance, supported by the fire of a considerable number of heavy guns."[18] For nearly a month the war in the north had seemingly come to a dead halt but it was now time to go back to work.

The union of Major-General George Izard's Right Division and Major-General Jacob Brown's Left Division was not easily accomplished. When Brown made a surprise visit to Izard at Batavia on 27 September, Izard told him that it was his intention "to besiege Fort Niagara with his division," while Brown was to remain on the Canada side to watch and amuse Drummond."[19] Brown was not too happy with this decision but decided not to argue it at that point. When Izard, however, began a detailed examination of what was required to undertake the siege, he came to the conclusion that he did not have sufficient heavy guns to do so and that the commencement of the operation would have to be delayed. In the meantime, he marched his division from Batavia toward the village of Lewiston using the Ridge Road, which was a longer route, "in order to approach Fort Niagara with less fatigue to the men."[20] This made no sense to Colonel Cromwell Pearce of the Sixteenth Infantry because the movement took more than a week to complete "and, thus instead of marching directly" toward Lewiston, the division "made a very circuitous and very fatiguing march of almost 100 miles."[21] On the other hand, Lieutenant Jacob Norton of the Fourth Infantry was pleased as the Ridge Road appeared "to be a natural turnpike to facilitate the settlement of this very fertile country."[22]

As has been discussed above, many American senior officers believed that Izard's heart was not in offensive action and his somewhat dilatory movements may have been a result. That this was the case is possibly born out by the fact that, before he even initiated any operation, Izard was already thinking of going into winter quarters. On 28 September, the day after he met with Brown and Porter, Izard wrote Secretary of War James Monroe that

> The experience of the last campaign proves the necessity of adopting timely measures for the accommodation and comfort of the troops during the winter. ...... The force now assembling on this frontier, small as it is in numbers, is great in value to the United States. It should not be forgotten that they were raw recruits only a few months ago, and that they have been engaged in active service ever since. Their instruction as soldiers is consequently far from what it might be, although the essentials of soldiership – as obedience, hardihood and courage – are theirs. In the repose of winter quarters they can acquire what is yet alone wanting to render them equal, if not superior, to any troops on earth.[23]

This was a curious comment to make as Izard still had at least four weeks of campaigning weather left, but then George Izard seems to have preferred war in the abstract to war in the flesh, and to training soldiers rather than leading them into battle.

In any case, when his division reached Lewiston on 5 October, the village presented "a deplorable scene of desolation," according to Norton of the Fourth Infantry, as every "house was burnt last year by the British, and the place is left without an Inhabitant."[24] Norton and his comrades amused themselves by observing the British officers on the Canadian bank of the Niagara – among whom may have been Le Couteur of the 104th. The two parties "took a look at each other," Norton remembered, and most likely traded insults or news as the Niagara River was so narrow at this point that "we could hail each other very distinctly."[25]

At Lewiston, Izard received another visit from Brown, who brought with him the newly-promoted Major-General Peter B. Porter of the New York militia. These two officers, both combat veterans, prevailed on Izard to relinquish any thought of mounting a siege of Fort Niagara, which, if successful, would only give him "a useless fortress and a few convalescents and invalids, who made up the garrison," – while it would give the British "time to get supplies and reinforcements from Kingston."[26] The three general officers decided that Izard would cross the Niagara and "concentrate our whole force on Drummond's position." Brown and Porter believed that if the two divisions combined at Chippawa and hit Drummond hard, they could drive him out of the Niagara and take the forts at the mouth of the river or even the British supply depot at Burlington before the season was over.[27]

At least that was how the two Left Division generals understood the plan. Unfortunately, on 6 October, the day after he met with Brown and Porter, Izard received a letter from Secretary of War Monroe informing him that he was to take command of both divisions as military operations in the north "must be combined and directed to one result, which can only be done, by being placed in the hands of one commander."[28] Armed with this power, Izard seems to have decided to do the least possible and then go into winter quarters without any hard fighting. Never an officer to move quickly, on 8 October he marched from Lewiston up the American side of the river to Schlosser, where boats were supposedly ready to convey his division to the Canadian side of the Niagara. He found them to be inadequate as "they would not contain above one fourth of my force; and to cross in the face of the enemy's batteries and intrenchments at Chippawa, by small detachments, would have been madness."[29] Izard decided instead to march to Black Rock, where on 10 and 11 October he crossed his army into Canada on a single scow and a raft, which took considerable time. Izard now assumed command in the Niagara and reorganized his forces: the Right Division became the First Division, and the Left Division the Second Division of a new Northern Army. Six weeks, two days and 630 miles had passed since he had marched out of Plattsburgh bound for the Niagara.[30]

The newcomers had a day or so to look around Fort Erie, which, as Lieutenant Norton of the Fourth Infantry remarked, had been rendered famous by the "gallant defence which Genl Brown has made against the enemy at this place." "The loss of the British," he was told, "while besieging this fort was very great, averaged 20 per day" and "a great number of dead bodies of the enemy still lay unburied in the woods, and others only partly buried."[31]

On 13 and 14 October Izard pushed north with an army that numbered 5,500 regular troops and 800 New York volunteers. The retreating British destroyed the bridges over the streams, which were booming because of the recent heavy rain, and this delayed progress until what Norton of the Fourth Infantry called "boat bridges" or pontoon bridges could be built to bear the weight of artillery and wagons.[32] Awed by the size of this force, most of the local civilians decided "to abandon their homes and property."[33] Izard tried to treat those who remained correctly, informing Monroe that, although he paid for anything his men took and spared "no pains to protect the wretched people from being plundered," some "excesses" had been committed "by the irregulars and riflemen, but they are remedied as much as possible; and if repeated (after the orders I have given on the subject) shall not go unpunished."[34] The orders referred to stated that Izard, having learned "with extreme concern" that some Canadians "had been plundered or ill treated by soldiers of the U.S.," forbade all officers or enlisted men from entering any house or dwelling without the written permission of their commanding officers.[35] By nightfall on 14 October, the army was on Samuel Street's farm, the site of the battle of Chippawa and of the Left Division's former provision store, which it had destroyed before withdrawing to Fort Erie on 26 July.

The following morning, Izard and his senior staff reconnoitred the British defences at Chippawa. Izard then ordered an artillery officer to take a field piece forward and attempt to draw the enemy's fire. This was done and although the gun detachment fired several rounds into the British defences, there was no response. A discussion now broke out among the senior officers as to whether the British had abandoned or were about to abandon their position. To test the validity of this hypothesis, Izard ordered Captains Nathan Towson and Samuel Archer to bring their artillery companies forward and open fire on the enemy works. Towson brought three 6-pdr. guns and a 5.5-inch howitzer into action, while Archer opened up with two 18-pdr. guns. In Izard's words,

> Nothing could be more gallant than the proceeding of this little band. They advanced through the open ground in full view of the enemy's batteries of twenty-four and twelve pounders, formed the line without any cover whatever, and commenced a cool and correct cannonade, which was immediately answered by their adversaries. The vast superiority of our artillerists was discernible to the most inexperienced eye. Every shot told. One of their batteries was silenced. The intended effort was produced, and it was plain that so far from abandoning their forts, the British were in strength, and superior in weight of metal, and number of guns. The firing continued till dusk, when I directed our pieces to be withdrawn for the night.[36]

Drummond, who was on the north side of the Chippawa that day, believed that the British artillery fire had deterred Izard from making a serious attack and of that he was glad, as the defensive works at Chippawa were far from finished.

A similar demonstration was mounted on the following day, 16 October, with the same result. That night Brown visited Izard to discuss a plan for future operations. To Brown, who was always looking for an opportunity for aggressive action, it was quite simple: the Northern Army, now concentrated and "being in high spirits and discipline, and little short of double the number of enemy," should immediately attack Drummond, "who had neither received as yet, reinforcements or supplies, and who, as our information stated – was even badly off for ammunition."[37] Brown proposed that one division ford the Chippawa upstream and turn the British right flank, forcing Drummond to send troops from Chippawa to bolster that flank, and when that happened, the other division would launch an assault straight over the river at the weakened British defences. This was actually a variation of the tactics Brown had used to get over the Chippawa a little more than three months previous. After much discussion, Izard "gave rather a reluctant assent, but he did give one" and Brown left to make preparations.[38] A short while later, however, Izard called Brown back and informed him that, "on further reflection," he had changed his mind and had decided to "act on the *defensive*" for two reasons: "*the imminent danger that threatened the fleet*, now that it was driven into port; and the importance of *keeping the strength of the army entire for the next campaign* [season]."[39] "Want of decision" on the part of his superior, Brown later commented, "and a system of procrastination would ultimately lead to difficulties and disgrace" and this being the case, he decided he would no longer trouble Izard with "importunities" or suggestions for offensive action.[40]

During the morning of 17 October Izard continued to demonstrate in front of the Chippawa, "in the hope of drawing the enemy out into the field; – but in vain."[41] The intelligence that Chauncey had withdrawn into Sackets Harbor, however, seems to have dampened what little aggressive spirit Izard possessed. In his opinion, the loss of naval superiority on Lake Ontario "defeats all the objects of the operations by land in this quarter" because, even if he got across the Chippawa and Drummond retreated, "every step I take in pursuit, exposes me to be cut off by large reinforcements" and it was "in the power of the enemy" to attack "my flank or rear." For the secretary of war, he catalogued his problems: "the artillery and all the ordnance stores on this frontier, are inadequate to the siege of one of the enemy's fortresses" while three quarters of the arms of Brown's Second Division were "unfit for service" and, of course, the "severe season is approaching." George Izard was clearly a commander who saw only problems and not possibilities. "I confess, sir," he wrote Monroe

Memorial to Cook's Mills. Today, a National Historic Sites Monument in the little hamlet of Cook's Mills commemorates the action fought on 19 October 1814. (Author's photograph)

that I am greatly embarrassed. At the head of the most efficient army which the United States have possessed during this war, much must be expected from me – and yet I can discern no object which can be achieved at this point, worthy of the risk which will attend its attempt. The relief of Major General Brown's force is completely effected. I have presented the army under my command in the open field, and under the enemy's intrenchments for battle, which he prudently declines.[42]

This being the case, "should no opening present itself in a few days, to obtain an immediate advantage over the enemy," Izard proposed "to commence preparations for the distribution of the troops in winter quarters."

During the afternoon of 17 October, Drummond reported, the enemy's troops "disappeared" to the south. The British commander pushed out patrols of dragoons and light infantry who informed him that the Americans had withdrawn up the River Road, crossed the swaying boat bridges over the creeks and were now in the vicinity of Black Creek. Deserters told Drummond that the retreat "was owing to finding our position at the mouth of the Chippawa so much stronger than they expected," but Drummond was not so sure. In the afternoon two boats, whose American crews did not know of Izard's withdrawal, crossed the Niagara from Schlosser and one was captured. To everyone's great joy, it was found to contain a cargo of "fresh meat, bread, and spirits," sufficient for a brigade. [43]

In the afternoon of 18 October Drummond began receiving reports that "a large body of the enemy" was moving up Black Creek in the direction of Cook's Mills, a hamlet located at the junction of that waterway and Lyon's Creek, and about ten miles west of Chippawa. Drummond immediately dispatched Colonel Christopher Myers with the Glengarry Light Infantry and seven companies of the 82nd Foot toward that place. When Myers reported early in the evening that the Americans appeared to be in strength and had occupied Cook's Mills, Drummond reinforced him with Tweeddale's light brigade – consisting of the flank companies of the 89th and 104th Foot and the 100th Foot – as well as a field gun and the remaining three companies of the 82nd. Myers was ordered "to act with caution" but to "feel" the enemy "so as accurately to ascertain their strength and the direction of their movement." Myers's orders were written at 9 P.M. but by the time the units involved were ready to march it was nearly dawn.[44]

The cause of all this excitement was a decision made by Izard on the morning of 18 October. Having learned that "a considerable quantity of grain collected for the British troops" was stored at Cook's Mills, the American commander ordered Brigadier-General Daniel Bissell to take his Second Brigade of the First Division to that place, seize the grain and either destroy it or, if practicable, remove it.[45] Bissell set out immediately with his formation, consisting of the Fifth, Fourteenth, Fifteenth and Sixteenth Infantry, a company of the Fourth Rifles under Captain Armstrong Irvine and a detachment of dragoons under Lieutenant Philip Anspach. Bissell's force, with a strength of about a thousand men, reached their objective late in the afternoon, brushed a picket of Canadian militia out of the hamlet and occupied it. Bissell posted strong pickets consisting of two companies of infantry and Irvine's riflemen on the far side of Lyon's Creek and then camped for the night on the opposite side. Sometime in the darkness hours, the Glengarry Light Infantry attacked the picket commanded by Lieutenant John Gassaway of the Fifth Infantry, but were beaten off.[46]

While this scrapping was going on, Myers's command was near the Mills and Tweeddale's small brigade was moving up to support him. Le Couteur remembered that march:

> We had hardly laid down and got into sound sleep … when [Lieutenant James] Coates ran down & awoke me, "Le C[outeur]. dont flatter yourself you are going to sleep, rouse up, we are going to surprise a picquet!" Packed up my haversack and off in a Jiffy to Olsen's – it is hardly worth repeating that we were marching knee deep in mud in a pitch dark night – over rough and smooth – an exquisite enjoyment for those who have never tried it. We slept in the wet for about half an hour while the 100th [Regiment] and others were crossing the river in batteaux. They then halted. We awoke cold and shivering & crossed, then marched on rapidly about nine miles through a horrid, swampy road, then halted on a sort of clearing at P___. Ordered to light camp fires, cook and sleep – we did both with a will.[47]

When dawn broke on 19 October, Myers reconnoitred and discovered that Bissell's advance posts were provided with a strong support posted on the right bank of a ravine, which runs to Lyon's Creek, a small distance from the Mills. A part of the Glengarry Regiment turned round a small wood which covered the front of the enemy and crossed the head of the ravine, whilst the remainder passed through the wood. By this movement the enemy's light troops were driven back in admirable style, whilst a part of his force crossed the Lyon's Creek for the purpose of annoying our left.[48]

He ordered the Glengarries to push back Bissell's advance posts, which, in Bissell's words, "sustained the whole fire of the enemy for about fifteen minutes with the greatest gallantry" until he could move troops up to support them. As his brigade came across Lyon's Creek on the bridge, Bissell ordered the Fifth Infantry to skirt the woods – around which the ensuing action would take place – and attack the British right while the Fourteenth was ordered to support the advance troops on the far side of the woods. Finally he ordered the Fifteenth and Sixteenth Infantry "to act as circumstances might require."[49]

Myers decided to pull the Glengarry Light Infantry back "in the hope of drawing the enemy forth to the open ground, and, if circumstances would justify it, to bring him to a more general action."[50] This, however, did not work as the Americans only advanced to the skirt of the woods, moving two columns "on our left and one on our right, opening a heavy fire of small arms and which from the distance we sparingly returned but from the fire of the six-pounder and the rockets the enemy's column on our left suffered severely." Having ascertained that the Americans numbered about 1,500 men (which, as we know, was too high a figure) but had no artillery, Myers decided that Bissell had no intention of making a serious attempt to turn the British flank nor did the enemy plan to establish themselves in Cook's Mills. Having accomplished his purpose, Myers ordered his troops to retire and they did so in good order.

Bissell, of course, saw it somewhat differently. As he reported to Izard:

> The well directed fire of the elite corps, riflemen, and gallant charge of the 14th soon compelled the enemy to give ground and on discovering that his

Brigadier-General Daniel Bissell (1768-1833). The American commander at the action at Cook's Mills or Lyon's Creek, Bissell was a veteran army officer who had first been commissioned in 1799. His military career, if not stellar, was steady and he remained in the postwar army until 1821. (Courtesy, Missouri Historical Society)

right flank was turned by the intrepid move of Colonel Pinckney, he retreated in the utmost confusion, leaving some killed, wounded and prisoners. We pursued to a ravine some distance from the scene where the action commenced.[51]

For his part, Tweeddale recalled that he formed the 100th Foot into line

with ordered arms 5 or 6 hundred yards from a wood in which the enemy were. We made a dash with a company which caused the enemy to drive them backward to form on the border of the wood. ..... I placed the other regiments so that they could all support the 100th if they were attacked. Having ascertained the strength of the enemy my object was gained and we returned to Headquarters.[52]

One of the most colourful accounts of this brisk little engagement is provided by John Le Couteur. He recalled that Tweeddale's brigade reached the battlefield about 8 A.M.

when the Glens [Glengarry Light Infantry] became suddenly engaged in our front. The Ground was a fine large clearing with the Chippawa Creek on our left, a gentle slope to the front and bank of the creek. About a mile in front were woods and to the extreme left we could perceive the American Army moving over a pontoon or temporary bridge which they had thrown over the river.

About four hundred of them had engaged our advance, the 82nd and 100th [Foot] were formed into line. We were thrown in extended order on the left and in support of [Lieutenant Thomas] Carter with a [6-pdr] Field piece and four Rockets. The Americans getting stronger and their fire overpowering the Glens, we were ordered to advance, extended, to turn the American right. Our men dashed into the ravine in good style and engaged the Yankees in our front, who soon gave way, for a short distance.

But they, in turn, being supported by about four hundred fresh troops, We had to give way in turn and retreated in good order a little way, when the 82nd Light bobs [light company] came to our aid, when both companies cheered and checked the enemy again. The rocket brigade was then brought up very opportunely and a volley plunging into a Column not yet deployed threw it into confusion, as well they might. This checked their further advance. Our Gun was very ill-placed behind a little wood and only barked without biting. We halted for a short while, drawn up securely behind a rail fence, a capital protection, when soon after the Marquis [of Tweeddale] ordered us to retire by alternate wings.

The line formed, and we flankers extended on the Flanks, covering the line, Rockets and Gun. The Americans came out of the woods. Officers and men did not fire and I verily believe cheered us while admiring the beautiful Military movement we were executing in slow time. It was altogether the prettiest little affair any of us had ever seen.[53]

A British soldier who most certainly did not do his duty that day for King and Country was Private George Ferguson of the 100th Foot. A devout Methodist lay preacher who never ceased upbraiding his fellow soldiers for their sinful ways, particularly their liking for strong drink and women of malleable virtue, Ferguson was present at Cook's Mills. He was absolutely sure, however, that he did not hurt anybody – including Americans – during the action. In fact he later confessed that he only "fired but one shot during the whole war and my mind was so intensely engaged with God, I scarcely knew which way I fired" and was "sure I never killed or wounded a human being in my life" and this was, of course, a "cause of thankfulness."[54] George Ferguson was the kind of soldier whose comrades fervently hoped would desert from the British army and join the American.

With the British withdrawal, Bissell considered his work done and the next day returned to the main army after burning 150-200 bushels of wheat that he found at the grist mill in that place. Curiously, he destroyed neither that mill nor the lumber mill in the village, even though they were legitimate targets of war. Drummond commented to Prevost that in recent weeks the enemy "had been studiously cautious in abstaining from his burning and plundering system," which he attributed "to the retaliation inflicted at Washington and on the coast" of the United States for the American depredations at Long Point and St. David's earlier in the year.[55]

The engagement at Cook's Mills had been hot while it lasted and the opposing commanders could feel satisfied that they had done their duty and accomplished their objectives. Mercifully, the casualties were light: Bissell reported the loss of 11 men killed and 57 wounded while Myers's casualties were 1 man killed and 35 wounded.[56]

The men of both armies had a miserable time carrying out this little operation as it rained heavily during their approach marches to Cook's Mills, during the action itself and during the withdrawal. When Izard heard the sound of musketry in his camp on the morning of 19 October, he dispatched Brown's Second Brigade, consisting of the Twenty-First and Twenty-Third Infantry, to Bissell's assistance. As that inventive speller, Captain Benjamin Ropes of the Twenty-First Infantry, recalled, it was a dreadful experience:

We Advanced in the morning [of 19 October] through the worst road I ever traviled without anything to eat or Drink we encamped the first night near a farm Conl [Colonel] [William] King bough[t] a young creature [calf] of the Owner of thee Farm which was all he could Spare except 3 or 4 Sheep which escaped, the Men bult fires and sat by them During the Night as our bagage wagons were three Mile in the rear, & it rained hard we commenced our March in the Morning, about Ten Oclock [on 20 October] we met the Troops returning, we then returned to Camp having our Labour for our pains and very much Fatigued....[57]

Sergeant Amasiah Ford of the Twenty-Third echoed Ropes's complaints about this nightmare march. He remembered that

We had not been long on the way before the rain began to fall very fast. We continued our march through a most dismal swamp in the mud up to our knees & at length arrived about sunset on the opposite shore in a cleared field without anything to eat or cover our wearied bodies with as we had left our knapsacks behind and brought nothing with us but our muskets and cartridge boxes well filled with powder and ball

Here we encamped for the night & built up large fires of rails, &c. to warm ourselves by, as it was now October & the weather very cold. Our stomachs now began to crave for food for we had not had anything to eat; but at length our officers procured a beef. We killed it & every officer & soldier helped himself to what he needed & roasted it in the fire by means of a sharpened stick & ate it without any salt to season or bread to eat it with. ......

The next morning we took our breakfast as usual on fresh beef without salt but we found a substitute for bread by roasting pumpkins in the fire & eating them with our beef. We lived in this situation for two days & nights lying on the cold wet ground without anything to cover us but the bare curtain of heaven while the rain was pouring down in torrents upon us.[58]

When Ford got back to the main camp and drew rations, he recalled it was "the best meal I ever ate for it consisted of raw pork & bread."

The misery was not all on the American side. Le Couteur recalled that after his unit withdrew from Cook's Mills to the east on 19 October,

We continued our retrograde march to Olsen's, and crossed the Creek and were quartered for the night about a quarter of a mile on – no bedding, not a thing to eat. Sent an imploring message to the 89th [Regiment] for relief but found that they were quite as miserably off as ourselves. Gave it up in despair when our Noble Marquis [Tweeddale], hearing of our distress, saved us from starvation by sending us a fine shoulder of mutton and a loaf of bread which were divided by my little sharp sabre, there not being one Knife, much less a fork, among us.[59]

This impromptu banquet was followed by a "dreadful cold night of suffering [with] no blankets, the fire out, and frost on the ground." The next day, 20 October, was Le Couteur's 20th birthday and he offered thanks to God "for having preserved me in safety through many dangers."

Four days earlier, on 16 October, Yeo had finally emerged from Kingston. Prevost had, "with difficulty," convinced him to embark half the 90th Foot and a small quantity of provisions and ordnance stores and take them to the Niagara.[60] As soon as he was out on the lake, Yeo ordered two hours of gun drill, a practical exercise although it was not likely that Chauncey was going to emerge from Sackets Harbor and fight. Yeo thought his new flagship handled well but the weather did not co-operate and adverse winds and squalls delayed the squadron's progress – the same stormy weather of wind and rain that was making life miserable for the troops on land. During the evening of 19 October, the commodore nearly lost the *St. Lawrence* when, as Lieutenant David Wingfield, RN, recalled, the squadron was lashed

by a tremendous squall, and every ship in the Squadron had their sails blown to ribbons, which were set at the time. The hands were turned up to clear the wreckage, and the Quarter deck being nearly full of men clearing up the remnants of the sails, a terrific flash of lightning struck the mainmast, cutting through the iron hoops with which it is bound, though nearly an inch thick, and killing seven, and wounding 22, all the hands being knocked down on the Quarter deck by the violence of the concussion. We were under the greatest apprehension about a hanging magazine of powder containing several hundred filled cartridges for the 32 pounders, which was situated on the orlop [or lowest] deck just abaft the mainmast. Had the lightning communicated to them we should have all taken our departure. The storm continued about a quarter of an hour attended with the most vivid flashes of lightening, the loudest thunder, and the heaviest rain I ever experienced in the whole course of my seafaring life, but not further damage was done than happened at its first commencement.[61]

Struggling with this weather, the squadron did not reach the mouth of the Niagara until the following day. Yeo, impatient to be relieved of his human and other cargo, immediately began to land the troops and supplies, a very difficult task given the wind-lashed lake. Drummond, who was anxious to get fresh troops as well as provisions and ammunition, suggested that the naval commander send on shore some of the small but elite battalion of Royal Marines that had recently been broken up to serve on his squadron. Yeo's response was quick and negative; in fact he was concerned that Drummond "should make a request that I cannot comply with without exposing the honor of the flag, the interest of the country, and my own reputation to most eminent danger."[62] In other words, the answer was a flat "no" and the reason given was that Yeo might have to fight a fleet action and his marines were "the most efficient part" of his ships' companies. As it was not likely that Chauncey, himself a very cautious officer, would challenge the leviathan of the lake until he had something bigger and meaner in the water, Yeo's reply was more than a little specious. It was yet another indication that the naval commander was not fighting the same war as his army counterparts.

Drummond himself visited the *St. Lawrence* on 23 October but there is no record of what was said between the two officers. Their conversation likely concerned Drummond's wish to have Yeo bring up more replacements and take away from the Niagara many of the regiments he considered burned out and in need of a rest. On his list to be shifted out was almost every unit that had been in the peninsula prior to 15 August. As it was, Drummond managed to get Yeo to take the 8th Foot and the flank companies of the 104th Foot back to Kingston when he sailed on 22 October. John Le Couteur remembered that the 104th was suddenly ordered to "embark all in a hurry at 8 A.M. without our breakfast" but were "right happy to do so." "Huzza! Huzza!" was the young officer's delighted reaction.[63]

On land, meanwhile, Drummond had no contact with Izard's troops until 21 October when the Americans reappeared before the British position at Chippawa. Izard, having heard of the arrival of the British squadron, had thought that his enemy might "be encouraged to accept the battle I had so frequently offered him."[64] This offer, like all the others, was refused, however, and Drummond stayed within his defences. Izard withdrew later in the day to a position directly across the river from Black Rock. Brown was now convinced that "all active service" in the theatre was at an end because, as he drily remarked, it appeared that "the strength of Drummond's army was to be kept entire, as well as that of our own, for the next campaign."[65] He therefore requested an order from Izard to march his division to Sackets Harbor, just a few miles from Brown's own residence at Brownville. Izard, who had just received a series of letters from Chauncey and other officers at the Harbor expressing their concern for the security of the naval base, "immediately granted" this request and on 24 October the former Left Division marched away from the Niagara, where it had done much hard fighting, established an enviable record of success and restored the reputation of the American soldier.[66]

With his strength now significantly reduced, Izard pondered whether it was worth his while to retain Fort Erie. Other than "being a trophy," he could find no reason justifying

> exposing in a weak, ill planned, and hastily repaired redoubt (it scarcely deserves even that humble designation,) some hundreds of valuable officers and men, with the cannon, and various stores, which if it were taken would necessarily fall with it into the hands of the enemy. It is as much unprotected in the winter by a force on this side, as if it were fifty miles off. It commands nothing, not even the entrance to the strait [the Niagara River]; and should by an untoward accident, the naval superiority on lake Erie be recovered by the enemy, the garrison must at any season and in a very short time, throw open their gates to any body that will furnish them with the means of subsistence.[67]

He consulted several of his senior officers – none of whom had served at Fort Erie during the siege – and, without exception, their opinion was that it should be destroyed and the army cross back into the United States and go into winter quarters. Pleased with this response, Izard gave orders for the defence works to be prepared for demolition, and within a week he was gratified to receive a dispatch from Monroe that not only approved of his decision but also stressed that "the preservation of the Troops we now have" was important, not only for the defence of the northern frontier but also as "a School of instruction and a model for the much greater Army which it is contemplated to raise."[68]

The weather at this time was abysmal, which should come as no surprise as the one common feature of the latter part of the Niagara campaign of 1814 was that it was wet. It rained incessantly during the last five days of October and intermittently during the first week of November. It was so damp at Fort Erie that Major Joseph Totten of the engineers, responsible for the demolition of the fort, found that it was impossible to dig shafts in which to plant explosive charges anywhere in the fort "without meeting water in almost every instance of our attempts."[69] Finally, on 5 November Totten was ready, the fuzes were lit and most of the defence works were destroyed in billowing clouds of mud, dirt, wood and stone. "The explosion was tremendous," commented Lieutenant Norton, "and worth seeing."[70] A few minutes later, the last American troops crossed the Niagara River to commence the construction of winter quarters.

Drummond made no attempt to interfere with Izard's army during its last days in Canada. "The weather has been so bad, and my information so defective," he reported, that he thought it "inexpedient to harass" his troops "by any

His Majesty's White Elephant. Finally completed, HMS *St. Lawrence* leads the Lake Ontario squadron in the autumn of 1814. Yeo's insistence on building this large warship severely strained the logistical lifeline for the British army in Upper Canada. (Painting by Peter Rindlisbacher, courtesy of the artist)

forward movement towards the enemy."[71] Yeo returned on 3 November but the uncertain weather made him so nervous that he cut short the offloading of troops and supplies and sailed away with a 9-pdr. artillery brigade (battery) and considerable quantities of badly-needed provisions and ammunition. On 5 November Drummond wrote to Prevost explaining why he thought that an attack on Fort Erie was not advisable because he had no wish "to pay a price" for an objective "beyond what I consider to be its real value."[72] These words had hardly been put on paper when intelligence arrived that Fort Erie had been blown up and the enemy had evacuated Canadian soil – causing the British commander to offer "sincere congratulations" to Prevost.[73] After 125 days of hard fighting, the Niagara campaign of 1814, the longest and bloodiest military operation of the War of 1812, had finally ended.

But not the war in the north. For the past several days Drummond had been receiving confusing reports that a large American mounted force was moving through the western part of Upper Canada and seemingly heading for the major British supply depot at Burlington Heights. More fighting lay ahead.

VOLUNTEERS.

G. R. III.

God Save the King.

LET us, who are Englishmen, protect and defend our good KING and COUNTRY against the Attempts of all *Republicans* and *Levellers*, and against the Designs of our NATURAL ENEMIES, who intend in this Year to invade OLD ENGLAND, *our happy Country*, to murder our gracious KING as they have done *their own*; to make WHORES of our *Wives* and *Daughters*; to rob us of our Property, and teach us nothing but the *damn'd Art of murdering one another.*

ROYAL TARS
Of OLD ENGLAND.

If you love your COUNTRY, and your LIBERTY, now is the Time to shew your Love.

REPAIR,

All who have good Hearts, who love their KING, their COUNTRY, and RELIGION, who hate the FRENCH, and damn the POPE,

T O

Lieut. W. J. Stephens,

At his Rendezvous, SHOREHAM,

Where they will be allowed to Enter for any SHIP of WAR,

AND THE FOLLOWING

BOUNTIES will be given by his MAJESTY,
in Addition to Two Months Advance.

To Able Seamen,	-	-	-	*Five Pounds.*
To Ordinary Seamen,	-	-	-	*Two Pounds Ten Shillings.*
To Landmen,	-	-	-	*Thirty Shillings.*

Conduct-Money paid to go by Land, and their Chests and Bedding sent Carriage free.

Those Men who have served as PETTY-OFFICERS, and those who are otherwise qualified, will be recommended accordingly.

LEWES, PRINTED BY W. AND A. LEE.

Royal Navy recruiting poster. Contrary to popular myth, the Royal Navy acquired a considerable proportion of its personnel by recruiting, not impressment. (Courtesy Parks Canada)

PART FIVE

The Last Battles in the North and the Coming of Peace

OCTOBER 1814–FEBRUARY 1815

Winter march. From mid-November to April, campaigning in the north almost ceased as troops went into winter quarters. There was the occasional winter movement as depicted in this painting by G. A. Embleton. (Courtesy, Parks Canada)

Cavalry charge at Moraviantown, 5 October 1813. Major-General William H. Harrison's troops make the charge that broke the British line at this crucial battle. The dress of these mounted riflemen was very similar to that worn one year later by McArthur's raiders. (Painting by Kenneth Riley, U.S. National Guard Heritage, Washington)

CHAPTER FIFTEEN

The War in the West
and McArthur's Raid

OCTOBER–NOVEMBER 1814

Let Bacchus's sons be not dismayed,
But join with me each jovial blade,
Come, booze and sing and lend me aid,
To help me with the chorus.
  Instead of spa we'll drink down ale,
  And pay the reckoning on the nail,
  For debt no man shall go to jail,
  From Garryowen and glory.

We'll break windows, we'll break doors,
The watch knock down by threes and fours,
Then let the doctors work their cures,
And tinker up our bruises.
  Instead of spa we'll drink down ale, etc.

Our hearts so stout have got us fame,
For soon 'tis known from whence we came,
Where'er we go they dread the name,
Of Garryowen in glory.
  Instead of spa we'll drink down ale, etc.[1]

To understand the military operations that took place in western Upper Canada in October and November 1814, it is necessary to first discuss the background of the conflict in that part of the province. The area had suffered grievously during the war. Sparsely settled with only about 4,000 inhabitants in 1812, it was partly surrounded by American territory and vulnerable to invasion. Matters were made worse by the fact that the settled areas, mostly clustered along the Detroit, Grand, Thames and St. Clair Rivers, as well as the north shore of Lake Erie, were riven with political and personal dissension and rivalries. These tensions were increased because this part of the province had a higher proportion of recent American immigrants, compared to those of British or Loyalist stock, than in other parts and their allegiance to the Crown was not as strong.

This fact became apparent in July 1812, when General William Hull launched the first American invasion of Canada. After crossing the Detroit River, Hull issued a proclamation addressed to the people of the western part of the province promising the security of their "persons, property and rights" if they remained at home pursuing their peaceful avocations and did not raise "their hands against their brethern."[2] Many men took advantage of this promise and refused to turn out for militia service and some, including two prominent locals, Simon Watson and Andrew Westbrook, joined Hull's army and were soon leading American scouting parties. The American incursion did not last long, however, as Hull withdrew to Detroit, where he was accosted on 15 August by a small British and Canadian army under the command of Major-General Isaac Brock, the British commander in Upper Canada. Brock was weaker in numbers than Hull but had a strong contingent of aboriginal warriors led by Tecumseh. Playing on this fact, Brock demanded that Hull surrender or the warriors would be beyond his control when the fighting started. To Brock's utter amazement Hull offered to surrender, not only his army (including detachments not at Detroit) but the entire Michigan Territory. This surrender was quickly accepted, of course, and Hull's army went into the bag although Watson and Westbrook managed to escape.[*3]

There was consternation in Washington when the government learned of this disaster. Orders were given to Brigadier-General William H. Harrison, the governor of the Indiana Territory, to retake Detroit and invade Canada. Although Washington expected him to mount an autumn offensive, Harrison, an experienced wilderness campaigner, moved carefully and first took care to establish logistical support. He was also distracted by a series of raids launched against frontier posts and communities by the members of Tecumseh's aboriginal confederacy who, heartened by the fall of Detroit and Mackinac Island, now actively supported Britain. Harrison slowly advanced toward Detroit but his subordinate, Brigadier-General James Winchester, moved his separate force more aggressively, isolating himself from Harrison and possible reinforcement. This did not escape the notice of Colonel Henry Procter, the British commander on the Detroit, who launched a surprise attack on Winchester at Frenchtown

---

* Hull was court-martialled for his actions in 1812, found guilty and condemned to death but his sentence was commuted by the president.

Major-General William Henry Harrison (1773-1841). A skilled frontier governor and militia officer, Harrison was appointed to the command in the Northwest in late 1812. It took him a year to do it, but by the autumn of 1813 he had broken the back of Tecumseh's confederacy and recovered lost territory. (Print after portrait by Charles Wilson Peale)

on the River Raisin, on 22 January 1813. After a bloody engagement, Winchester surrendered but unfortunately Tecumseh was not present and the warriors got out of control and murdered American prisoners, an event that shocked the republic and gave birth to a vengeful new battle cry, "Remember the Raisin!"[4]

Most of Harrison's troops were militia and volunteers, enlisted only for short periods of service, and as their terms expired, his strength began to dwindle. In March 1813 Secretary of War John Armstrong ordered Harrison to suspend all offensive action until the U.S. Navy acquired superiority on Lake Erie. Harrison therefore moved much of his army into a large fortified position he constructed at Fort Meigs on the Maumee River in Ohio. It is interesting to note that the engineer officer who designed this fortification was Major Eleazar D. Wood, who would play a prominent part at Fort Erie the next year. In May 1813 British and aboriginal forces under the newly-promoted Brigadier-General Procter and Tecumseh besieged Fort Meigs, and again it is worthy of comment that Wood constructed earthen traverses to prevent British artillery from being able to rake the entire perimeter, as was to be done at Fort Erie. When Harrison received reinforcements, Procter broke off the siege but returned in late July to try unsuccessfully to draw the garrison out of their defence works. After an attempt to assault nearby Fort Stephenson failed miserably at the cost of heavy casualties, Procter withdrew to Fort Malden at Amherstburg on the Canadian side of the Detroit River. Being at the very end of the British supply line, he received only a trickle of reinforcements – and many of these were siphoned off by British commanders farther east – and he was short of almost every article needed to properly defend the Detroit frontier against a determined invasion. Harrison, meanwhile, under orders to wait for the navy, had spent the remainder of the summer amassing a force to carry out an invasion of Canada. By early September he had gathered an army of 5,650 regular, militia and volunteer troops (and a patriotic pig who had followed one Kentucky unit all the way from the bluegrass state) and was awaiting the outcome on the lake.[5]

Commander Robert H. Barclay, RN, (1786-1837). A veteran naval officer, Barclay was appointed to command the British Lake Erie squadron in 1813. Yeo ignored his frequent appeals for personnel, equipment and weapons, forcing Barclay to fight a battle against a superior enemy that he was almost certain to lose. Nonetheless, the battle of Lake Erie was a hard fought and close action. (Toronto Reference Library, T-15259)

Commander Robert Barclay, RN, the British naval commander on Lake Erie, was a veteran officer who had lost an arm at the battle of Trafalgar in 1805. He spent much of the summer of 1813 blockading the American naval base at Presque Isle Bay, Pennsylvania. There, an energetic young American naval officer, Master Commandant Oliver Hazard Perry, was overseeing the construction of a squadron that would rival the British naval force on the lake. Barclay's appeal to the army commander in Upper Canada, at that time Major-General Francis De Rottenburg, for troops to carry out an attack on Presque Isle, was rejected and he had to content himself with a blockade, hoping to catch his opponents while they crossed the sand bar at the mouth of Presque Isle Bay, which would necessitate the removal of the ships' armament, making them vulnerable. Unfortunately, for reasons that have never been properly explained, Barclay was absent for part of the time this process took place and did not see fit to interfere with it when he returned on 4 August.[6]

With the American squadron out on the lake, a battle was inevitable because Perry could interdict the British supply line. Barclay's squadron was much weaker than that of his opponent. Barclay commanded six vessels with 35 guns and 28 carronades with a broadside weight of 459 lb. against Perry who had vessels mounting 15 guns and 35 carronades with a broadside weight of 896 lb. To make matters worse, Yeo had starved the Lake Erie squadron of seamen and equipment

Master Commandant Oliver H. Perry, USN (1785-1819). Still a young man in 1813 when he was appointed to command the American squadron on Lake Erie, Perry built and equipped it in a period of a few months. On 13 September he defeated and captured the entire British squadron after a hard fought battle with heavy casualties on both sides. (Library of Congress)

to build up his command on Lake Ontario, and Barclay only had ten seamen in each of his vessels, the remainder being soldiers. He had made repeated requests to Yeo for more seamen, writing no fewer than eight letters between June and September 1813 but never receiving a reply. In desperation Barclay appealed to Prevost, who tried to obtain trained seamen from Admiral John Warren, the naval commander on the Atlantic coast, to no avail but did provide Barclay with soldiers to fill out his ships' companies.[7] Barclay had other shortages: he had no locks for his ordnance and his flagship, HMS *Detroit*, was armed with a hodge-podge of weaponry, much of it taken from the ramparts of Fort Malden. The odds were not attractive and, writing to his brother in early September, the British naval commander commented that he had "never underestimated my enemy" and would "therefore expect a sanguinary contest."[8] "Times are serious," he added,

> and the want of exertion on the part of Government have made them almost dangerous. It is unpardonable, the neglect of not having sent seamen to this Lake. I am in the command of a squadron that might raise the envy of any officer, was that squadron well manned. As I am, I have the whole charge almost of this province on my shoulders (for without the command of the Lake, we must be starved) – and am chiefly manned with soldiers, brave to excess, I own a soldier's character; but they are not the crew for a British man of war.[9]

Three days later, the two squadrons met at Put-In Bay on the Ohio shore. On board his flagship the USS *Niagara*, Perry hoisted a special dark blue flag, which bore a motto in white letters: "Don't Give Up the Ship" – the dying appeal of Captain James Lawrence when his frigate, the USS *Chesapeake*, had fought the British frigate *Shannon* the previous June. The battle at Put-In Bay lasted two hours and it was a hard-fought action. Years later Gunner David Bunnel, who served on board the USS *Niagara*, recalled some of the scenes he witnessed that day on Lake Erie:

> My comrades fell on all sides of me. One man who stood next to me, was most shockingly wounded – having both his legs shot off ... and a number of the spikes from the bulwark drove into his body. ......
>
> At last my gun got so warm that it jumped entirely out of its carriage, which rendered it useless. Five of my men out of eight were either killed or wounded. I went to the next gun and found there but one man left, but by the assistance of my three she was soon made to play again. I could now hear an occasional gun fired from our vessel. I looked up to see if our flag

The battle of Lake Erie, 10 September 1813. The two squadrons met at Put-In-Bay near the western end of the lake to commence a vicious, obstinate action that cost heavy casualties on both sides. In the end, Perry prevailed and Lake Erie was now controlled by the United States. (Painting by Peter Rindlisbacher, courtesy of the artist)

was still flying, and with pleasure beheld, partly obscured by smoke, the star spangled banner yet waving ……

During the action, a shot struck a man in the head, who was standing close by me; his brains flew so thick in my face, that I was for some time blinded, and for a few moments was at a loss to ascertain whether it was him or me who was killed.

We had pease boiling for dinner – our place for cooking was on deck, and during the action a shot had penetrated the boiler, and the peas were rolling all over the deck, – we had several pigs loose on deck, and I actually saw one of them eating peas that had both his hind legs shot off – and a little dog belonging to one of the officers, that was wounded, ran from one end of the vessel to the other, howling in the most dreadful manner.[10]

Barclay, who was wounded twice, had to give up command and his successor surrendered the British squadron to save lives because it was clear that Perry had a overwhelming advantage. The losses were sixty-five killed or wounded on both sides and Lake Erie was now controlled by the United States. Perry sent a terse note to inform Harrison that "We have met the enemy and they are ours – two ships, two brigs, one schooner, and a sloop."[11]

Barclay's defeat put Procter in an impossible position and he began to prepare for a withdrawal. This did not please Tecumseh, who publicly chastized the British general for being a coward:

> Our ships have gone one way, and we are much astonished to see our Father tying up every thing and preparing to run the other, without letting his red children know what his intentions are. You always told us to remain here and take care of our lands; it made our hearts glad to hear that was your wish. Our Great Father, the King, is the head and you represent him. You always told us that you would never draw your foot off British ground; but now, Father, we see you are drawing back, and we are sorry to see our Father doing so, without seeing the enemy. We must compare our Father's conduct to a fat animal that carries its tail upon its back; but when affrighted, it drops it between its legs and runs off.[12]

Be that as it may, Procter began to retreat on 24 September, first north to Sandwich and then east up the Thames River, which was navigable along most of its length. He was accompanied by Tecumseh's warriors, whose numbers dwindled on a daily basis, and encumbered by baggage, supply wagons and dependants. Progress was slow and Procter, not believing that Harrison would pursue him, did not even bother to destroy the bridges over the many creeks that had to be crossed.

Unfortunately for the British general, Harrison was actually hot on his trail. With the assistance of Perry's squadron, he had landed his army at Malden three days after the British had abandoned that place. All his army, that is, except for the patriotic pig from Kentucky, who positively refused to embark for Canada – her conduct being attributed "to constitutional scruples" because "she knew it was contrary to the constitution to force a militia pig" over the border, and she was therefore permitted to remain on American soil.[13] Harrison encouraged his men to "Remember the river Raisin; but remember it only, whilst victory is suspended" because the "revenge of a soldier can not be gratified on a fallen enemy."[14] As they approached Amherstburg, one American recalled, "instead of the red coats and war whoop of the Indians, a group of well-dressed ladies advanced to meet us, and to implore mercy and protection."[15] After Harrison's senior officers assured the women that the forces of the United States "came not to make war upon women and children but to protect them," Harrison's troops marched through the village "to the thunder of 'Yankee Doodle.'"[16] Harrison then set out in pursuit of the retreating enemy and by 4 October was close to the Moravian mission at Fairfield when he learned that Procter's army was at that place.

Procter knew that he had to make a stand and chose a position that was flanked on the left by the Thames River and on the right by a swamp and woods. He placed his 450 regulars, mainly the 41st Foot with some small detachments of other units and one field gun, on the left by the river and Tecumseh's 500 warriors in the woods on the right. Procter's deployment was curious and his regulars ended up poorly positioned with gaps in their line. This became apparent during the afternoon of 5 October when Harrison arrived with about 3,000 men, one third of them on horseback. The approach to the British position was fairly flat and open and, after some skirmishing, Harrison sent Colonel Richard Johnson's mounted regiment, nearly a thousand strong, directly at the 41st Foot, which fired a volley and collapsed. Captain Robert McAfee of Johnson's unit recalled that

the trumpet then sounded and we charged on horseback about fifty yards when the spys fired and were fired on by the British, they nearly all dismounted and began to fire from behind trees which gave us a check and we had to halt our danger thus on horseback in column was immediately seen, the spys were ordered to mount and charge every officer exerted himself and Genl. Harrison exclaimed charge them my brave Kentuckians and the Indian yell was raised and we rushed upon them like a storm and received a heavy fire by the whole British line when at the distance of twenty steps, but it only inspired us with fresh courage and before they could reload we broke their lines & one half of the Battalion wheeled to the left and the other to the right & completely surrounded the British who immediately surrendered as fast as they could throw down their arms.[17]

Private Shadrach Byfield of the 41st Foot, who was on the receiving end of this mounted tidal wave, remembered that,

after exchanging a few shots, our men gave way. I was in the act of retreating, when one of our sergeants exclaimed, "For God's sake, men, stand and fight." I stood by him and fired one shot, but the line was broken and the men were retreating. I then made my escape farther into the wood, where I met some Indians, who said that they had beaten the enemy on the right, but that ... [Tecumseh] ... was killed, and they then retreated.[18]

Having disposed of the regular troops, Harrison turned his attention to Tecumseh's warriors on the British right. Here the combat was more obstinate and both sides took casualties. When Tecumseh was killed, however, his followers lost heart and began to melt away. In this part of the field, the fighting was vicious – a Kentucky rifleman remembered one of his comrades "shot an Indian on the other side of the river Thames, swam over and scalped him and swam back."[19]

Procter lost 634 men in the battle of Moraviantown* but only 25 were killed or wounded, the remainder being prisoners. Harrison reported 7 killed and 22 wounded. In the following few weeks, about 250 British officers and enlisted men straggled into the British post at Burlington Heights. Almost to a man, they complained about their commander and Prevost had trouble getting a coherent report from Procter as to what had happened. Procter himself laid part of the blame on the 41st Foot, whose conduct "was not such as I have on other occasions witnessed with pride and satisfaction," nor did he feel that he received the "cordial aid I sought and was entitled to."[20] This did not fool his superiors and Procter was eventually court-martialled on charges relating to his conduct of the retreat and the battle. He was found partly guilty, publicly reprimanded for his actions and never again employed on active service.[21]

The battle of Moraviantown lasted no more than forty-five minutes but it radically changed the course of the war in the west. Harrison's victory had destroyed the power of Tecumseh's confederacy and permanently restored American control in the Northwest. Satisfied with his victory, Harrison did not mount a serious pursuit of the retreating British but on the following day retraced his steps to Detroit. Before he did so he burned to the ground the Moravian brothers' mission to the Lenapi (Delaware) people at Fairfield.†

On his return, most of Harrison's volunteer troops went home as their terms of service expired. Harrison was lionized throughout the United States and, in a triumphal journey through New York to Washington to discuss future plans, he was accorded every possible honour the republic could bestow before returning to Detroit in January 1814. Unfortunately, his acclaim incurred the jealousy of Secretary of War John Armstrong, who deliberately set out to provoke Harrison into retiring by using such calculated insults as issuing orders to his subordinates without informing him and trying to get him relegated to a lesser post. The result was that an exasperated Harrison submitted his resignation in May 1814 and the United States lost the services of a very good officer.[22]

---

* The action fought on 5 October 1813 is known as the battle of Moraviantown in Canada but as the battle of the Thames in the United States. As these words are being written in Canada, we will go with the former.

† This was unfortunately the third disaster the Moravians and their Lenapi congregation had experienced. The Moravian mission to the Christian Lenapi at Gnadenhutten, Pennsylvania, was massacred by the French in 1755 and, again, by the Pennsylvania militia in 1782. Ironically, the order had relocated it to Upper Canada, believing it to be more secure.

Death of Tecumseh at the battle of Moraviantown (or the Thames), 5 October 1813. The great aboriginal leader was killed in this engagement, which ended the power of his confederacy. This 19th century print purports to show him being killed by Colonel R. M. Johnson but this has never been verified. (Print by John L. McGee, author's collection)

For the people of western Upper Canada, the American victory at Moraviantown was a disaster as it ushered in a period of uncertainty and fear. British commanders more or less abandoned the area west of the Grand River, contenting themselves with establishing outposts of militia or regulars at Delaware, Dover, Long Point and Port Talbot. The Americans, who now occupied Amherstburg and Sandwich, created similar outposts and the area in between became a "no man's land" patrolled from time to time by both sides and also by robbers, smugglers and deserters.

Those who remained suffered at the hands of American raiders, who became very active. In November the Norfolk County militia were able to turn away a force of the Canadian Volunteers, Joseph Willcocks's renegade unit, when it tried to raid along the Grand River. In December a detachment of militia from Kent, Middlesex and Norfolk Counties, commanded by Lieutenant Henry Medcalf, surrounded and attacked a patrol from the Twenty-Sixth Infantry at McCrae's house on the banks of the Thames east of Sandwich. In the resulting action Medcalf's men killed one American and captured thirty-four officers and men.[23]

But these were the last British or Canadian successes in the west for some time as in 1814 the Americans and their renegade auxiliaries became very aggressive. Andrew Westbrook made a daring raid into Delaware Township in late January and captured the same militia officer, Captain Daniel Springer, who had tried to arrest him in 1812. The following month a force of 200 British regulars and Canadian militia attacked an entrenched party of 160 American regulars at the battle of the Longwoods but were beaten off with the loss of 14 killed and 51 wounded. Warmer weather brought more incursions and Westbrook was back in April, leading a mounted raid that penetrated as far as the Oxford settlement and caught Major Sykes Tousley, the local militia commander, in bed sound asleep with his wife. Mrs. Tousley, as one historian has told the tale,

> awoke first to stare at the barrel of a pistol which was pointed at her husband's head. Holding the pistol was none other than Andrew Westbrook, the Marauder! Before she could scream, Westbrook hissed his warning to her, "If you scream, I shall blow your husband's brains out!"
>
> Fortunately, Mrs. Tousley stifled her scream and attempted to control her terrified emotions. Nudging her husband awake with the pistol, Westbrook bade him to dress and come with him as Tousley was a prisoner of war.[24]

Things got worse in May. On the 14th of that month, a major American raid took place in the Long Point area. The USN squadron on Lake Erie landed a force of 800 regulars and volunteers, commanded by Lieutenant-Colonel John B. Campbell, which, guided by officers of the Canadian Volunteers, burned mills, houses and barns in the village of Dover and the surrounding area. Captain Samuel White, a volunteer officer, recalled that when the Americans approached Dover, they

> found it deserted by all but a few women, who had white clothes hanging upon broomsticks suing for peace. The only hostile demonstration on our part was the destruction of some mills employed in milling flour for the army, together with some houses used as stores, and those belonging to some officers, who, it had been ascertained, had been on the expedition of the burning of Buffalo and Black Rock some time previous. Every possible respect was paid to the women and children, and the best part of the furniture in the houses, which were destroyed, was even carried out by the troops previous to their being burned.[25]

Amelia Ryerse, whose widowed mother had certainly never taken part in the burning of Buffalo in December 1813, always remembered the following morning when Campbell's men arrived:

Mother and myself were at Breakfast, the Dogs made an unusual barking. I went to the door to discover the cause. When I looked up I saw the hillside and the fields as far as the eye could reach covered with American soldiers. They had landed at Patterson's Creek, Burnt the Mills and village of Port Dover and then marched to Ryerse.

Two men stepped from the ranks, selected some large chips, came into the room where we were standing and took coals from the hearth, without speaking. My mother knew instinctively what they were going to do. She went out and asked to see the commanding officer, a gentleman rode up to her and said he was the person she asked for. She entreated Him to spare her property and said that she was a widow with a young family. He answered her civilly & respectfully and regretted that his orders were to Burn, but that He would spare the house, which He did, & said in justification that the Buildings were used as Barracks and the mill furnished flour for British Troops.

Very soon we saw [a] column of dark smoke arise from every Building and what at early morn had been a prosperous homestead, at noon there remained only smouldering ruins.[26]

Many of Campbell's men were disgusted by his actions and he was subjected to a court of inquiry which admonished him for burning private dwellings, but that was all the punishment he received.[27]

In the late summer Andrew Westbrook became very aggressive, leading several raids in August and September on the Talbot settlement, the community established by the aristocratic Thomas Talbot on the north shore of Lake Erie east of Amherstburg. The local militia and the small detachments of regulars posted in the vicinity of the Grand River proved powerless to stop or even hinder this activity as they were either greatly outnumbered or assembled too late to catch the raiders. Many of these incursions were made to acquire foodstuffs as the Americans regarded western Upper Canada as their own granary. This was made official on 26 September when Colonel John Miller of the Seventeenth Infantry, commanding at Fort Detroit, issued a proclamation ordering all Canadian farmers in the vicinity of the Detroit and St. Clair rivers to bring any surplus grain, "more than is absolutely necessary for the use and consumption of their families and stock," to selected places by 1 November, where American agents would purchase it at a fair price.[28] Miller warned that any Canadian who withheld "such supplies of flour or grain," or failed "to deliver within the time prescribed, shall be severely punished." On the other side, Drummond declared limited martial law with regard to the procuring of foodstuffs for the British forces, which required farmers in the Grand River area to sell their surplus grain to the army commissary officers at a fair price fixed by local magistrates.[29]

The Canadian renegades such as Westbrook and Watson who led or accompanied these raids benefited from accurate information given to them by sympathizers who remained on British soil and they often took the opportunity to settle some personal scores, trying to kidnap militia officers or looting or burning their property. In late October, a party of marauders led by one John Dickson (or Dixon), a former resident of Norfolk, and an associate of Willcocks and Mallory of the Canadian Volunteers, surrounded the house of Captain William Francis at night and shouted for him to come out. Francis said

> he would surrender himself a prisoner, but begged them to spare his life, which they [Dickson's men] declared they would not. He then looked out of the upper window to see if there was any way to escape and was shot through the head. The family heard him fall. They then desired them [the Francis family] to take out the goods [the family's possessions], but would not suffer his remains to be removed, which was burned with the house.[30]

This act of cold-blooded murder shocked Francis's neighbours, and Lieutenant-Colonel Thomas Talbot, the senior militia officer in western Upper Canada, appealed to his superiors to "order out a greater force of militia for the guards."[31] Many civilians, however, fearful that they might suffer a similar fate, simply abandoned their property and withdrew to the security of the British garrison at Burlington Heights.

In September and early October American raiding parties came very close to that place without encountering any strong British or Canadian military presence.[32] This intelligence was given to Brigadier-General Duncan McArthur at Detroit, who had succeeded Harrison. He began to plan a raid into western Upper Canada that would be the largest mounted operation of the War of 1812.

Born in New York state, the 42-year-old McArthur had worked his way west as a young man and fought as a volunteer in the frontier conflicts with the aboriginal peoples waged in the 1790s. McArthur decided to settle in Ohio, where he worked as a surveyor and, through careful land speculation, became a wealthy man. He was elected to the state legislature in 1805 and was also active in militia affairs, rising to the rank of Ohio major-general. He commanded a volunteer regiment which joined Hull's army and, although not at Detroit, was surrendered along with his regiment by Hull in August 1812. Released on parole, he gained a seat in the House of Representatives in early 1813 but opted in-

Brigadier-General Duncan McArthur (1772-1839).
A frontier politician and militia officer before the war,
McArthur was brought into the regular army in 1813.
In the autumn of 1814, he planned and led the largest
mounted operation of the War of 1812, penetrating
deeply into British territory. (Courtesy, Ohio Historical
Society)

stead to accept a commission as a brigadier-general in the regular army. McArthur commanded
an Ohio volunteer brigade in Harrison's successful offensive during the autumn of 1813 and succeeded that officer as commander in the Northwest in May 1814.[33]

Harrison's victory at Moraviantown had broken up Tecumseh's confederacy
and in July 1814 a treaty was signed at Greenville, Ohio, between the United
States and many of the aboriginal nations that had fought against the republic.
Not only did these nations make peace, but they promised to fight against the
British and their aboriginal allies. Some nations refused, however, to come to
terms, notably the Potawatomi people, and in early August Secretary of War
John Armstrong, who was still in office at that time, ordered McArthur to carry
out a punitive expedition "of mounted men and friendly Indians against the
Potawatomie tribe inhabiting the country on both sides of Lake Michigan."[34]
Armstrong authorized the raising of 1,000 men to undertake this expedition
and McArthur immediately called on the governors of Kentucky and Ohio for
volunteers. Over the next few weeks, however, he began to have doubts about
the planned operation as information about the strength of the Potawatomi
was inaccurate and the republic's new aboriginal allies gained by the Treaty of
Greenville displayed a marked reluctance to fight their kindred people.[35]

The situation also changed following the failure of the Mackinac expedition
in late August 1814. Captured by the British at the outbreak of the war, Mackinac was the commercial centre of the Upper Great Lakes, and whichever nation held it would have much influence with the aboriginal nations resident in
the area. In the summer of 1814 the United States launched a major operation to
recover the island but it was repulsed and this gave heart to the aboriginal peoples allied to Britain, whose support of the Crown had been diminished by the
defeat at Moraviantown. McArthur suggested that the force he was assembling
at Detroit might be used against Mackinac but this proposal was turned down
by Washington. In October McArthur learned from raiding parties who had
penetrated into Upper Canada as far east as Oxford, forty miles from Burling-

ton Heights, that there were no strong British forces, either regular or militia, between that point and Detroit. Faced with a possible resurgence of aboriginal aggression, and having lost his two strongest regular units, the Seventeenth and Nineteenth Infantry, which had been transferred to the Niagara, McArthur decided that the best defence was a good offence. As he informed Secretary of War Monroe, it was "expedient, from the ardor and species of the force, that the mounted volunteers should be actively employed in the territory of the enemy, with a view to destroying their resources" and to "paralyze any efforts which might be made against this place during the winter."[36] In other words, he would take the war to the enemy before they brought it to him.

By late October McArthur had assembled a force of over 700 men at Detroit. It comprised a battalion of Kentucky volunteers and a battalion of Ohio volunteers, whose combined strength was 600 men, a company of U.S. Rangers, 50 men strong, under Captain Samuel McCormick, as well as a few Michigan Rangers and Michigan militia volunteers. Included in the force was a party of 74 Lenapi, Shawnee and Wyandot warriors led by three chiefs: Civil John (Corachcoonke) of the Seneca and Wolf (Piasek) and Captain Lewis (Quitawepahh) of the Shawnee people.[37] The entire force was mounted and shortly before their departure McArthur advised his men "to take special care of their horses; to prepare for a short, rapid and brilliant expedition – one which may be attended with danger and will require, fortitude to produce a successful issue."[38] He trusted few of the residents along the Detroit River on either side of the border and had no great opinion of them, finding their society truly "disageeable."[39] Since he knew that all military movements in the Detroit area "were rapidly communicated" to the British by spies and sympathizers, he took pains to conceal the purpose and direction of his planned move by pretending that "it was destined against the Indian towns at Saguina [Saginaw, Michigan]."[40]

To promote that idea, McArthur reported, "boats were prepared for the reception of artillery, to be conveyed through Lake St. Clair, up that river into Lake Huron, and to co-operate with the mounted troops in the attack."[41] So secret did McArthur keep his intentions that when his command rode out of Detroit on 22 October 1814, only a few of his senior officers knew the true destination. It was only four days later, while camped on the shore of Lake St. Clair, that he informed his men of the real objective of their mission.

Using the boats that had moved with him from Detroit, McArthur crossed his troops into Canada on 27 October and captured the settlement of Baldoon. Established by Lord Selkirk ten years earlier, this struggling community of Scots emigrants had been raided before and had precious little worth looting. Nonetheless McArthur's men confiscated portable property and horses and this was to set a pattern throughout the raid. McArthur had brought sufficient rations to feed his men and horses for about a week, but after that his command "lived entirely on the enemy."[42] Although he claimed that no more private property was taken or destroyed "than was absolutely necessary for the support of the troops," he did admit that "there were some partial abuses produced by the unfortunate examples presented by the Indians."[43] The detailed war loss claims filed by civilian sufferers preserved in the Canadian archives demonstrate that the raiders took from the helpless civilians anything they wanted or needed, particularly horses to replace their own tired mounts, and livestock and forage to provide sustenance for man and beast.[44]

Baldoon was isolated from the rest of western Upper Canada by Bear Creek, which was very high at that time of year, so its inhabitants could not alert the province. Knowing this, McArthur opted to stay off the main roads and ride thirty miles southeast across country to a point on the north bank of the Thames River near the Moravian settlement at Fairfield, which Harrison had destroyed the previous year. The raiders arrived at Fairfield, on 30 October and spent the night there before heading east on the road through the Longwoods, which ran parallel to the Thames on its north bank. The Longwoods was a massive primal forest nearly thirty miles in length, containing tall and thick stands of high ash, birch, chestnut, hickory, oak and walnut trees, with foliage so rich that the sun could not penetrate and travellers moved in perpetual shade. Just before entering the Longwoods, McArthur's advance guard seized a mounted British sergeant who was taking news of the raid to the garrison at Burlington. This stroke of luck meant that McArthur could move up the Thames without fearing an ambush, as the defenders would have no clear warning of his approach.[45]

Without concrete information, the British reaction to McArthur's raid was slow. It appears that the first news of the American movement came to the attention of Lieutenant-Colonel William Smelt at Burlington in the form of a message that an American party had landed at the mouth of the Grand River. In reporting this information Smelt advised that, if true, this landing would "be nothing more than a marauding [party] as I do not conceive they would venture so far into this country unless they had a very large raiding force, which I do not hear to be the case."[46] Smelt added an interesting postscript to his message: "P.S. I forgot to mention that there is a report of another party coming down from Detroit." Smelt's message was passed up the chain of command to Drummond at Chippawa, who had for some time been hearing rumours from "various sources" of an American plan to "push on a party of mounted men" from Detroit up the Thames River to Burlington.[47] Now he had news of another enemy force landing at the mouth of the Grand but, as he reported to Prevost, he felt that these reports were "confused and indistinct, and I doubt not will prove that the parties in question are a small number of plunderers whom the armed settlers of the country ought to repel."[48] Smelt's message was also relayed to Lieutenant-Colonel John Goulston Price Tucker, the same "Brigadier Shindy" who had been defeated at Conjocta Creek the previous August and was now commanding at York. Tucker believed that the enemy's objective was to seize Burlington and York and that the 6,300 troops under Izard's command on the Niagara were really "only displayed as a mask for the projected operations against Burlington."[49] For lack of accurate intelligence, however, nothing was done.

McArthur took two days to traverse the Longwoods but encountered no opposition. By 2 November he was approaching the settlement of Delaware on the south bank of the Thames and ordered his advance guard to cross the river and post vedettes on all roads and paths leading out of the place so that no warning could be sent to neighbouring communities. There was some delay getting the main body over the river, but it eventually crossed using an old scow and rafts to carry the heavy baggage. McArthur only tarried in Delaware a short time, during which his men relieved the inhabitants of much property and burned at least one of the local mills. At this point, many of the Michigan militia, worried about the distance they had travelled and feeling that they were not being treated well by McArthur, left the expedition and went home. During the night of 3 November, the raiders camped between Delaware and Oxford, the next community, and then pushed on for the latter place, 150 miles from Detroit and fifty miles from Burlington.[50]

On the morning of 4 November McArthur's men rode into Oxford before the residents "knew that a force was approaching."[51] The people of Oxford "were promised protection to their persons and property upon condition that they remained peaceably at their respective homes," otherwise "they were assured that their property should be destroyed." Two Canadians, George Nichol and Jacob Wood, decided to warn the people of Burford, the next community. Leaving their homes at 3 A.M. and evading McArthur's sentries and vedettes, they made their way to Burford and informed Lieutenant-Colonel Henry Bostwick, the commanding officer of the 1st Regiment of Oxford Militia, that a strong American mounted force was on his doorstep. Bostwick decided that his best course was take up a position on high ground at Malcolm's Creek, ten miles south of Burford, which was a convenient place where detachments from the Middlesex and Norfolk Regiments could reinforce Bostwick's small force of only 150 Oxford militia.[52]

Unfortunately for Nichol and Wood, on the morning of 5 November an informer named Bazely reported their activity to McArthur, who immediately ordered their property – "consisting of two dwelling houses, two barns, and one shop" – set on fire.[53] The same informer identified the residences of several other militia officers and men who were absent on service, and McArthur had their property put to the torch. He then ordered his command to proceed to Burford and on the way "this horde of undisciplined partisans spread out over the country like a flight of locusts, to pillage and devour the lon[e]ly settler along the side roads and back concessions."[54] The raiders rode into Burford during the afternoon, and in later years a local historian, who spoke with the people of the village who were present that day, wrote that the Americans were mounted "mostly on Canadian horses stolen from the inhabitants during their passage, their worn out and useless mounts having been discarded" and there "were many led horses, loaded with plunder of every description."[55] Although Burford was a well-settled community, McArthur did not tarry there after he learned that the militia had been embodied and were gathering at Malcolm's Creek to the south. Having no intention of fighting an action he did not have to fight, McArthur collected "his noisy, threatening, thieving rabble, most of whom were dressed in their hunting outfits and equipped with scalping knives, tomahawks and long rifles," and started for the Grand River, five miles to the east and twenty-five miles from Burlington Heights, his intended objective.[56]

By now the British and Canadian military were waking – as well they should have – to the fact that a large enemy mounted force had penetrated deep into Upper Canada. Various reports had filtered into Burlington which gave Lieutenant-Colonel William Smelt, the senior officer at that place, an accurate picture of the size of McArthur's force and its probable objective. Smelt moved forward with 200 men of the 103rd Foot and a large force of militia drawn from the Burlington Heights

Upper Canada militiaman, 1814. As the war went on and more regular troops arrived from overseas or were raised in Canada, the militia became less important to the defence of British North America. They could be called on in an emergency as they were at Malcolm's Mills in the autumn of 1814. Lacking uniforms, they identified themselves by fastening strips of cloth around their arm as shown here. (Painting by Eric Manders, courtesy Parks Canada.

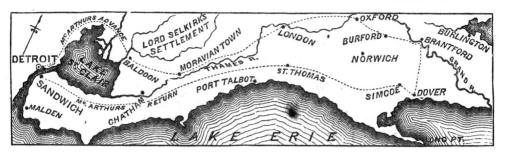

McArthur's Raid, October–November 1814. McArthur's incursion into western Upper Canada was the largest mounted operation of the war. From Detroit he penetrated 200 miles into British territory, riding more than 400 miles. (From Benson Lossing, *Pictorial Field-Book of the War of 1812*)

area, and a contingent of Six Nations warriors from the Grand River nations. He had also ordered up two 6-pdr. field guns in support. Major Adam Muir of the 41st Foot – captured at Moraviantown and only recently released – assembled a small force of about a hundred Lincoln militia and warriors at Brant's Ford on the Grand River, the most likely crossing spot for the raiders. Muir sank the scow used for ferrying and positioned his force on the east bank of the river. Meanwhile, reinforcements from the 1st and 2nd Norfolk, 1st Oxford and 1st Middlesex marched into Bostwick's position at Malcolm's Creek. Bostwick had ripped up the planks of the bridge spanning the waterway, which powered a nearby sawmill, and deployed his force, which would eventually number about 400, on a ridge south of the creek, where they built crude breastworks of logs and rails. Behind these defences he might be able to successfully hold the creek against a mounted force superior in numbers, delaying McArthur long enough for Smelt to assemble a force of regulars to deal him a decisive blow.[57]

McArthur's horsemen reached Brant's Ford late in the afternoon of 5 November, the first Americans to enter this area during the war. His scouts immediately came under fire from Muir's people on the opposite bank. There was an exchange of musketry but McArthur was fortunate to capture a prisoner, who provided him with much useful intelligence that caused him to alter his plans. As he later reported, it had been his

> intention to cross [the] Grand River as soon as possible, without regarding the Militia collected at Malcolm's mills, and attack Burlington. To my great mortification, upon our arrival at the river we found it high and rapid from the late excessive rains. ……
>
> No means were presented of even passing the river on rafts, and had it been effected, upon our return, the [Canadian] militia, contemptible as they

were, might have been encouraged to attack when a rapid river divided us. Major Muir, with about fifty Indians and fifty militia, was preparing to contest the passage. A battery was also erecting, as we understood, for three pieces of artillery, distant twelve miles on the road from Burlington.[58]

McArthur also learned that Izard had withdrawn the greater part of his army to the United States. Taking everything into consideration, the American commander decided not to attempt to cross the Grand and push on to Burlington Heights, but to turn south and "attack and defeat or disperse" Bostwick's militia at Malcolm's Creek and then move south to Long Point and burn the mills in that vicinity before returning to American territory "either by a movement across Grand River at the mouth to Fort Erie or along Talbot's street [road] to the Thames."[59] This decision made, McArthur camped for the night near the ford but out of sight of Muir's force.

On the following morning, 6 November, he rode south along the Long Point road toward Bostwick's position. McArthur left Captain Martin Wickcliffe's company from Nelson County, Kentucky, as a rearguard at Brant's Ford to cover the movement. Wickcliffe's orders were to demonstrate against Muir for two hours and then catch up with the main body, and he carried out these orders to the letter. It was around noon when McArthur's scouts reached Malcolm's Creek and reconnoitered Bostwick's position. It was a strong one. "We found the enemy," McArthur later reported, "fortified on commanding ground beyond a creek, deep and difficult of passage except at a bridge immediately in front of their works, which was destroyed."[60] Assessing the situation, McArthur decided to simultaneously attack both the front and rear of Bostwick's force:

> Arrangements were made for a joint attack on the front and rear. The Ohio troops with the advance guard and the Indians were accordingly thrown across the creek under cover of a thick wood, to approach the enemy in the rear, while the Kentucky troops were to attack in front as soon as the attention of the enemy was engaged by the attack in the rear.[61]

The manoeuvre took time to carry out and it was late afternoon before everyone was in place. McArthur accompanied the Ohio volunteers and the warriors, who moved down the north side of Malcolm's Creek looking for a place to ford. At one point, thinking that his men were too reluctant to test the water, he plunged into it but had only taken a few steps when it came up to his shoulders, which convinced him "that his men could not cross there and keep their ammunition dry."[62] Farther downstream, the party found a pile of driftwood in the waterway which provided a convenient means to cross over to the south side. Although Bostwick had posted sentries on both his flanks, McArthur's plan worked almost to perfection and was only spoiled at the last minute by "an unfortunate yell by our Indians" which gave away "the approach of the detachment destined to attack their rear." As Garrett Oakes of the Norfolk militia remembered, it was all over very fast:

> The first information we had of their proximity was by our sentinels firing and running in [to the position]. They continued firing upon us fully ten minutes before we could form into line, but providentially we were far down the hill side, so that they over shot us, and out of thousands of shots only three took effect, killing three of our men, one of them a sergeant of the regulars [Sergeant Collins of the 41st] that joined us that same day; the second, a neighbour of mine, Edwin Burtow [Edwin Barton] and one more. As they had the advantage of us in numbers and position we were ordered to retreat, which we did. I thought our commander acted wisely, for we were all raw to the business, without discipline, and armed with no better implements of war than old muskets, rifles and shot guns which had to be charged from powder horn and bullet pouch with tow for wadding, a slow process against cartridges.[63]

Most of the militia were able to escape captivity, only 111 being rounded up and forced to sign paroles before being released to their homes. There is some disagreement over the casualties. McArthur reported one killed and six wounded, while later research records two killed and two wounded on the Canadian side. A British detachment, which arrived on the field three days later, reported that the bodies of both Barton and Collins were "mutilated in a most horrible manner" with Barton being "actually butchered" and "scalped and cut shockingly."[64]

The Americans camped on the battlefield that night and on the following day rode south toward Long Point. On the way, they stopped and torched Malcolm's Mills and three other mills and searched every farmhouse for weapons. They also forced every male of military age to sign certificates that they had "been paroled not to bear arms against nor do anything prejudicial to the interests of the U.States during the present war until regularly exchanged," that is to say until the British released an American militiaman whom they had captured from his parole.[65] As these certificates basically exempted the bearer from militia service for long periods, some men were not unhappy to receive them as, by this time, many in Upper Canada – particularly in the western part of the province – had pretty well had a belly full of the war.

During the night of 7 November the raiders stayed at William Culver's Tavern, a few miles from Lake Erie in Woodhouse Township. According to Culver family legend McArthur's men, particularly the Kentuckians, had a good time and, after filling themselves full of "budge" or homebrew and "committing all the 'deviltry' they could think of, they 'borrowed' Mrs. Culver's favourite New Jersey horse, and proceeded on their home-pillaging tour."[66]

On the following day, 8 November, McArthur made an important decision. He had become apprehensive about being able to feed his men if he moved toward Fort Erie and about trying to cross the mouth of the Grand River, which was in full flood. He was also unsure about the military situation on the Niagara so he decided to turn west and move along the Talbot Road, which paralleled the north shore of Lake Erie. His men must have greeted this decision enthusiastically as by now they had been more than two weeks in the saddle. It took the raiders nearly another week to reach Detroit and on the way his command continued to merrily loot and pillage. Much too late, Drummond ordered strong forces of regular troops to move west of the Grand but by the time they crossed the river, McArthur was far beyond reach.

McArthur's force arrived at Sandwich on 17 November and crossed over to Detroit on the following day. McArthur praised his men for their conduct during a raid that had covered

> more than four hundred miles, one hundred and eighty of which is a wilderness and a considerable part of that distance too without any road. The Detachment, consisting of not more than seven hundred and twenty effectives, penetrated two hundred miles into the enemy's territory, destroyed upward of two hundred stands of arms, defeated and dispersed four or five hundred of their militia, encamped in a strong position …[67]

It had been a well planned and well conducted operation and McArthur did not exaggerate when he stated that

> The resources of the enemy have been essentially affected by the fact that the detachment subsisted entirely upon them, this circumstance together with the destruction of the five valuable mills in the vicinity of the Grand river, which were employed in the support of the enemy in the [Niagara] peninsula, will present objections to any attempts during the winter against this place [Detroit].[68]

It was no less than the truth and indeed Drummond's immediate concern was that as a result of the raid he would be unable to feed his troops during the winter. From Kingston, where he had shifted his headquarters in early November, Drummond appealed to Yeo for help, explaining that because of the destruction by the enemy of all the resources (and the mills) of the country to the westward of the Grand River, from which we had calculated upon receiving the principal part of the supplies destined to support the regular troops and Indians during the approaching winter, it becomes absolutely necessary that the means of feeding them should be forwarded from hence before the close of the navigation. I cannot exactly state the quantity of transport which will be required but I can, without hesitation, say that nothing less then the aid of the whole squadron will be sufficient to relieve the urgent wants of the right division of the army.[69]

Believing that Yeo could only "assent to a proposition which is so immediately connected with the preservation of an important part of the province," Drummond ordered the commissariat to actually begin loading the squadron "with every barrel of provisions which can possibly be spared." He need not have bothered as Yeo, having made two cruises to the Niagara, was not going to risk his flagship or his squadron by undertaking a third before winter because of possible bad weather. On 14 November Yeo turned Drummond down flat, expressing regret that while he had "at all times, from motives of duty and inclination, been ready and solicitous to co-operate and assist the army to the utmost of my means and ability," he felt even more distressed "that it is not in my power to comply with your request without exposing His Majesty's squadron to the most imminent danger, such as no officer would be warranted in risking."[70]

Drummond's reaction to this letter can only be imagined and he might be forgiven if he had torn it to shreds and stamped on it. The land commander must have controlled his temper, however, because Yeo's letter ended up in the official records. As it happened, the naval commander did permit some of the smaller ships of the squadron to make a third voyage to the Niagara but not his beloved *St. Lawrence*. At the time this correspondence took place, there were no fewer than 5,000 boat-loads (perhaps as much as 15,000-20,000 tons) of supplies waiting at Montreal for transport to Kingston. They might have been delivered if Yeo had not placed such a heavy strain on the supply system to build his leviathan.[71]

It was becoming clear that the campaign season in the northern theatre had ended. "We had now entered upon November," the British aboriginal leader John Norton recalled, "and from the Nature of the Climate" and the American evacuation of the Canadian side of the Niagara, the British, Canadian and aboriginal defenders of Canada "had reason to expect that we might pass the Winter in tranquility."[72] This was a wish heartily shared by their opponents as, in terms of military operations in the northern theatre, 1814 had been a very long year.

HMS *St. Lawrence* in winter. Yeo's leviathan of the lake only made two operational cruises before being laid up for the winter of 1814. After the war ended, she rendered excellent service as the venue for a large ball to celebrate the coming of peace. Taken out of service after the war, she was later sold for scrap for the exorbitant price of £25 ($125). (Painting by Peter Rindlisbacher, courtesy of the artist)

CHAPTER SIXTEEN

"Oh I would that the wars were all done"

WINTER QUARTERS AND THE COMING OF PEACE, NOVEMBER 1814–JUNE 1815

In the meadow one morning when pearly with drew
A fair pretty maid plucked violets blue.
I heard her clear voice making all the woods ring:
"Oh my love is in Flanders to fight for the king,
    And I would that the wars were well over,
    Oh I would that the wars were all done."

"I'll pluck the red robin so jaunty and gay;
Yet I have my Robin, but he's far away.
His jacket is red – and his cheeks – as the rose;
He sings of his Nell as to battle he goes."
    And I would, etc.

Ten thousand of bluebells now welcome the spring;
Oh when will the church bells for victory ring?
And the soldiers return and all England rejoice?
Oh then I'll be wed to the lad of my choice.
    And I would, etc.[1]

The first snow of the winter of 1814-1815 fell in early December. For this reason, Major-General George Izard's men were glad that he put them to work building huts for winter quarters as soon as they had withdrawn from Canada. Izard cantoned his infantry regiments between Buffalo and Black Rock and his artillery and cavalry units in outlying villages. Lieutenant Jacob Norton of the Fourth Infantry was disgusted when, just as the soldiers of his regiment were finishing their huts, it was ordered to move from Black Rock to a location closer to Buffalo. It seemed to be "an established rule of our feeble commanders," Norton complained, "that preparation for comfort is a sure presage of movement."[2] Such is life in the service but Norton was also unhappy about being too close to Buffalo, which he regarded as "a nest of villains, rogues, rascals, pickpockets, knaves & extortioners."[3]

Colonel Cromwell Pearce of the Sixteenth Infantry had a particular concern. "Generals and Subalterns," he noted, "obtained leave of absence before a hut was constructed to protect the soldiers from the inclemency of the winter, in a short time scarcely a General or Field Officer was to be found in the camp."[4] This was no exaggeration for Izard found himself bombarded with requests from officers for permission to leave the frontier over the winter to attend to "urgent private affairs." He refused most of them and, as he wrote to the secretary of war, thus "exposed myself to the ill-will of many individuals by resisting their importunities" but found that officers to whom he refused leave, simply contacted friends in the War Department who granted it.[5] By mid-December there were only two officers above the rank of major in Izard's division at Buffalo.

Izard's other problem was getting his men paid. "More than six months have elapsed," he wrote Monroe in January 1815, "since any of the troops have been paid; some of them have a twelve-month's pay due" but all were "astonishingly patient."[6] The men had still not received their salaries when Pearce took over the division at the end of January after Izard left the Niagara area. Pearce recalled that a good deal of unrest was beginning "to show itself" among the troops so he ordered double rations of bread and whisky, which gave "general satisfaction, and reconciled all difficulties."[7]

Major-General Jacob Brown's Second Division, the other component of the Northern Army, experienced a terrible march from the Niagara to Sackets Harbor in late October and early November. Captain Benjamin Ropes of the Twenty-First Infantry recalled that "it rained & snowed half of the time we ware on this March which made the roads intolerably bad & Mud very Deep."[8] The arrival of Brown's veterans at the Harbor reduced the great anxiety on Chauncey's part that his base would be attacked by Yeo. Brown's troops built their own winter quarters while, nearby, dockyard workers finished the hull of the battleship *New Orleans*, to be armed with eighty-seven guns, and there was talk of plans to build other large warships as Chauncey had no intention of being outgunned by Yeo when navigation resumed in the spring. In the meantime the American naval commander had a most interesting visitor, Lieutenant James McGhie, RN, the former commanding officer of HMS *Chubb*, the British sloop captured at Plattsburgh the previous September. McGhie had deserted – a rare thing for a British naval officer – because he felt that Yeo had unjustly reprimanded him for the loss of his command and was now earnestly seeking "employment" in the United States Navy. Wisely, Chauncey did not trust the man and ordered him to leave the Harbor under pain of arrest, which McGhie did, although he was seen later that winter at a ball in the nearby village of Denmark, still in British uniform.[9]

Sackets Harbor. The best deep anchorage on the American shore of Lake Ontario, Sackets Harbor was the major U.S. naval base on Lake Ontario and the headquarters of Commodore Isaac Chauncey during the war. Chauncey worried constantly about its security and he was right do so as it was attacked twice by the British. (From the *Naval Chronicle,* 1814)

Drummer Jarvis Hanks of the Eleventh Infantry found a profitable pastime at the Harbor that winter. "During the cold season," Jarvis recalled, "I was, much of my time, engaged in drawing plans of battles, fortifications, cantonments and harbors, on paper with water colours."[10] His officers encouraged Jarvis's budding artistic endeavours "by purchasing what I had, and commissioning me to execute more, under their direction," paying the boy one dollar for each completed work. Since Jarvis was only paid $9 a month, these commissions resulted in a substantial boost to his income.

About twenty-five airline miles across Lake Ontario from where Drummer Hanks carried out his artistic endeavours, Lieutenant John Le Couteur of the 104th Foot was a very happy man. He had regained his old lodging in Kingston with the Widow Robison, where he had stayed the previous winter, and whose family had taken him to their heart. In the four months Le Couteur had been absent in the Niagara, he found that Kingston had been "greatly strengthened" with "Six blockhouses and a stout picketing all round it besides the batteries – it is safe from a *coup de main* without the fleet."[11] Shortly after his return, however, the young officer was afflicted with attacks of rheumatism and dysentery that prostrated him for nearly six weeks. When he had recovered his health Le Couteur enjoyed dinners at his own or other regimental messes, dancing, either at private parties or the public assemblies, and reading

– Richardson's *Sir Charles Grandison* and Knox's *Elegant Extracts* were two of the books he records as having read that winter. Le Couteur also skated on the frozen lake and one day visited Yeo's squadron anchored off Point Frederick, finding it a "curious feeling to be able to glide close up to ships of War, reduced to wooden fortresses on a field of ice."[12]

The biggest military excitement Le Couteur experienced during the cold months was leading a patrol that apprehended a number of deserters. The biggest domestic excitement was created by his soldier servant, Private Cornelius Mills, who

> played me and my friend Mrs. [George Shore] a vile trick by getting her maid in the family way. I and He wished [Mills] to marry her but Cap[tain]. [George] S[hore]. never would consent to it which I was exceedingly angry at. However both the poor girl & child died. He was very penitent and really wished to do what He ought but was prevented – shamefully, I think.[13]

In Lower Canada, meanwhile, the winter of 1814-1815 proved a long one for the 88th Foot, which was stationed first at Three Rivers and then Sorel. The Ranger officers were lionized by local society and were popular guests, particularly with mothers having single daughters on their hands, who saw an excellent opportunity to make a good match for them, as a British officer was a prime target in the Canadian marital market. Unfortunately for such maternal ambitions, the 88th was transferred late in the winter to Saint John (modern St. Jean, Quebec) and only two Ranger officers were "hooked" into committing matrimony at Sorel although "several others were partly engaged."[14] There seemed little danger of a similar peril being encountered at Saint John, as it was known to be a dull sort of place – dull that is, until the first night the 88th Foot was in town.

As Lieutenant William Grattan of the Rangers tells the story, the officers of the regiment were invited that evening to dine with Major-General Thomas Brisbane. Although Brisbane was only 42, Grattan, with the self-satisfaction of the young, refers to him as an "old general of brigade." In any case, the company broke up at about 10 P.M. and the Rangers made their way back to their quarters. It seems that four officers – Lieutenants John Fairfield and Christopher Hilliard, and Ensigns John Hickson and Charles Morgan, to be precise – happened upon a brightly-lit hotel from which came "the sound of two or three fiddles" while visible at the windows were "the passing figures of several ladies." All this told plainly that a ball was taking place inside and it was just too good an opportunity to pass up so, without hesitating, the four Rangers plunged through the front doors of the hotel and climbed the stairs to the ball room on the first floor, with the same determination that the 88th Foot had shown when they had stormed the breach at the Spanish city of Ciudad Rodrigo some three years before. They emerged in the middle of a large chamber adorned with a fine display of young pulchritude, whose bright eyes lit up at the sight of scarlet uniforms. Unfortunately, what the Rangers did not know was that this ball had been organized by a number of American smugglers who had come over the border to sell provisions to the British army – and the Jonathans were not happy with the intrusion, even if redcoats were good customers.[15]

Almost immediately, so Grattan informs us, "a tall, raw-boned Yankee, about six feet five inches in height," approached the Rangers and demanded, in language "not the most polite, even for a Yankee," what "in h[el]l's d[amnatio]n brought them there?" Lieutenant Fairfield courteously replied that he and his comrades had just arrived in Saint John and hearing the music, thought this was a public ball and wished to join in the fun. The American retorted that the Rangers were "d[amnabl]y mistaken," that this was a private affair, and – at this point the Doodle unfortunately made a fatal mistake – "the sooner you make yourselves scarce the better, or we'll take the liberty of kicking you down the stairs." That was definitely the wrong thing to say to a British officer, particularly an infantry officer, and even more particularly an officer of the Connaught Rangers. There was but one correct response and it was quick in coming – Fairfield floored the rude Yankee with a single blow.

"A general row," says Grattan, now erupted as the Rangers engaged five times their number of Jonathans, while "men shouted" and "ladies screamed." Ensign Morgan, a strong fellow, finding himself battling half a dozen Doodles on his own, pulled the pipe down from the red hot stove in the middle of the room and flung it at them, which no doubt gave them pause to reflect. Unfortunately, in doing so, Morgan knocked over the stove, which "tumbled about the room, discharging its contents, and, in fine, setting fire" to the ballroom, which became "one mass of flame." Things now started to get truly riotous as

all the ladies, and several of the men, attempted to hurry out towards the street, but the passages were blocked up and all egress was denied them; for Morgan, Hickson, Hilliard and Fairfield, were combatting fiercely on the lobby [landing]. Several of the townspeople came rushing up the stairs, some from curiosity, others to assist in extinguishing the flames, but the moment they made their appearances they were knocked down.

The affair now assumed a very serious appearance, and even the most turbulent and refractory became cool. The ladies, one-half of them fainting, while the others were screaming, and endeavouring to get down stairs, in which attempt they lost the greater part of their dresses.

Fortunately, at this point, a sergeant arrived with the guard from the post, extinguished the fire and sent for a surgeon to tend the wounded.

The four Ranger officers – visions of courts martial dancing in their heads – were worried about the ramifications of this affair, as well they might be. The aggrieved Jonathans, as litigious as are most citizens of the republic, hired a Canadian lawyer – so much for patriotism – to bring a lawsuit against their Hibernian adversaries. It was dismissed on the ground that the Yankees had offered the first insult. What could not be so easily ignored was that a woman had been injured in the fray, and there was also a bill for damages from an apothecary whose shop was below the ballroom and who claimed the loss of "as many bottles of physic as would have drenched the stomachs of all the inhabitants of Lower Canada put together." In the end, all the officers of the 88th Foot dug into their own pockets to find the sum of £240 – three years' pay for an infantry lieutenant – which was presented to the aggrieved parties and the matter was closed. It was not forgotten, however, and the "battle of the ball" was told round the Rangers' mess table for years afterwards with considerable satisfaction because there had been some annoyance in the 88th that, with the exception of the light company which had fought at Plattsburgh, the Rangers had never got a chance to take on the Yankees. Thanks to Fairfield, Hickson, Hilliard and Morgan, they had now done so, vindicating the honour of the regiment.

Major-General Thomas Brisbane, of course, had more important things to concern him than to inquire too deeply into the behaviour of certain Connaught Ranger officers. Brisbane was actively planning an attack on Macdonough's Lake Champlain squadron now frozen in the ice at Whitehall, New York, at the head of the lake. Brisbane planned to transport 7,000 troops in a thousand sleighs up the frozen lake and capture or destroy Macdonough's ships, overturning at one blow the defeat suffered at the naval battle of Plattsburgh. It was a daring plan, which excited Prevost's interest but it was reluctantly shelved after Izard sent reinforcements to the garrison at the request of Secretary of War Monroe.[16]

For his part, Commodore James Yeo had ambitious plans for the spring of 1815. He wanted to build three frigates and two brigs at Isle-aux-Noix to again contest control of Lake Champlain. He also wished to construct a frigate at a dockyard that would be established at Penetanguishene on Georgian Bay, after the army had cut a road across country from York. With this vessel and others to be built at the same place, Yeo intended to battle for control of the Upper Great Lakes. At Kingston, late in the year, he completed the frigate HMS *Psyche*, which had been sent from Britain in a dismantled state and re-assembled. He also laid down the keels of another frigate and two ships of the line nearly as large as the *St. Lawrence,* as well as some transports and gunboats. To man these new vessels he requested the Admiralty to send him 868 seamen.[17]

Prevost approved most of these plans but he was not happy with the naval commander. Relations between the two men had soured, particularly after newspapers in Britain and Canada began publishing articles critical of Prevost, some of which were clearly based on leaks from naval sources. Other press attacks were so outlandish that it was clear they were complete fabrications, such as the London paper which assured its readers that, at Plattsburgh, Macomb

> was preparing to surrender, when the [British] retreat commenced. Sir George is severely censured in the private letters for this result. It was rumoured that General Robinson has been put under arrest, and that Generals Brisbane and Power have tendered their resignations to Sir G. Prevost. A general dissatisfaction prevailed against the latter, and had been openly manifested.[18]

In fact, Yeo had indeed been corresponding with the Admiralty on the subject of Plattsburgh, particularly after Captain Robert Barclay's court-martial for the loss of the Lake Erie squadron. In this process, which was held at Portsmouth in September, Barclay produced eight letters he had written to Yeo over a three-month period requesting assistance, not one of which had been answered by their addressee. The court cleared Barclay of all charges and attributed the loss of his command partly to the shortage of trained seamen, which Barclay "had repeatedly and earnestly requested to be sent to him."[19] This was not a reference to Prevost, who had personally tried to reinforce Barclay; it was a reference to Yeo and the naval commander was beginning to get nervous about his own career.

For Prevost, the major objective of an 1815 campaign would be Sackets Harbor, fulfilling the British government's orders of the previous June. Having grown more than a little weary of Yeo's intransigence toward supporting the army, he complained to London that the construction of the *St. Lawrence* had "absorbed almost the whole of the Summer Transport Service from Montreal leaving the Materials for an undertaking of the magnitude of the Destruction of Sacketts harbor" uncertain because Kingston was "at the extremity of the Line of Communication."[20] Reiterating yet again that in North America, military operations depended on naval operations, Prevost stressed that many naval commanders "consider themselves as directing Squadrons which by a trial of strength were to decide the fate of the War" when, in fact, they were forgetting that their most important role was to support "the Land Force for the general prosperity of the common cause." The result was that, "instead of that zealous, prompt, & cheerful cooperation so essential in the movement and very existence of H[is] M[ajesty]'s Troops on this widely extended frontier," every request for transport, "either of Men or Stores, is considered as hampering the powers of the Fleet and endangering its safety.[21]

There is no doubt that these words referred to Yeo and his behaviour during the campaign that had just ended. Prevost suggested that an admiral be sent to assume overall command on the lakes. This officer would work closely with the army staff to develop objectives and would direct the squadron commanders. This way, the army would not have to depend on a squadron commander – and again this was a direct reference to Yeo – "whose situation might on some occasions give him a bias incompatible with the real good of the service."[22]

B risbane was not the only senior officer planning a surprise raid that winter. At Sackets Harbor, Commodore Isaac Chauncey had come up with a novel way of reducing British naval superiority on Lake Ontario – he sent a party of men to blow up the *St. Lawrence*. On 12 November Midshipman James McGowan and a party of ten men crossed the lake in a boat. They sheltered in and among the many islands off Kingston until 16 November, when they prepared to make their final approach in darkness to the British naval base at Point Frederick. Their plan was to get as close as possible to the target ship at night and affix a "torpedo" (a mine in modern language) to her hull, light

Winter quarters, 1814-1815. If they had warm quarters for the winter, the soldiers of both nations looked forward to a period of rest and relaxation. Depicted here is a typical tavern scene in Lower Canada with soldiers and civilians engaging in a jollification. (Painting by Eugene Leliepvre, courtesy Parks Canada)

James Monroe (1758-1831). One of the most effective members of the Madison administration, Secretary of State Monroe took over the War Department after John Armstrong resigned in September 1814. He brought much common sense to his new post, but by this time the perilous financial state of the republic precluded his plans for a major offensive against Canada. (Library of Congress)

the fuze and then pull hard for some distant place. Unfortunately, McGowan's party was discovered by two British guard boats, which approached to make a closer investigation. Their British crews, however, promptly surrendered when McGowan's men rushed them after they landed. As McGowan now had eleven prisoners, he had to end his mission as he could not take the prisoners with him to Kingston and he could not leave them on the island, as he did not have enough men to guard them. He therefore returned to the Harbor with his prizes and prisoners, and shortly thereafter received a well-earned promotion to lieutenant.[23]

Secretary of the Navy William Jones favoured more conventional methods of regaining naval superiority on Lake Ontario. He authorized the construction of three ships-of-the-line at Sackets Harbor, each mounting nearly as many guns as the *St. Lawrence*. But Jones was also starting to have doubts about this "war of carpenters" being waged fast and furious at dockyards on the Great Lakes. He reminded President James Madison that the republic was "at War with the most potent Naval power in the world," an enemy that could land anywhere on the Atlantic or Gulf coasts, and felt that the American naval strength should be deployed on those coasts. In the secretary's opinion, the naval war on the lakes was "greatly overrated" and "further sacrifices in the struggle would be incompatible with the public interest."[24] Instead, he suggested the United States seize a point on the St. Lawrence River that, "well fortified and held with a strong force, would effectually cut off all transportation either of troops or stores from below," thus severing the logistical throat of the British forces to the west. "Of what consequence then," he asked the president, "would the Naval Command of Lake Ontario be to the enemy."[25]

An attempt to cut the St. Lawrence was dreaded by any British soldier or sailor with the sense to know that the preservation of that lifeline was absolutely crucial to the survival of Canada. As one British officer put it:

Not only provisions, but every kind of Military and Naval Stores, every bolt of canvas, every rope yarn, as well as the heavier articles of guns, shot, cables, anchors, and all the numerous etceteras for furnishing a large squadron, arming forts, supplying arms for the militia and the line, had to be brought from Montreal to Kingston, a distance of nearly 200 miles, by land in winter, and in summer by flat-bottomed boats, which had to tow up the rapids, and sail up the still parts of the river, (in many places not a mile in breadth, between the British and American shores,) exposed to the shot of the enemy without any protection; for with the small body of troops we had in the country, it was utterly impossible that we could detach a force sufficient to protect the numerous brigades of boats that were daily proceeding up the river, and we must have been utterly undone, had not the ignorance and inertness of the enemy saved us.[26]

Izard stressed the vulnerability of the St. Lawrence to Secretary of War James Monroe and suggested that "the object of our first operations next campaign should be the establishment of a respectable fortress on that river, which would interrupt its navigation and thus paralyze the Upper Province."[27]

Monroe called both Brown and Izard to Washington to discuss plans for the coming year. In late December 1814, however, Izard indicated his wish to resign from the army because "attempts have been made to lessen the confidence of government, as well as the public, in my ability to execute the important duties intrusted to me."[28] Izard had recently come under criticism in the press for his actions during the 1814 campaign and, being a sensitive man, felt his "voluntary retirement" would relieve the War Department from embarrassment. Monroe refused to accept Izard's resignation before discussing it personally.[29] In the end, however, it was Brown who met with the secretary to contemplate strategy for the forthcoming campaign. This pleased Izard as he had great admiration and respect for Brown, who he felt was "a brave, intelligent and active officer" and had earlier suggested to Monroe that Brown assume command in the north.[30] As we have seen, Brown did not reciprocate Izard's feelings.

In late January Monroe met with Brown, discussing options for the 1815 campaign season. The two men envisaged a major offensive to be carried out by no fewer than 15,000 regulars and 30,000 New York and Vermont militia under Brown's overall command. Brown would either first cut the St. Lawrence, most likely at Ogdensburg, and then mop up, both east and west, or would drive from Lake Champlain directly on Montreal. As Monroe explained it:

The great object to be attained, is to carry the war into Canada, and to break the British power there, to the utmost practicable extent. After making due allowance for the number of British forces, for the difficulties attending the passage of the Saint Lawrence, and the immature state of our preparations, I think that we may enter Canada, and gain a decided superiority this next campaign. To what extent it may be carried, is uncertain, as it will depend upon many circumstances, of which we can form no estimate at this time. It seems probable, however, that if we secure the landing of a great force, and beat them completely in the field at any point between *Kingston and Montreal, or wherever we may select, we shall be able to drive them into Quebec* ......

At every other point above [west of] Kingston, our superiority may be whatever we choose to make it; and altho' it will [not] consist principally, or in any considerable force of regular troops, it will be of a character to press the enemy, interrupt his supplies, fight and demolish him...

If we succeed in the invasion of Canada, we take the war from our seaboards at once. It is only by making a defensive war there [i.e., on the northern frontier] that we enable the enemy to detach troops here.[31]

It was a good plan, featuring concentration of force against the most important and vulnerable areas of Canada, but it ignored actual reality. By January 1815 the British forces defending Canada amounted to 25,772 British and Canadian regulars formed in three strong divisions and a number of independent brigades and garrisons, commanded by competent generals and backed by a numerous militia.[32] Monroe must also have known that, given the state of the republic, the plan could never be carried out.

The truth was that by the last days of 1814 and the first of 1815, the United States was bankrupt and on the verge of disintegration. In September 1814 Secretary of the Treasury George Campbell stated that $23 million were required to continue the war effort for the remainder of that year. He then resigned and his successor, Alexander Dallas, proposed that a national bank be chartered to solve a serious financial crisis but ran into entrenched congressional opposition and the matter was debated for more than four months without a solution being found. By the end of 1814 the War Department had run out of money and there were no funds available for the prosecution of the war effort in 1815. Shortage of money also meant that Secretary of War Monroe's efforts to increase the strength of the regular army came to nothing and he too encountered determined resistance in congress when he tried to introduce a limited form of conscription – the best he was able to get was a bill passed permitting the president to call out 40,000 state troops for twelve months' service but they could not be employed outside their own or an adjoining state without the permission of the governor of the state that had raised them. At best, these would be home defence troops, completely unsuitable for an offensive war against British North America and their use would vest in the state governors even more influence on how the war was to be conducted.[33]

Finally, the New England states, which had been resolutely opposed to the war since the outset, held a convention in December 1814. Ostensibly it was to discuss matters of local defence but many feared that the opposition Federalist governors of the area would push for secession from a union governed by Republicans. As it turned out, the Hartford Convention, whose delegates did not include representation from New Hampshire or Vermont, did not do much more than criticize Madison's administration of the war and repeat many of the complaints New England had been making against the Republican party since it came to power in 1800.[34]

The effect of all these problems – money, manpower and federal–state relations – more or less ensured that there would be no major campaign against Canada in the spring of 1815. The republic no longer had the capability of waging offensive war because, as one historian has noted, thirty months of conflict "had weakened the capacities of the federal government more than it had strengthened them."[35] There was also a more pressing problem facing Madison's administration – a major British invasion was underway in Louisiana.

The Louisiana campaign of 1814–1815 is one of the most studied episodes of the War of 1812 and the present author, who is concerned with the war in the northern theatre, sees little point in examining it in any great detail. Suffice it to say that it originated with a plan of the senior British naval officer in North America, Vice-Admiral Alexander Cochrane, – which he had inherited from his predecessor, Admiral John Warren – to seize the city of New Orleans, a commercial centre that was also the gateway to navigation of the Mississippi. An unspoken reason, but never far from either Cochrane's mind or that of the other senior naval officers involved, was that their share of the prize money from the seizure and sale of commercial goods in the city would be very large. Cochrane had always had a reputation for being avaricious and he had made himself a very wealthy man from his previous appointment in the West Indies. Over the last half of 1814 the operation evolved as the small army repulsed at Baltimore was gradually reinforced and transported by Cochrane's fleet to Louisiana. It advanced on New Orleans by way of Lake Borgne but was brought up short on 22 December at a strong American defensive position a few miles east of the city. This position was held by 4,400 regulars, militia and volunteers under the command of Major-General Andrew Jackson.[36]

Andrew Jackson was, like Jacob Brown and William Henry Harrison, a prewar militia officer from a frontier area, and he had a good record as a combat leader during the war. His campaigns against the Creek Confederacy in 1813 and 1814, which had culminated in the battle of Horseshoe Bend the previous spring, had broken the power of that aboriginal alliance and the 47-year-old Jackson had been brought into the regular army and given command in the Gulf states and territories. Knowing that his troops, many of whom were basically civilians, could not face British regulars in a stand-up fight in the open, Jackson entrenched them on both sides of the Mississippi on the ground of the Villere Plantation. For more than two weeks, the British force, which eventually came under the command of Major-General Edward Pakenham, the Duke of Wellington's brother-in-law, tried various ways of getting through or around Jackson's position. Finally, on 8 January 1815, Pakenham with just under 7,000 troops launched a major assault against Jackson's 4,400 well-entrenched men. The result was a complete and bloody disaster as just about everything went wrong that day that could go wrong for the British. At the end of it, Pakenham and another British general were dead and 1,939 officers and men were killed or wounded. Jackson's losses were 45 killed and wounded, making the battle of New Orleans possibly the most one-sided victory in the history of modern warfare.[37]

Naturally, Jackson's army was elated – a British officer recorded the following conversation between an American and one of his opponents who had been sent after the battle to negotiate a truce to bury the dead:

A fellow in the shape of an officer asked Colonel Smith, (I think it was,) "Well, what do you think of we Yankees? Don't you think we could lick any of the troops of the continent easily?" – "I don't know that," says our officer – "Why, I'll prove to you," says Jonathan, "that we have shown ourselves the best troops in the world. Didn't the French beat the troops of every other continental nation? Didn't you beat the French in the Peninsula? and haven't we beat you just now?"[38]

It may not have been true but one cannot fault the American's impeccable logic.

The British army, now under the command of Major-General John Lambert, stayed for some time in Louisiana, only re-embarking on 27 January, nearly three weeks after the battle. The campaign had not yet ended, however, and on 8 February Lambert landed troops on Dauphin Island and prepared to lay siege to Fort Bowyer, which guarded the entrance to the port of Mobile. Four days later the fort surrendered and most of the Second Infantry, who garrisoned it, became prisoners. Opinion in Lambert's army was divided about the appearance of the Americans: Major Harry Smith of the staff thought "they looked very like French soldiers, for their uniforms were the same, and much of the same cut as to buttons, belts and pipe clay," while Colonel Alexander Dickson of the Royal Artillery, on the other hand, was not impressed. Dickson thought the prisoners "were very dirty and both in dress and appearance looked much like Spaniards."[39] Two days later, on St. Valentine's Day 1815, a British warship arrived with the thrilling information that a peace treaty had been signed between the United States and Britain. It still had to be ratified by the American government, but for the time being hostilities were to cease. Captain Harry Smith and his comrades were very pleased with this news as they had realized "that neither fame nor any military distinction" could ever "be acquired in this species of milito-nautico-guerilla-plundering warfare" being waged in North America.[40]

The peace treaty had resulted from a breakthrough in the negotiations at Ghent. When we were last with the peace commissioners, the American delegation was preparing to pack its bags, convinced the negotiations were finished because they had just refused to even discuss recent British proposals, which would mean the United States would cede a large amount of her national territory. Such an early end to the negotiations, however, did not please the British government, which disapproved of the actions of its commissioners. Furthermore, if there was to be an end to negotiations, Britain wanted it to be blamed on the United States and did not want it said "that we have brought forward points as ultimata, which were only brought forward for discussion."[41] On instructions from London, therefore, the British delegation scaled back its demands and, in place of an aboriginal buffer state, suggested a simple article in any treaty restoring to all the aboriginal nations the rights and privileges they possessed before the war. News of the fall of Washington reached Ghent in early October and the British delegation, assuming more good news was forthcoming from Prevost on Lake Champlain, pressed for a settlement of the war on the basis of *uti possidetis*, meaning both nations would retain whatever territory they currently held. Since Britain held more American territory than the United States held British, this meant that Britain would emerge as the clear victor. The American delegation, however, refused to negotiate on this basis as they had no instruction from their government to do so.[42]

On 17 October London learned of a string of defeats in North America: the failed 15 August assault on Fort Erie, the rebuff of Ross's army at Baltimore and the defeat and subsequent withdrawal from Plattsburgh. A week later, the American delegation sent a note that definitely rejected any treaty on the basis of *uti possidetis* and the British government now faced what it did not want – a continuation of a costly conflict in North America. "Looking to a continuance of the American war," Lord Liverpool, the British prime minister, wrote to the

Duke of Wellington, it would cost £10,000,000* and the government was already receiving complaints about the heavy taxation of nearly two decades of war with France that was being "continued for the purpose of securing a better frontier for Canada."[43]

If the war was to be prolonged, however, the British government decided it would send its top soldier to prosecute it and in early November offered the command in North America to the Duke of Wellington. As always Wellington's response was to the point:

> I feel no objection to going to America, though I don't promise to myself much success there. I believe there are troops enough there for the defence of Canada forever, and even for the accomplishment of any reasonable offensive plan that could be formed from the Canadian frontier. I am quite sure that all the American armies of which I have ever read would not beat out of a field of battle the troops that went from Bordeaux last summer, if common precautions and care were taken of them. That which appears to me to be wanting in America is not a [British] general, or a general officer and troops, but a naval superiority on the Lakes.[44]

Furthermore, Wellington did not believe that the British government had any right "to demand any concession of territory from America" as Britain had

> not been able to carry it [the war] into the enemy's territory, notwithstanding your military success and now undoubted military superiority, and have not even cleared your own territory on the point of attack. You cannot on any principle of equality in negotiation claim a cession of territory excepting in exchange for other advantages which you have in your power.

Most simply put, in the duke's eyes, the results of Britain's recent North American military operations did not entitle her to retain territory on the basis of *uti possidetis* and therefore it was better for her to settle on the basis of *status quo ante bellum*.

This advice from the foremost soldier of his time, coupled with the financial burden of the American war, plus problems with Russia and Prussia at the Congress of Vienna (which was proceeding at the same time), combined to persuade the British government to change its attitude. A proposal was therefore sent to the American commissioners that they compose a draft treaty and, although there was still much discussion over certain points, a final treaty of peace was signed by both nations on Christmas Eve 1814. Four days later, it

---

* $50 million.

was ratified on behalf of Britain by the Prince Regent, the head of state in the absence of his indisposed father, King George III. A copy was given to a special messenger, who took passage on the sloop-of-war HMS *Favorite* to carry it to Washington.

The *Favorite* did not make a swift crossing and only docked at New York on 11 February. The draft treaty reached Washington two days later, a week or so after the news of the Jackson's victory at New Orleans and thus that battle and the peace treaty which ended the war became inextricably linked in the minds of many Americans (and still are, for that matter). The treaty was quickly ratified by the Senate on 16 February and, as news of the coming of peace spread throughout the United States, there were impromptu celebrations, fireworks, speeches, parades and band concerts. This was to be expected because, as militiaman Eber Howe of Buffalo remarked (paraphrasing Shakespeare's *Richard III*):

> Now was the winter of our discontent
> Made glorious by the men of Ghent.[45]

Typical was the reaction in Boston, where three days after word of the treaty arrived in the city, there was a huge firework display with a large arch proclaiming in big letters, "PEACE."[46]

The news took longer to reach the northern frontier – at Buffalo, Colonel Cromwell Pearce recalled, it arrived on 24 February 1815 and was celebrated by "a discharge of artillery" and friendly visits being "exchanged between the American and British officers."[47] Within a few days, American merchants had crossed the Niagara River to sell their goods to Canadians, and the people of both nations were pleasantly surprised by the immediate drop in prices and a resulting decrease in the cost of living. The news was received at Sackets Harbor at about the same time as Buffalo and a delegation of American army and naval officers immediately travelled to Kingston to spread the word. They were invited to dinner by the officers of the garrison and many toasts were drunk to both nations, while a British regimental band played "Yankee Doodle."[48]

The conflict had been unpopular in most quarters and once it was over the parties began. In Boston a ball was held the same day the Senate ratified the Treaty of Ghent and the officers of the blockading British squadron were invited. Elizabeth Quincy, the daughter of a prominent Federalist, remembered that they attended in full uniform and were soon "actively employed in flirting and dancing," although "not in the most graceful manner" – still they seemed "favorite partners among the young ladies."[49] A similar invitation was extended to a ball held at Hartford in late March but Captain George Howard

The Duke of Wellington (1769-1852). The foremost soldier of the age and the man who pounded a stake through the heart of Bonaparte's imperial ambitions, Wellington also served as military advisor to the British government. It was Wellington who told that government to stop fooling about and make peace with the United States, as there were more serious problems in Europe. (Print after portrait by Thomas Lawrence, author's collection)

of the Twenty-Fifth Infantry, a veteran of the Niagara campaign, was not amused to see the Royal Navy being lionized by "the fair daughters of Federalism and the worships of admiring Sycophants," nor did he like the Britishers being offered "the feast of calves and the flow of wine" in return for souvenir "crown and anchor" buttons from their uniforms.[50] On the Niagara frontier, where both sides of the river had suffered much devastation, there was less celebration and, if there was a celebration, it was probably limited to a few fiddles in the largest room available and as much "budge" as could be scraped together at short notice.

Things were much grander at Kingston, where on 5 March 1815 Commodore James Yeo found a practical peacetime use for HMS *St. Lawrence* – as the newspapers reported, she made a simply splendid ballroom:

> Yesterday an elegant fete was given on board His Majesty's Ship St. Lawrence by the officers of the wardroom to the gentry of Kingston and its vicinity. The entertainment commenced at one o'clock with an exhibition of fire works, and dancing until four o'clock, when upwards of Ninety Ladies and Gentlemen descended to the middle deck of this beautiful Ship, fitted up on an appropriate manner, and partook of a sumptuous dinner; after which dancing re-commenced, and with the assistance of a late supper kept up the brilliant liveliness of this (to us handsome) naval scene of festivity to an early hour the next morning; when all retired highly gratified with the hilarity of the occasion and the polite attention of their entertainers.[51]

Lieutenant-General Gordon Drummond was not present at this affair as he had been ordered to Quebec to take over the vice-regency from Prevost, who had been recalled to Britain. One wonders, however, if the army officers who danced and dined on board the *St. Lawrence* did not make a few *sotto voce* comments about what the construction of the finest floating ballroom in

North America had really cost, in terms not only of money but also in terms of its negative effect on the campaign of the previous year. If they did, however, they were probably tactfully quiet remarks because, when offered free drink, it is very rude to insult your host – at least until it has all been consumed. In any case, Yeo did not have much longer to pace the decks of the leviathan of the lake as he too had been recalled to Britain to answer certain questions concerning his command in North America. He left Kingston on 23 March and travelled by way of Sackets Harbor at the invitation of his late enemy, Commodore Isaac Chauncey, who proved to be such an excellent host that Yeo extended his stay in the American naval base.[52]

It seems that the finest party, at least in the former northern theatre of war, took place in Montreal in early March. The host was Lieutenant-Colonel George Hay, Marquis of Tweeddale, the aristocratic and wealthy commanding officer of the 100th Foot, who organized a large costume ball, which was professionally catered. Tweeddale made sure to invite Juliana De Rottenburg, the wife of Major-General Francis De Rottenburg and the reigning beauty of British North America. Juliana was twenty-eight that spring, had been married to General "God-for-damn" (three decades her senior) for thirteen years, and was so beautiful that she turned to ice-cream the brains of almost every male over the age of fourteen who clapped eyes on her. Montreal society swirled around Juliana De Rottenburg and Tweeddale made sure that she and her husband were on the invitation list, even if he had to listen to the old German veteran banging on about how soft the modern army had become compared to when he was a young officer in the 1780s. Le Couteur was present at this affair, which he characterized as "delightful," with no fewer than seven hundred persons in costume ranging "from the Devil to his darling, a Monk," and an officer dressed as a rooster whose "strutting up & pecking his way down to invite a partner to dance was delectable."[53]

A reporter from the Montreal *Herald* was also there – no doubt blessing his luck as he scarfed down the free food and drink – and filed a lengthy report on the entertainment and costumes. "Mrs. Colonel Murray," whose husband, Colonel John Murray, had raided Plattsburgh and captured Fort Niagara in 1813, enchanted all present "by a display of various talents in several characters; all of which were supported with spirit" and "rendered more interesting still by her songs: accompanied by the pleasing sounds of the tinkling Guitar."[54] The ladies' costumes included a "good Soldier's Wife", an "interesting Flower Girl," a "modern young lady of Fashion," an "Augustin Nun," an "inviting Peasant Girl," a "Newmarket jockey of feather weight," a "Columbine of the old Theatre" and, of course, the lovely Mrs. De Rottenburg, who was "an interesting Squaw."

When "the fair revealed their charms," Juliana's beauty "was conspicuous, and shone forth unrivalled in spite of the savage costume, which in vain attempted to hide the Symmetry of her Person."*

At 1 A.M., writes our reporter, "the company unmasked & proceeded to Supper; where all the delicacies and art of the maitre de cuisine was laid out in a style seldom before witnessed in this country." Le Couteur remembered that there was "a Pandora's box in the Centre of the table which some lady was desired to open." She did so "to distribute its favours or evils" and "out flew a number of Canaries and other birds that flew at all the Candles and almost left us in darkness, charging and extinguishing them in succession."[55] Dancing then resumed "till the brightness of the sun eclipsed the dim light of the Chandeliers," at which time everyone carried out "a Promenade in mask" through the streets of Montreal "to the wonder of the industrious peasant, as he came to market."[56] No doubt about it, the Marquis of Tweeddale knew how to throw a party.†

The war being over, both nations began to reduce their armed forces and a massive demobilization began as units were disbanded and their men paid off. Private Charles Fairbanks of the Forty-Fifth Infantry was discharged at Sackets Harbor and given $2.25 and 22.5 days to get to Albany to collect the six months pay owing to him but, as Fairbanks said, he and his comrades "were used to hardships."[57] Private Jonathan Philips of the Glengarry Light Infantry remembered his regiment, which was stationed at Adolphustown, a small settlement west of Kingston, being paraded one day at the Court House, "paid off and discharged," with each man drawing "100 acres of land in Upper Canada, farming utensils and a year's provisions."[58] Lieutenant Jonathan Kearsley of the Fourth Rifles, who had lost his leg at Fort Erie, went home on a mattress in a carriage driven by his father, who had come to fetch him. Private Shadrach Byfield of the 41st Foot, who had lost an arm at Conjocta Creek, was sent across the Atlantic on a military transport with other invalids to appear before a medical board at the Chelsea Hospital in London, which awarded him a pension of 9 pence a day. There were many similar stories.[59]

The immediate postwar period was perhaps hardest on the aboriginal peoples, most of whom had fought as allies of Great Britain. Their losses, mainly through starvation, were considerable and numbered in the thousands. As

---

* The term "symmetry," when applied to a description of a lady's charms, was early 19th-century shorthand for her figure and, from all surviving accounts, Mrs. De Rottenburg was truly a fine figure of a woman.

† Of course, it might have been livelier if the Connaught Ranger officers had been invited, but history is silent on that subject.

Chetanwakanmani or Little Crow, a chief of the Mdewkanton Sioux, expressed it to British officers, one half of his people "have died of hunger with shreds of skin in their mouths for want of other Nourishment" and the cause was "the troubles you have with the Americans."[60] When Prevost learned of the Treaty of Ghent, he instructed the officers of the Indian Department to hold meetings with all the nations that had fought alongside Britain during the conflict, to explain its terms to them and to assure them that the King would not abandon his allies. Makataimeshekiakiak, or Black Hawk, a war chief of the Sauk nation, which was resident on American territory, reminded the British that "at the Commencement of the War we were loath to take up the Tomahawk and did not until you absolutely threatened us seriously with your displeasure" and promised that "those bad spirits the Americans were entirely driven off our Lands and those of our Ancestors."[61] This had not happened and although the Indian Department officers was assuring the Sauks and other nations from the Northwest who had taken shelter in Upper Canada that they could return to their homes, the Big Knives or Americans "according to their stories are Masters of us and our lands." Black Hawk stressed that the Americans "have Sweet Tongues " and "have cheated us all." When he contemplated the future, he warned that "some bad blood that remains in my heart jumps up to my throat" and, if it were not for the British wish for peace, he would "free myself of it" by attacking the Americans.[62] But the war had broken the military power of the aboriginal peoples east of the Mississippi and they now set foot on that wretched downward spiral marked by forced resettlement, reservations and white schools, a spiral which has only recently been arrested.

The postwar period was also difficult for the officers and men of the British army in North America, who wanted to get to their homes on the other side of the Atlantic, even though, as Surgeon Dunlop commented, the officers had "half pay staring us in the face."[63] The British government, hoping to attract these men as settlers, created a number of "military settlements" in the Canadas and many regulars took advantage of the free land offered and the Crown support to become pioneers – notably the foreigners of De Meuron's and De Watteville's Regiments.[64] Far to the south, on Dauphin Island, the officers of Lambert's army, having nothing much to do except hunt alligators, of which there was no shortage, wiled away the hours in an elaborate role-playing game. They divided themselves into opposing kingdoms and constructed two elaborate fortresses from pine trees and boughs, complete with ditches, drawbridges and secret passages. They then insulted each other by written communications and fought pitched battles using pine cones as ammunition and pine branches as weapons, after which they wrote long and untruthful reports about the outcome. That grown men – many veterans of Bladensburg, Baltimore and New Orleans (and even blooodier actions in Portugal and Spain) – could engage in such behaviour can only be attributed to a dangerous combination of too much time and drink, or to some deeply-hidden psychological origin, which the present author will not explore as there are barriers to knowledge beyond which it truly is not wise to pass.[65]

The British regulars' anxiety to leave became worse in late April 1815 when North America learned the "Most Extraordinary News" that Bonaparte had escaped his place of exile in Elba, landed in France and proclaimed himself emperor.[66] The nations at the Congress of Vienna promptly declared war on a man they termed an "outlaw," not on the nation he claimed to rule. London sent orders for the immediate recall of the veteran units in North America but, as it happened, only four battalions, all from Lambert's command, returned in time to fight at Waterloo, where Wellington and Blucher ended, once and for all, the Corsican's imperial ambitions. None of the British regiments which served in Canada in 1814–1815 were able to get back in time to fight with Wellington at that famous engagement, causing Surgeon William Dunlop of the 89th Foot to quip, "Thank God he managed to do without us."[67]

Getting paid off. As soon as the conflict had ended, both Britain and the United States quickly demobilized their forces as both nations faced astronomical war debts. Here, the men of the Canadian Voltigeurs collect their final pay before departing to begin new lives as civilians. (Painting by Eugene Leliepvre, courtesy Parks Canada)

Memorials at Fort Erie and Plattsburgh. The memorial at Fort Erie (left) was erected in 1939 to mark the graves of 150 British and Canadian soldiers and three Americans which were discovered when the fort was reconstructed. It is possible that Lieutenant-Colonel William Drummond's remains lie near this memorial. The impressive limestone Macdonough Memorial (right), 135 feet high and topped by a victorious American eagle was completed in 1926 to commemorate the victory at Plattsburgh. (Author's photographs)

"In Peace in Chelsea Quarters"

THE FATE OF MEN, WOMEN, WARSHIPS AND BATTLEFIELDS

Come hear an old campaigner's song,
A British soldier's story,
Who oft has trained his martial throng
To noble deeds of glory,
But let not boasting swell my praise,
Who's faced hot balls and mortars
In hopes to spend my latter days
In Peace in Chelsea Quarters.

On swampy grounds and burning lands,
In march and counter-marches,
I've met in fight the hostile band,
And sunk beneath my gashes,
Yet innate valour cheers my heart,
'Tis fear the coward slaughters,
And he that takes a soldier's part
Secured me in Chelsea Quarters.

And Heavens bless his Majesty
Who leaves a veteran never;
Grown all and hacked up as you see
He's pensioned me for ever.
My rent is fixed at last for life,
And safe from mines and mortars;
Though kingdoms wage eternal strife
I'll ne'er quit Chelsea Quarters.[1]

When the war ended, the American, British, Canadian and aboriginal participants started to resume lives interrupted by more than three years of conflict. Most of the British soldiers and sailors who fought during the war were professionals who continued in service while many of the Americans, who had only joined to fight during the war, found they liked military service and became

333

regular soldiers. Some Canadians continued to serve in the British army but most returned to their peacetime pursuits, although their military experience ensured that for the next two decades the militia was much more effective than it had been prior to the war. As we have noted, however, the war had its most serious effect on the aboriginal peoples, particularly those who had been resident on American territory, as most were forced off their land and forcibly relocated.

Of the British participants, Lieutenant-General Sir George Prevost, the governor-general and commander-in-chief, perhaps fared worse than any of his subordinates when peace came. Worn down by the persistent criticism from his many enemies, his health was affected and he was a sick and weary man when he was recalled to Britain in April 1815. Worse was to come. In August 1815 a naval court martial was held for the officers of the Lake Champlain squadron. Yeo was present and there seems little doubt that he was involved behind the scenes coaching and advising the officers undergoing trial. The Prevost–Downie correspondence of 7 through 10 September 1814, described as "the very pressing Letters and communications" of the army's commander, was produced as evidence. The court honourably acquitted all those charged – with the exceptions of Lieutenants Raynham and James McGhie, who had deserted – and found that the loss of the squadron had been "principally caused" by it "having been urged into Battle previous to its being in a proper state to meet its Enemy by a promised Cooperation of the Land Forces, which was not carried into effect."[3] Prevost could not let such a damning verdict stand unquestioned and requested a court martial to clear his name. The Duke of York, the commander-in-chief, agreed and a date was set for early 1816. The board was to consist of two full generals and no less than fifteen lieutenant-generals. A list of witnesses was drawn up, which included every senior officer involved in the Plattsburgh expedition – Baynes, Brisbane, De Rottenburg, Power and Robinson among them. Ironically, both Macomb and Macdonough provided evidence in written form, stating that, even had the British captured the redoubts, they would not have been able to sway the outcome of the naval action because Macomb's shore-based batteries were unable to reach the British squadron. The court martial was scheduled to begin sitting on 5 February but, unfortunately, Prevost died from dropsy (probably pulmonary edema) on 5 January 1816 at the age of forty-eight.

His premature death meant that Prevost was unable to set the record straight, and since that time historians have generally excoriated him as an amiable but weak-willed nonentity. While it is true that the man made mistakes, his critics overlook the fact that Prevost's defence of British North America was successful – he was ordered to hold the line and he did so, for two long years. There is no doubt that his conduct of the Plattsburgh campaign was indecisive but Prevost was a defensive-minded general and it was difficult for him to switch gears to lead an offensive. Prevost has rarely received a fair hearing at the hands of historians, who, relying on witnesses of the time who were not privy to the higher strategic councils, roundly condemn him and compare him unfavourably with Wellington, the most successful British general of the time. Prevost's "military reputation would have stood higher," one of his biographers has astutely remarked, "had his exploits been compared not to those of Wellington, but to those of the opposing generals."[4] In recent years, fortunately, historians have begun to take a second look at this oft-maligned officer and a more balanced assessment of his record has now appeared.[5] Its author renders this judgment on his subject:

> Far from home, with irregular communication, and responsible for the defense of a massive and complex theater, he commanded a mix of regular soldiers, sailors, locally-raised forces, and indigenous peoples with prudence and economy that completely thwarted his opponent's plans.[6]

The other British generals involved in the 1814 Niagara and Plattsburgh campaigns had less controversial postwar careers. Lieutenant-General Gordon Drummond succeeded Prevost as governor-general and captain-general of British North America in 1815. Troubled by a stomach ailment, he relinquished this appointment at his own request and returned to Britain. Drummond never again saw active service but reached the rank of general by seniority when he died in London in 1854 at the age of eighty-two.[7]

Major-General Francis de Rottenburg was recalled to Britain in 1815 and never again saw active service, being promoted lieutenant-general by seniority in 1819. He died at Portsmouth in 1832 at the age of eighty-five. The lovely Juliana survived her husband by thirty-two years, dying at Southsea in Hampshire at the age of eighty-one.*[8]

Major-General Louis de Watteville succeeded Drummond as the commander in Upper Canada but retired from service in 1816 and spent the remainder of his live at Rubingen in Switzerland where he died in 1836 at the age of sixty.[9]

Major-General Thomas Brisbane returned to Britain in 1815 and married in 1819 at the age of forty-seven. In 1821 he was appointed governor of New South Wales in Australia and he served in that capacity until 1825. Brisbane devoted much of his later life to the study of science, particularly astronomy.

---

*Juliana's daughter, Frances, said to be even more beautiful than her mother, if possible, married Captain William Paget, RN. It was not a happy marriage and Frances became involved in a notorious legal case involving her possible adultery with the Earl of Cardigan, which was brought by her husband. It was dismissed and Cardigan went on from this mess to command the Light Brigade when it made its gallant but suicidal charge at the battle of Balaclava in 1854.

Brisbane died at the age of eighty-seven in 1860. The Australian city of Brisbane is named after him.[10]

Major-General Manley Power served in the occupation force in France from 1815 to 1818 before being appointed governor of Malta in 1820. He died at the age of fifty-three in Switzerland in 1826 while travelling back to Britain.[11]

Major-General Frederick P. Robinson succeeded de Watteville as the commander in Upper Canada in 1815 and, the following year, was appointed the governor of Tobago, where he served until 1828. He had reached the rank of full general by seniority when he retired in 1841. Robinson died at the age of eighty-nine in 1852, and was at that time the longest serving soldier in the British army.[12]

Colonel Viktor Fischer of De Watteville's Regiment, who led one of the assault columns during the night attack on Fort Erie, retired from the army in 1815 and died in Switzerland in 1821.

Colonel Christopher Myers, who commanded the British forces in the action at Cook's Mills in October 1814, died at Quebec in November 1817.

Lieutenant-Colonel Thomas Pearson, badly wounded during the sortie of 17 September 1814, took a long time to recover. He passed his convalescence at his father-in-law's estate near Fredericton, New Brunswick, and eventually regained his sight but remained partially deaf for the rest of his life. In 1817 Pearson was appointed commanding officer of the 23rd Foot and retained that appointment until 1830 when he was promoted to major-general. Pearson was a lieutenant-general when he retired in 1841 and he died at the age of sixty-six at Bath in 1847. As has been noted, Thomas Pearson was the only British officer to fight in the four major battles of the northern theatre of war – Crysler's Farm, Chippawa, Lundy's Lane and Fort Erie – and was wounded in two of them. He also participated in the attack on Oswego in May 1814 but, most importantly, he held the St. Lawrence for the Crown from October 1812 to April 1814, preserving the logistical lifeline of British North America. Despite this, Pearson was not even accorded an entry in the *Dictionary of Canadian Biography* nor is there any reference in modern Canada to him beyond a small plaque at Fort Wellington which notes that he was first commander of that post (he actually oversaw its construction).[*][13]

Lieutenant-Colonel John Harvey, Drummond's adjutant-general, reached the rank of major-general by 1828. He then entered the colonial service, serving as lieutenant-governor of Prince Edward Island, New Brunswick, Newfoundland and Nova Scotia from 1831 to his death in Halifax in 1852. Harvey proved

---

* The present author has initiated a request to the National Historic Sites and Monuments Board of Canada for a plaque to be struck to honour this brave but bad-tempered soldier. Let us hope.

to be a very able administrator who was able to conciliate warring factions in all four colonies. Harvey died in 1852 and is buried in Halifax.[14]

Lieutenant-Colonel George Hay, the Marquis of Tweeddale, possibly British North America's best host, returned to Britain in 1815. Tweeddale married in 1816, had seven sons and six daughters, and was apparently too busy siring children to have much time for his military career although he continued to be promoted by seniority. By 1842, when he was appointed commander-in-chief of the Madras army in India, Tweeddale was a full general. He died at the age of eighty-nine in 1876.[15]

The remains of Lieutenant-Colonel William Drummond were buried, along with other fatal casualties of the assault of 15 August 1814, in a common grave in the ditch of Fort Erie. Today that grave is believed to be located near the memorial to the British and Canadian dead erected in late 19th century. There is a plaque to Drummond at Saint John, New Brunswick.[16]

Commander Alexander Dobbs, RN, who led a daring "cutting-out" expedition at Fort Erie in August 1814, was appointed the commander at Isle-aux-Noix late in 1814. When the war ended, he was briefly a transport agent at Quebec before returning to Britain. Dobbs was made a post captain in 1819 but died at Malta in 1827.[17]

Major James Campbell, who served on Brisbane's staff in 1814 during the Plattsburgh campaign, reached the rank of lieutenant-colonel when he retired in 1826. He later wrote a book about the British army, which contained a brief account of the campaign.[18]

Lieutenant Joseph-David Mermet of De Watteville's Regiment, who was captured during the sortie, was released in February 1814 when the war ended. He retired on half-pay in 1816 and returned to France, his native country, where he apparently lived in poverty. Sources differ at to when he died, stating anywhere from the 1820s to 1858.[19]

Lieutenant George Philpotts continued to serve in the Royal Engineers, slowly clawing his way up the ranks as promotion in that corps went by seniority. He had reached the rank of brevet colonel when he died at Bermuda in 1853.[20]

Plaque dedicated to William Drummond. The officers of the 104th Foot never forgot their heroic commanding officer, who was killed during the assault of 15 August, and dedicated this plaque to him in St. Anne Chapel in Fredericton, New Brunswick. (Photograph, Brent Wilson)

Grown older but not bolder. Colonel John Le Couteur, wearing the uniform of the Queen's Aide de Camp for Jersey, at the age of sixty-one in 1855. To the end of his life Le Couteur liked to recount his adventures in North America during the War of 1812. (Courtesy, Societé Jersiaise)

Lieutenant John Le Couteur retired from the army with the rank of captain and returned to his native Jersey in 1818 and married his cousin. He lived a wonderfully active life, involved in many civic projects, including establishing the breeding points of the Jersey cow, no small matter in a community that prided itself on the quality of its cattle. A prodigious diarist, Le Couteur worked for many years on a memoir of his service in the War of 1812, which was possibly one of the most exciting periods of his life and certainly one to which he made constant reference.* John Le Couteur died at the age of eighty-two in 1875 surrounded by children, grandchildren and great-grandchildren.[21]

Surgeon William Dunlop went on half pay in 1817 and remained on it for nearly a decade, during which time he was an editor and contributor to *Blackwood's Magazine*. He returned to Canada in the 1840s and wrote a witty memoir of his wartime service, which is still a delight to read. Dunlop never lost his sense of humour – possibly because he was wise enough to remain single – and was famous for his skills as a raconteur. Dunlop died in 1848 at the young age of fifty-six.[22]

Of the naval officers who participated in the 1814 Plattsburgh and Niagara campaigns, Commodore James Lucas Yeo, RN, emerged unscathed from the court martial of the Plattsburgh naval officers. He might not have got off so easily if the Prevost court martial had gone forward but, as it did not, his career suffered no ill effects. The Admiralty placed him in command of an anti-slaving squadron and in early 1816 Yeo began patrolling the mid-Atlantic slave routes. Unfortunately, he contracted yellow fever in Jamaica in 1818 and died at the age of thirty-six while on passage to Britain. In contrast to Prevost, Yeo has been treated kindly by historians, one of his biographers lauding him as a "brilliant officer" who "deserves well of his country" for his wartime services.[23] Just as Prevost's reputation is starting to undergo revision, historians are now starting to take a more critical look at Yeo.[24]

Commander Daniel Pring, RN, was promoted to post captain following his

---

* The present author discovered this memoir on Jersey in 1993 and published it with annotations as *Merry Hearts Make Light Days: The War of 1812 Journal of Lieutenant John Le Couteur, 104th Foot.*

acquittal at the Plattsburgh court martial. He was appointed to command the RN establishment on Lake Erie in 1816 but, when it was closed in 1817, he went on half pay and remained there until 1836, when he received a series of commands. He was senior naval officer in Jamaica when he died, possibly of yellow fever, in 1846 at the age of fifty-eight.[25]

Commander Robert H. Barclay, RN, who lost his squadron in the 1813 battle of Lake Erie, was completely exonerated by a court martial held in 1814. The Admiralty, however, did not see fit to employ him again until 1824 when he was briefly given command of a bomb vessel. This was Barclay's last command and, although promoted to post captain, he remained on shore until his death in 1837 at the age of fifty-one.[26]

History is unfortunately silent about whether Sergeant and Mrs. Patrick Anthony of the 88th Foot, married in haste at Quebec in August 1815, lived happily ever after but one certainly hopes so. As for Anthony's regiment, the Connaught Rangers returned to Britain in 1815 and for more than a century served in almost every major conflict which involved the British army: the Crimea, the Indian Mutiny; the Zulu War, the Sudan, South Africa and the First World War. The Regimental Colour was adorned with many famous Battle Honours including TALAVERA 1809, BADAJOZ 1812, SALAMANCA 1812, ALMA 1854; INKERMAN 1854; THE MARNE 1914; THE SOMME, 1916; and FRANCE AND FLANDERS, 1914-1918. With the creation of the Republic of Eire in 1921, however, the regiment could no longer recruit in Connaught and chose to disband the following year.

Alicia Cockburn, the observant but sharp-tongued commentator on the scene around her, became Lady Cockburn when her husband was knighted after the war. She accompanied him to his various diplomatic postings as governor of Curaçao and then the Bahamas. On his retirement, the couple settled in Dover, where Alicia died in 1854 at the age of seventy-two.[27]

George Nichol and Jacob Wood of Oxford, whose property had been burned by McArthur after they had evaded the American sentries to bring a warning to Burford, received $200 from the Loyal and Patriotic Society of Upper Canada to help rebuild.[28]

John Norton, the aboriginal leader, was given a pension for his wartime services. After the war he wrote a lengthy memoir of his wartime experiences which was also a history of the aboriginal peoples of eastern North America. Norton returned to Canada but after killing a man in a duel, he went to live with the Cherokee people and is believed to have died in the 1830s.[29]

Black Hawk, the Sauk or Sac war chief who upbraided the British for abandoning his people at the end of the war, was angered when they were dispossessed of their lands. In 1832 he raided white settlements in Iowa and commenced the "Black Hawk" war, which lasted five months before the aboriginal leader was defeated by Illinois, Iowa and Michigan militia. Taken prisoner, Black Hawk dictated his life story to a white journalist and it became a bestseller after it was published. Black Hawk returned to the Sauk settlements in southern Iowa, where he died in 1838.[30]

Of the Americans, former Secretary of War John Armstrong retired to his estate at Red Hook, New York. In 1815 he failed to win an election to the senate and retired from public life, devoting himself to agricultural pursuits. In 1836 Armstrong published *Notices of the War of 1812*, his account of the war, which contains vicious criticism of almost every major officer in the war including his once good friend Jacob Brown. Armstrong died in 1843 at the age of eighty-four.[31]

James Monroe, Armstrong's successor as secretary of war, became the fifth president of the United States and held that office until 1825. During Monroe's presidency the United States expanded to the Pacific, and Florida was purchased from Spain. Monroe is best known for the "Monroe Doctrine," which originated in a proposal from Britain, and holds that the United States will resist any European power that attempts to intervene in the Americas. It is interesting to note that Monroe's vice-president during his two terms was Daniel D. Tompkins, the wartime governor of New York. Monroe died in 1831 at the age of seventy-three.[32]

Regarded as a national hero, Major-General Jacob Brown was given command of the Northern Division, where he served until 1821 when he was appointed general-in-chief. In 1815 Brown drew up court martial charges against Ripley but was persuaded not to go forward with them by senior members of the cabinet, who were anxious to smooth over any problems as Ripley was one of the few senior officers from New England. Ripley, however, hearing of these charges, demanded and received a court of inquiry but it had just begun when it was discharged by the president. Senior members of the cabinet then persuaded Brown to write an official letter exonerating Ripley from any criticism contained in his official report on the battle of Lundy's Lane. This letter was supposed to remain confidential but Ripley's adherents promptly had it published, much to Brown's fury. By this adroit manoeuvring Ripley defused the case against him and there was nothing the straightforward Brown could do about it. Brown's later years were marred by illness and financial problems and he died at the very young age of fifty-three in 1828. Brown was the best American general of the War of 1812, and certainly the one most respected by his opponents.[33]

Major-General William Henry Harrison refused the post of secretary of war when it was offered by President Monroe in 1817. He served in a number of administrative and diplomatic roles and also in the Ohio state senate and the federal senate. He was an unsuccessful candidate for the presidency in 1836 but won election in 1840. Unfortunately, Harrison died at the age of sixty-eight, just 30 days after his inauguration in March 1841.[34]

Major-General George Izard resigned from the army in 1815 and devoted himself to private pursuits. In 1825 he was appointed governor of the Arkansas Territory and he died there three years later at the age of fifty-two.[35]

Brigadier-General Alexander Macomb was promoted to major-general in 1814 and, after the war, commanded the Corps of Engineers until 1828, when, following the death of Jacob Brown, he was appointed general-in-chief, a position he held until his own death in 1841 at the age of fifty-nine.[36]

Brigadier-General Duncan McArthur resigned from the army to attend to his business affairs. He served intermittently as a member of the Ohio legislature and the House of representatives. In 1830 he was elected governor of Ohio but did not seek re-election when his term expired. McArthur died at the age of sixty-seven in 1839.[37]

Brigadier-General Edmund P. Gaines had a long and active career in the postwar army although it was marred by a never-ending feud with Major-General Winfield Scott. Gaines served mainly on the frontier, where Scott was rarely to be seen. He raised some eyebrows in 1839 when he married for the third time to a woman more than thirty years younger. Gaines died in New Orleans from cholera a the age of seventy-two in 1849. The city of Gainesville, Florida, is named after him.[38]

Brigadier-General Eleazar Ripley took some time to recover from the wound he had suffered during the sortie. He received a brevet promotion to major-general but his reputation had suffered from his actions during the Niagara campaign. After he outmanoeuvred Brown, Ripley was sent to serve in the Southern Department to keep him away from that general. In 1820 he resigned from the army because of ill health and returned to the practice of law and was elected from Louisiana to the House of Representatives. Ripley was fifty-seven when he died in 1839.[39]

Brigadier-General Daniel Bissell remained in the army after the war but took his discharge to manage the large estate he had carefully built up at St. Louis, Missouri. He built a fine house which remained in the possession of his descendants for generations after his death in 1833 at the age of sixty-five. In the 1960s the Bissell family presented it to the state of Missouri and it is now a museum.[40]

Brigadier-General James Miller, whose regiment captured the British artillery at Lundy's Lane and who led one of the assault columns during the sortie of 17 September, remained in the army after the war. He resigned his commission in 1819 after he was appointed the first governor of the Arkansas Territory but gave up this post in 1823 because of ill health and was appointed collector of the port of Salem, Massachusetts. Miller resigned from this post after he had a stroke in 1849 and died at the age of seventy-three in 1851.[41]

Colonel Cromwell Pearce left the army in 1815 and returned to his home in Chester County, Pennsylvania, where he served as the sheriff until 1825, when he was elected an associate judge of the county court. Pearce died in 1852 at the age of eighty.[42]

Lieutenant-Colonel Thomas Aspinwall, who was wounded at the sortie of 17 September 1814, left the army in 1815 and served as the American consul in London until 1852. Becoming wealthy from his participation in trans-Atlantic shipping, Aspinwall returned to Boston, where he became a strong supporter of the Massachusetts Historical Society before dying in 1876 at the age of ninety-one.[43]

Major Thomas S. Jesup of the Twenty-Fifth Infantry received a brevet promotion to colonel and in 1818 was appointed quartermaster general. He served in this appointment until his death in 1860 at the age of seventy-two.[44]

Major William McRee received a brevet promotion to colonel and went on a European inspection tour after the war. He worked on coastal fortifications before resigning from the army in 1819 to become surveyor general of the United States. McRee died, unmarried, in 1833, in St. Louis at the young age of forty-six.[45]

Major John Wool of the Twenty-Ninth Infantry remained in the regular army after the war and held various posts, including inspector-general. He reached the rank of brigadier-general in 1841 and commanded a division during the Mexican War where he played a prominent part in the battle of Buena Vista in 1847, which brought him promotion to brevet major-general. One of his staff officers in Mexico was Captain Robert E. Lee of the Corps of Engineers. After the end of that conflict, Wool served in various campaigns against the aboriginal peoples and

The very model of a modern major-general. John Wool, who conducted a fine delaying action north of Plattsburgh on 6 September 1814, stayed in the army after the war. He had risen to the rank of major-general and was still in active service at the age of seventy-seven when this photograph was taken in 1861. (Library of Congress)

was still in service when the Civil War broke out in 1861. He was instrumental in securing Fortress Monroe for the federal government and was promoted full major-general at the age of seventy-nine in 1863 when he commanded the military force that put down the draft riots in New York. Shortly afterward, he retired from the army after more than a half century of service and died at the age of eighty.[46]

Major George Brooke of the Twenty-Third Infantry ended the war as a brevet colonel. He remained in the army after the war, was promoted brigadier general in 1824 and major general in 1848. Brooke's last command was Texas and he died at the age of sixty-six in San Antonio in 1851. Fort Brooke in Florida is named after him.[47]

Major William A. Trimble, who held the stone fort during the night assault of 15 August 1814, reached the rank of lieutenant-colonel by the end of the war. He remained in the army and preferred charges against Major-General Edmund Gaines, who he felt had not properly acknowledged the part played by Trimble and his men during the assault. The charges were flimsy and the resulting court martial honourably acquitted Gaines but the transcript of the proceedings provides excellent evidence for the historian of the siege. Trimble resigned from the army in 1819 after being elected to the U.S. senate but died two years later at the young age of thirty-five.[48]

Captain Nathan Towson ended the war as a brevet lieutenant colonel. He became paymaster general in 1819 and remained in this position for thirty-four years. Towson died at the age of seventy at his home in Washington in 1854.[49]

Captain Benjamin Birdsall recovered from his mouth wound suffered during the assault and remained in the army after the war, only to be murdered by one of his own soldiers in July 1816. He left a widow and four children.[50]

Lieutenant David Bates Douglass received a brevet promotion to captain and was appointed to the faculty of the military academy at West Point. He resigned from the army in 1831 and joined the staff of New York University as professor of civil engineering. In the 1840s Douglass began delivering a series of popular lectures on his wartime experiences which were later published. Douglass died suddenly from a stroke in 1849 at the age of sixty.[51]

Lieutenant Jonathan Kearsley of the Fourth Rifle Regiment was given a brevet promotion for gallantry at Fort Erie. In 1819 Kearsley moved from his native Pennsylvania to Detroit to assume the position of Receiver of the U.S. Land Office, a position he held for thirty years. In 1819 he was elected mayor of Detroit and, in 1836 was appointed regent of the University of Michigan, a post he held until his death in 1859 at the age of seventy-three.[52]

Lieutenant John G. Watmough, the only officer to survive from the defend-

The last resting place of Drummer Hanks. Jarvis was buried in Woodland Cemetery in Cleveland and in 2003 a group of interested citizens procured a military headstone for him. It is shown here shortly after it was dedicated, decorated for Memorial Day. (Photograph, courtesy Michelle A. Day)

ers of the northeast bastion during the assault of 15 August, resigned from the army in 1816, was elected to Congress in 1831 and served until 1835 but failed to secure re-election. He was appointed the sheriff of Philadelphia in 1835 and later served as the surveyor of the city's port. He named one of his sons Pendleton Gaines after his former commanding officer, Edmund Pendleton Gaines. Watmough died in 1861 at the age of sixty-eight.[53]

Following his discharge from the army in 1815, Jarvis Hanks wanted to go to West Point but his parents would not hear of it so Jarvis drifted around for a time, working as an itinerant artist and sign painter. For a time he studied portraiture under Thomas Sully, but after he married, Jarvis tried to find a more steady means of income. In 1835 Jarvis and his wife, Charlotte, moved to the Cleveland area, where they purchased a small farm and raised ten children. Jarvis hung out his shingle as a portrait artist but would undertake any kind of work, including sign lettering. An accomplished violin player, Jarvis also gave music lessons. He was active in his local church and in the temperance and anti-slavery movements. He died at the age of fifty-four in 1853.[54] *

Robert White, the 20-year-old private who lost his forearms to a roundshot during the siege of Fort Erie, received a federal pension of $480 *per annum*, a very generous settlement. White lived in Vermont after the war, married the young widow of another soldier killed during the siege and raised a large family. White devised a contraption by which he could write using a pen held in his teeth but his penmanship failed when these went. White always wore artificial tin arms and hands when going outside his house. Both he and his wife were still alive in 1867 when they communicated with the historian Benson Lossing.[55] †

---

* The present author edited his wartime memoir for publication in 1996 and in 2003 a group of local people procured a military headstone for Jarvis's grave in Woodland Cemetery in Cleveland.

† It is interesting that, during the excavation of the wartime American military cemetery near Fort Erie in 1987, the bones of a pair of forearms and hands were uncovered. Whether or not these are the limbs that were removed from White by a roundshot has never been established.

Master Commandant Thomas Macdonough, USN, the victor of the naval battle of Plattsburgh, was promoted captain and given command of a frigate in the Second Barbary War. In 1818 he was the first captain of the 74-gun ship of the line, USS *Ohio*, and stayed with that ship until 1823. A year later he took over the USS *Constitution* but had to give up command at Gibraltar in 1825 because of illness and died on the return voyage to the United States.[56]

Master Commandant Oliver Perry, USN, was promoted captain after his September 1813 victory on Lake Erie and given command of the 44-gun frigate, USS *Java*. He was preparing her for sea at Baltimore in the summer of 1814 when he became caught up in the British invasion of the Chesapeake and participated in the defence of the city. Perry commanded the *Java* in the Second Barbary War and was later promoted commodore and sent on a diplomatic mission to South America but contracted yellow fever and died in 1819 at the age of thirty-four.[57]

Lieutenant Silas Duncan, USN, survived the terrible wound he had received at Plattsburgh after having been struck by a Congreve rocket. He received the thanks of Congress and a pension for his wound but returned to active service, eventually reaching the rank of commander before his death in 1834 at the age of forty-six.[58]

Major-General Peter B. Porter of the New York militia, who led the largest component of the sortie of 17 September 1814, was elected to Congress in 1815 and spent a year as secretary of war in the cabinet of President John Quincy Adams. In the 1830s Porter retired from political life and died at the age of seventy-one in 1844.[59]

Eleazar Williams, who had operated an intelligence service for Macomb during the Plattsburgh campaign, served as an Episcopal missionary to the aboriginal peoples at Green Bay, Michigan, until 1839 when he became a schoolmaster at the St. Regis settlement near Cornwall. About this time Williams claimed to be the son of Louis XVI of France, executed during the French Revolution, and thus the rightful king of that nation. This claim was thoroughly debunked by the time of Williams's death in 1858 at the age of seventy.[60]

Captain Nathaniel Platt, the septuagenarian who taunted the British staff officers billeted in his house in September 1814, died in 1816.[61]

Henry K. Averill, the 16-year-old boy who joined Captain Martin Aitken's company of teenagers and fought at Plattsburgh in September 1811, became a lawyer. He practised in Plattsburgh, where he was also involved in politics and business matters until the 1850s when he moved to Iowa. He returned to live with his daughter in Morrisonville near Plattsburgh, where he died in 1881 at the age of eighty-two. Averill wrote a memoir of his experiences during the battle, which has recently been published.[62] In 1826 Congress approved the presentation of a rifle to every member of Aitken's company "for Gallantry at the Siege of Plattsburgh.

Andrew Westbrook, the Canadian traitor, settled in Michigan after the war, where he was given large tracts of land by the federal government and appointed Supervisor of Highways by the state governor. He became the subject of an historical novel by John Richardson titled *Westbrook the Outlaw, or, the Avenging Wolf* published in 1851. One of the characters in this novel was Captain Daniel Stringer, Westbrook's worst enemy. This was a thinly veiled reference to militia officer and justice of the peace Captain Daniel Springer, who during the war had tried to kill or capture Westbrook and who acquired his Canadian property, about 4,000 acres of prime farmland after the war. Westbrook died in 1835 at the age of fifty-four.[63]

The American and British squadrons on Great Lakes did not long survive the war. As soon as hostilities ended, both Britain and the United States took steps to reduce their fleets and both nations used a similar approach, selling or scrapping smaller vessels while large vessels were either roofed over to serve as barracks or sunk in shallow water to preserve them. In 1817 the Rush-Bagot Treaty effectively "de-militarized" the lakes, restricting each nation to one small warship with one gun on each of Lakes Champlain and Ontario and two on the upper lakes. This agreement spelled the end of the remaining vessels of the wartime fleets as those vessels not already disposed of simply rotted at their moorings. The unfortunate *Confiance* was demolished in 1824 and the *Detroit*, Perry's first flagship at the battle of Lake Erie was purchased in 1841 by a group of businessman who tried to send her over Niagara Falls as a publicity stunt, but she ran aground and was knocked to pieces by the current. The *St. Lawrence*, Yeo's leviathan, lingered on until 1831 when she was sold for scrap for £25 ($125); the naval officer who did so reported that he could have got a better price but the purchaser was required to remove the ship from the naval dockyard, which, if the navy had been forced to do it, would have cost more than she was worth. The mighty *St. Lawrence* ended up as a dock until she was sunk in shallow water off Kingston, where her remains are still regularly visited by divers. The guns and equipment from the squadron at Kingston were stored in a building constructed in 1820, which was called the "Stone Frigate," a traditional British naval term for a shore establishment. It is now a cadet residence of the Royal Military College of Canada, which occupies the site of the wartime British naval dockyard. Perhaps the last of the wartime vessels to meet its fate was the incomplete American ship-of-the-line *New Orleans,* which survived in a special-

Niagara fires a broadside. The reconstructed brig USS *Niagara*, a living museum of naval history, fires a broadside on Lake Erie. (Courtesy, Erie Maritime Museum, Pennsylvania History and Museum Commission)

ly constructed boathouse on land at Sackets Harbor until 1884, when, after part of the boathouse had blown away, the vessel was accidentally demolished by a contractor who bought the hull.[64]

A century after the 1813 naval battle of Lake Erie, the hull of the USS *Niagara*, Perry's second flagship at the engagement, was excavated from where she had been sunk for preservation. This created a wave of interest in the sailing warships of the War of 1812 and the *Niagara* was reconstructed at Erie, Pennsylvania, as a static display in time for the 150th Anniversary of the battle. A second reconstruction of the *Niagara* was begun in 1988 and this brig sails on summer tours throughout the Great Lakes and along the Atlantic seaboard. A beautiful thing to see under full sail, the *Niagara* is a living monument to the naval War of 1812 on the Great Lakes and the men who fought it.[65]

With the exception of Conjocta Creek, which has become a post-industrial wasteland, most of the battlefields and forts described in this book are still in existence. In the Depression years, the governments of Canada and the province of Ontario funded the reconstruction of many wartime forts as employment projects and thus both Forts Erie and George rose again. At the same time, Fort Niagara on the American side of the river was rebuilt using private funds.

The interested reader can today walk through the stone mess buildings at Fort Erie and stand in the northeast demi-bastion where so many men died in the early hours of 15 August 1814. Most of the extended American defence perimeter has been eaten up by development although if the visitor stands in the southwest demi-bastion, particularly in the autumn, he or she can make out the line of earthworks that once ran down to Snake Hill, which has disappeared.

A splendid new interpretation centre has recently been opened at Fort Erie complete with a display that interprets the siege (and is surprisingly accurate, which is not always the case with historic site interpretation). An outside annex features partially rebuilt battery positions complete with artillery pieces and Congreve rockets, as well as a representative of the type of primitive huts the besiegers lived in for almost two months. The only thing missing is the nearly constant downpour of rain, but perhaps in future a sprinkler system could be installed to enhance the visitor's experience. Besides the many historic sites, the Niagara region of Canada and the United States have much to offer the visitor, and if one gets tired of the past, the numerous wineries in the area provide a convenient place to rest and catch up on one's historical note taking.

On Lake Champlain, Plattsburgh is definitely worth a visit. Except for a new interstate highway, the road system from the Canadian border to Plattsburgh has not altered that much and the interested visitor can follow the route of the British army through East Beekmantown, Culver Hill and Halsey's Corners, and it is not hard to see why Major John Wool of the Twenty-Ninth chose his delaying positions. Captain Nathaniel Platt's house still exists and it does not take much imagination to see him sitting on his porch, grimacing in disgust as the Britishers marched by on their way to the Saranac.

Plattsburgh itself has grown considerably but it is still a very pretty place. Two of the three redoubts have been removed but plaques have been erected on their location. The remains of Fort Brown are still visible. There is a bridge over Pike's Ford, which is now in the middle of the town, but the ford can clearly be made out. Plattsburgh was for many years a major military post and later a Strategic Air Command base and this has resulted in much of the historic

Wartime graves, Plattsburgh Cemetery. The large, raised flat stone is that of Captain Robert Downie, RN, and clustered around it are the graves of the British and American officers killed in the land and lake battles. (Author's photograph)

ground on the south side of the Saranac being preserved although it is being encroached on by development. A fine museum dedicated to the battle has recently been established and contains many interesting displays.

The town cemetery at Plattsburgh contains the graves of many of those who were killed in the battle, including Captain Robert Downie, RN, the ill-fated British squadron commander, Captain Alexander Anderson of the Royal Marines, Lieutenant Peter Gamble of the *Saratoga*, Lieutenant Colonel James Willington of the 3rd Foot and Captain John Purchas of the 76th Foot.

The best time to visit Plattsburgh is in the early autumn on the weekend closest to 11 September when the town holds its annual battle commemoration and street festival which is a combination of homage to history and old-fashioned small town pride. And if one gets tired of the War of 1812, the nearby Adirondacks State Park beckons with six million acres of hills, woodland and wildlife.

Returning to the Niagara, the Lundy's Lane Cemetery in Niagara Falls, Canada, is not only the site of one of the bloodiest battles of the War of 1812; it contains the graves of British officers who were killed in the siege of Fort Erie, including Lieutenant-Colonel John Gordon of the 1st Foot and Captain Robert Pattison of the 82nd Foot.

In nearby Buffalo, Forest Lawn Cemetery, which is a wonderful 19th century creation, comprises 269 acres of lawns, ponds and woods and many, many

Cemetery, Lundy's Lane, Niagara Falls, Canada. The cemetery at Lundy's Lane is not only the last resting place of many British and Canadian officers killed in the 1814 Niagara campaign but also the site of one of the bloodiest battles of the war. Interred on its grounds are Lieutenant-Colonel John Gordon of the 1st Foot and Captain Robert Pattison of the 82nd Foot, both killed during the sortie of 17 September 1814. (Author's photograph)

Soldier's Memorial, Forest Lawn Cemetery, Buffalo. Near this monument are the unmarked graves of many American officers killed during the siege including Major Lodowick Morgan, the victor at Conjocta Creek, and one Canadian, the renegade Joseph Willcocks. (Author's photo)

tombs and graves. Many of the American officers killed during the siege of Fort Erie are interred here. They were first buried in a cemetery in the middle of the village of Buffalo, but when this was threatened by development, they were removed in 1852 to the newly-opened Forest Lawn site. A marble memorial obelisk dedicated to the veterans of the war was erected near the new mass grave site and it includes the names of Major Lodowick Morgan of the Rifles and Captain Alexander Williams of the artillery. It is noteworthy that Conjocta Creek (as the present author insists on calling it), which Lodowick Morgan so ably defended, flows through Forest Lawn Cemetery not far from his last resting place. Less noteworthy is the fact that, among the remains of those relocated from the older cemetery are those of the Canadian traitor Joseph Willcocks.

Other wartime graves, not as well marked, became obliterated and lost over time as wooden headstones or markers crumbled and disintegrated. The remains of a British soldier were discovered in the vicinity of Culver Hill north of Plattsburgh in the late 19th century. He was found to have a small stash of gold and silver coins in a pocket, probably his life savings, and was given a decent reburial.[66]

Monument to Eleazar D. Wood, West Point. Major-General Jacob Brown commissioned and paid for this monument to Wood, which was erected on the grounds of the United States Military Academy shortly after the war. (Photograph by Pat Kavanagh)

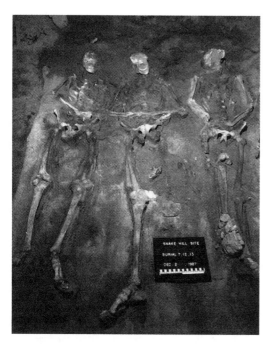

Last resting place. Three of the remains in the wartime American burial ground discovered near the site of the Snake Hill battery in 1987. Investigation revealed that 28 of the 31 sets of remains were definitely Americans and they were repatriated to the United States in a moving ceremony in June 1988. (Courtesy, Ron Williamson and Archaeological Services Incorporated)

Below **An American soldier of the War of 1812.** Forensic reconstruction was carried out on the skull of one set of remains and the result was this head. This is the face of an American soldier who served at Fort Erie. (Photograph by Dianne Graves)

In May 1932 workmen excavating near the stone Fort Erie uncovered three wooden coffins containing the remains of three men who were identified by bits of silver and gold braid and buttons as an officer of the 8th Foot, an American officer and an American enlisted man. The only officer of the 8th Foot who died at the siege was Lieutenant Charles Barstow, a personal friend of John Le Couteur of the 104th Foot. Barstow was killed during the sortie of 17 September 1814. This raises the question whether the remains of the American officer might be those of Major Eleazar Wood, who also died shortly after he was captured during the sortie. On 14 August 1932 a guard of honour

from the Toronto Regiment (now the Royal Regiment of Canada), which is allied to the King's Regiment (the successor of the 8th Foot), was present when these remains were re-interred in the Soldiers' Plot of the Fort Erie Cemetery under a memorial to the dead of the War of 1812. As the history of the Royals records: "The guard of honour rested on their arms reversed, a firing party fired three volleys, and regimental buglers sounded 'Last Post.'"[67]

And All Their Glory Past. Bedecked with the Stars and Stripes, the coffins of the 28 American soldiers disinterred at Fort Erie lie in state before the fort, awaiting repatriation to the United States on 30 June 1988. They were re-interred at the National Cemetery at Bath, New York. (Courtesy, Ron Williamson and Archaeological Services)

In October 1987 an American military burial ground from the 1814 siege was discovered near what was once Snake Hill. Archaeological excavations uncovered the remains of thirty-one persons, of whom twenty-eight were positively identified as Americans from buttons on their clothing. Many of the remains revealed evidence of serious wounds, some having amputated limbs, etc. After a thorough forensic examination conducted by American and Canadian pathologists, on 30 June 1988 the remains of the Americans were returned to the United States. Following a brief ceremony at the stone fort mounted by Canadian military units, the coffins, each draped with the American flag, were placed into twenty-eight hearses, which drove in column across the Peace Bridge linking the town of Fort Erie and the city of Buffalo while Phantom jets of the Air National Guard flew overhead in the "missing plane" formation. Finally home, the remains of these veterans of the siege were re-interred with ceremony at the National Cemetery in Bath, New York.[68]

And all their glory past, they lie there now – but they are not forgotten.

THE END

Weapons and Weapons Performance, 1814

INFANTRY WEAPONS

British Short Land Musket, India Pattern

Furniture:	brass
Calibre of bore:	.75 (.75 of an inch)
Calibre of projectile:	.71 (.71 of an inch)
Projectile:	lead ball, just over 1 ounce in weight
Range:	
Theoretical maximum:	250 yards
Effective maximum:	
Volley (100 rounds):	150 yards
Single round:	100 yards
Favoured range:	50-75 yards
Weight:	9 lb. 11 oz.
Optimum effect at 30 yards:	penetrate 3/8 inch of iron or 5 inches of seasoned oak
Rate of fire by trained infantry:	
Optimum:	4-5 rounds per minute
Actual:	2-3 rounds per minute
Rate of misfire:	20-40% depending on conditions

American 1795 Springfield Musket, or Later Variants

Furniture:	steel
Calibre of bore:	.69 calibre
Calibre of projectile:	.65 calibre
Projectile	soft lead ball just under 1 ounce or a "buck and ball" combination with one musket ball and three buck shot
Range (for ball ammunition)	
Theoretical maximum:	less than 250 yards
Effective maximum:	
Volley (100 rounds)	less than 150 yards
Single round:	less than 100 yards
Favoured range:	50-75 yards
Weight:	11 lb. with bayonet
Effect	less than that of British ounce ball
Rate of fire and misfire:	same as British musket

Note: Depending on quality of powder and flint, the touch-holes of these muskets had to be manually cleaned every 15 to 20 rounds and the flint replaced every 10 to 15 rounds. After 15 or so repeated rounds the barrel became too hot to handle with comfort, and if the soldier did not have gloves, he usually wrapped the carrying strap around the barrel as a protection.

American 1803 Harper's Ferry Rifle

Overall length:	49 inches
Furniture:	brass
Calibre of bore:	.54 (.54 of an inch)
Calibre of projectile:	.53 (.53 of an inch)
Projectile:	soft lead ball, half an ounce in weight
Range:	
Theoretical maximum:	300 yards
Effective maximum:	200 yards
Favoured range:	100-125 yards
Weight:	9 lbs

LAND ORDNANCE

Brass 24-pdr. Gun

Weight on carriage:	4963 lb.
Number of horses in team:	6 to 8
Service life:	500-600 rounds at service charge
Gun detachment:	
Trained gunners:	3
Assistants:	5
Calibre:	
Bore:	5.8 in./148 mm.
Projectile (round shot):	5.53 in.
Weight of projectile (round shot):	24 lb./52.8 kg.
Range:	
Round shot:	
Theoretical maximum:	2000 yds.
Effective maximum:	1000-1200 yards
Favoured range:	800-1000 yards
Canister:	600 yards
Effectiveness:	under optimum conditions, a 24-pdr. round shot could penetrate 40 human beings.
Rate of fire:	one round per minute.
Ammunition scales:	probably 60-70 rounds, 75% round shot, with more in immediate supply.

Brass 6-pdr. Gun

Weight: gun, carriage and limber:	3080 lb.
Number of horses in team:	4 to 6
Service life:	500-600 rounds at service charge
Gun detachment:	
Trained gunners:	2-3
Assistants:	3-4
Calibre:	
Bore:	3.66 in./83 mm.
Projectile (round shot):	3.49 in.
Weight of projectile (round shot):	6 lb./13.2 kg.
Range:	
Round shot:	
Theoretical maximum:	1000 yards
Effective maximum:	600-800 yards
Favoured range:	600-800 yards
Canister:	200-600 yards
Effectiveness:	under optimum conditions, a 6-pdr. round shot could penetrate 19 human beings.

Rate of fire:	1-2 rounds per minute.
Ammunition scales:	40 round shot and 10 rounds of canister with the gun and limber. The ammunition carriage contained 92 round shot, 18 canister and 20 shrapnel rounds.

Iron 6-pdr. Gun (American)

Weight of gun and carriage:	2000 lb.
Number of horses in team:	4 to 6
Service life:	estimated 1000 rounds at service charge
Gun detachment:	
Trained gunners:	3
Assistants:	6
Calibre of bore:	3.66 in./83 mm.
Projectile (round shot):	3.49 inches
Weight of projectile (round shot):	6 lb./13.2 kg.
Range and effectiveness:	see figures for British brass 6-pdr. gun.
Rate of fire:	1-2 rounds per minute.
Ammunition scales:	18 round shot on carriage and 62 round shot and 30 canister rounds in their caissons.

Iron 8-inch Mortar

Weight of mortar:	896 lb.
Calibre of bore:	8 inches
Calibre of projectile:	7.5 inches
Range:	
Theoretical maximum:	1720 yards
Effective maximum:	1300 yards

Brass 5.5 inch Howitzer

Weight: howitzer, carriage, limber:	3052 lb.
Number of horses in team:	4 to 6
Service life:	500-600 rounds at service charge
Gun detachment:	
Trained gunners:	2-3
Assistants:	3-4
Calibre of bore:	5.5 in./139.7 mm.
Weight of shell:	15.5 lb.
Range:	
Theoretical maximum:	1200 yards
Effective maximum:	800-1000 yards
Favoured range:	600-800 yards
Rate of fire:	1 round per minute.
Ammunition scales:	62 shells and 8 canister and case shot shells with the gun, limber and ammunition cart.

Iron 5.5 inch Howitzer (American)

Weight of howitzer and carriage:	2100 lb.
Number of horses in team:	4 to 6
Service life:	estimated 1000 rounds at service charge.
Gun detachment:	
Trained gunners:	2-3
Assistants:	3-4
Calibre of bore:	5.5 in./139.7 mm.
Weight of projectile shell	15.5 lb.
Range, effectiveness and rate of fire:	same as British 5.5 inch howitzer.

Congreve Rockets

32-pdr. shell rocket
  Maximum range: 3000 yards at 50 degrees elevation
32-pdr. case shot (canister) rocket, containing 200 balls
  Maximum range: 2600 yards at 55 degrees elevation
32-pdr. explosive rocket
  Maximum range: 2500-3000 yards at 5 degrees
12-pdr case shot (canister) rocket containing 72 balls
  Maximum range: 2000 yards at 45 degrees of elevation
Note: Congreve rockets were likely to fly in any direction after being fired and they often doubled back on the rocket detachment

NAVAL ORDNANCE

32-pdr. Iron Carronade

Length:	4 feet
Weight of tube:	1908 lb.
Diameter of bore:	6.35 inches
Diameter of round shot:	6.106 inches
Gun crew:	6 men permanent with occasional assistance from several more
Maximum range with shot:	1087 yards at full charge with 5 degrees of elevation
Effective range:	600-800 yards
Penetration:	10 inches of elm at 1600 yards at full charge

24-pdr. Iron Gun

Length:	9 feet
Weight of tube:	5724 lb.
Diameter of bore:	5 8/10 inch
Diameter of round shot:	5 6/10 inch
Gun crew:	6 men permanent with occasional assistance from 9 more
Maximum range with shot:	2020 yards at full charge with 7 degrees of elevation
Effective range:	1400-1800 yards
Recoil:	10-12 feet
Penetration:	41.5 inches of elm at 1600 yards with full charge

24-pdr. Iron Carronade

Length:	3 feet
Weight of tube:	3804 lb.
Diameter of bore:	5.68 inches
Diameter of round shot:	5.475 inches
Gun crew:	6 men permanent with occasional assistance from several more
Maximum range with shot:	1050 yards at full charge with 5 degrees of elevation
Effective range:	600-800 yards
Penetration:	9 inches of elm at 1600 yards with full charge

18-pdr. Iron Gun

Length:	8 feet
Weight of tube:	4704 lb.
Diameter of bore:	5 3/10 inch
Diameter of round shot:	5 1/10 inch
Gun crew:	6 men permanent with occasional assistance from 9 more
Maximum range with shot:	2610 yards at full charge with 5 degrees of elevation

Effective range:	1400-1800 yards
Recoil:	10-12 feet
Penetration:	37.5 inches of elm at 1600 yards with full charge

12-pdr. Iron Gun

Length:	7 feet
Weight of tube:	3804 lb.
Diameter of bore:	4 7/10 inch
Diameter of round shot:	4 5/10 inch
Gun crew:	6 men permanent with occasional assistance from several more
Maximum range with shot:	1600 yards at full charge with 6 degrees of elevation
Effective range:	1200-1400 yards
Recoil:	8 feet
Penetration:	32 inches of elm at 1600 yards at full charge

Sources

Muskets and Rifles: Howard Blackmore, *British Military Firearms, 1650-1850* (London, 1961); René Chartrand, *Uniforms and Equipment of the United States Forces in the War of 1812* (Youngstown, 1992); William Duane, *American Military Library* (2 vols., Philadelphia, 1809); William Greener, *The Gun; or, A Treatise on the Various Descriptions of Small Fire-Arms* (London, 1808); James Hicks, *Notes on U.S. Ordnance* (Mt. Vernon, 1940); and B.P. Hughes, *Firepower, Weapons Effectiveness on the Battlefield, 1630-1850* (London, 1974); George Moller, *American Military Shoulder Arms. Volume II. From the 1790s to the End of the Flintlock Period.* (Author's publication, 2011); Joseph W. Shield, *From Flintlock to M1* (New York, 1954).

Land Ordnance: Ralph W. Adye, *The Bombardier and Pocket Gunner* (London, 1813); Henri Othon De Scheel, *Treatise on Artillery* (Philadelphia, 1800); Jean-Jacques Basiline de Gassendi, *Aide-Memoir, à l'usage des Officiers de l'artillerie de France* (2 vols., Paris, 1801); [Amos Stoddard], *Exercise for the Garrison and Field Ordnance, Together with Manoeuvres of Horse Artillery …* (Philadelphia, 1812); and Louis de Tousard, *American Artillerist's Companion, or Elements of Artillery* (2 vols., Philadelphia, 1809).

Naval Ordnance: Theophilus S. Beauchant, *The Naval Gunner* (London, 1828); Howard Douglas, *A Treatise on Naval Gunnery*, (London, 1819); Robert Simmons, *The Sea-Gunner's Vade-Mecum* (London, 1812); Spencer Tucker, *Arming the Fleet: U.S. Navy Ordnance in the Muzzle-Loading Era* (Annapolis, 1989).

Opposing Forces, Assault on Fort Erie, 15 August 1814

BRITISH ARMY AND ROYAL NAVY
Commanding general Lieutenant-General Gordon Drummond

Assault Columns

Southern Column, LCol Viktor Fischer

89th Foot, flank companies	90
100th Foot, flank companies	80
8th Foot	670
De Watteville's Regiment	1,000
Detachment, Royal Artillery	13
Strength	1,853

Northern Column, Colonel Hercules Scott

103rd Regiment of Foot	750
1st Foot, flank companies	130
Strength	880

Northern Mixed Column, LCol William Drummond

41st Foot, flank companies	110
104th Foot, flank companies	77
Detachment, Royal Navy seamen	90
Detachment, Royal Marines	50
Detachment, Royal Artillery	13
Strength	340

Pickets and Demonstration Force

Regular troops	300
Aboriginal warriors	200
Strength	500

Reserve, Lieutenant-Colonel John Tucker

19th Light Dragoons	100
Royal Artillery	100
1st Foot	535
Glengarry Light Infantry	492
Incorporated Milita	350
Strength	1,577
Less infantry assigned to demonstration force	300
Revised strength	1,277

Recapitulation

Assault Forces	3,073
Demonstration Forces	500
Reserve	1,277
Total	4,850

Total Strength of Right Division, 14 August 1814   4,850

LEFT DIVISION, UNITED STATES ARMY
Commanding General Brigadier-General E.P. Gaines

Divisional Troops

Light Dragoons	48
Artillery	est. 250
Bombardiers	60
Strength	358

1st Brigade, Lieutenant-Colonel Henry Aspinwall

9th Infantry	200
11th Infantry	300
22nd Infantry	240
25th Infantry	230
Strength	970

2nd Brigade, Brigadier-General E.W. Ripley

1st Infantry	150
21st Infantry	450
23rd Infantry	300
Strength	900

Unbrigaded Regular Units

19th Infantry	150
Detachment, 1st and 4th Rifle Regiments	200
Strength	350

Volunteer Brigade, Brigadier-General Peter B. Porter

New York volunteers & Canadian Volunteers	250

Recapitulation

Divisional Troops	358
1st Brigade	970
2nd Brigade	900
Unbrigaded Regular Troops	350
Volunteer Brigade	250
Total	2,828

Total Strength of Left Division: 2,828

Comments on British Order of Battle

Almost all the British strength figures, except those for the 104th Foot, are estimates based on the best available evidence. The closest British strength return to 14 August 1814 is the monthly return of the forces dated 25 July 1814, which can be found in NAB, WO 17, vol. 1517. At this time the British army was paid and mustered on the 25th of every month and these general monthly returns are available for the entire period, 1812-1815. Unfortunately, 25 July was also the date of the battle of Lundy's Lane, in which the Right Division suffered some 800 casualties. The question thus resolves itself whether the monthly return was compiled before or after the battle. After studying it for some time, I have concluded that it was taken before the battle and, therefore, I have deducted the lossess suffered by units in that battle (and also Conjocta Creek) to arrive at the figures above. Note that these figures do not include those on the sick list, which is normally about ⅛ of a healthy's army's strength. Therefore, the Right Division's totals might be reduced by ⅛.

Comments on American Order of Battle

The figures for the Left Division are easier to establish than those for their British opponents as we have two reliable strength returns taken after the battle of Lundy's Lane. The biggest problem is establishing a strength for the unbrigaded units and their figures are estimates based on the best available evidence. Note that it appears that one or more of the regular infantry units were stationed on the American side of the Niagara but there is no concrete evidence as to which one was stationed there on 14/15 August 1814.

Sources:

British: LAC, RGp 8 I, vol. 685: Arrangement of Assault Forces, 14 August 1814; Harvey to Fischer, 14 August 1814, Drummond to Prevost, 15 August 1814, Fischer to Prevost, 15 August 1814, List of Casualties, 15 August 1814, Drummond to Prevost, 16 August 1814; NAB, WO 17, Monthly Returns, July and August 1814; Le Couteur, *Merry Hearts,* 191.

American: Adams History, vol. 8: 69, Monthly Return of Troops under Major General Brown, Fort Erie, 31 July 1814 and, 83, Strength of the Army at Fort Erie, 31 August 1814; Gaines CM, Evidence of Trimble and Hindman.

Myths of the Siege of Fort Erie

William Drummond's Actions during the Assault of 15 August

The reputation of Lieutenant-Colonel William Drummond of the 104th Foot has suffered at the hands of 19th-century American historians, who often portray him as a stone-cold killer. This unflattering assessment originated in the report on the assault of 15 August 1814 written by Brigadier-General E. P. Gaines, the American commander, who damned Drummond as "a hardened murderer" for his refusal to grant quarter (to take prisoners).[1] This refrain was taken up by others and became a common feature of early American histories of the war. In his *Pictorial Field-Book of the War of 1812*, published in 1869, Benson Lossing claimed that

> the exasperated Drummond, goaded almost to madness by the murderous repulses which he had endured, had given orders to show no mercy to the "damned Yankees," and had actually stationed a body of painted savages near, with instructions to rush into the fort when the regulars should get possession of it, and assist in the general massacre.[2]

It appears that Drummond's reputation is still slightly black among Americans – the author of a recent history of the War of 1812 terms him "a cheerfully bloody-minded light infantry officer."[3]

This negative assessment of William Drummond's actions during the assault – particularly his orders to give "no quarter" (take no prisoners) – is flawed because it fails to take into account the military "laws," or customs and usages of Napoleonic warfare. There were, of course, no international agreements such as the Hague or Geneva Conventions in 1814, but by that time a fairly elaborate tradition had been constructed around the attack and defence of fortified places. It held that the garrison of a besieged place which surrendered would be taken prisoner. But, if a fortified place, "after being duly summoned, refuses to surrender, and is taken by assault, those found in it are obliged to submit to the discretion of the victor" and the best they might hope for would be "to have their lives spared, if they immediately lay down their arms."[4]

By extension, if a fortified place was taken by assault without being summoned – as the British attempted to do at Fort Erie – the tradition was that the attacker was not expected to take prisoners. In 1820 no less an authority than the Duke of Wellington stated that "it has always been understood that the defenders of a fortress stormed have no claim to quarter, and the practice which prevailed during the last century of surrendering fortresses when a breach was opened in the body of a place" was based "on this understanding."[5] The British soldiers who attacked Fort Erie were well aware of this custom and saw no reason to make prisoners of men who might inflict terrible losses on them.

It should be noted that nowhere in the 1929 Geneva Convention, which was in force during the Second World War, is there a direction that a combatant must grant quarter to his enemy and take him prisoner, sparing his life. If a combatant does make an enemy prisoner, the Convention then goes into effect concerning the proper treatment of prisoners in that they must be placed in a safe area and removed from a combat zone, etc., but nowhere does the Geneva Convention state that prisoners must be taken. Many times during that war (and other wars), combatants resorted to the traditional British army response to a plea for mercy: "Too late, chum."

The Cause of the Explosion in the Northeast Bastion

Immediately after the assault, and in the weeks, months and years that followed, many extravagant and fanciful claims were made about the cause of the explosion under the floor of the northeast bastion. For example, exactly one week after the failed attack, a Canadian officer claimed that

> a corporal of the American Artillery, having got on a red coat and cap of a British deserter, and while it was scarce daylight, got in amongst our men, who were principally in and near this bastion, and appeared to make himself busy in working the gun, which by this time had been turned against the enemy and in the bustle he got under the platform and effected his purpose with a slow match. He had but just time himself to slink off and get behind a stone building in the fort when this unfortunate explosion took place.[6]

Most officers and men in the Right Division were convinced that the explosion was due to a deliberate act, that gunpowder had been stowed under the bastion to act as a gigantic "mine." For example, to the end of his days, Lieutenant John Le Couteur believed that he had been "blown up" by a mine.[7]

Neither Gaines nor any of his subordinates claimed to have deliberately caused the explosion but, nonetheless, many stories circulated that attributed it to:

a) the mortally wounded McDonough, whose dying act was to fling a torch into the magazine. McDonough's mother firmly believed this to have been the case;

b) an unidentified American officer who claimed that "I could blow them all to hell in a moment" and did so – but how he did so, is not known;

c) an unidentified lieutenant of Bombardiers, who volunteered to set fire to a trail of powder laid into the bastion. It proved so difficult to light that he had to go closer to the bastion and was killed in the resulting explosion;

d) a lieutenant of the artillery or bombardiers commanding a gun in another bastion of the stone fort who turned his weapon and fired at a basket of artillery cartridges placed under the floor of the bastion which was open at the rear. He hit it and the bastion exploded but he was killed in subsequent fighting and his deed never properly acknowledged.[8]

It is not difficult to reject these claims. McDonough died long before the explosion, so could not have been responsible for it. No officer of the bombardiers was killed during the assault and the only artillery officers killed were Williams and McDonough, and they both died well before the magazine ignited. Furthermore it is nearly impossible to bring artillery fire into the northeast bastion from any other part of the fort, and even if it were, the basket of cartridges would have been obscured by the men in the bastion and the dim light. As for "blowing them all to hell," no further evidence has ever been produced to identify this officer or his method.

There is a strong possibility, however, that the explosion was entirely accidental and caused by either

e) an artillery cartridge being broken while being handled, which created an accidental powder train to the magazine. This train later caught fire, again by accident, and exploded the magazine;[9] or

f) the British discharging the guns in the bastion or their own muskets, which resulted in flaming fragments from the muzzle blast being communicated to, and igniting the magazine below the bastion floor.[10]

Lieutenant-General Gordon Drummond believed that the explosion was caused by the discharge of the guns of the bastion inside the fort. In his words: "some ammunition which had been placed under the platform caught fire from the firing of the guns to the rear and a most tremendous explosion followed."[11] There is a very strong possibility that this is what ignited the magazine as we know that Lieutenant George Charlton, RA, swung one of the guns in the bastion and fired at least two rounds *within* it.[12] We also have the testimony of Major Jacob Hindman, the American artillery commander, that the magazine exploded shortly after Charlton fired within the bastion.[13]

In fact, we shall never know what caused the explosion and, as one historian has remarked, so many reasons have been given, the individual "will doubtless find no difficulty making a satisfactory choice, for each has this merit – it cannot be successfully controverted."[14]

Opposing Forces during the Plattsburgh Campaign, September 1814

BRITISH FORCES

BRITISH ARMY IN NORTH AMERICA
Commander in Chief: Lieutenant-General Sir George Prevost

Left Division, British Army in North America
Commanding General: Major-General Francis De Rottenburg

Cavalry
Commanding Officer: Lieutenant-Colonel John O'Neill
2 Squadrons, 19th Light Dragoons,   266

Artillery
Senior Officer: Major John Sinclair   534
    Major William Gordon's company, attached to 1st Brigade
    Captain William Green's company, attached to 2nd Brigade
    Captain Henry Jackson's company, atached to 3rd Brigade
    Train of Artillery (including a RMA rocket detachment)

Infantry
1st Brigade
Commander: Major-General F.P. Robinson
    3/27th Foot; 1/39th Foot; 76th Foot; 1/88th Foot
Brigade strength   1,221

2nd Brigade
Commander: Major-General Thomas Brisbane
    2/8th, 13th and 49th Foot; De Meuron's Regiment;
    Voltigeurs Canadiens; Chasseurs Canadiens:
Brigade strength   2,952

3rd Brigade
Commander: Major-General Manley Power
    3rd Foot, 1/5th Foot, 1/27th Foot and 1/58th Foot:
Brigade strength   3,094

Total strength, Left Division at Plattsburgh, 6 September 1814   9,067

THE ROYAL NAVY, LAKE CHAMPLAIN SQUADRON
Commander: Captain George Downie, RN

Vessel	Rig	Armament
HMS *Confiance*	ship	27 × 24-pdr guns, 4 × 32-pdr carronades and 6 × 24-pdr. carronades
HMS *Linnet*	brig	16 × 12-pdr. guns
HMS *Chubb*	sloop	3 × 6-pdr. guns, 18 × 18-pdr. carronades
HMS *Finch*	sloop	6 × 18-pdr. carronades, 4 × 6-pdr. and 1 × 18 pdr. "Columbiads

Gunboats

Beckwith	lugger	1 × 18-pdr. gun
Beresford	lugger	1 × 32-pdr. carronade
Blucher	lugger	1 × 24-pdr. gun, 1 × 32-pdr. carronade
Brock	lugger	1 × 32-pdr. carronade
Drummond	lugger	1 × 18-pdr. gun
Murray	lugger	1 × 18-pdr. gun
Popham	lugger	1 × 32-pdr. carronade
Prevost	lugger	1 × 24-pdr. gun, 1 × 32-pdr. carronade
Simcoe	lugger	1 × 32-pdr. carrpmade
Wellington	lugger	1 × 18-pdr. gun, 1 × 18-pdr. carronade
Yeo	lugger	1 × 24-pdr. gun, 1 × 32-pdr. carronade

AMERICAN FORCES

UNITED STATES ARMY
Commanding General: Brigadier-General Alexander Macomb

Artillery

Capt Luther Leonard's Company, Regiment of Light Artillery	100
Capt Alexander S. Brooks, two companies, Corps of Artillery	200

Infantry

Lt-Col. Daniel Appling's battalion, 1st Rifle Regiment	150
Major J. Sproull's detachment, 13th Infantry	200
Captain G. McGlassin's Company, 15th Infantry	50
Major A. Sizer's detachment, 29th Infantry	100
Captain Shell's company, 6th Infantry	80

Detachments at the forts
    Fort Moreau
        6th & 29th Infantry under Col. Melancton Smith
    Fort Brown
        30th & 31st Infantry under Lt.Col. H. Storrs
    Fort Scott
        33rd & 34th Infantry under Lt.Col. T. Vinson   1,771

Invalids of the Light Artillery, Dragoons, 4th, 5th, 10th, 12th, 14th, 15th, 16th and 45th Infantry   803

Estimated Strength of Regular Units   3,454

NEW YORK STATE MILITIA
Commanding General: Major-General Benjaminn Mooers
    Elements of 40th and 42nd Brigades, 9th, 36th and 37th Regiments and Sanford's Independent Battalion

Estimated Strength of New York Militia: 700

VERMONT VOLUNTEERS
Commanding General: Major-General Samuel Strong
    1st Regiment, 11 companies
    2nd Regiment, 6 companies
    3rd Regiment, 5 companies
    4th Regiment, 5 companies

Estimated strength of Vermont Militia: 2,200

Recapitulation, American Land Forces

United States Army:	3,454
New York Militia:	700
Vermont Volunteers:	2,200
Total Strength:	6,354

UNITED STATES NAVY

Commanding Officer, Lake Champlain: Master Commandant Thomas Macdonough

Name	Rig	Armament
USS *Saratoga*	ship	8 × 24-pdr. guns, 12 × 32-pdr. & 6 × 42-pdr. carronades
USS *Eagle*	brig	8 × 18-pdr. guns, 12 × 32-pdr. carronades
USS *Ticonderoga*	schooner	8 × 12-pdr. guns, 4 × 18 pdr. guns, 5 × 32 pdr. carronades
USS *Preble*	sloop	7 × 9-pdr. guns

Gunboats (lateen rigged)

Allen	1 × 24-pdr. gun, 1 × 18-pdr. "Columbiad"
Borer	1 × 24-pdr. gun, 1 × 18-pdr. "Columbiad"
Burows	1 × 24-pdr. gun, 1 × 18-pdr. "Columbiad"
Centipede	1 × 24-pdr. gun, 1 × 18-pdr. "Columbiad"
Nettle	1 × 24-pdr. gun, 1 × 18-pdr. "Columbiad"
Viper	1 × 24-pdr. gun, 1 × 18-pdr. "Columbiad"

Gunboats (lugger rigged)

Alwyn	1 × 12-pdr. gun
Ballard	1 × 12-pdr. gun
Ludlow	1 × 12-pdr. gun
Wilmer	1 × 12-pdr. gun

Comments

See Appendix E for an analysis of the composition and strength of the British army at Plattsburgh and the sources on which it is based.

Establishing accurate figures for the American forces is difficult because there do not seem to exist any musters for the New York or Vermont militia (at least none have yet surfaced). The figures for the regular units are at best estimates, most of which were made at the time. Although it appears that more Americans were available to defend Plattsburgh than is commonly stated, one must take into consideration that the high number of invalids could only provide imited service and the militia were not really trained to fight British regulars in the open. Even many of the so-called regulars under Macomb's command were really only recruits who had been in service for about six months.

Sources

British army figures are from Weekly State of the Left Division, 6 September 1814, and Return of the Left Division, Odeltown, 15 September, LAC, appended to Prevost to Bathurst, 1 April 1815, LAC, CO 42, vol. 131. Royal Navy figures from Comparative State of the Flotilla on Lake Champlain, 11 September 1814, LAC, CO 42, vol. 128-2, 258.

American land strength figures from Alan Everest, *The War of 1812 in the Champlain Valley* (Syracuse, 1981), 164-166; Keith Herkalo, *The Battles at Plattsburgh, September 11, 1814* (Charleston, 2012), 79-80; George Izard, *Official Correspondence with the Department of War* (Philadelphia, 1816), 144. American Naval Strength Figures from Thomas Macdonough, *Master of Command in the Early U.S. Navy* (Annapolis, 2003), 119.

APPENDIX E

Strength, Composition and Desertion Rate
of the British Army at Plattsburgh, 1814

There is a prevalent myth on the part of many American historians that Prevost's army was a red-coated juggernaut composed of 15,000 veterans of Wellington's army, hundreds of whom deserted during the campaign. Some years ago, the author published a study on the strength, composition and desertion rate of this force and what follows is a summary of that study.[1]

The Strength of the British Army

In April 1815, as one of his last acts before being relieved as the commander-in-chief in British North America, Prevost dispatched a number of documents to London at the request of his superiors. Among them were two strength returns, one being a "Weekly State of the Left Division under the Command of Major General de Rottenburg," dated "Headquarters Platsburg [sic] 6th September 1814."[2] At first glance, therefore, this return would seem to be accurate evidence of the strength of the British army at the battle of Plattsburgh. The devil, however, is often found in the details and a closer examination of this document reveals some interesting facts.

The return of 6 September is broken down by the standard British method of separate figures for officers, sergeants, drummers, and "rank and file" (privates and corporals). It shows that on 6 September Prevost's infantry comprised 14 battalions of infantry organized into three brigades, two squadrons of light dragoons, and three artillery companies and a train of artillery (which probably included a Royal Marine Artillery rocket detachment). The total strength of the army on 6 September was 11,349 officers and men.

From this figure, however, deductions must be made. First, the number of men on the sick list must be taken away and, although the return of 6 September does not include figures for officers, it shows 136 enlisted men as unable to perform their duties on 6 September 1814 because of sickness.

The second deduction that must be made is for those officers and men "on command," or detached from their brigades and regiments. Of the 14 infantry battalions in the army, the 6 September return lists 13 battalions as having officers and men "on command." In nine of these units, the average number of "rank and file" so detached is 16 men – clearly small parties – but in four battalions the numbers "on command" are much larger. From Robinson's 1st Brigade, only 60 "rank and file" each from the 1/39th and 1/88th Foot are present under arms at Plattsburgh on 6 September, the remainder being listed as "on command." The fact that the greater part of these units had been detached is confirmed by Major-General Frederick Robinson's journal of the campaign, which states that the 39th and 88th Foot were left on lines of communication duties at Chazy and Champlain, New York, and only their light infantry companies were present with the main army.[3] From Major-General Thomas Brisbane's 2nd Brigade, one-third of the 49th Foot and one half of De Meuron's Regiment are listed as "on command" and not at Plattsburgh on 6 September. Finally, a "division" or half one of the three field artillery brigades or companies had been detached, an estimated 50 men. In total, no fewer than 2,146 enlisted men were "on command" on 6 September and must be deducted from the figure of 11,349 officers and men in the division at Plattsburgh.

Taking all this into consideration, and deducting the figures for the sick and "on command," the strength of Prevost's army present and fit for duty at Plattsburgh on 6 September was 9,062 officers and men. This figure would not have changed substantially when the battle was fought five days later as the four infantry units and one artillery unit "on command" remained so and it is doubtful that the number of sick increased appreciably over this short period.

The Composition of the Army

Contrary to the popular myth that the British army at Plattsburgh consisted primarily of veteran units from Wellington's army, only 6 of the 14 infantry battalions were actually from the Peninsular army. Robinson's 1st Brigade was composed entirely of these troops while Power's 3rd Brigade had two Peninsular battalions (1/3rd and 1/5th Foot) and two non-Peninsular units: the 1/27th Foot and the 1/58th, which came from Bentinck's "East Coast" army in Spain. Brisbane's 2nd Brigade was composed entirely of British units that had been serving in North America for some time or Canadian units. Finally, as has been pointed out above, only the light companies of two Peninsular units, the 39th and 88th Foot, ever reached Plattsburgh during the campaign. None of the four artillery companies or part companies under Sinclair's command were from the Peninsula nor was Prevost's sole cavalry regiment, the 19th Light Dragoons. Extrapolating from the figures in the return of 6 September 1814, therefore, only 2,625 (or about 29%) of the 9,062 officers and men reported fit for duty that day were Peninsula veterans.[4]

British Losses during the Plattsburgh Campaign

When turning to the question of losses suffered during the campaign, we have additional evidence from two returns compiled on 14 and 15 September, as well as the return for 6 September.[5] One of these new documents is a "Return of the Killed Wounded and Missing of the Left Division ... from the 6th to the 14th September 1814, Inclusive," and was appended to Prevost's official report on the battle, which he dated 11 September. It states that 37 men were killed, 150 wounded and 55 went missing between 6 and 14 September.

This document, however, was compiled within a few days of the end of the campaign before an accurate accounting of all casualties was available – many of those it lists as being wounded on 11 September would later have died. It is also notable that, in contrast to the returns of 6 and 15 September, which break down the "missing" category into those taken prisoner and those who deserted, this document simply lists them as "missing" – reason unspecified.

On balance, because they were prepared six months later when more reliable information was available, the returns for 6 and 15 September can be regarded as more accurate. They list the following casualty statistics:

British Losses, September 1814

Returns	Killed	Wounded	Prisoner	Deserted
6 Sept 1814	14	94	2	5
15 Sept 1814	33	127	68	234
Totals	47	221	70	239

Some comment should be made here about the period covered by these two returns. That for 6 September 1814 notes that the casualty figures are those "since the last return" and, since the British army was mustered and paid on the 25th of every month, the two returns thus cover the period 25 August to 15 September 1814, or the duration of the Plattsburgh campaign. In sum, therefore, Prevost suffered 577 losses of all types during those three weeks, or 5.6% of the army he led across the international border.

When contemplating these figures, those for desertion immediately attract the eye. Much has been made of the high rate of desertion in Prevost's army during the retreat back to Canada and the implication has been made that the prime culprits were the Peninsula veterans who, disgusted with poor leadership of a "colonial" general, took the opportunity to undergo instant conversion to republicans. Certainly the figure of five deserters (a very low rate) prior to 6 September compared to 234 deserters after that date would seem to be an indication of low morale in the army during its retreat. A closer examination of the return for 15 September, however, reveals some interesting facts about the matter of desertion.

Desertion in Prevost's Army, 7-15 September 1814 (Asterisks indicate former units of Wellington's Peninsular army)

Formation and Unit	Number
1st Brigade	
3/27th Foot*	–
1/39th Foot*	–
76th Foot*	–
1/88th Foot*	–
2nd Brigade	
2/8th Foot	39
13th Foot	22
49th Foot	18
De Meuron's Regiment	74
Canadian Voltigeurs	4
Canadian Chasseurs	–
Brigade total:	157
3rd Brigade	
1/3rd Foot*	12
1st/5th Foot*	3
1/27th Foot	48
1/58th Foot	12
Brigade total:	75
Artillery	–
Cavalry (19th Light Dragoons)	2
Total:	**234**

These figures demonstrate that, without question, the rate of desertion among the Peninsular units was non-existent or very low. They remained steadfast to the colours – and this is perhaps an indication of both high unit morale and superior (that is, veteran) junior leadership. About 60% of the total desertion occurs in the 2nd Brigade, the non-Peninsular formation, which does not speak well for its leadership and the implication is that these troops, who had been serving in North America for some time (more than a decade in the case of the 49th Foot), were no longer enamoured with life in the wilderness. The two Canadian units, however, are the exception to that statement as their desertion rate was much lower than the British regulars in the 2nd Brigade. This is surprising as, throughout the War of 1812, the desertion rate for regular and near-regular units recruited in the Canadas was generally higher than British units.

What is really intriguing is that just three units – 2/8th Foot and De Meuron's Regiment from the 2nd Brigade and the 1/27th Foot from the 3rd Brigade – account for 161 deserters or 68% of the total desertion in the army. To answer why that should be so – or at least to postulate why it should be so – requires an investigation of the background of these three regiments and this was done in the study from which this appendix is summarized.[6]

In the matter of desertion, therefore, the Peninsular units were almost blameless. The greater part of the deserters came from the 2nd Brigade composed of non-Peninsular units, and three regiments contributed nearly 70% of the total number of deserters.

Conclusions

The cherished legend of an invincible redcoated juggernaut composed of as many as 15,000 of Wellington's veterans coming to grief in the forests of northern New York and deserting in large numbers as a result, is a myth. The British strength at Plattsburgh was 8,389 all ranks, much lower than is usually stated but still a figure that compares well with the 3,454 regulars under Macomb's command.[7] Only 6 of Prevost's 14 battalions were veteran units from Wellington's Peninsular Army and, of these veterans, only four complete battalions and two companies, totalling 2,625 officers and men, were present at Plattsburgh on the day of the battle. While there is no doubt that Prevost's army suffered a fairly high rate of desertion, 234 men, only 15 of those men absconded from Peninsular units. Finally, the regiment with the highest desertion rate, nearly a third of the total, was not British but a nominally Swiss unit.

Organization and Strength of Opposing Forces, Sortie from Fort Erie, 17 September 1814

LEFT DIVISION, UNITED STATES ARMY
Commanding General: Major-General Jacob Brown

Porter's Force
Commander: Major-General Peter B. Porter

Advance Force, Gibson	
Detachment, 1st and 4th Rifles:	est. 200
Party, aboriginal warriors	est. 25
Right Column, Major Eleazar D. Wood	
23rd Infantry	est. 250
1st Infantry	est. 150
New York volunteers	
Left Column, Davis	
New York volunteers	500
Miller's Force	
Commander: Brigadier-General James Miller	
9th Infantry	
11th Infantry	
19th Infantry	est. 750
Fort Erie, Major T.S. Jesup	
25th Infantry,	est. 250
Light Dragoons	est. 30
Artillery	est. 200
Bombardiers	est. 35

Recapitulation

Sortie assault forces:	1,875
Fort Erie and reserves	515
Recapitulation:	2,390

RIGHT DIVISION, BRITISH ARMY IN NORTH AMERICA
Commanding General: Major-General Louis de Watteville

Divisional Troops	
19th Light Dragoons	est. 100
Royal Artillery	est. 110
1st Brigade, LCol John Gordon	
1st Foot	810
6th Foot	690
82nd Foot	696
2/89th flank coys	est. 110
Brigade strength	2,196

2nd Brigade, LCol Viktor Fischer	
8th Foot	650
De Watteville's Regiment	714
Brigade Strength:	1,364
Light Demi-Brigade, LCol Thomas Pearson	
Glengarry Light Infantry	300
Incorporated Militia Battalion	211
Brigade strength	511

Recapitulation

Divisional Troops:	210
1st Brigade:	2,916
2nd Brigade:	1,364
Light Demi-Brigade	511
Total strength:	5,001

Comments

The strength of the Left Division is extrapolated from the closest returns and some intelligent estimates. Note that the Twenty-Second Infantry were on the east bank of the Niagara, as well as a sizeable force of militia.

Strength of the Right Division extrapolated from the Monthly Return of 25 August and reliable secondary sources. Note, however, that the strengths of the British regulars include their sick and the actual figures fit for duty would be much lower. Although part of the light demi-brigade, the Incorporated Militia were not involved in the battle as they were being employed as labour troops from Fort Erie to Chippawa.

Sources

American sources from: Strength of the Army at Fort Erie, 31 August 1814, in Henry Adams, *History of the United States in the Administration of James Madison, Book VII* (New York, 1930), 83; Porter to Brown, 23 September 1814 and Brown to Secretary of War, in E.A. Cruikshank, *Documentary History of the Campaign on the Niagara Frontier in 1814* (Welland, n.d, c. 1906), 211; and Left Division Strength by Ration Abstracts, in Joseph Whitehorne, *While Washington Burned. The Battle for Fort Erie, 1814* (Baltimore, 1992), 116.

British sources from: NAB, WO 17, Monthly Muster, 25 August 1814; LAC, RG 8 I, vol. 685, De Watteville to Drummond, 19 September 1814 and Drummond to Prevost, 19 September 1814; Richard Feltoe, *Redcoated Ploughboys: The Volunteer Battalion of Incorporated Militia of Upper Canada, 1813-1815* (Toronto, 2012), 313; Winston Johnston, The Glengarry Light Infantry, 1812-1816 (Charlottetown, 1998).

Weather in the Niagara, 26 July–21 September, and Incidence of Combat at Fort Erie, 3 August–21 September 1814

Date	Weather	Action
July		
26	Rain at night	
27		
28		
29		
30		
31		
August		
1	Rain at night	
2		
3		Action at Conjocta Creek
		Reconnaisance of Fort Erie
4		
5		
6	Heavy rain at night	Outpost action
7		
8		
9		
10	Thunderstorm and heavy rain	Outpost action
11	Rain	
12		
13	Rain during day	Outpost action
14	Rain at night	
15	Rain	Assault repelled
16		
17	Rain	
18		Outpost action
19	Heavy rain	Outpost action
20	Heavy rain	Outpost action
21		
22	Very cold at night	Outpost action
23		Outpost action
24		Outpost action
25	Rain	

26		Outpost action
27		Outpost action
28	Rain in morning	
29		
30		
31		

September

1		
2		
3		
4	Rain in evening	Outpost action, Willcocks killed
5		Outpost action
6		
7		Outpost action
8	Rain	
9	Rain	Outpost action
10	Rain	
11	Rain	
12	Rain	
13	Rain	
14		Outpost action
15	Intensely cold	
16		
17	Rain	American sortie
18	Rain	
19	Rain at night	
20		
21	Rain at night	

Comments

Formally, the siege lasted only from 3 August to 21 September 1814 but this table runs from the day after the battle of Lundy's Lane as the book starts on that day and ends with the British withdrawal from Fort Erie. During this 58-day period, it rained on at least 25 days and there were outpost actions or skirmishes on 17 of those days and two major actions on 15 August and 17 September.

Sources

LAC, RG 8I, vols 684 & 685, Drummond to Prevost, letters dated 31 July, 4, 8, 12, 13, 15, 16, 21, 24 August and 5, 8, 11, 14, 17, 19, 21 and 24 September 1814; and Donald E. Graves, ed. *Merry Hearts Make Light Days. The War of 1812 Journal of Lieutenant John Le Couteur, 104th Foot* (Montreal, 2012), 183-199.

Endnotes

Abbreviations Used in the Endnotes

AO	Archives of Ontario, Toronto
Adams, *History*	Henry Adams, *History of the United States during the Administration of James Madison*. Books VII and IX. New York: 1930
ADM	Admiralty
BECHS	Buffalo and Erie County Historical Society, Buffalo
Brown, *Documents*	Ernest Cruikshank, ed., *Documents Relating to the Invasion of the Niagara Peninsula by the United States Army, commanded by Major-General Jacob Brown in July and August, 1814*. Niagara-on-the-Lake: 1920.
Brown, Memoranda	Memoranda of Occurrences and Some Important Facts Attending the Campaign on the Niagara, Gardner Papers, New York State Library, Albany
CLUM	Clements Library, University of Michigan, Ann Arbor
CO	Colonial Office
Doc. Hist. Nav.	Michael J. Crawford, ed., *The Naval War of 1812. A Documentary History*. Washington: 2003.
Doc. Hist.	Ernest A. Cruikshank, ed. *Documentary HIstory of the Campaigns upon the Niagara Frontier in 1814*. Volumes 1 and 2, Welland: 1896).
Douglass, "Reminiscences"	David B. Douglass, "Reminiscences of the Campaign of 1814, on the Niagara Frontier," *The HIstorical Magazine*, August-October, 1873.
Dunlop, *Recollections*	William Dunlop, *Recollections of the American War of 1812-1814*. Toronto: 1905.
GCM	Court Martial of Brigadier-General E. P. Gaines, New York, 1816, USNA, Record Group 153, K2, Records of the Judge Advocate General
GHS	Geneva Historical Society, Geneva
Izard, *Correspondence*	George Izard, *Official Correspondence with the War Department*. Philadelphia: 1816.
LAC	Libary and Archives Canada, Ottawa
Le Couteur, *Merry Hearts*	Donald E. Graves, *Merry Hearts Make Light Days. The War of 1812 Journal of Lieutenant John Le Couteur, 104th Foot*. Montreal: 1994, 2012
MG	Manuscript Group
Micro	Microfilm
NAB	National Archives of Britain, Kew
Norton, *Journal*	J. J. Talman and C. F. Klinck, eds., *The Journal of John Norton, 1816*. Toronto: 1970.
NYSL	New York State Library, Albany
PCM	Plattsburgh Court Martial. Court-Martial of Commander Daniel Pring, *et al.*, August 1815 from NAB, Admiralty 1, vol. 5430, transcript in W. H. Wood, ed. *Select British Documents of the Canadian War of 1812*. vol. 3, part 1, 400-496,
Philpotts, Journal	Journal of Lt. Philpotts, RE, Fort Erie, August to September 1814, in War Office 55, Ordnance Office, Miscellaneous, National Archives of Britain
RG	Record Group
RMC	Royal Military College of Canada, Kingston
USNA	United States National Archives, Washington
WO	War Office

Prologue: "A complete drubbing before peace is made"

1. "North Americay," a British soldier's song from the Revolutionary War that remained popular thoughout the early 19th century, with its words often altered to fit changing circumstances as they have been here. See Roy Palmer, ed., *The Rambling Soldier: Life in the Lower Ranks, 1750-1900, through Soldier's Songs and Writing* (London, 1985), 157-158.

2. Quebec *Courier*, 20 June 1814.

3. On British trans-Atlantic troop movements, see Donald E. Graves, "'The Redcoats are Coming!': British Troop Movements to North America in 1814," *Journal of the War of 1812*, vol. 6, no. 5 (Summer 2001), 12-18.

4. Canadian newspapers were not the only North American publications to follow the war in Europe closely; American newspapers often printed more information about the European war than the American conflict.

5. Wellington to Liverpool, 3 Aug 1813, in John Gurwood, ed., *The Dispatches of Field Marshal The Duke of Wellington*, vol. 10 (London, 1837), 591.

6. On the action at El Bodon, see Charles Oman, *History of the Peninsular War*, vol. IV (Oxford, 1902), 564-570. On the 3rd Foot at Albuera, see Donald E. Graves, *Fix Bayonets! A Royal Welch Fusilier at War, 1795-1815* (Toronto, 2006), 183-252. On the nicknames of British regiments and the reasons for them, see H.L. Wickes, *Regiments of Foot: A Historical Record of all the foot regiments of the British Army* (Southampton, 1974).

7. William Grattan, *Adventures with the Connaught Rangers* (London, 1902), 87.

8. James McGrigor, *The Autobiography and Services of Sir James McGrigor* (London, 1861), 259.

9. George Wood, *The Subaltern Officer: A Narrative* (London, 1825), 234.

10. John Cooke, *Narrative of Events in the South of France, and the Attack on New Orleans in 1814 and 1815* (London, 1852), 40.

11. G.C. Moore Smith, ed., *The Autobiography of Lieutenant-General Sir Harry Smith* (London, 1901), 181. On the social activities in the Gironde and the amiability of the local women, see J. Leach, *Rough Sketches of the Life of an Old Soldier* (London, 1831), 368-369. On the quantities of wine available in the Gironde in 1814, see Jonathan Crook, ed., *The Very Thing. The Memories of Drummer Richard Bentinck, Royal Welch Fusiliers, 1807-1823* (London, 2011), 120.

12. General Order, 26 Apr 1814, quoted in Charles Oman, *Wellington's Army, 1809-1814* (London, 1913), 276n.

13. William Grattan, *Adventures of the Connaught Rangers, 1808-1814* (2 vols, London 1847), vol.

2, 203. Note this is a different book than the same author's *Adventures* with *the Connaught Rangers*.

14. Edward Costello, *The Adventures of a Soldier, Written by Himself* (London, 1852), 136.

15. John Cooke, *Narrative of Events*, 38-39.

16. Grattan, *Adventures of the Connaught Rangers*, vol. 2, 275.

17. Grattan, *Adventures of the Connaught Rangers*, vol. 2, 275.

18. Quebec *Gazette*, 30 June 1814.

19. Grattan, *Adventures with the Connaught Rangers*, vol. 1, 50.

20. Anonymous, *The Military Adventures of Johnny Newcome* (London, 1904), 14n.

21. Edward Sabine, ed., *Letters of Colonel Sir Augustus Simon Fraser* (London, 1859), 128.

22. Sabine, *Letter of Frazer*, 128.

23. Grattan, *Adventures with the Connaught Rangers*, vol. 1, 50.

24. *Military Adventures of Johnny Newcome*, 14n.

25. Grattan, *Adventures of the Connaught Rangers*, vol. 2, 276.

26. Alicia Cockburn to Charles Sandys, 28 June 1814, LAC, MG 24, I28.

27. Cochrane to Bathurst, 14 July 1814, WO 1, vol. 3, 131, in *Doc. Hist. Naval*, vol. 3, 131.

Chapter 1: "An ugly customer"

1. "Old England Forty Years Ago," a broadsheet song of the War of 1812 published by L. Denning of Boston in 1814.

2. D.E. Graves, ed., *Soldiers of 1814: American Enlisted Men's Memoirs of the Niagara Campaign* (Youngstown, 1996), Memoir of Jarvis Frary Hanks, 19-20.

3. Graves, Hanks, 38.

4. The events of the Niagara campaign of 1814 up to the battle of Lundy's Lane are described in the second volume of the "Forgotten Soldiers" trilogy, *Where Right and Glory Lead: The Battle of Lundy's Lane, 1814* (Toronto, 1997).

5. Jacob Brown, Memoranda of Occurrences and Some Important Facts Attending the Campaign on the Niagara, NYSL, Gardner Papers.

6. Brown, Memoranda

7. Brown, Memoranda

8. Gaines to Armstrong, 20 July 1814, Brown Papers, Library of Congress; Graves, *Where Right and Glory Lead*, 212-214; John Morris, *Sword of the Border. Major General Jacob Jennings Brown, 1775-1828* (Kent, Ohio, 2000), 134-137; Joseph Whitehorne, *While Washington Burned: The Battle for Fort Erie, 1814* (Baltimore, 1992), 57. Whitehorne points out that Brown had decided to call for Gaines to come to the Left Division before the battle of 25 July.

9. Douglass, "Reminiscences," 128. On the retreat, see Graves, *Where Right and Glory Lead*, 190-192.

10. Sketch of Nathan Towson, in John Livingston, ed. *Portraits of Eminent Americans, now living … *(New York, 1854), 408.
11. Sketch of Towson, in Livingston, *Portraits*, 408.
12. Sketch of Towson, in Livingston, *Portraits*, 408.
13. Brown, Memoranda.
14. Brown to Ripley, 27 July 1814, Brown *Documents*, 87.
15. Brown to Ripley, 31 July 1814, Brown *Documents*, 92.
16. Brown, Memoranda.
17. Brown, Memoranda.
18. On the strength of the Left Division, see Brown, Memoranda; strength returns, 31 July 1814, in Adams, *History*, 68-69; Diary of Hugh Dobbin, 28 July 1814, GHS; Miller to wife, 28 July 1814, War of 1812 Mss. CLUM.
19. On the history of the different forts, see David Owen, *Fort Erie (1764-1823): An Historical Guide* (Fort Erie, 1988).
20. Douglass, "Reminiscences," 181.
21. Douglass, "Reminiscences," 182.
22. Brown, Memoranda.
23. Porter to Tompkins, 9 Aug 1814, *Doc. Hist*, vol. 2, 431.
24. Graves, *Where Right and Glory Lead*, 211-215.
25. Drummond to Prevost, 10 July 1814, LAC, RG 8 I, vol. 684, 59.
26. Harvey to Riall, 23 July 1814, LAC, RG 8 I, vol., 684, 169.
27. Bathurst to Prevost, 3 June 1814, LAC, CO 43, vol. 23, 153.
28. Prevost to Drummond, 31 July 1814, LAC, RG 8 I, vol. 1222, 94.
29. Drummond to Prevost, 31 July 1814, LAC, RG 8 I, vol. 684, 29.
30. Robert Malcomson, ed., *Sailors of 1812: Memoirs and Letters of Naval Officers and Lake Ontario* (Youngstown, 1997), Memoir of James Richardson, 36-37.
31. On problems with Yeo, see John Grodzinski, *Defender of Canada: Sir George Prevost and the War of 1812* (Norman, 2013), 140-143, 148-152; and Robert Malcomson, *Lords of the Lake* (Toronto, 1998), 305-310.
32. J.J. Talman and C.F. Klinck, eds., *The Journal of John Norton, 1816* (Toronto, 1970), 359.
33. Graves, *Where Right and Glory Lead*, 211-212.
34. General Order, 1 Aug 1814, LAC, RG 8 I, vol. 231, 128.
35. General Order, 1 Aug 1814, LAC, RG 8 I, vol. 231, 128.
36. Drummond to Prevost, 4 Aug 1814, LAC, RG 8 I, vol 685, 38.
37. Harvey to Conran, 2 Aug 1814, LAC, RG 8 I, vol. 685, 31.
38. Le Couteur, *Merry Hearts*, 183
39. Le Couteur, *Merry Hearts*, 183.

40. Morgan to Brown, 5 Aug 1814, *Doc. Hist.*, vol 1, 121.
41. John C. Fredriksen, ed., *The War of 1812 in Person* (Jefferson, 2010) Memoir of Major Jonathan Kearsley, 60.
42. Shadrach Byfield, *A Narrative of a Light Company Soldier's Service in the Forty-First Regiment of Foot* (New York, 1910), 91.
43. Le Couteur, *Merry Hearts*, 183.
44. Byfield, *Narrative*, 91.
45. Norton, *Journal*, 360.
46. Le Couteur, *Merry Hearts*, 184.
47. Tucker to Conran, 4 Aug 1814, LAC, RG 8 I, vol. 685, 34.
48. District General Order, 5 Aug 1814, in *Doc Hist.* vol. 2, 427.
49. Drummond to Prevost, 4 Aug 1814, LAC, RG 8 I, vol. 685, 38.
50. Fredriksen, *War of 1812 in Person*, Memoir of Kearsley, 61-62.
51. Le Couteur, *Merry Hearts*, 184.
52. Le Couteur, *Merry Hearts*, 188

Chapter 2: "Steady my lads, not a shot till I tell you to fire"
1. "A Soldier's Life," by Charles Dibdin (1745-1814), whose patriotic songs were immensely popular in Britain during the Napoleonic Wars. This is from a broadsheet, see Palmer, *Rambling Soldier*, 157-158.
2. Thomas Jones, *History of the Sieges Carried on by the Army under the Duke of Wellington, in Spain, During the Years 1811 to 1814* (3 vols., London, 1846), vol. 1, vii.
3. Drummond to Prevost, 4 Aug 1814, LAC, RG 8I, vol 685, 38.
4. Graves, *Fix Bayonets*, 101-105; Jones, *Sieges*, vol 2:209, 378-379, 389-390, 438-439; and M.E.S. Laws, The Royal Artillery at Martinique 1809," *Journal of the Royal Artillery Institute*, 78, no. 1 (Jan 1950), 70-81.
5. William Napier, *History of the War in the Peninsula and the South of France … Volume 3* (London, 1840), 532.
6. Wellington to Liverpool, n.d. [7 Apr 1812], quoted in Oman, *Wellington's Army*
7. Dunlop, *Recollections*, 63.
8. Philpotts, Journal, 5 Aug 1814.
9. Le Couteur, *Merry Hearts*, 184-185.
10. Le Couteur, *Merry Hearts*, 185.
11. Dunlop, *Recollections*, 61.
12. On Gaines, see John C. Fredriksen, *The United States Army of the War of 1812* (Jefferson, 2009), 96-98.
13. General Order, 5 Aug 1814, War of 1812 Papers, BECHS.
14. On Gaines, see James Silver, *Edmund Pendleton Gaines: Frontier General* (Baton Rouge, 1949).
15. Testimony of Gaines at his court martial, GCM 469.

16. Gaines to Brown, 10 Aug 1814, BECHS, War of 1812 Papers.
17. Armstrong to Brown, 19 Aug 1814 and Brown to Armstrong, 25 Aug 1814, in Brown, *Documents*, 67, 70.
18. Brown to Tompkins, 1 Aug 1814, *Doc. Hist*, vol 1, 103.
19. Brown to Tompkins, 1 Aug 1814, *Doc. Hist*, vol 1, 103.
20. McIntyre to Holmes, 1 Aug 1814, in Fredriksen, *The War of 1812 in Person*, Letters of Captain Rufus McIntrye, 133.
21. Chauncey to Brown, 10 Aug 1814, *Doc. Hist. Naval*, 554.
22. Brown to Chauncey, 4 Sept 1814, *Doc. Hist. Naval*, 581.
23. Drummond to Prevost, 12 Aug 1814, LAC, RG 8 I, vol. 685, 76.
24. Drummond to Prevost, 16 Aug 1814, LAC, RG 8 I, vol. 685, 101.
25. Drummond to Prevost, 12 Aug 1814, LAC, RG 8 I, vol. 685, 76.
26. Drummond to Prevost, 12 Aug 1814, LAC, RG 8 I, vol. 685, 76.
27. Scott to brother, 12 Aug 1814, LAC, MG 24, F15.
28. Mermet to Viger, 31 July 1814, LAC, MG 24, L8, Viger Papers, volume 4.
29. Norton, *Journal*, 350.
30. Harvey to Baynes, 6 Aug 1814, AO, MU 2057, Harvey Papers.
31. Drummond to Prevost, 8 Aug 1814, LAC, RG 8 I, vol. 685, 47.
32. See Appendix G for the frequency of skirmish actions.
33. Dunlop, *Recollections*, 67.
34. Fredriksen, *War of 1812 in Person*, Memoir of Kearsley, 62.
35. Fredriksen, *War of 1812 in Person*, Memoir of Kearsley, 62.
36. Dunlop, *Recollections*, 67.
37. Norton, *Journal*, 361.
38. Le Couteur, *Merry Hearts*, 184.
39. Dunlop, *Recollections*, 78.
40. Drummond to Prevost, 12 Aug 1814, LAC, RG 8 I, vol. 685, 76.
41. Donald Melhorn, "'A Splendid Man:' Richardson, Fort Meigs and Metossa, *Northwest Ohio Quarterly*, vol. 69, no. 3 (Summer 1997), 151.
42. Dunlop, *Recollections*, 69-70.
43. Dunlop, *Recollections*, 68-69.
44. Le Couteur, *Merry Hearts*, 186-187.
45. Fredriksen, *War of 1812 in Person*, Memoir of Kearsley, 62.
46. Gaines to Armstrong, 13 Aug 1814, *Doc. Hist.*, vol. 1, 137.
47. Douglass, "Reminiscences," 230.
48. Philpotts, Journal, 11 Aug 1814.
49. Drummond to Prevost, 12 Aug 1814, LAC, RG 8 I, vol. 685, 76.
50. Return of deserters attached to Drummond to Prevost, 27 Aug 1814, LAC, RG 8 I, in *Doc. Hist.* vol. 1, 188-189.
51. Fredriksen, *War of 1812 in Person*, Memoir of George McFeely, 37.
52. Conckling to Kennedy, 16 Aug 1814, *Doc. Hist. Naval*, vol. 3, 500.
53. Conckling to Kennedy, 16 Aug 1814, *Doc. Hist. Naval*, vol. 3, 500.
54. Mermet to Viger, 8 Aug 1814, LAC, MG 24, L8, Viger Papers, volume 4.
55. Fredriksen, *War of 1812 in Person*, Memoir of George McFeely, 37.
56. Le Couteur, *Merry Hearts*, 187.
57. Douglass, "Reminiscences," 230.

Chapter 3: "That went as swift as any goose egg!"
1. "The Patriotic Diggers" by Samuel Woodworth (1785-1842), sung to an old Scots-Irish air, first appeared in print in 1812 and was very popular in the United States during the war. This version is from William McCarty, *Songs, Odes and Other Poems of National Subject* (n.p., 1842).
2. Philpotts, Journal, 14 Aug 1814.
3. Le Couteur, *Merry Hearts*, 188.
4. Dunlop, *Recollections*, 64.
5. Drummond to Prevost, 4 Aug 1814, LAC, RG 8 I, vol. 685, 38.
6. Philpotts, Journal, 11, 14 Aug 1814.
7. On British ordnance at Fort Erie, see Dunlop, *Recollections*, 64; and Drummond to Prevost, 12 Aug 1814, LAC, RG 8 I, vol. 685, 26.
8. Letter to the editor signed "Artillero Viejo" in *United Service Magazine*, 1841, Part I, 555.
9. Dunlop, *Recollections*, 64.
10. Dunlop, *Recollections*, 65-66. On the identification of McKay, see Winston Johnston, *The Glengarry Light Infantry, 1812-1816* (Charlottetown, 1998), 245.
11. Graves, Hanks, 40.
12. *A Brief Sketch of the Services of John G. Watmough, during and subsequent to the Campaigns of 1814-1815* (Philadelphia, 1838). 7
13. Weeks to Pearson, 18 Aug 1814, Weeks Papers, Dartmouth College Library, Hanover, New Hampshire.
14. Douglass, "Reminiscences," 180-181.
15. White to Johnson, n.d, Benson Lossing, *Pictorial Field-Book of the War of 1812* (New York, 1869), 843n.
16. Graves, Hanks, 42.
17. Graves, Hanks, 43.
18. Philpotts, Journal, 14 Aug 1814
19. Douglass, "Reminiscences," 197.
20. Eber Howe, "Recollections of Pioneer Printer," *Buffalo Historical Society Publications*, vol. 9 (1906), 397.
21. Sketch of Towson, in Livingston, ed. *Portraits of Eminent Americans*, 408-409.

22. Dunlop, *Recollections*, 71

23. Dunlop, *Recollections*, 80.

24. Morning District General Order, 13 Aug 1814, *Doc. Hist.*, vol. 1, 135.

25. Harris Hailes, "The Assault on Fort Erie, or Two Ways of Telling the Same Story," *United Service Journal*, 1841, Part 3, 88.

26. Gaines to Armstrong, 23 Aug 1814, *Doc. Hist.*, vol. 1, 152.

27. Douglass, "Reminiscences," 131.

28. Gaines to Armstrong, 23 Aug 1814, *Doc. Hist.*, vol. 1, 152.

29. Drummond to Prevost, 15 Aug 1814, LAC, RG 8 I, vol. 685, 94.

30. Philpotts, Journal, 14 Aug 1814.

31. Drummond to Prevost, 15 Aug 1814, LAC, RG 8 I, vol. 685, 94.

32. On the history of De Wattteville's Regiment, see Antoine de Courten, *Canada 1812-1814: Fighting the British Banner. The Swiss Regiments de Watteville and de Meuron on the Fronts of Niagara and Montreal* (Montreal, 2009).

33. The 8th Foot would have mustered about 670 all ranks at this time, while De Watteville's Regiment would have mustered about a thousand all ranks, see NAB, WO 17, Returns of the Army, 25 July 1814.

34. Harvey to Fischer, 14 Aug 1814, LAC, RG 8 I, vol. 685, 90.

35. Harvey to Fischer, 14 Aug 1814, LAC, RG 8 I, vol. 685, 90.

36. Harvey to Fischer, 14 Aug 1814, LAC, RG 8 I, vol. 685, 90.33.

37. Arrangement for the Attack on Fort Erie, 14 Aug 1814, LAC, RG 8 I, vol. 685, 83.

38. Arrangement for the Attack on Fort Erie, 14 Aug 1814, LAC, RG 8 I, vol. 685, 83.

39. Scott to brother, 12 Aug 1814, LAC, MG 24, F15.

40. Le Couteur, *Merry Hearts*, 187.

41. Le Couteur, *Merry Hearts*, 187.

42. Dunlop, *Recollections*, 63.

43. Viger to wife, 6 June 1813, LAC, MG 24, L8, Viger Papers, volume 4.

44. Norton, *Journal*, 361.

45. Dunlop, *Recollections*, 82.

46. Dunlop, *Recollections*, 82.

47. Dunlop, *Recollections*, 83.

48. Dunlop, *Recollections*, 83.

49. Young to Scott, 18 Aug 1814, LAC, MG 24, F15.

50. Dunlop, *Recollections*, 81.

51. Mermet to Viger, 15 Aug 1814, MG 24, L8, Viger Papers, volume 4.

52. Arrangement for the Attack on Fort Erie, 14 Aug 1814, LAC, RG 8 I, vol. 685, 83.

53. Douglass, "Reminiscences," 131.

54. Douglass, "Reminiscences," 131.

55. Sketch of Towson, in Livingston, *Portraits*, 412.

56. Douglass, "Reminiscences," 131.

57. Douglass, "Reminiscences," 131-132.

58. Mary R. Cate, "Benjamin Ropes' Autobiography," *Essex County Historical Collections* 91 (1955), 122.

59. Belknap to Brown, 21 Feb 1821, quoted in Carolyn T. Foreman, "General William Goldsmith Belknap, Commandant at Fort Gibson, Fort Washita and Fort Smith, *Chronicles of Oklahoma*, vol. 20, no. 2 (June 1942), 125.

60. Belknap to Brown, 21 Feb 1821, in Foreman, "General … Belknap," 125.

Chapter 4: "Bravery, coolness, ingenuity and perseverance were useless"

1. "Thus We Soldiers Live," another song by the popular British songwriter Charles Dibdin (1745-1814), from Thomas Dibdin, ed., *Songs, Naval and National of the Late Charles Dibdin* (London, 1841), 37.

2. Belknap to Brown, 21 Feb 1821, in Foreman, "General … Belknap," 125.

3. Towson to Belknap, n.d. (c. 1841), in Sketch of Towson, in Livingston, *Portraits*, 412. On the height of the Snake Hill battery, see Douglass, "Reminiscences," 132.

4. Belknap to Brown, 21 Feb 1821, in Foreman, "General … Belknap," 125.

5. Drummond to Prevost, 16 Aug 1814, LAC, RG 8 I, vol. 685, 101.

6. GCM, evidence of Douglass, 408.

7. GCM, evidence of Marston, 162; Cate, "Ropes' Autobiography," 122-123.

8. Gaines to Armstrong, 23 Aug 14, in *Doc. Hist.*, volume 1, 151.

9. GCM, 162, evidence of Marston, and 469, evidence of Gaines.

10. Cate, "Ropes' Autobiography," 121.

11. GCM, 162, evidence of Marston.

12. Douglass, "Reminiscences," 132.

13. Le Couteur, *Merry Hearts*, 183

14. Drummond to Prevost, 16 Aug 1814, LAC, RG 8 I, vol. 685, 101; Fischer to Drummond, 15 Aug 1814, LAC, RG 8 I, vol. 685, 97.

15. Fischer to Drummond, 15 Aug 1814, LAC, RG 8 I, vol. 685, 97.

16. Drummond to Prevost, 16 Aug 1814, LAC, RG 8 I, vol. 685, 101

17. Mermet to Viger, 15 Aug 1814, LAC, MG 24, L8, Viger Papers, volume 4.

18. GCM, evidence of Marston.

19. Killed, Wounded and Missing of the Right Division at Fort Erie on the Morning of 15 Aug, 1814, LAC, CO 42, vol. 128-1, 182a.

20. Norton, *Journal*, 362.

21. Norton, *Journal*, 362.

22. Norton, *Journal*, 362.

23. Douglass, "Reminiscences," 132.

24. Porter to Gaines, 15 Aug 1814, in *Doc. Hist.* vol. 2, 431.

25. Douglass, "Reminiscences," 132.

26. GCM: evidence given by: Hill, 276,381; Cessna, 241; Cass, 342; McIlwain, 258; Trimble, 53; Douglass, 403; Trimble to Gaines, n.d, 599; Trimble to Crawford, 15 Aug 1815, 615; Watmough, *Sketch*, 8-9.
27. GCM, evidence of Douglass, 403.
28. Watmough, *Sketch,* 7-9.
29. GCM, evidence of Childs, 331.
30. Douglass, "Reminiscences," 131-132.
31. GCM, evidence of Broughton, 424.
32. Douglass, "Reminiscences," 132.
33. Watmough, *Sketch*, 9-10.
34. Watmough, *Sketch*, 10.
35. Watmough, *Sketch*, 10.
36. Douglass, "Reminiscences," 132.

Chapter 5: "Give the damned Yankees no quarter!"
1. "Ye Parliament of England, a song popular in the United States during the War fo 1812, sets out the American side of the conflict.
2. *Rules and Regulations for the Formations, Field-Exercise, and Movements of His Majesty's Forces* (London, 1793), 13-14, 38-47.
3. Calculations of the projectiles in Douglass's gun extrapolated from R.W. Adye, *The Bombardier and Pocket Gunner* (London, 1813), 6-14.
4. GCM, 424, evidence of Broughton.
5. Henderson to unknown, 18 Sept 1814, Henderson Papers, Lily Library, University of Indiana.
6. Hailes, "Assault on Fort Erie," 88.
7. Le Couteur, *Merry Hearts*, 188.
8. GCM, 276, evidence of Hill.
9. GCM, 241, evidence of Cessna.
10. GCM, 241, evidence of Cessna.
11. Trimble to Gaines, n.d., GCM, 599.
12. GCM: 381, evidence of Hill; 342, evidence of Cass; 241, evidence of Cessna.
13. Douglass, "Reminiscences," 133.
14. GCM, 424, evidence of Broughton.
15. Dunlop, *Recollections*, 83.
16. Dunlop, *Recollections*, 84.
17. GCM, 223, evidence of Watmough.
18. Watmough, *Sketch*, 6-7.
19. Watmough, *Sketch*, 7; GCM, 223, 251, evidence of Watmough.
20. Douglass, "Reminiscences," 133.
21. GCM, 331, evidence of Childs.
22. Douglass, "Reminiscences," 133.
23. GCM, 258, evidence of McIlwain.
24. GCM, 258, evidence of McIlwain.
25. GCM, 258, evidence of McIlwain.
26. GCM, 276, evidence of Hill.
27. Le Couteur, *Merry Hearts*, 188; GCM, 342, evidence of Cass.
28. Hailes, "Assault on Fort Erie," 88.
29. GCM, evidence of: 336, 453, Brady; 207, Foster; and 258, McIlwain.
30. GCM, 387, evidence of Birdsall.

31. GCM: 387, evidence of Birdsall; 442, Hall; and 615, Trimble to Crawford, 15 Aug 1814.
32. Hailes, "Assault on Fort Erie," 89.
33. GCM, 196, evidence of Watmough.
34. GCM, 84, evidence of Hindman; Drummond to Prevost, 15 Aug 1814, LAC, RG 8 I, vol. 685, 94; Donald E. Graves, "William Drummond and the Battle of Fort Erie, " *Canadian Military History* 1 (1992), 1-18.
35. Gaines to Armstrong, 23 Aug 1814, *Doc. Hist.*, vol. 1, 152; GCM: evidence of 387, Birdsall; 442, Hall; 84, Hindman; and "Biographical Sketch of Major Thomas Biddle," *Illinois Monthly Magazine*, vol. 1, 557.
36. Douglass, "Reminiscences," 134.
37. "War of 1812 Reminiscences of a Veteran Survivor," *Geneva Gazette*, 29 Nov 1878.
38. Douglass, "Reminiscences," 134; Whitehorne, *While Washington Burned*, 161.
39. Le Couteur, *Merry Hearts*, 189.
40. Dunlop, *Recollections*, 85.
41. Le Couteur, *Merry Hearts*, 189.
42. Le Couteur to H. Le Couteur, 24 July 1861, *Doc. Hist.*, vol. 1, 168.
43. Fredriksen, *War of 1812 in Person*, Memoir of Kearsley, 66.
44. GCM, 255, evidence of Jones.
45. Norton, *Journal*, 362-363.
46. Dunlop, *Recollections*, 86.
47. Le Couteur, *Merry Hearts*, 190.
48. Le Couteur, *Merry Hearts*, 190.

Chapter 6: "Oh God! what a scene!"
1. "Savourneen deelish" ("Sweet Love"), a sad and wistful song with words written by George Coleman for the 1791 opera "The Surrender of Calais." It was a favourite of the many Irishmen serving in the British army during the Napoleonic period. On the evening of 6 Apr 1812, the band of the 88th Foot played it and other traditional Irish airs as the regiment waited to mount a night assault on the French-held city of Badajoz in Spain. Unfortunately, one eyewitness remembered, the effect was to dampen the spirits of the men who were reminded of better times. The 88th Foot had reason to be sad because when dawn came the following day, 144 were dead or wounded. See Grattan, *Adventures with the Connaught Rangers*, vol. 1, 196-197
2. Louis L. Babcock, *The War of 1812 on the Niagara Frontier* (Buffalo, 1927), 205.
3. Douglass, "Reminiscences," 134.
4. Fredriksen, *War of 1812 in Person*, Memoir of Kearsley, 66.
5. Graves, Hanks, 39.
6. Douglass, "Reminiscences," 134.
7. Graves, Hanks, 40.
8. Lossing, *Field-Book*, 832.
9. GCM, 416, evidence of Belton.

10. *Columbian Centinel*, 27 Aug 1814.
11. GCM, 258, evidence of McIlwain.
12. Memoir of Lieutenant Samuel Tappan, 23rd Infantry, U.S. Army Military History Institute, Carlisle.
13. Cate, "Ropes' Autobiography," 123.
14. Dunlop, *Recollections*, 53.
15. W.E. Horner, "A Military Hospital at Buffalo, New York, in the year 1814," *The Medical Examiner and Record of Medical Science*, vol. 8, (1852), 770.
16. Fredriksen, *War of 1812 in Person*, Memoir of Kearsley, 66.
17. Howe, "Recollections," 399.
18. Horner, "Military Hospital," 769.
19. Horner, "Military Hospital," 772.
20. George Guthrie's major works were *A Treatise on Gun-Shot Wounds* (London, 1827) and *Commentaries on the Surgery of War* (London, 1855). Dominique Larrey's major works were *Memoirs of Military Surgery, and the Campaigns of the French Army on the Rhine, in Corsica, Catalonia, Egypt and Spain, at Boulogne, Ulm, and Austerlitze, in Saxony, Prussia, Poland, Spain and Austria* (2 vols, Baltimore, 1814). There is also a substantial secondary literature on both men.
21. Amasa Trowbridge, "Gun-Shot Wounds," *Boston Medical and Surgical Journal*, vol. 18, no. 22 (July 1838), 341-342.
22. Horner, "Military Hospital," 23.
23. Horner, "Military Hospital," 23.
24. Horner, "Military Hospital," 4.
25. Killed, Wounded and Missing of the Right Division at Fort Erie on the Morning of 15 Aug, 1814, LAC, CO 42, vol. 128-1, 182a.
26. Young to Scott, 18 Aug 1814, LAC, MG 24, F15.
27. Le Couteur, *Merry Hearts*, 191. On the casualties of the 41st Foot, see the British casualty return dated 15 Aug 1814, LAC, CO 42, vol. 128-1, 182a.
28. Drummond to Prevost, 15 Aug 1814, LAC, RG 8 I, vol. 685, 94.
29. Drummond to Prevost, 16 Aug 1814, LAC, RG 8 I, vol. 685, 101.
30. Prevost to Drummond, 26 Aug 1814, *Doc. Hist.* vol. 1, 175.
31. Prevost to Drummond, 26 Aug 1814, *Doc. Hist.* vol. 1, 175.
32. Mermet to Viger, 28 Aug 1814, LAC, MG 24, L8, Viger Papers, volume 4.
33. Hailes, "Assault on Fort Erie," 88.
34. Le Couteur, *Merry Hearts*, 190.
35. Killed, Wounded and Missing of the Left Division ... in the Action of 15 Aug 1814, *Doc. Hist.*, vol. 1, 150.
36. Gaines to Armstrong, 15 Aug 1814, *Doc. Hist.*, vol. 1, 149.
37. Gaines to Armstrong, 23 Aug 1814, *Doc. Hist.*, vol. 1, 151.
38. Gaines to Armstrong, 23 Aug 1814, *Doc. Hist.*, vol. 1, 151.
39. Douglass, "Reminiscences," 135-136.
40. Cate, "Ropes' Autobiography," 123.
41. Brown to Tompkins, 19 Aug 1814, in Brown, *Documents*, 67.

Chapter 7: Entr'acte (1): "No peace with James Madison!"

1. "James Madison, my Joe, Jim," sung to the tune of the Scots song "John Anderson, my Joe," was a satirical assault on Madison's conduct of the war. This version appeared in the *Connecticut Herald*, 21 Mar 1815. I am grateful to Dr. David Hildebrand, Scott Sheads, Steven H. Smith and Vince Vaise for helping me track down the lyrics.
2. My summary of the origins of the War of 1812 is based on the two standard scholarly American studies of the conflict, which tend to complement each other. See Donald Hickey, *The War of 1812: A Forgotten Conflict* (Chicago, 1989, revised 2012), 29-45; and John Stagg, *Mr. Madison's War: Politics, Diplomacy, and Warfare in the Early American Republic, 1783-1830* (Princeton, 1983), 110-119.
3. Information on the naval war on the high seas from Brian Arthur, *How Britain Won the War of 1812: The Royal Navy's Blockades of the United States, 1812-1815* (Woodbridge, 2011), 131-203; and Andrew Lambert, *The Challenge: America, Britain and the War of 1812* (London, 2012), 380-402.
4. Jefferson to Short, 28 Nov 1814, quoted in Arthur, *How Britain won the War*, 201. Statistical information is from the same source, 163-203 and appendices; and Lambert, *Challenge*, 393-401. Informaton on Canadian privateering contained in an email communication to author dated 5 Nov 2012 from Faye Kert, author of *Pride and Prejudice: Privateering and Naval Prize in Atlantic Canada in the War of 1812* (St. John's, 1997).
5. London *Times*, 15 Apr 1814, quoted in Adams, *History*, vol. 9, 3.
6. Letter dated Washington, 24 June 1814, in the *Columbian Centinel*, 29 June 1814.
7. John Stagg, "The Politics of Ending the War of 1812," in R.A. Bowler, ed., *War Along the Niagara: Essays on the War of 1812 and Its Legacy* (Lewiston, 1991), 93-104.
8. Cabinet Memorandum, 26 Dec 1813, in Charles K. Webster, ed., *British Diplomacy, 1813-1815: Select Documents Dealing with the Reconstruction of Europe* (London, 1921), 126.
9. Dundee *Courier*, 6 Nov 1814.
10. Stagg, "Politics," 99-100.
11. Report of the Army, Its Strength and Distribution. Previous to the 1st of July, 1814, *American State Papers: Military Affairs*, vol. 1 (Washing-

ton, 1832), 536; Stagg, *Madison's War*, 403-407.

12. Madison to Armstrong, 18 July 1814, in Stagg, *Madison's War*, 404.

13. Report of the Army, Its Strength and Distribution. Previous to the 1st of July, 1814, *American State Papers: Military Affairs*, 536; and Stagg, *Madison's War*, 405-407.

14. George Izard, biographical entry in "The Encyclopedia of Arkansas History & Culture, *http://www:encyclopediaofarkansas.net*. On Izard's performance in 1813, see the author's book, *Field of Glory: The Battle of Crysler's Farm, 1813* (Toronto, 1999).

15. Izard to Armstrong, 7 May 1814, in Izard *Correspondence*, 2

16. Izard to Armstrong, 7 May 1814, in Izard *Correspondence*, 2

17. System of Discipline for the Army, 23 Nov 1814, *American State Papers, Military Affairs*, vol. 1, 523. On the subject of infantry tactical doctrine in the wartime U.S. Army, see the author's articles: "'Dry Books of Tactics': U.S. Infantry Manuals of the War of 1812 and after," Part I, *Military Historian*, vol. 38, no. 2 (Summer, 1986), 50-61; Part II, *Military Historian*, vol. 38, no. 4 (Winter, 1986), 173-177; and "From Steuben to Scott. The Adoption of French Infantry Tactics by the U.S. Army, 1807-1816," *Acta* of the International Commission of Military History, no. 13 (Helsinki, 1991), 223-235.

18. Fredriksen, *War of 1812 in Person*, Fairbanks Memoir, 259.

19. Fredriksen, *War of 1812 in Person*, Fairbanks Memoir, 259.

20. Order of the Division of the Right, Izard *Correspondence*, 6; Robert Quimby, *The U.S. Army in the War of 1812: An Operational and Command Study* (2 vols, Lansing, 1998), vol 2, 602-605.

21. Izard to Armstrong, 19 July 1814, Izard *Correspondence*, 55.

22. Izard to Armstrong, 19 July 1814, Izard *Correspondence*, 55.

23. Armstrong to Izard, 2 Aug 1814, Izard *Correspondence*, 65.

24. Izard to Armstrong, 11 Aug 1814, Izard *Correspondence*, 65.

25. Armstrong to Izard, 12 Aug 1814, Izard *Correspondence*, 69

26. Izard to Armstrong, 20 Aug 1814, Izard *Correspondence*, 69.

27. Fredriksen, *War of 1812 in Person*, Pearce Memoir, 91.

28. Quimby, *U.S. Army*, vol. 2, 606-607.

29. Joseph Whitehorne, *The Battle for Baltimore 1814* (Baltimore, 1997). This badly mistitled book is actually a study of the War of 1812 in the Chesapeake in 1813-1814. Balanced, factual and well researched, it remains one of the best works on this subject.

30. Cochrane to Bathurst, 14 July 1814, NAB, WO 1, vol. 3, 131, in *Doc. Hist. Naval*, vol. 3, 131.

31. Bathurst to Barnes, 20 May 1814, enclosed in Croker to Cochrane, 21 May 1814, Cochrane Papers, National Library of Scotland MS 2343, in *Doc. Hist. Naval*, vol. 3, 72. These orders, originally addressed to Barnes, were later transferred to Ross.

32. Whitehorne, *Battle of Baltimore*, 122-125.

33. George De Lacy Evans, Memorandum of operations on the shores of the Chesapeake in 1814, National Library of Scotland.

34. James Scott, *Recollections of a Naval Life* (3 vols, London, 1834), vol. 3, 280; Evans, Memorandum; strength of opposing forces, from Christopher George, *Terror in the Chesapeake: The War of 1812 on the Bay* (Shippensburg, 2001), 83.

35. Thomas Parker, A Narrative of the Battle of Bladensburg in a Letter to Henry Banning, n.d, U.S. Military History Institute, quoted in Whitehorne, *Battle of Baltimore*, 136.

36. James Madison, Memorandum, 24 Aug 1814, in Gaillard Hunt, ed., *The Writings of James Madison*, vol. 8 (New York, 1908), 295.

37. Eric M. Smith, "Leaders who Lost: Case Studies of Command under Stress," *Military Review*, 61 (Apr 1981), 45.

38. Whitehorne, *Battle of Baltimore*, 128-132.

39. Smith, *Autobiography of Harry Smith*, vol. 3, 283.

40. On Bladensburg, see Quimby, *U.S. Army*, vol. 2, 684-691; and Whitehorne, *Battle of Baltimore*, 127-135; and Glen Williams, "The Bladensburg Races," *Military History Quarterly*, vol. 12, no. 1 (1999).

41. Smith, *Autobiography*, vol. 3, 283.

42. *National Intelligencer*, 31 Aug 1814.

43. Pringle to the editor of the Edinburgh *Evening Courant*, 29 Oct 1833 in *Letters by Major Norman Pringle … vindicating the Character of the British Army employed in North America in the Years 1814-1815* (Edinburgh, n.d. [c. 1835]), 2.

44. Ross to Bathurst, 30 Aug 1814, NAB, WO 1, vol. 141, 31, in *Doc. Hist. Naval*, vol. 3, 233.

45. Cockburn to Cochrane, 27 Aug 1814, NAB, Adm 1, vol. 506, 606, in *Doc. Hist. Naval*, vol. 3, 220.

46. Martin Garrod, "Amphibious Warfare: Why?," *Journal of the Royal United Services Institute*, 113, (Winter 1988), 26.

47. Stagg, *Madison's War*, 420-423.

48. Proclamation of President Madison, 1 Sept 1813, *Niles' Weekly Register*, 10 Sept 1814.

Chapter 8: "O how high the pulse of hope beat at that moment"

1. "Noble Lads of Canada," written by Miner Lewis, who farmed north of Plattsburgh during the invasion, became quite popular in the

Lake Champlain area and later throughout the United States. Lewis's friends would always ask him to sing it "in the evening after an election" and he "would stand up in a chair" and do so. See Alan Everest, ec., *Recollections of Clinton County and the Battle of Plattsburgh, 1800-1840* (Plattsburgh, 1964), 42-43.

2. Wellington to Bathurst, 22 Feb 1814, in Gurwood, ed., *Dispatches*, vol. 10, 525.

3. Bathurst to Prevost, 3 June 1814, LAC, CO 43, vol. 23, 153.

4. Bathurst to Prevost, 3 June 1814, LAC, CO 43, vol. 23, 153.

5. Bathurst to Prevost, 3 June 1814, LAC, CO 43, vol. 23, 153.

6. On the subject of the confusing objectives presented by London to Prevost, see Grodzinski, *Defender of Canada*, 145-153.

7. The best and most recent examination of the life and career of Prevost is Grodzinski, *Defender of Canada*. The author was privileged to see this book in manuscript.

8. Prevost to Bathurst, 5 Aug 1814, LAC, CO 43, vol. 157, 136.

9. Bathurst to Prevost, 22 Aug 1814, LAC, CO 43, vol. 23, 111.

10. York to Prevost, 15 Oct 1814, LAC, RG 8 I, vol. 686, 28.

11. Prevost to Bathurst, 5 Aug 1814, LAC, CO 43, vol. 157, 136.

12. Prevost to Drummond, 16 Sept 1814, LAC, RG 8 I, vol. 1222, 194.

13. Prevost, being born in North America and having a half-brother who was an American citizen, was very aware of public opinion about the war in the northern states.

14. Viger to wife, 14 June 1813, LAC, MG 24, L8, Viger Papers, volume 4.

15. On De Rottenburg, see his entry in *DCB*, volume 6 (Toronto, 1987).

16. Information on Brisbane, Power and Robinson from the relevant volumes of the *Dictionary of National Biography*.

17. On the strength and composition of the British Left Division, see General Order, 7 Aug 1814, LAC, RG 8 I, vol. 1171, 333; General Order, 15 Aug 1814, LAC, RG 8 I, vol. 1171, 349; General Order, 22 Aug 1814, LAC, RG 8 I, vol. 1172, 22 Aug 1814; and Donald E. Graves, "The Redcoats are Coming!" 12-18.

18. Alicia Cockburn to Charles Sandys, 28 June 1814, LAC, MG 24, I28.

19. For example, see the diary of Lieutenant James Pringle, 81st Foot, who found the young ladies of Montreal "remarkably pretty," see Pringle diary, LAC, MG 24, I29. On many occasions the author has had reason to make similar observations about the pulchritude and fashion sense of the *belles jeunes filles* of Montreal, observations that, in his experi-

ence, cannot be made about the young women of any other large Canadian city which he has lived in or visited – although the *jolies jeunes filles* of Quebec City come a very close second.

20. Grattan, *Adventures of the Connaught Rangers*, vol. 2, 267-268.

21. Grattan, *Adventures of the Connaught Rangers*, vol. 2, 269.

22. General Order, 23 Aug 1814, LAC, RG 8 I, vol. 1171a, 54.

23. William Napier, *The Life and Opinions of General Sir Charles James Napier*, (4 vols., London, 1857) vol. 1, 221.

24. Alicia Cockburn to Charles Sandys, 2O Oct 1814, LAC, MG 24, I28.

25. James Campbell, *A British Army, As It Was, Is, and Ought To Be* (London, 1840), 271.

26. Journal of F.P. Robinson, RMC Robinson Papers, 261.

27. For recent accounts of the naval war on Lake Champlain in 1812-1814, see David S. Skaggs, *Thomas Macdonough: Master of Command in the Early U.S. Navy* (Annapolis, 2003), 59-106; and Robert Malcomson, *Warships of the Great Lakes, 1754-1834* (London, 2001), 119-131.

28. Yeo to Croker, 17 Sept 1814, Adm 1, vol. 2737, 179, LAC, MG 12.

29. Grodzinski, *Defender of Canada*, 168; also Robert Malcomson, *Historical Dictionary of the War of 1812* (Lanham, 2006), 618-619.

30. Downie to Upton, 1 Sept 1814, quoted in Grodzinski, *Defender of Canada*, 168.

31. Grodzinski, *Defender of Canada*, 167-168.

32. Prevost to Bathurst, 18 Oct 1814, LAC, CO 42, vol. 128-2, 316.

33. PCM, statement of Robertson, 469.

34. Anne Elinor Prevost Diary, 30 Aug 1814, LAC, MG 24, A9.

35. Izard to Armstrong, 23 Aug 1814, Izard, *Correspondence*, 74.

36. Macomb to Armstrong, 15 Sept 1814, USNA, RG 107, Micro 221, reel 62.

37. Macomb to Armstrong, 31 Aug 1814, USNA, RG 107, micro 221, reel 64.

38. On Macomb, see Fredriksen, *The United States Army in the War of 1812*, 109-112.

39. John Hanson, *The Lost Prince, Facts Tending to Prove the Identity of Louis the Seventeenth, of France and the Rev. Eleazer Williams* (New York, 1854), 258, Williams Diary, 19 Aug 1814.

40. Hanson, *Lost Prince*, 260, Williams Diary, 27 Aug 1814.

41. Hanson, *Lost Prince*, 260, Williams Diary, 26 Aug 1814.

42. Hanson, *Lost Prince*, 260, Williams Diary, 26 Aug 1814.

43. Beaumont to his brother, 1 Sept 1814, Beaumont Papers, Yale Medical Library, New Haven, quoted in Allan Everest, *The War of 1812*

in thge Champlain Valley (Syracuse, 1981), 162.

44. Hanson, *Lost Prince*, 260, Williams Diary, 27 Aug 1814.
45. On the strength and disposition of Macomb's forces see Macomb to Armstrong, 15 Sept 1814, USNA, RG 107, Micro 221, reel 62; General Order, 5 Sept 1814, *Plattsburgh Republican* 24 Sept 1814, cited in Everest, *War in the Champlain Valley*, 164-165.
46. Everest, *War in the Champlain Valley*, 163.
47. Charles W. Dolan, ed., "Extracts from the Diary of Joseph Heatley Dulles," *Pennsylvania Magazine of History and Biography*, vol.35, no. 3 (1911), 279.
48. Hanson, *Lost Prince*, 257, Williams Diary, 3 Aug 1814.
49. Hanson, *Lost Prince*, 261, Williams Diary, 29 Aug 1814.

Chapter 9: "The eyes of America are on us"
1. "The Noble Lads of Canada," written by Miner Lewis of Clinton County, New York, who watched Prevost's army march by his farm. See Everest, *Recollections*, 42n.
2. Proclamation, 2 Sept 1814, *Niles' Weekly Register*, vol. 7, 1 Oct 1814.
3. Brigade General Order, 30 Aug 1814, *Niles' Weekly Register*, 19 Sept 1814.
4. Campbell, *British Army*, 272.
5. Journal of F.P. Robinson, RMC Robinson Papers.
6. Everest, *Recollections*, 21.
7. Everest, *War in the Champlain Valley*, 171.
8. Hanson, *Lost Prince*, 267, Williams Diary, 6 Sept 1814.
9. Everest, *Recollections*, 24.
10. Macomb to Armstrong, 15 Sept 1814, USNA, RG 107, Micro 221, reel 62.
11. On Wool, see Harwood Hinton, *The Military Career of John Ellis Wool, 1812-1863* (Madison, 1960).
12. Journal of F.P. Robinson, RMC Robinson Papers.
13. Macomb to Armstrong, 15 Sept 1814, USNA, RG 107, Micro 221, reel 62.
14. Keith Herkalo, ed., *The Journal of H.K. Averill Sr.* (Plattsburgh, 2001), 6.
15. Herkalo, *Averill Journal*, 6
16. Rochester to father, 9 Sept 1814, in Gladys Nelson, ed., "The Battle of Plattsburgh," *University of Rochester Library Bulletin*, vol. 3, no. 2 (1948).
17. Macomb to Armstrong, 15 Sept 1814, USNA, RG 107, Micro 221, reel 62.
18. Keith Herkalo, *The Battles at Plattsburgh, September 11, 1814* (Charleson, 2012), 84-85.
19. Macomb to Armstrong, 15 Sept 1814, USNA, RG 107, Micro 221, reel 62.
20. Macomb to Armstrong, 15 Sept 1814, USNA, RG 107, Micro 221, reel 62.

21. Campbell, *British Army*, 267.
22. Campbell, *British Army*, 267.
23. *American State Papers: Naval Affairs*, vol. 2 (Washington, 1860), 460.
24. William Apess, *A Son of the Forest: The Experience of William Apes, A Native of the Forest* (New York, 1829), 64.
25. Journal of F.P. Robinson, RMC Robinson Papers. The emphasis is in the original.
26. Journal of F.P. Robinson, RMC Robinson Papers. The emphasis is in the original.
27. Everest, *Recollections*, 9.
28. Peter Sailly, *History of Plattsburgh, N.Y.* (Plattsburgh, 1877), 33.
29. Journal of F.P. Robinson, RMC Robinson Papers.
30. Journal of F.P. Robinson, RMC Robinson Papers.
31. Journal of F.P. Robinson, RMC Robinson Papers. This wording actually differs from the letter Prevost sent that day, which is in PCM, 466. As Robinson was normally careful with his statements, it might well be that Prevost toned down the sentiments in the final draft of his letter.
32. Prevost to Downie, 7 Sept 1814, PCM, 466.
33. Prevost to Bathurst, 22 Sept 1814, LAC, CO 42, vol. 128-2, 254.
34. PCM, Aug 1815, evidence of Brydon; 421, evidence of Cox; Everest, *War in the Champlain Valley*, 179.
35. Downie to Prevost, 7 Sept 1812, PCM, 379.
36. "Plattsburg. (1814). From the Diary of J.H. Wood," *Women's Canadian Historical Society*, Transaction No. 5 (1905), 10.
37. Journal of F.P. Robinson, RMC Robinson Papers.
38. "Diary of J.H. Wood," 11; Letter of William Robinson, 10 Sept 1814, RMC, Robinson Papers.
39. "Diary of J.H. Wood," 11.
40. Apess, *Son of the Forest*, 65.
41. Prevost to Downie, 7 Sept 1814, PCM, 466-467; and Sinclair to Baynes, 20 Mar 1815, LAC, CO 42, vol. 131, 162.
42. Macomb to Armstrong, 15 Sept 1814, USNA, RG 107, Micro 221, reel 62; "Diary of J.H. Wood," 12.
43. Sinclair to Baynes, 20 Mar 1815, LAC, CO 42, vol. 131, 162; and "Diary of J.H. Wood," 12.
44. Hanson, *Lost Prince*, 260, Williams Diary, 6 Sept 1814.
45. General Order, 5 Sept 1814, quoted in Herkalo, *Battles at Plattsburgh*, 81-82.
46. Rochester to father, 9 Sept 1814, in Nelson, "Battle of Plattsburgh".
47. Division Order, 18 Sept 1814, quoted in Everest, *War in the Champlain Valley*, 175.
48. General Order, 5 Sept 1814, quoted in Herkalo, *Battles at Plattsburgh*, 81-82.

49. Herkalo, *Battles at Plattsburgh*, 100.
50. Macomb to Chittenden, 31 Aug 1814, in *Mr. H.C. Dennison's Resolution Calling on the Governor for Copies of Any Correspondence He May Have Had with Military Officers* (Montpelier, 1814).
51. Affidavit of Herman Green, 1859, USNA, RG 94-E 125, file 15026, contained in Jack Bilow, ed., *A War of 1812 Death Register* (a.p., Plattsburgh, 2011), 144-145.
52. Everest, *War in the Champlain Valley*, 177.
53. Jonathan Stevens to Benjamin Stevens, "Vermont Letters," *Proceedings of the Vermont Historical Society* 6 (Mar 1938), 15-20.
54. Everest, *Recollections*, 30.
55. Everest, *Recollections*, 18.
56. Neil Sullivan and David Martin, *A History of the Town of Chazy, Clinton County, New York* (a.p., 1970), 102.
57. Everest, *Recollections*, 31.
58. Everest, *Recollections*, 9.
59. Prevost to Downie, 8 Sept 1814, LAC, CO 42, vol. 129, 161.
60. Coore to Yeo, 26 Feb 1815, in W.H. Wood, ed., *Select British Documents of the Canadian War of 1812* (4 vols, Toronto, 1920-1928), vol. 3, part 1, 394.
61. Downie to Prevost, 8 Sept 1814, LAC, CO 42, vol. 129, 162.
62. PCM, 470, statement of Robertson.
63. PCM, 412, evidence of Brydon.
64. PCM, 469, statement of Robertson.
65. Abstract of the Crew of His Majesty's Late Ship Confiance, PCM, 481.
66. Prevost to Downie, 9 Sept 1814, LAC, CO 42, vol. 129, 163.
67. Downie to Prevost, 9 Sept 1814, LAC, CO 42, vol 129, 165.
68. Journal of F.P. Robinson, RMC Robinson Papers.
69. PCM, 470, statement of Robertson.
70. Prevost to Downie, 10 Sept 1814, LAC, CO 42, vol. 129, 166.
71. PCM, 442. evidence of Pring.
72. PCM, 442-443, evidence of Pring.
73. In fact, it was eventually to cost Prevost his appointment as governor-general of British North America.
74. Hanson, *Lost Prince*, 265, Williams Diary, 10 Sept 1814.
75. Norman Ansley, *Vergennes, Vermont and the War of 1812: The Battle of Lake Champlain* (Severna Park, 1999), 20-22: and Skaggs, *Thomas Macdonough*, 117.
76. PCM, 470, statement of Robertson.
77. Journal of F.P. Robinson, RMC Robinson Papers.
78. Journal of F.P. Robinson, RMC Robinson Papers.
79. Letter of William Robinson, 10 Sept 1815, RMC

Robinson Papers. The addressee is not intelligible. Calculation of daily issue as laid out in the general orders based on strength of division at Plattsburgh, which was just over 9,000 men and estimated number of horses with the division, about a thousand. On rations for the army in North America, see General Order, 20 Jan 1814, RG 8 I, vol. 1172a, 43.
80. Letter of William Robinson, 10 Sept 1815, RMC Robinson Papers. The addressee cannot be positively identified.

Chapter 10: "A signal victory on Lake Champlain"

1. More verses from "The Noble Lads of Canada," by Miner Lewis of Clinton County.
2. PCM, 470, statement of Robertson.
3. At the court martial of the Royal Navy officers who fought at Plattsburgh, there was some discussion about whether Downie did indeed send a message to Prevost or whether he was depending on the noise of the scaling of the guns to alert the army to the squadron's movement.
4. Unless otherwise noted, the description of clearing the *Confiance* for action is taken from *Regulations and Instructions Relating to His Majesty's Service at Sea* (London, 1808), 191-197, 205-236, 250-2153, 265-285, 418-436; and statistics for weapons performance from Samuel Atkinson, *The Naval Pocket Gunner, or Compendium of Information Relating to Sea Service Gunnery ...* (London, 1814).
5. Naval *Regulations and Instructions* 1808, 228.
6. PCM, 421, evidence of Cox.
7. Naval *Regulations and Instructions* 1808, Appendix.
8. Naval *Regulations and Instructions* 1808, 274.
9. Instruments of a Naval Surgeon, from Roger Hart, *England Expects* (London, 1972), 94.
10. Naval *Regulations and Instructions* 1808, 274-275.
11. PCM, 421, evidence of Cox.
12. PCM, 412-413, evidence of Brydon; and Theodore Roosevelt, *The Naval War of 1812* (1882, reprinted Annapolis, 1987), 347-348.
13. PCM, 471, statement of Robertson.
14. Etienne-Paschal Taché, "Bataille Navale du Lac Champlain," 1859, quoted in Skaggs, *Thomas Macdonough*, 117.
15. PCM, 413, evidence of Brydon; 471, statement of Robertson.
16. PCM, 414, evidence of Brydon.
17. PCM, 471, statement of Robertson.
18. Prayer to be said before a fight at Sea, *Book of Common Prayer*, Episcopalian Church (Boston, 1789).
19. William R. Folsom, "The Battle of Plattsburgh," *Vermont Quarterly* 20 (Oct 1952), 253.
20. Apess, *Son of the Forest*, 64.

21. Journal of F.P. Robinson, RMC Robinson Papers; Sinclair to Baynes, 20 Mar 1815, LAC, CO 42, vol. 131, 162; and "Diary of J.H. Wood," 11.
22. Journal of F.P. Robinson, RMC Robinson Papers.
23. Journal of F.P. Robinson, RMC Robinson Papers.
24. "Diary of J.H. Wood," 11.
25. Journal of F.P. Robinson, RMC Robinson Papers.
26. PCM, 472, statement of Robertson.
27. Skaggs, *Thomas Macdonough*, 129.
28. PCM, 407, evidence of Drew.
29. PCM, 123, evidence of Bodell.
30. Roosevelt, *Naval War*, 349.
31. Skaggs, *Thomas Macdonough*, 130.
32. PCM, 442, evidence of Eyre.
33. PCM, 491, statement of Hicks.
34. Quoted in Herkalo, *Battles at Plattsburgh*, 110.
35. Macdonough to Jones, 13 Sept 1814, *Doc. Hist. Naval*, 614.
36. On the British gunboats, see PCM, 429-431, evidence of Bell; and 432-436, evidence of Robertson.
37. Firing procedure for firing a large naval gun adapted from description in Dudley Pope, *England Expects: Nelson and the Trafalgar Campaign* (London, 1959), 280; and instructions for gun crews in Atkinson, *Naval Pocket Gunner*.
38. Ship Muster Rolls, HMS *Confiance*, NAB, Adm 37, vol. 5631. The author is trying to establish the name of this brave woman.
39. Samuel Leech quoted in Henry Baynhamn, *From the Lower Deck: The Old Navy, 1780-1840* (London, 1972), 75-79.
40. Apess, *Son of the Forest*, 64-65.
41. *Plattsburgh Republican*, 1 Feb 1879, quoted in Everest, *War in the Champlain Valley*, 185.
42. Logbook, USS *Eagle*, USNA, RG 45, quoted in Kenneth Crisman, *The Eagle: An American Brig on Lake Champlain during the War of 1812* (Annapolis, 1987), 86.
43. A.S. Barker, "An Incident from the War of 1812," *Navy* (1914), 66-67.
44. PCM, 473, statement of Robertson.
45. Macdonough to Jones, 13 Sept 1814, *Doc. Hist. Naval*, 614.
46. PCM, 473, statement of Robertson.
47. PCM, 473, statement of Robertson.
48. PCM, 474, statement of Robertson
49. Pring to Yeo, 12 Sept 1814, LAC, CO 42, vol. 129, 174.
50. PCM, 464, statement of Pring.
51. Macdonough to Jones, 13 Sept 1814, *Doc. Hist. Naval*, 614.
52. Condition of Prize Frigate Confiance, Sloop War Linnet, Sloops Chubb and Finch in Lake Champlain, 21 Nov 1814 in Bilow, *War of 1812 Death Register*, 87-88.
53. Everest, *War in the Champlain Valley*, 185; Return of the Killed and Wounded of His Majesty's Late Squadron, 11 Sept 1814, LAC CO 42, vol. 129, 190.
54. Macdonough to Jones, 11 Sept 1814, *Doc. Hist. Naval*, 607.
55. Prevost to Bathurst, 11 Sept 1814, LAC, CO 42, vol. 128-1, 220.
56. Journal of F.P. Robinson, RMC Robinson Papers.
57. Journal of F.P. Robinson, RMC Robinson Papers.
58. Journal of F.P. Robinson, RMC Robinson Papers.
59. Lynch to Robinson, 30 Sept 1814, RMC, Robinson Papers.
60. Journal of F.P. Robinson, RMC Robinson Papers.
61. Statement of Herman Green, in Bilow, *War of 1812 Death Register*, 144.
62. Lynch to Robinson, 30 Sept 1814, RMC, Robinson Papers.
63. Baynes to Robinson, 11 Sept 1814, RMC, Robinson Papers.
64. Journal of F.P. Robinson, RMC Robinson Papers.
65. Journal of F.P. Robinson, RMC Robinson Papers.
66. Sinclair to Baynes, 20 Mar 1815, LAC, CO 42, vol. 131, 162.
67. "Diary of J.H. Wood," 13.
68. Campbell, *British Army*, 271-272.
69. Hanson, *Lost Prince*, 266, Williams Diary, 27 Aug 1814.
70. Rochester to father, 12 Sept 1814, in Nelson, "The Battle of Plattsburgh."
71. Rochester to father, 12 Sept 1814, in Nelson, "The Battle of Plattsburgh."
72. Jonathan Stevens to Benjamin Stevens, 5 Dec 1814, "Vermont Letters."
73. Prevost to Bathurst, 22 Sept 1814, LAC, CO 432, vol. 128-2, 254.
74. Campbell, *British Army*, 273.
75. J.H. Wood, "Reflections on Plattsburg," *Women's Canadian Historical Society*, Transaction No. 5 (1905), 15.
76. Macomb to Armstrong, 15 Sept 1814, USNA, RG 107, Micro 221, reel 62; also "Diary of J.H. Wood," 12-13; Sinclair to Baynes, 20 Mar 1815, LAC, CO 42, vol. 131, 162; Everest, *Recollections*, 9, 31.
77. Macomb to Armstrong, 15 Sept 1814, USNA, RG 107, Micro 221, reel 62.
78. Everest, *Recollections*, 19-20.
79. *Plattsburgh Republican*, 1 Feb 1879, quoted in Everest, *War in the Champlain Valley*, 185.
80. Everest, *Recollections*, 49.
81. Memoir of Benajah Phelps, in Bilow, *War of 1812 Death Register*, 91.
82. Bilow, *War of 1812 Death Register*, 56.

83. *Plattsburgh Republican*, 19 Mar 1892, quoted in Bilow, *War of 1812 Death Register*, 89.

84. *Plattsburgh Republican*, 19 Mar 1892, quoted in Bilow, *War of 1812 Death Register*, 89.

85. Herkalo, Battles of Plattsburgh, 141.

86. Campbell, *British Army*, 274.

87. Diary of Lt. John Lang, 12 Sept 1814, Special Collections Library, Duke University.

88. Grattan, *Adventures of the Connaught Rangers*, vol. 2, 277.

89. Everest, *Recollections*, 26.

90. Campbell, *British Army*, 275.

91. Hanson, *Lost Prince*, 267, Williams Diary, 12 Sept 1814.

92. Return of the Killed, Wounded and Missing of the Left Division … 6 to 14 Sept 1814, LAC, CO 42, vol. 128-1, 235a; Quimby, *U.S. Army*, vol. 2, 626.

93. Campbell, *British Army*, 275.

94. General Order, 13 Sept 1814, McCord Museum, Montreal, War of 1812 Collection, Garrison Orders, vol. 4.

95. Campbell, *British Army*, 275.

96. Campbell, *British Army*, 276.

Chapter 11: Entr'Acte (2): Baltimore, Washington, London, Ghent and the Northern Theatre

1. "Old John Bull," a broadsheet from the War of 1812 published by the Boston firm of Leonard Diming in 1814.

2. Anne Elinor Prevost Diary, Sept 1814, LAC, MG 24, A9.

3. Grodzinski, *Defender of Canada*, 207-219

4. Particulars of the Late Disastrous Affair on Lake Champlain, Montreal *Herald*, 17 Sept 1814. The author of this article was later identified as Stephen Sewell, a Montreal businessman who held a grudge against Prevost.

5. Extract from an unidentified Halifax newspaper, contained in Alicia Cockburn to her cousin Charles, 20 Oct 1814, LAC, MG 24, I 28.

6. *Annual Register* 1814, 332, quoted in Adams, *History*, II, 112.

7. Alicia Cockburn to her cousin Charles Sandys, 20 Oct 1814, LAC, MG 24, I 28.

8. Wellington to Bathurst, 30 Oct 1814, in F.L. Bickley, ed., *Report on the Manuscripts of Earl Bathurst* (London, 1923), 302.

9. Wellington to Murray, 22 Dec 1814, in Gurwood, ed., *Dispatches of Wellington*, vol. 12 (London, 1838), 224.

10. Philip Stanhope, *Notes of Conversations with the Duke of Wellington* (London, 1866), 252.

11. Yeo to Croker, 24 Sept 1814, LAC, CO 42, vol. 129, 173.

12. Yeo to Croker, 29 Sept 1814, LAC, CO 42, vol. 129, 157.

13. The best analysis of Yeo's attempts to shift the blame for the failure at Plattsburgh to Prevost's shoulders will be found in Grodzinski, *Defender of Canada*, 208-214.

14. *Buffalo Gazette*, 20 Sept 1814.

15. Bathurst to Barnes, 20 May 1814, enclosed in Croker to Cochrane, 21 May 1814, Cochrane Papers, National Library of Scotland MS 2343, *Doc. Hist. Naval*, vol. 3, 72.

16. Cochrane to Croker, 17 Sep 1814, Adm 1, vol. 507, 171, in *Doc. Hist. Naval*, vol. 3, 286.

17. Whitehorne, *Battle for Baltimore*, 173, 184.

18. Whitehorne, *Battle for Baltimore*, 183. My account of North point is based on this source, 175-183.

19. Quoted in Whitehorne, *Battle for Baltimore*, 188.

20. Whitehorne, *Battle for Baltimore*, 188-189.

21. Ralph Eschelman, *In Full Glory Reflected: Discovering the War of 1812 in the Chesapeake* (Annapolis, 2012), 162-164.

22. Capitulation of Washington County, 13 Sept 1814, LAC, RG 8 I, vol. 685, 276.

23. George Stanley, *The War of 1812: Land Operations* (Ottawa, 1983), 396.

24. On the economic problems of the United States, see Adams, *History*, Book VIII, 238-262.

25. General Monthly Return …, 25 Sept 1814, NAB, WO 17, vol.1517.

26. On problems of recruitment in 1814 and unrest in New England, see Adams, History, Book VIII, 216, 235 and 263-281; and John Stagg, *The War of 1812: Conflict for a Continent* (Cambridge, 2012), 130-138, 147-150.

27. U.S. Commissioners to Monroe, 12 Aug 1814, in *American State Papers: Foreign Relations*, vol. 3, 705.

28. U.S. Commissioners to Monroe, 19 Aug 1814, in *American State Papers: Foreign Relations*, vol. 3, 709.

29. U.S. Commissioners to Monroe, 19 Aug 1814, in *American State Papers: Foreign Relations*, vol. 3, 709.

30. Note of British Commissioners, 19 Aug 1814, in *American State Papers: Foreign Relations*, vol. 3, 709.

31. Izard to Monroe, 7 Sept 1814, in Izard *Correspondence*, 76.

32. Fredriksen, *War of 1812 in Person*, Memoir of Charles Fairbanks, 262.

33. Izard to Brown, 13 Sept 1814, Izard, *Correspondence*, 84-85.

34. Brown to Armstrong, 31 Aug 1814, in John Armstrong, *Notices of the War of 1812* (2 vols., New York, 1840), vol. 2, 100. The emphasis is in the original.

35. Brown to Armstrong, 31 Aug 1814, in Armstrong, *Notices of the War of 1812*, 100.

36. Brown to Armstrong, 28 Nov 1814, in John Armstrong, *Notice of Mr. Adams' Eulogiium on the Life and Character of James Monroe* (Washington, 1832), 27

37. Brown to Izard, 10 Sept 1814, in Izard, *Correspondence*, 86.
38. Brown to Izard, 11 Sept 1814, in Izard, *Correspondence*, 87.
39. Brown to Izard, 11 Sept 1814, in Izard, *Correspondence*, 87.
40. Izard to Monroe, 17 Sept 1814, in Izard, *Correspondence*, 89.
41. Fredriksen, *War of 1812 in Person*, Memoir of Fairbanks, 262.
42. Izard to Monroe, 20 Sept 1814, in Izard, *Correspondence*, 91.
43. Fredriksen, *War of 1812 in Person*, Memoir of Fairbanks, 262.
44. Izard to Monroe, 28 Sept 1814, in Izard, *Correspondence*, 92.

Chapter 12: "I have twenty toads beneath my feet, a hundred grasshoppers on my clothes"
1. An unattributed poem or drinking song which, judging by the words, appears to date from the last decades of the 18th century but in any case expresses a laudable sentiment. LAC, MG 23, GIII, vol. 3, part 3.
2. Drummond to Prevost, 21 Aug 1814, LAC, RG 8 I, vol. 685, 123.
3. Robinson to Prevost, 27 Aug 1814, enclosed in Prevost to Bathurst, 27 Aug 1814, LAC, RG 8 I, vol. 1219, 276.
4. Cochran to James Stewart, 4 Nov 1814, LAC, MG 24, B16.
5. Cochran to James Stewart, 4 Nov 1814, LAC, MG 24, B16.
6. Yeo to Prevost, 13 Apr 1814, LAC, RG 8 I, vol. 683, 19.
7. Robinson to Prevost, 27 Aug 1814, Doc. Hist., vol. 1, 180.
8. Weight of armament for the *St. Lawrence* based on data for a vessel of 100 guns contained a list of Guns and Carronades on Each Deck of Every Rate contained in Robert Simmons, *The Sea-Gunners Vade-Mecum, Being a New Introduction to Practical Gunnery* (London, 1812, 165-168.
9. Malcomson, *Lords of the Lake*, 303, 305.
10. Yeo to White, 2 July 1814, LAC, MG 24, F58.
11. Yeo to Croker, 14 Oct 1814, LAC, MG 12, Adm 1, vol. 2737.
12. I base this statement on the shipbuilding capability and expertise of the RN Dockyard at Kingston, as described in Malcomson, *Warships of the Great Lakes*, 100-118. These frigates would have had to have been laid down by April 1814.
13. Prevost to Drummond, 18 Aug 1814, LAC, RG 8 I, vol. 118, 141.
14. Yeo to Croker, 14 Oct 1814, Adm 1, vol. 2737, 221, in *Doc. Hist. Naval*, vol. 3, 625.
15. Malcomson, *Lords of the Lake*, 208.

16. Drummond to Prevost, 24 Aug 1814, LAC, RG 8 I, vol. 685, 134.
17. Militia General Order, 25 Aug 1814, *Doc. Hist.*, vol 1, 187.
18. Drummond to Prevost, 21 Aug 1814, LAC, RG 8 I, vol. 685, 123.
19. C.P. Stacey, "Upper Canada at War, 1814: Captain Armstrong Reports," *Ontario History*, vol. 48 (1956), 40.
20. Le Couteur, *Merry Hearts*, 192-193.
21. Dunlop, *Recollections*, 66.
22. Sketch of Towson, in Livingston, *Portraits*, 409.
23. Sketch of Towson, in Livingston, *Portraits*, 409.
24. Le Couteur, *Merry Hearts*, 193.
25. Le Couteur, *Merry Hearts*, 193.
26. Philpotts, Journal, 30 Aug 1814.
27. Dunlop, *Recollections*, 67.
28. Drummond to Prevost, 30 Aug 1814, *Doc. Hist.*, vol. 1, 189.
29. Douglass, "Reminiscences," 138.
30. Graves, Hanks, 42.
31. Douglas, "Narrative," 137.
32. Douglas, "Narrative," 136.
33. Aspinwall to father, 1 Oct 1814, in Hugh D. Hamilton, *History of Norfolk County, Massachusetts* (Philadelpia, 1884), 864.
34. Drummond to Prevost, 30 Aug 1814, *Doc. Hist.*, vol. 1, 189.
35. Drummond to Prevost, 30 Aug 1814, *Doc. Hist.*, vol. 1, 189.
36. Drummond to Prevost, 2 Sept 1814, *Doc. Hist.*, vol. 1, 190.
37. Letter of Douglass dated 9 Sept 1814, in Douglass, "Reminiscences," 138n.
38. Douglass, "Reminiscences," 138n.
39. Douglass, "Reminiscences," 139.
40. Le Couteur, *Merry Hearts*, 191-192.
41. Le Couteur, *Merry Hearts*, 192.
42. Mermet to Viger, 28 Aug 1814, LAC, MG 24, L8, Viger Papers, volume 4.
43. Dunlop, *Recollections*, 74.
44. Memoir of Tappan, U.S. Army Military History Institute, Carlisle.
45. Fredriksen, *War of 1812 in Person*, Memoir of Kearsley, 67.
46. Norton, *Journal*, 363-364.
47. Drummond to Prevost, 21 Aug 1814, LAC, RG 8 I, vol. 685, 123.
48. Fredriksen, *War of 1812 in Person*, Memoir of Kearsley, 66-67.
49. Le Couteur, *Merry Hearts*, 193.
50. Dunlop, *Recollections*, 76.
51. Le Couteur, *Merry Hearts*, 193.
52. Mermet to Viger, 28 Aug 1814, LAC, MG 24, L8, Viger Papers, volume 4.
53. This was possibly Captain Thomas FitzGerald of the Glengarry Light Infantry, see Johnston, *Glengarry Light Infantry*, 222.

54. Dunlop, *Recollections*, 59.
55. Dunlop, *Recollections*, 40.
56. Dunlop, *Recollections*, 73.
57. Dunlop, *Recollections*, 73.dun pear
58. Le Couteur, *Merry Hearts*, 194.
59. Le Couteur, *Merry Hearts*, 192.
60. Graves, Hanks, 41.
61. Douglass, "Reminiscences," 136n.
62. Douglass, "Reminiscences," 136n.
63. General Order, 27 Aug 1814, Dobbins Papers, Genessee HIstorical Society.
64. Douglass, "Reminiscences," 137n.
65. Sketch of Towson, in Livingston, *Portraits*, 410.

Chapter 13: "As sure as there is a God in heaven, the enemy shall be attacked"

1. "How Happy the Soldier," from the 1783 opera "The Poor Soldier" by Richard Shield and John O'Keefe, was popular in both armies during the War of 1812.
2. Babcock, *War of 1812*, 213.
3. Porter to the Militia of Western New York, 21 Aug 1814, *Buffalo Gazette*, 30 Aug 1814.
4. General Order, State of New York, *Buffalo Gazette*, 30 Aug 1814.
5. On Jacob Brown, man and general, the most recent and best study is Morris, *Sword of the Border*.
6. Brown, Memoranda.
7. Babcock, *War of 1812*, 213.
8. Fleming to Porter, 4 Sept 1814, *Doc. Hist.*, vol. 2, 443.
9. Thomas Jesup, Memoir of the Campaign on the Niagara, Jesup Papers, Library of Congress.
10. Jesup, Memoir of the Campaign on the Niagara.
11. Brown, Memoranda.
12. Brown to Tompkins, 20 Sept 1814, *Doc. Hist.*, vol. 1, 207. Memoir of the Campaign on the Niagara.
13. Jesup, Memoir of the Campaign on the Niagara.
14. Yates to Tompkins, 3 Sept 1814, *Doc. Hist.* vol. 1, 192.
15. Howe, "Recollections," 400.
16. Cate, "Ropes' Autobiography," 124.
17. The residue of the militia augmented Colonel Hugh Brady's Twenty-Second Infantry, which had been shifted to the American bank of the Niagara.
18. Cate, "Ropes' Autobiography," 124.
19. Douglass, "Reminiscences," 139, 159.
20. Drummond to Prevost, 2 Sept 1814, *Doc. Hist.*, vol. 1, 190.
21. Philpotts, Journal, 7 Sept 1814.
22. Drummond to Prevost, 8 Sept 1814, *Doc. Hist.* vol. 1, 195.
23. Philpotts, Journal, 16 Sept 1814.
24. Matteson to Ripley, 5 Sept 1814, *Doc. Hist.* vol. 2, 445.
25. General Order, 6 Sept 1814, *Doc. Hist.* vol. 1, 194.
26. Harvey to Strachan, 8 Sept 18145, Strachan Papers, AO; also General Order, 6 Sept 1814, *Doc. Hist.* vol. 1, 194; Matteson to Ripley, 5 Sept 18143, Doc. Hist., vol. 2, 445; Le Couteur, *Merry Hearts*, 194; Philpotts, Journal, 4 Sept 1814.
27. De Watteville Journal, 4 Sept 1814, LAC, MG 24, F96, De Watteville Papers.
28. Drummond to Prevost, 8 Sept 1814, *Doc. Hist.* vol. 1, 195.
29. Philpotts, Journal, 10 Sept 1814.
30. Norton, *Journal*, 365.
31. Philpotts, Journal, 7 Sept 1814.
32. Drummond to Prevost, 11 Sept 1814, *Doc. Hist.* vol. 1, 198.
33. Confidential Memorandum, 10 Sept 1814 & Memorandum, 16 Sept 1814, in LAC, MG 24, F96, De Watteville Papers.
34. Drummond to Prevost, 11 Sept 1814, *Doc. Hist.* vol. 1, 200.
35. Drummond to Prevost, 11 Sept 1814, *Doc. Hist.* vol. 1, 200.
36. Drummond to Prevost, 11 Sept 1814, *Doc. Hist.* vol. 2, 225.
37. Philpotts, Journal, 16 Sept 1814.
38. Brown to Monroe, 29 Sept 1814, *Doc. Hist.* vol. 1, 211.
39. Douglass, "Reminiscences," 140.
40. Brown, Memoranda.
41. *Articles of War, Military Laws, and Rules and Regulations for the Army of the United States* (Albany, 1816), articles 10, 12 and 24. This publication contains the 1806 Articles of War.
42. Brown, Memoranda.
43. Douglass, "Reminiscences," 140.
44. Organization of American forces for the sortie from Porter to Brown, 23 Sept 1814, *Doc. Hist.* vol. 1, 208; and Brown to Monroe, 29 Sept 1814, *Doc. Hist.* vol. 1, 211.
45. Brown to Monroe, 29 Sept 1814, *Doc. Hist.* vol. 1, 211.
46. Dunlop, *Recollections*, 79.
47. Dunlop's statements about the unreliability of De Watteville's Regiment should be contrasted with the comments of Lieutenant Joseph-David Mermet of that unit.
48. Howe, "Recollections," 400.
49. Dunlop, *Recollections*, 74.
50. Graves, ed., *Soldiers of 1814*, Memoir of Amasiah Ford, 57.
51. Porter to Brown, 23 Sept 1814, *Doc. Hist.* vol. 1, 208; and Philpotts, Journal, 17 Sept 1814.
52. Graves, Hanks, 45.
53. Aspinwall to father, 1 Oct 1814, in Hamilton, *History of Norfolk County*, 864.
54. Names and Ranks of Officers Killed, Wounded and Missing at Fort Erie, 17 Sept 1814, *Doc. Hist.*, vol. 1, 214.

55. Graves, Hanks, 45.
56. Commins to Davidson, 28 Aug 1815, in Norman Lord, "The War of 1812 on the Niagara Frontier. Letters Written by Sergt. James Commins, 8th Foot," *Journal of the Society for Army Historical Research*, 18 (1939), 210.
57. Philpotts, Journal, 17 Sept 1814.
58. Porter to Brown, 23 Sept 1814, *Doc. Hist.* vol. 1, 208.
59. Dunlop, *Recolletions*, 75. Remarkable as this statement may seen to the modern reader, it is confirmed Le Couteur of the 104 th Foot (Le Couteur, *Merry Hearts*, 202). The behaviour of the 82nd Foot can be explained in part by the fact that in the heat of battle, soldiers are much less willing to forgive the shooting of one of their officers after they believed that the enemy had surrendered. Moreover, the 82nd had recently served in the Peninsula where the fighting was more savage than in North America.
60. Le Couteur, *Merry Hearts*, 198.
61. Dunlop, *Recollections*, 77.
62. Graves, Ford, 57.
63. *Niles' Weekly Register*, Vol. 7, 124, in *Doc. Hist*, vol. 2, 221.
64. Brown, Memoranda.
65. Brown to Monroe, 29 Sept 1814, *Doc. Hist.* vol. 1, 211.
66. *Niles' Weekly Register*, Vol. 7, 136, in *Doc. Hist*, vol. 2, 222.
67. Brown to Monroe, 29 Sept 1814, *Doc. Hist.* vol. 1, 211.
68. Dunlop, *Recollections*, 77.
69. De Watteville to Drummond, 19 Sept 1814, *Doc. Hist.* vol. 1, 203.
70. Dunlop, *Recollections*, 72.
71. Dunlop, *Recollections*, 72-73.
72. Brown to Monroe, 29 Sept 1814, *Doc. Hist.* vol. 1, 211.
73. Norton, *Journal*, 365.
74. Report of the Killed, Wounded and Missing in the above Action, attached to Brown to Monroe, 29 Sept 1814, *Doc. Hist.* vol. 1, 214; and Return of Casualties of the Right Division, 17 Sept 1814, *Doc. Hist.* vol. 2, 219.
75. Jesup, Memoir of the Campaign on the Niagara.
76. Drummond to Prevost, 21 Sept 1814, LAC, RG 8 I, vol. 1, 685, 259 and Memorandum on Dispositions of Troops, 261.
77. Drummond to Prevost, 24 Sept 1814, LAC, RG 8 I, vol. 1, 685, 266.

Chapter 14: "The prettiest little affair any of us had ever seen"
1. "The Soldier's Prayer," a poem which was possibly the work of Sergeant Archibald (Bauldy) Corson, a recruiter with the 10th Regiment, North British Militia, an Edinburgh unit in the 1790s. Bauldy Corson sang the words but the tune has been lost. Corson was described as a man "who could give a damn with singular bravado" and who "was a blackguard of great grace" who "drank whisky after a most enticing manner." On Corson, see John McTaggart, ed., *The Scottish Gallovidian Encyclopedia* (London, 1878), 50-56. The word "claise" in the first verse is Scots dialect for "clothes."
2. Drummond to Prevost, 21 Sept 1814, LAC, RG 8 I, vol. 1, 685, 259; Memorandum on Dispositions of Troops, 261; and to Prevost, 24 Sept 1814, LAC, RG 8 I, vol. 1, 685, 266.
3. Drummond to Prevost, 28 Sept 1814, *Doc. Hist.*, vol. 2, 235.
4. Le Couteur, *Merry Hearts*, 199-200.
5. On the details of the *St. Lawrence*, see Malcomson, *Warships of the Great Lakes*, 112-117; Malcomson, *Lords of the Lake*, 301-304 and, in particular, "HMS St. Lawrence: Commodore Yeo's Unique First-Rate," *Fresh Water: A Journal of Great Lakes Marine History*, vol. 6 (1991), 27-35.
6. Malcomson, *Lords of the Lake*, 309.
7. Drummond to Prevost, 6 Oct 1814, LAC, RG 8 I, vol. 686, 5.
8. Prevost to Drummond, 11 Oct 1814. Prevost wrote two letters of this date to Drummond and they will be found in *Doc. Hist*, vol. 2, 243-244.
9. Drummond to Prevost, 11 Oct 1814, LAC, RG 8 I, vol. 686, 19.
10. Drummond to Prevost, 15 Oct 1814, LAC, RG 8 I, vol. 686, 31.
11. Louis Einstein, ed., "Recollections of the War of 1812 by George Hay, Eighth Marquis of Tweeddale," American Historical Review, vol. 32 (1926), 75. On British disposiitions, see Drummond to Prevost, 10 Oct 1814, Doc. Hist. vol. 2, 241, and District General Order, 11 Oct 1813, Doc. Hist., vol. 2, 246.
12. Le Couteur, *Merry Hearts*, 203.
13. Le Couteur, *Merry Hearts*, 202-204.
14. Le Couteur, *Merry Hearts*, 200-201.
15. Le Couteur, *Merry Hearts*, 201.
16. Le Couteur, *Merry Hearts*, 202.
17. Drummond to Prevost, 15 Oct 1814, LAC, RG 8 I, vol. 686, 34.
18. Drummond to Prevost, 18 Oct 1814, LAC, RG 8 I, vol. 686, 34.
19. Brown to Armstrong, 2 Nov 1814, quoted in Morris, *Sword of the Border*, 150.
20. Izard to Monroe, 28 Sept 1814, Izard, *Correspondence*, 92.
21. Fredriksen, *War of 1812 in Person*, Memoir of Pearce, 92-93.
22. Norton to father, 6 Oct 1814, in David R. Porter, ed, "Jacob Porter Norton: A Yankee on the Niagara Frontier," *Niagara Frontier* (Summer 1965), 52.

23. Izard to Monroe, 28 Sept 1814, 92.
24. Norton to father, 6 Oct 1814, in Norton, "Jacob Porter Norton," 52.
25. Norton to father, 6 Oct 1814, in Norton, "Jacob Porter Norton," 52.
26. Brown to Armstrong, 28 Nov 1814, in *Notice of Adams' Eulogiium*, 27. Emphasis in the original.
27. Brown to Armstrong, 28 Nov 1814, in *Notice of Adams' Eulogiium*, 27.
28. Monroe to Izard, 27 Sept 1814, Izard, *Correspondence*, 95.
29. Izard to Monroe, 16 Oct 1814, Izard, *Correspondence*, 100.
30. The distance calculations are mine.
31. Norton to father, 6 Oct 1814, in Norton, "Jacob Porter Norton," 52.
32. Norton's Journal, 14 Oct 1814, in Norton, "Jacob Porter Norton," 53; Izard to Monroe, 16 Oct 1814, Izard, *Correspondence*, 100.
33. Drummond to Prevost, 11 Oct 1814, LAC, RG8 I, vol. 686, 19.
34. Izard to Monroe, 16 Oct 1814, Izard, *Correspondence*, 100.
35. General Order, 16 Oct 1814, Dobbins Papers, Genessee Historical Society.
36. Izard to Monroe, 16 Oct 1814, *Correspondence*, 100.
37. Brown to Armstrong, 28 Nov 1814, in *Notice of Adams' Eulogiium*, 27.
38. Brown to Armstrong, 2 Nov 1814, Brown Papers, Massachusetts Historical Society, quoted in Morris, *Sword of the Border*, 151.
39. Brown to Armstrong, 2 Nov 1814, Brown Papers, Massachusetts Historical Society, quoted in Morris, *Sword of the Border*, 151.
40. Brown to Armstrong, 28 Nov 1814, in *Notice of Adams' Eulogiium*, 27.
41. Izard to Monroe, 16 Oct 1814, Izard, *Correspondence*, 1814.
42. Izard to Monroe, 16 Oct 1814, Izard, *Correspondence*, 1814.
43. Drummond to Prevost, 18 Oct 1814, LAC, RG 8 I, vol. 686, 34.
44. Drummond to Prevost, 18 Oct 1814, LAC, RG 8 I, vol. 686, 34; Harvey to Myers, 18 Oct 1814, LAC, RG 8 I, *Doc. Hist.*, vol 2, 258.
45. Izard to Monroe, 23 Oct 1814, Izard, *Correspondence*, 104. Unless otherwise noted, my account of the battle of Cook's Mills is based on Myers to Drummond, 19 Oct 1814, *Doc. Hist.*, vol. 2, 260; and Bissell to Izard, 22 Oct 1814, *Doc. Hist.*, vol. 2, 270.
46. Bissell to Izard, 22 Oct 1814, *Doc. Hist.*, vol. 2, 270. Le Couteur, *Merry Hearts*, 204.
47. Le Couteur, *Merry Hearts*, 204.
48. Myers to Drummond, 19 Oct 1814, *Doc. Hist.*, vol. 2, 260
49. Bissell to Izard, 22 Oct 1814, *Doc. Hist.*, vol. 2, 270

50. Myers to Drummond, 19 Oct 1814, *Doc. Hist.*, vol. 2, 260.
51. Bissell to Izard, 22 Oct 1814, *Doc. Hist.*, vol. 2, 270
52. Einstein, ed., "Recollections of the War of 1812 by George Hay, 76.
53. Le Couteur, *Merry Hearts*, 205-206.
54. Journal of the Reverend George Ferguson, Victoria University Archives, Toronto.
55. Drummond to Prevost, 20 Oct, 1814, LAC, RG 8 I, vol. 686, 77; Bissell to Izard, 22 Oct 1814, *Doc. Hist.*, vol. 2, 270
56. Myers to Drummond, 19 Oct 1814, *Doc. Hist.*, vol. 2, 260; and Return of the Killed and Wounded of the Second Brigade, 19 Oct 1914, *Doc. Hist.*, vol. 2, 272.
57. Cate, "Ropes' Autobiography," 125.
58. Graves, Ford, 58-59.
59. Le Couteur, *Merry Hearts*, 206-207.
60. Prevost to Bathurst, 18 Oct 1814, LAC, CO 42, vol. 128-2, 316.
61. Memoir of David Wingfield, LAC, MG 24, F1.
62. Yeo to Drummond, 19 Oct 1814, *Doc. Hist.*, vol. 2, 263.
63. Le Couteur, *Merry Hearts*, 207.
64. Izard to Monroe, 2 Nov 1814, *Correspondence*, 104.
65. Brown to Armstrong, 28 Nov 1814, in *Notice of Adams' Eulogiium*, 27.
66. Brown to Armstrong, 28 Nov 1814, in *Notice of Adams' Eulogiium*, 27.
67. Izard to Monroe, 2 Nov 1814, Izard, *Correspondence*, 104.
68. Monroe to Izard, 24 Oct 1814, Izard, *Correspondence*, 107.
69. Totten to Izard, 1 Nov 1814, *Doc. Hist.*, vol. 2, 282.
70. Norton to father, 12 Nov 1814, in Norton, "Jacob Porter Norton," 54.
71. Drummond to Prevost, 30 Oct 1814, LAC, RG 8 I, vol. 686, 114.
72. Drummond to Prevost, 5 Nov 1814, LAC, RG 8 I, vol. 686, 134.
73. Drummond to Prevost, 5 Nov 1814, LAC, RG 8 I, vol. 686, 134.

Chapter 15: The War in the West and McArthur's Raid

1. "Garry Owen," placed here because this chapter concerns a major mounted operation, has so long been associated with the U.S. cavalry and, latterly, the air cavalry, that many Americans believe it dates from the Civil War. The song actually originated in the Irish city of Limerick in the 1780s and was sung by a gang of wealthy hooligans who liked to drink in the fashionable Limerick suburb of Garryowen (*Garrai Eoin* or "the garden of John") and smash property other than their own. The rollicking tune spread to the British army dur-

ing the French wars of 1793-1815 and became the second most popular quick march in that army after "The British Grenadiers." On the origins and history of "Garry Owen" see Lewis Winstock, *Songs & Music of the Redcoats, A History of the War Music of the British Army, 1642-1902* (London, 1970), 103-105. "Spa" was a period term for mineral water.

2. Hull's proclamation, 12 July 1812, in E.A. Cruikshank, ed., *Documents Relating to the Invasion of Canada and the Surrender of Detroit, 1812* (Ottawa, 1912), 85.

3. On the first year of the war in the west, see Glenn Stott, *Greater Evils: The War of 1812 in Southwestern Ontario* (Arkona, 2001), 17-29. On Brock and the Detroit campaign, see Jonathon Riley, *A Matter of Honour: The Life, Campaigns and Generalship of Isaac Brock* (Montreal, 2012), 168-200.

4. J.M.Hitsman, *The Incredible War of 1812*, (1965, revised Toronto, 1999), 126-127. On the nature of the atrocities at the River Raisin, see Sandor Antal, "The River Raisin! Anatomy of a Demon Myth," *War of 1812 Magazine* (online) Issue 10 (Oct 2008) for an important corrective to the myth.

5. Hitsman, *Incredible War*, 169-171. On the patriotic pig, see A. Bryce Wallace, *History of Fort Wayne from the Earliest Known Accounts of the Past to the Present Period* (Fort Wayne, 1868), 270.

6. Hitsman, *Incredible War*, 166-171.

7. Grodzinski, *Defender of Canada*, 235-236.

8. Barclay to brother, 7 Sept 1813, Manuscript Sketch of Career of Robert H. Barclay, McCord Museum, Montreal.

9. Barclay to brother, 7 Sept 1813, Manuscript Sketch of Career of Robert H. Barclay, McCord Museum, Montreal.

10. David Bunnell, *The Travels and Adventures of David C. Bunnell* (Palmyra, 1831), 113-117.

11. Perry to Jones, 10 Sep 1813, *Doc. Hist. Naval*, vol. 2, 287.

12. Speech of Tecumseh, supposedly given on 18 Sept 1814, LAC, MG 13, WO 71, Court Martial of Major-General Henry Procter, Appendix 7.

13. Robert McAffee, *History of the Late War in the Western Country* (1816, reprinted Bowling Green, 1919), 415.

14. Wallace, *History of Fort Wayne*, 270. A. Bryce Wallace, *History of Fort Wayne from the Earliest Known Accounts of the Past to the Present Period* (Fort Wayne, 1868), 270.

15. John McDonald, *Biographical Sketch of General Duncan McArthur,* (Dayton, 1851), 138.

16. McDonald, *Sketch of McArthur*, 138.

17. Entry for 5 October 1813 in Journal of Captain Robert B. MaAfee's Mounted Company in Colonel Richard M. Johnson's Regiment, 1813, Kentucky Historical Society.

18. Byfield, *Narrative*, 80.

19. Fredriksen, *War of 1812 in Person*, Memoir of William Greathouse, 244.

20. Procter to De Rottenbureg, 23 Oct 1813, LAC, RG 8 I, vol. 680, 273.

21. Court Martial of Major-General Henry Procter, LAC, MG 13, WO 71. With referenc to this court martial see the note by Stewart Sutherland in Hitsman, *Incredible War*, 343-334.

22. On Harrison and Armstrong, see A.J. Languth, *Union 1812: The Americans Who Fought the Second War of Independence* (New York, 2006), 291-292; and Stagg, *Madison's War*, 398-399.

23. Stott, *Greater Evils*, 84-87.

24. Stott, *Greater Evils*, 126.

25. Samuel White, *A History of the American Troops during the Late War under Colonel Fenton* (Baltimore, 1829), 7.

26. Memoir of Amelia Ryerse, Harris Papers, D.B. Weldon Library, Western University, Ontario.

27. On Campbell's raid and its consequences see Graves, *Soldiers of 1814*, Memoir of Alexander McMullen, 66; Armstrong to Brown, 2 June 1814, USNA, RG 107, Micro 6; and General Order, 30 June 1814, Left Division Order Book, New York State Library, Albany, l.

28. Proclamation, 26 Sept 1814, contained in Stott, *Greater Evils*, 165.

29. Proclamation, 12 Apr 1814, reproduced in George Sheppard, *Plunder, Profit and Paroles: A Social History of the War of 1812 in Upper Canada* (Montreal, 1994), 170.

30. Salmon to Parry, 22 Oct 1814, *Doc. Hist.*, vol. 2, 275.

31. Talbot to Parry, n.d. [c. late Oct 1814], *Doc. Hist.*, vol. 2, 275.

32. Stott, *Greater Evils*, 163-165.

33. Fredriksen, *United States Army*, 106-108.

34. Armstrong to McArthur, 2 Aug 1814, Library of Congress, McArthur Papers, quoted in Stewart Rammage, *The Militia Stood Alone: Malcolm's Mills, 6 November 1814*, (Summerland, 2000), 31.

35. Rammage, *Militia*, 31.

36. McArthur to Monroe, 18 Nov 1814, *Doc. Hist.*, vol. 2, 308.

37. McArthur to Monroe, 18 Nov 1814, *Doc. Hist.*, vol. 2, 308.

38. General Order quoted in Rammage, *Militia*, 37.

39. McArthur to Woodbridge, 17 Nov 1814, quoted in Stott, *Greater Evils*, 564.

40. McArthur to Monroe, 18 Nov 1814, *Doc. Hist.*, vol. 2, 308.

41. McArthur to Monroe, 18 Nov 1814, *Doc. Hist.*, vol. 2, 308.

42. McArthur to Monroe, 18 Nov 1814, *Doc. Hist.*, vol. 2, 308.

43. McArthur to Monroe, 18 Nov 1814, *Doc. Hist.*, vol. 2, 308.
44. Stott, *Greater Evils*, 167-169
45. Stott, *Greater Evils*, 176.
46. Smelt to officer commanding at York, 26 Oct 1814, *Doc. Hist.*, vol. 2, 278.
47. Smelt to officer commanding at York, 26 Oct 1814, *Doc. Hist.*, vol. 2, 278.
48. Drummond to Prevost, 26 Oct 1814, LAC, RG8 I, vol. 686, 108.
49. Tucker to Harvey, 27 Oct 1814, *Doc. Hist.*, vol. 2, 278.
50. Stott, *Greater Evils*, 168-169.
51. McArthur to Monroe, 18 Nov 1814, *Doc. Hist.*, vol. 2, 308.
52. Rammage, *Militia*, 89-90.
53. Stott, *Greater Evils*, 170.
54. R.C. Muir, *The Early Political and Military History of Burford* (Quebec, 1913), 237.
55. Muir, *History of Burford*, 237.
56. Muir, *History of Burford*, 237-238.
57. Unless otherwise noted, my account of the action at Malcom's Mill, 6 Nov 1814, is based on Rammage, *Militia*, 97-109.
58. McArthur to Monroe, 18 Nov 1814, *Doc. Hist.*, vol. 2, 308.
59. McArthur to Monroe, 18 Nov 1814, *Doc. Hist.*, vol. 2, 308.
60. McArthur to Monroe, 18 Nov 1814, *Doc. Hist.*, vol. 2, 308.
61. McArthur to Monroe, 18 Nov 1814, *Doc. Hist.*, vol. 2, 308.
62. McAfee, *War in the Western Country*, 486.
63. George Thorman and Frank Clark, eds. *Garret Oakes, Tales of a Pioneer* (Elgin, 1991), 9.
64. Rammage, *Militia*, 105.
65. Certificate of Noah Fairchild, dated Long Point, 9 Nov 1814, reproduced in Rammage, *Militia*, 118.
66. E.A. Owen, *Pioneer Sketches of the Long Point Settlement* (Toronto, 1898), 561.
67. General Order, 18 Nov 1814, in Rammage, *Militia*, 128.
68. General Order, 18 Nov 1814, in Rammage, *Militia*, 128
69. Drummond to Yeo, 13 Nov 1814, *Doc. Hist.*, vol. 2, 303.
70. Yeo to Drummond, 14 Nov 1814, *Doc. Hist.*, vol. 2, 303.
71. Cochran to James Stewart, 4 Nov 1814, LAC, MG 24, B16.
72. Drummond to Yeo, 13 Nov 1814, *Doc. Hist.*, vol. 2, 303.

Chapter 16: "Oh I would that the wars were all done"

1. "I Would that the Wars were all Done," a British broadside ballad that dates to the late 18th century. A "robin" is a local term in Devon for a type of geranium. See Palmer, *The Rambling Soldier*, 225-226.
2. Norton, Journal, 2 Nov 1814, "Jacob Porter Norton," 53.
3. Norton, Journal, 8 Nov 1814, "Jacob Porter Norton," 53.
4. Fredriksen, *War of 1812 in Person*, Pearce Memoir, 93.
5. Izard to Monroe, 16 Dec 1814, Izard, *Correspondence*, 126.
6. Izard to Monroe, 15 Jan 1814. Izard, *Correspondence*, 132.
7. Fredriksen, *War of 1812 in Person*, Pearce Memoir, 94.
8. Cate, "Ropes' Autobiography," 126.
9. McIntire to Holmes, 14 Dec 1814, in Fredriksen, *War of 1812 in Person*, Letters of Rufus McIntire, 137. On construction plans at Sackets Harbor, see Chauncey to Jones, 5 Nov 1814, *Doc. Hist. Naval*, vol. 3, 637. On McGhie, see McDonell to Beckwith, 4 Feb 1815, LAC, RG 8 I, vol. 687, 96.
10. Graves, Hanks, 45-46.
11. Le Couteur, *Merry Hearts*, 210.
12. Le Couteur, *Merry Hearts*, 211-217.
13. Le Couteur, *Merry Hearts*, 211.
14. Grattan, *Adventures of the Connaught Rangers*, vol. 2, 287. Of the three posts, Three Rivers (now Trois-Rivières) seems to be have been the most pleasant. A newspaper clipping survives that reveals that, on 11 February 1815, the officers of the 88th Foot gave a ball and supper at that place, with dancing commencing at 9.30 P.M., interrupted by dinner at 1 A.M., and then "continued with great life and effect" until dawn. The transparencies of battles that adorned the walls of the ballroom were "eclipsed by the efulgent glow, of interesting and vivid beauties, who at once gave gaiety and lustre to the room." See AO, F 922, Military Scrapbook. Unfortunately the name of the newspaper was cut out of the clipping but it was probably the Montreal *Herald*.
15. My account of the infamous ball at St. Jean is from Grattan, *Adventures of the Connaught Rangers*, vol. 2, 288-292.
16. Monroe to Macomb, 12 Jan 1815, *Doc. Hist. Naval*, vol. 3, 683; Brisbane to Prevost, 22 Dec 1814, Brisbane Papers, CLUM, in *Doc. Hist. Naval*, vol. 3, 681; Prevost to Brisbane, 24 Dec 1814 and 12 Jan 1815,, Brisbane Papers, CLUM; Homans to Macdonough, 27 Dec 1814, *Doc. Hist. Naval.*, vol 3, 683.
17. Yeo to Croker, 14 Oct 1814, *Doc. Hist. Naval*, vol 3, 624; Yeo to Prevost, 6 Jan 1815, LAC, RG 8I, vol. 734, 8.
18. Unidentified newspaper clipping in the Brisbane Papers, CLUM. I am grateful to John Grodzinski for bringing this item to my attention.

19. Malcomson, *Lords of the Lake*, 315.
20. Prevost to Bathurst, 18 Oct 1814, LAC, RG 8I, vol. 1219, 307.
21. Prevost to Bathurst, 18 Oct 1814, LAC, RG 8I, vol. 1219, 307.
22. Yeo to Croker, 14 Oct 1814, *Doc. Hist. Naval.*, vol. 3, 625, 627n; Prevost to Bathurst, 18 Oct 1814, LAC, RG 8I, vol. 1219, 307; and Prevost to Bathurst, 19 Nov 1814, LAC, CO 42, vol. 157, 360.
23. McGowan to Chauncey, 19 Nov 1814, *Doc.Hist. Naval.*, 665.
24. Jones to Chauncey, 24 Oct 1814, *Doc.Hist.Naval*, vol.3, 629; Jones to Madison, 28 Oct 1814, *Doc.Hist.Naval*, vol. 3, 629.
25. Jones to Madison, 28 Oct 1814, *Doc.Hist.Naval*, vol. 3, 629.
26. Dunlop, "Recollections," 35-36.
27. Izard to Monroe, 16 Dec 1814, Izard, *Correspondence*, 126.
28. Izard to Monroe, 18 Dec 1814, Izard, *Correspondence*, 130.
29. Monroe to Izard, 8 Jan 1815, Izard, *Correspondence*, 134.
30. Izard to Monroe, 20 Nov 1814, Izard, *Correspondence*, 119.
31. Monroe to Brown, 10 Feb 1815, contained in C.P. Stacey, "An American Plan for a Canadian Campaign," *American Historical Review*, vol. 46 (1941), 356-358.
32. Grodzinski, *Defender of Canada*, 207.
33. Stagg, *War of 1812*, 135-137.
34. Stagg, *War of 1812*, 147-150.
35. Stagg, *War of 1812*, 138.
36. On the background of the New Orleans campaign, see Robin Reilly, *The British at the Gates: The New Orleans Campaign in the War of 1812* (1974, reprinted Toronto, 2002), 162-177.
37. The best account of the battle of 8 Jan 1815, because it states the facts without dramatically embellishing them, remains Reilly, *British at the Gates*, 302-330.
38. John Surtees, *Twenty-Five Years in the Rifle Brigade* (1833, reprinted London, 1996), 380-381.
39. Moore Smith, ed., *Autobiography of Harry Smith*, 251; and Journal of Colonel Alexander Dickson, quoted in Robin Reilly, *The British at the Gates*, 342.
40. Moore Smith, ed., *Autobiography of Harry Smith*, 251.
41. Liverpool to Wellington, in Adams, *History*, vol. 9, 26.
42. Unless otherwise noted, my discussion of the negotiations leading to the Treaty of Ghent and the arrival of the treaty in the United States are based on Adams, *History*, vol. 9, 1-59; and Stagg, *War of 1812*, 139-147.
43. Liverpool to Wellington, 28 Oct 1814, quoted in Adams, *History*, vol. 9, 38.
44. Wellington to Castlereagh, 9 Nov 1814, in Adams, *History*, vol. 9, 40-41.
45. Howe, "Recollections," 407. Howe is quoting Shakespeare's "Richard III," Act 1, Scene 1.
46. Eliza Quincy, quoted in Dianne Graves, *In the Midst of Alarms: The Untold Story of Women and the War of 1812* (Montreal, 2007), 380.
47. Fredriksen, *War of 1812 in Person*, Pearce Memoir, 92.
48. Le Couteur, *Merry Hearts*, 217.
49. Eliza Quincy, quoted in Dianne Graves, *Midst of Alarms*, 380.
50. Journal of George Howard, 1815, in Gregory V. Kloten, *Captain George Howard, United States Army …* (Youngstown, 2013), 151-152.
51. *Montreal Herald*, 11 Mar 1815.
52. Malcomson, *Lords of the Lake*, 321.
53. Le Couteur, *Merry Hearts*, 222-223.
54. *Montreal Herald*, 11 Mar 1815.
55. Le Couteur, *Merry Hearts*, 222-223.
56. *Montreal Herald*, 11 Mar 1815.
57. Fredriksen, *War of 1812 in Person*, Fairbanks Memoir, 262-262.
58. Jonathan Phillips, quoted in Winston Johnston, *Glengarry Light Infantry*, 296.
59. On Kearsley and Byfield, see Fredriksen, *War of 1812 in Person*, Kearsely Memoir, 67; and Byfield, *Narrative*, 93-94.
60. Speech of Little Crow, June 1814, enclosed in Prevost to Bathurst, 18 July 1814, LAC, CO 42, vol. 157, 12.
61. Speech of Makataimeshekiakiak, or Black Hawk, 28 Jun 1815, LAC, RG 8 I, vo. 258, 285.
62. Speech of Makataimeshekiakiak, or Black Hawk, 28 Jun 1815, LAC, RG 8 I, vo. 258, 285.
63. Dunlop, "Recollections," 100.
64. The author resides in an area that was originally called the "Perth Military Settlement," in which several hundred veterans of the war were settled in 1816-1822. One of the largest groups of settlers was formed by veterans of De Watteville's and De Meuron's Regiments but most did not make good settlers and drifted away after a year or two. The men of the Glengarry Light Infantry, in contrast, which also contributed a large contingent, proved to be among the best military pioneers.
65. A detailed description of this elaborate fantasy game will be found in Cooke, *Narrative of Events*, 282-303. Cooke devotes more space in his book to this game, including many of the documents written by the opposing sides than he does to some of the major military actions in which he participated.
66. *Columbian Centinel*, 29 Apr 1815.
67. Dunlop, "Recollections," 101.

Epilogue: "In Peace in Chelsea Quarters"

1. "Chelsea Quarters," a British broadsheet ballad dating from the Napoleonic Wars. Found-

ed in 1682 by Charles II and still in operaton, Chelsea Hospital in London is a charitable establishment that houses and feeds indigent veteran soldiers.

2. PCM, verdict of the court martial board, 402.
3. PCM, verdict of the court martial board, 402.
4. On Prevost's last days, see Grodzinski, *Defender of Canada*, 208-240.
5. Peter Burroughs, "Sir George Prevost," *DCB*, vol. 5 (Toronto, 1976).
6. Grodzinski, *Defender of Canada*, 240-241.
7. "Sir Gordon Drummond," *DCB*, vol. 8 (Toronto, 1988).
8. "Baron Francis De Rottenburg," *DCB*, vol. 6 (Toronto, 1987).
9. "Louis de Watteville," *DCB*, vol. 7 (Toronto, 1985).
10. Thomas Brisbane entry in *Australian Dictionary of Biography* 4, vol. 1 (Melbourne, 1966).
11. Manley Power entry in *Dictionary of National Biography*, vol. 46 (London, 1891).
12. *Gentleman's Magazine*,(Feb 1852), 188-190.
13, Fischer entry in Stuart Sutherland, ed., *His Majesty's Gentlemen: A Directory of British Regular Army Officers of the War of 1812* (Toronto, 2000).
14. Myers entry in Sutherland, *His Majesty's Gentlemen*.
15. On Pearson's later life, see Graves, *Fix Bayonets!*.
16. "Sir John Harvey," *DCB*, vol. 8 (Toronto, 1988).
17. Andrew Leith Hay entry in *Dictionary of National Biography*, (London, 1891).
18. Robert Malcomson, "Dobbs and the Royal Navy at Niagara," *Fortress Niagara*, (June 2000), 710-713.
19. Campbell entry in Sutherland, *His Majesty's Gentlemen*. Campbell's book, *A British Army, As It Was, Is, and Ought To Be* was published in 1840.
20. Mermet entry in Sutherland, *His Majesty's Gentlemen*.
21. Philpotts entry in Sutherland, *His Majesty's Gentlemen*. Note that this man also spelt his name as Philpotts.
22. Le Couteur, *Merry Hearts*, 19-23.
23. "William Dunlop," *DCB*, vol. 7 (Toronto, 1985).
24. Yeo's biographical entry in *DCB*, vol. 7 (Toronto, 1985) is unusually adulatory but the present author flatly disagrees with this assessment.
25. "Daniel Pring" entry in *DCB*, vol. 6 (Toronto, 1987).
26. "Robert Barclay," *DCB*, vol. 6 (Toronto, 1987).
27. Dianne Graves, *Midst of Alarms*, 380.
28. *Report of the Loyal and Patriotic Society of Upper Canada* (York, 1815), 147-149, 160-162.
29. "John Norton" entry, *DCB*, vol. 6 (Toronto, 1987).
30. See Roger L. Nichols, *Black Hawk and the Warrior's Path* (Arlington Heights, 1992).
31. The standard biography, which is rather adulatory, is Carl Skeen, *John Armstrong Jr., 1758-1843: A Biography* (Syracuse, 1982).
32. A standard biography is Harry Ammon, *James Monroe: The Quest for National Unity* (New York, 1971).
33. The standard biography is John Morris, *Sword of the Border. Major General Jacob Jennings Brown, 1775-1828* (Kent, 2000)
34. Fredriksen, *The United States Army*, 42-47.
35. Fredriksen, *The United States Army*, 47-52.
36. Fredriksen, *The United States Army*, 109-112,
37. Fredriksen, *The United States Army*, 107-108.
38. Fredriksen, *The United States Army*, 96-98.
39. Graves, *Where Right and Glory Lead*, 244.
40. Fredriksen, *The United States Army*, 70-72.
41. Graves, *Where Right and Glory Lead*, 245.
42. Graves, *Field of Glory*, 324.
43. Graves, *Field of Glory*, 325.
44. Graves, *Where Right and Glory Lead*, 244.
45. Anonymous, *Memoir of Colonel William McRee, U.S.E.* (Wilmington, 1843).
46. Hinton, *Military Career of John Ellis Wool*.
47. Graves, *Where Right and Glory Lead*, 245.
48. William A. Trimble entry in Appleton's *Cyclopedia of American Biography*, vol. 6 (New York, 1900).
49. Graves, *Where Right and Glory Lead*, 241
50. *The Life and Dying Confession of James Hamilton, Executed for the Murder of Major Benjamin Birdsall, Nov. 6, 1818, at Albany* (Albany, 1818).
51. Graves, *Where Right and Glory Lead*, 241
52. Fredriksen, *War of 1812 in Person*, 51-53.
53. John G. Watmough Entry in *Biographical Directory of the United States Congress* on line.
54. Graves, *Where Right and Glory Lead*, 245-246.
55. Lossing, *Field-Book*, 846n.
56. Skaggs, *Thomas Macdonough*.
57. David Skaggs, *Oliver Hazard Perry: Honor, Courage and Patriotism in the Early U.S. Navy* (Annapolis, 2006).
58. *American State Papers: Naval Affairs*, vol. 2 (Washington, 1826), 460.
59. Graves, *Where Right and Glory Lead*, 245.
60. "Eleazar Williams," entry in *DCB*, vol. 8.
61. George Platt, *The Platt Lineage: A Genealogical Research and Record* (New York, 1891), 107.
62. Herkalo, *Averill Journal*, preface.
63. "Andrew Westbrook" entry in *DCB*, vol. 6. Canadian John Richardson, who had served as an officer in the 41st Foot during the war, wrote several novels with a War of 1812 theme, many modelled on historic characters and events. Although he was a prolific author, Richardson never made much money from his work and apparently died from starvation in New York in 1852, a not uncommon fate for authors. His novel *Westbrook, the Outlaw, Or,*

The Avenging Wolf, first appeared as a serial in the New York periodical the *Sunday Mercury*, in 1851. The author is distantly related to Westbrook's arch-enemy, Daniel Springer, and had the great pleasure of meeting Nicholas Westbrook, a descendant of Andrew, at an historical conference in Ogdensburg, NY, in 2011. Although Westbrook captured Springer during the war, Springer received Westbrook's property, more than 4,000 acres of fine farmland in western Upper Canada, in compensation.

64. Fate of Great Lakes warships from Robert Malcomson, *Warships of the Great Lakes*, 139-140; *Lords of the Lake*, 324-326, and "HMS St. Lawrence," 35.

65. Information from the Erie Maritime Museum and the Flagship Niagara Organization.

66. *Plattsburgh Republican*, 23 Sept 1906.

67. D.J Goodspeed, *Battle Royal: A History of The Royal Regiment of Canada, 1862-1962* (Toronto, 1962), 338-339.

68. *New York Times*, 30 June 1988.

Appendix C: Myths of the Siege of Fort Erie

1. USNA, RG 107, Micro 221, reel 60, Gaines to the Secretary of War, 23 Aug 1814.

2. Benson Lossing, *Pictorial Field-Book of the War of 1812* (New York, 1869), 834.

3. John Elting, *Amateurs to Arms: A Military History of the War of 1812*. (Chapel Hill, 1991), 248n.

4. Georg von Martens, *A Compendium of the Law of Nations*, (London, 1802), 305.

5. Wellington to Canning, quoted in Charles Calwell, "The Sacking of Ciudad Rodrgo, Badajoz and San Sebastian," *Blackwood's Magazine*, September 1913, 367-377.

6. MacMahon to Jarvis, 22 August 1814, *Doc. Hist.* vol. I, 166.

7. LeCouteur to H. Le Couteur, 29 July 1869, in *Doc. Hist.* I, 168.

8. On the various suggestions for the causes of the explosion, see Louis L. Babcock, *The War of 1812 on the Niagara Frontier* (Buffalo, 1927), 209-210.

9. Babcock. *War of 1812*, 210.

10. LAC, RG 8 I, vol. 685, Drummond to Prevost, 15 Aug 1814.

11. LAC, RG 8 I, vol. 685, Drummond to Prevost, 15 Aug 1814.

12. Donald E. Graves, "William Drummond and the Battle of Fort Erie," *Canadian Military History*, vol. 1, no. 1, (1992), 25-41.

13. GM, evidence of Hindman.

14. Babcock, *War of 1812*, 210.

Appendix E: Strength, Composition and Desertion Rate of the British Army at Plattsburgh...

1. Donald E. Graves, "'The Finest Army ever to Campaign on American Soil?': The Organization, Strength, Composition, and Losses of the British Land Forces during the Plattsburgh Campaign, September 1814, *Journal of the War of 1812*, vol. 7, no. 4 (2003), 6-13.

2. This return is appended to Prevost to Bathurst, 1 April 1815, LAC, CO 42, vol. 131.

3. Journal of Major-General F.P. Robinson, Royal Military College of Canada, Kingston.

4. On the number and origin of British units sent to North America in 1814, see Donald E. Graves, "'The Redcoats are Coming!': British Troop Movements to North America in 1814, Journal of the War of 1812, vol. 6, no. 5 (Summer 2001), 12-18.

5. The return of killed and wounded dated 14 September will be found in Prevost to Bathurst, 11 September 1814, LAC, CO 42, col. 128-1, 220. The Return for 15 September is appended to Prevost to Bathurst, 1 April 1815, LAC, CO 42, vol. 131, 165.

6. Graves, "The Finest Army ever to Campaign."

7. See Appendix D above.

Bibliography

PRIMARY SOURCES – ARCHIVAL

Archives of Ontario, Toronto
    MU 2057, Harvey Papers
    F 922, Military Scrapbook, Lee Pritzker Collection
    FU 983, John Strachan Papers
Buffalo and Erie County Historical Society, Buffalo
    Manuscripts Collection, War of 1812 Papers
Clements Library, University of Michigan, Ann Arbor
    Thomas Brisbane Papers, CLUM
Dartmouth College Library, Hanover, New Hampshire
    John W. Weeks Papers
Duke University Special Collections, Durham, North Carolina
    Diary of Lt. John Lang
Geneva Historical Society, Geneva, New York
    Papers of Lieutenant-Colonel Hugh W. Dobbins, New York Volunteers Dobbins Papers
Kentucky Historical Society, Louisville
    Journal of Captain Robert B. MaAfee's Mounted Company in Colonel Richard M. Johnson's Regiment, 1813
Library and Archives Canada, Ottawa
    Manuscript Group 11, Colonial Office 42 and 43
    Manuscript Group 23
        GIII, Loyalist Papers
    Manuscript Group 24
        A9 Anne Elinor Prevost Papers
        F1, Narrative of David Wingfield
        F15, Hercules Scott Papers
        F96, De Watteville Papers
            Journal, August-October 1814
        I28, Alicia Cockburn correspondence
        I29, Diary of Lt. James Pringle, 82nd Foot
        L8, Jacques Viger Papers
    Record Group 8I, British Military Records
Library of Congress, Washington
    Jacob Brown Papers
    Thomas W. Jesup Papers
        Memoir of the Campaign on the Niagara
Lily Library, University of Indiana, Bloomington
    Captain Joseph Henderson Papers
McCord Museum, Montreal
    General and Garrison Orders, War of 1812 Collection
    R.H. Barclay Biography files
National Archives of Britain, Kew Surrey
    Admiralty 37, Ships' Musters
    War Office 17, Monthly Returns

War Office 55, Ordnance Office, Miscellaneous
    Journal of Lt. Philpotts, RE
War Office 71, Records of the Judge-Advocate General
    Court Martial of Major-General Henry Procter
National Archives of the United States, Washington
    Record Group 107, Correspondence of the Secretary of War
    Record Group 153, Records of the Judge Advocate General
        Court-Martial of Brigadier-General E.P. Gaines
National Library of Scotland, Edinburgh
    Memorandum of Operations in the Chesapeke by George DeLacy Evans
New York State Library, Albany
    Mss. 11225, Left Division Order Book, 1814
    Papers of Colonel Charles K. Gardner
        Memoranda of Occurrences and Some Important Facts Attending the Campaign on the Niagara
Royal Military College of Canada, Kingston
    Papers of Major-General of F.P. Robinson
United States Army Military History Center
    Memoir of Lieutenant Samuel Tappan
Western University, Ontario, D.B. Weldon Library
    Memoir of Amelia Ryerse, Harris Papers
Victoria University, Toronto
    Journal of the Reverend George Ferguson

PRIMARY SOURCES – PUBLISHED

Newspapers & Periodicals

Annual Register, 1814-185
Columbian Centinel, 1814
Dundee Courier, 1814
Gentleman's Magazine, 1852
Quebec Courier, 1814
Quebec Gazette, 1814
London Times, 1814
Montreal Herald, 1815
National Intelligencer, 1814
New York Times, 1988
Niles' Weekly Register, 1814
Plattsburgh Republican 1814, 1879

Published Documents

Bickley, F.L., ed. *Report on the Manuscripts of Earl Bathurst*. London: 1923.
Crawford, Michael J., ed. *The Naval War of 1812. A Documentary History*. Washington: 2003.
Cruikshank, Ernest A., ed. *Documentary HIstory of the Campaigns upon the Niagara Frontier in 1814*. Volumes 1 and 2, Welland: 1896).
——. *Documents Relating to the Invasion of Canada and the Surrender of Detroit, 1812* Ottawa: 1912.
——. *Documents Relating to the Invasion of the Niagara Peninsula by the United States Army, commanded by Major-General Jacob Brown in July and August, 1814*. Niagara-on-the-Lake: 1920.
Mr. H.C. Dennison's *Resolution Calling on the Governor for Copies of Any Correspondence He May Have Had with Military Officers*. Montpelier: 1814.
Gurwood, John, ed., *The Dispatches of Field Marshal The Duke of Wellington*, vol. 10. London: 1835.
Izard, George. *Official Correspondence with the War Department*. Philadelphia: 1816.
Report of the Loyal and Patriotic Society of Upper Canada. York: 1815.
United States Congress. *American State Papers*. Washington: 1832-1837.
    Class I. Foreign Relations, vol. 3
    Class V. Militry Affairs, vols. 1 and 2
    Class VI. Naval Affairs, vols. 1 and 2

Webster, Charles K., ed., *British Diplomacy, 1813-1815: Select Documents Dealing with the Reconstruction of Europe.* London: 1921.

Wood, W.H., ed. *Select British Documents of the Canadian War of 1812.* 4 vols., Toronto: 1920-1928,

Published Diaries, Correspondence, Journals and Memoirs

Anonymous. *The Military Adventures of Johnny Newcome.* London: 1904.

———. "War of 1812 Reminiscences of a Veteran Survivor," *Geneva Gazette,* 29 Nov 1878.

Apess. William. *A Son of the Forest. The Experience of William Apes, A Native of the Forest.* New York: 1829.

"Artillero Viejo." *United Service Magazine,* 1841, Part I, 555.

Bunnell, David. *The Travels and Adventures of David C. Bunnell.* Palmyra: 1831.

Byfield, Shadrach. *A Narrative of a Light Company Soldier's Service in the Forty-First Regiment of Foot.* New York: 1910).

Cate, Mary R., ed. "Benjamin Ropes' Autobiography," *Essex County Historical Collections* 91 (1955).

Campbell, James. *A British Army, As It Was, Is, and Ought To Be.* London, 1840.

Cooke, John. *Narrative of Events in the South of France, and the Attack on New Orleans in 1814 and 1815.* London: 1852.

Costello, Edward. *The Adventures of a Soldier, Written by Himself.* London: 1852.

Crook, Jonathan, ed. *The Very Thing. The Memories of Drummer Richard Bentinck, Royal Welch Fusiliers, 1807-1823.* London: 2011.

Dolan, Charles W., ed. "Extracts from the Diary of Joseph Heatley Dulles," *Pennsylvania Magazine of History and Biography,* vol.35, no. 3 (1911).

David B. Douglass. "Reminiscences of the Campaign of 1814, on the Niagara Frontier," *The HIstorical Magazine,* August-October, 1873.

Dunlop, William. *Recollections of the American War of 1812-1814.* Toronto: 1905.

Einstein, Louis, ed. "Recollections of the War of 1812 by George Hay, Eighth Marquis of Tweedale," *American Historical Review,* vol. 32 (1926).

Folsom, William R. "The Battle of Plattsburgh," *Vermont Quarterly* 20 (Oct 1952).

Fredriksen, John C. ed. *The War of 1812 in Person.* Jefferson: 2010.

Grattan, William. *Adventures with the Connaught Rangers.* London: 1902.

———. *Adventures of the Connaught Rangers, 1808-1814.* 2 vols, London: 1847.

Graves, Donald E., ed. *Merry Hearts Make Light Days. The War of 1812 Journal of Lieutenant John Le Couteur, 104th Foot.* Montreal: 1994, 2012

———. *Soldiers of 1814: American Enlisted Men's Memoirs of the Niagara Campaign.* Youngstown: 1996.

———. *First Campaign of an A.D.C. The War of 1812 Memoir of Lieutenant William Jenkins Worth, United States Army.* Youngstown: 2012.

Hailes, Harris. "The Assault on Fort Erie, or Two Ways of Telling the Same Story," *United Service Journal,* 1841.

Hamilton, James. *The Life and Dying Confession of James Hamilton, Executed for the Murder of Major Benjamin Birdsall, Nov. 6, 1818, at Albany.* Albany: 1818.

Hanson, John. *The Lost Prince, Facts Tending to Prove the Identity of Louis the Seventeenth, of France and the Rev. Eleazer Williams.* New York: 1854.

Herkalo, Keith, ed. *The Journal of H.K. Averill Sr.* Plattsburgh: 2001.

Horner, W.E. Horner. "A Military Hospital at Buffalo, New York, in the year 1814," *The Medical Examiner and Record of Medical Science,* vol. 8, (1852).

Howe, Eber. "Recollections of Pioneer Printer," *Buffalo Historical Society Publications,* vol. 9 (1906).

Hunt, Gaillard. *The Writings of James Madison,* vol. 8. New York: 1908.

Kloten, Gregory V., ed. *Captain George Howard, United States Army* ... Youngstown: 2013.

Leach, J. *Rough Sketches of the Life of an Old Soldier.* London: 1831.

Lord, Norman, ed. "The War of 1812 on the Niagara Frontier. Letters Written by Sergt. James Commins, 8th Foot," *Journal of the Society for Army Historical Research,* 18 (1939), No. 2.

Malcomson, Robert, ed. *Sailors of 1812. Memoirs and Letters of Naval Officers and Lake Ontario.* Youngstown: 1997.

McGrigor, James. *The Autobiography and Services of Sir James McGrigor.* London: 1861.

Moore Smith, G.C., ed. *The Autobiography of Lieutenant-General Sir Harry Smith.* London: 1901.

Napier, William. *The Life and Opinions of General Sir Charles James Napier*. 4 vols., London: 1857.

Nelson, Gladys, ed.. "The Battle of Plattsburgh," *University of Rochester Library Bulletin*, vol. 3, no. 2 (1948).

Porter, David R., ed. "Jacob Porter Norton: A Yankee on the Niagara Frontier," *Niagara Frontier* (Summer 1965).

Pringle, Norman. *Letters by Major Norman Pringle ... vindicating the Character of the British Army employed in North America in the Years 1814-1815*. Edinburgh: 1835.

Sabine, Edward, ed. *Letters of Colonel Sir Augustus Simon Fraser*. London: 1859.

Scott, James. *Recollections of a Naval Life*. London: 3 vols, 1834.

Stacey, C.P., ed. "Upper Canada at War, 1814: Captain Armstrong Reports," *Ontario History*, vol. 48 (1956).

Stevens, Jonathan. "Vermont Letters," *Proceedings of the Vermont Historical Society*, vol. 6 (Mar 1938).

Surtees, John. *Twenty-Five Years in the Rifle Brigade*. London: 1833.

Talman, J.J. and C.F. Klinck, eds. *The Journal of John Norton, 1816*. Toronto: 1970.

Thorman, George and Frank Clark, eds. *Garret Oakes, Tales of a Pioneer*. Elgin: 1991.

White, Samuel. *A History of the American Troops during the Late War under Colonel Fenton* (Baltimore, 1829)

Wood, George. *The Subaltern Officer. A Narrative*. London: 1825.

Wood, John H., "Plattsburg. (1814). From the Diary of J. H. Wood," *Women's Canadian Historical Society*, Transaction No. 5 (1905).

———. "Reflections on Plattsburg," *Women's Canadian Historical Society*, Transaction No. 5 (1905).

Period Military, Naval and Medical Technical Literature

Adye, Ralph W. *The Bombardier and Pocket Gunner*. London: 1813.

Atkinson, Samuel Coate. *The Naval Pocket Gunner, or Compendium of Informaton Relating to Sea Service Gunnery ...* London: 1814.

Beauchant, Theophilus. *The Naval Gunner*. London: 1828.

Britain, Admiralty. *Regulations and Instructions Relating to His Majesty's Service at Sea* (London, 1808)

———. War Office. *Rules and Regulations for the Formations, Field-Exercise, and Movements of His Majesty's Forces*. London: 1793).

Duane, William. *American Military Library*. Philadelphia: 2 vols., 1809.

Douglas, Howard. *A Treatise on Naval Gunnery*. London: 1819.

Gassendi, Jean-Jacques Basiline de. *Aide-Memoire, à l'usage des Officiers de l'artillerie de France*. Paris: 2 vols., 1801.

Greener, William. *The Gun; or, A Treatise on the Various Descriptions of Small Fire-Arms*. London: 1808.

Guthrie, George. *A Treatise on Gun-Shot Wounds*. London: 1827.

———. *Commentaries on the Surgery of War*. London: 1855.

Larrey, Dominique. *Memoirs of Military Surgery, and the Campaigns of the French Army on the Rhine, in Corsica, Catalonia, Egypt and Spain, at Boulogne, Ulm, and Austerlitze, in Saxony, Prussia, Poland, Spain and Austria*. Baltimore: 2 vols, 1814.

Scheel, Henri Othon De. *Treatise on Artillery*. Philadelphia: 1800.

Simmons, Robert. *The Sea-Gunner's Vade-Mecum*. London: 1812.

[Stoddard, Amos]. *Exercise for the Garrison and Field Ordnance, Together with Manoeuvres of Horse Artillery....* Philadelphia: 1812.

Tousard, Louis de. *American Artillerist's Companion, or Elements of Artillery*. Philadelphia, 2 vols., 1809.

Trowbridge, Amasa. "Gun-Shot Wounds," *Boston Medical and Surgical Journal*, vol. 18, no. 22 (July 1838).

SECONDARY SOURCES

Biographical Encyclopedias, Dictionaries and Militry Unit References

Appleton's Encyclopedia of American Biography. New York: 7 vols, 1888.

The Encyclopedia of Arkansas History & Culture (online).

Askwith, W.H. *List of Officers of the Royal Regiment of Artillery From the Year 1716 to the Year 1899.* London: 1900.

Australian Dictionary of Biography. Canberra: 18 vols., 1967-2012.

Biographical Directory of the United States Congress (online).

Britain, War Office. *A List of all the Officers of the Army and Royal Marines on Full and Half-pay.* London: 1814, 1815.

Chichester, Henry and George Burgess-Short. *Records and Badges of the British Army.* London: 1902.

Dictionary of American Biography. New York: 22 vols., 1958-1964.

Dictionary of Canadian Biography. Volumes V–IX. Toronto: 1976-1988.

Dictionary of National Biography. London: 63 vols., 1885-1900.

Heitman, Francis B. *Historical Register and Dictionary of the U.S Army.* Washington: 2 vols, 1903.

Irving, L. Homfray. *Officers of the British Forces in Canada during the War of 1812-15.* Welland: 1908.

Laws, M.E.S. *Battery Records of the Royal Artillery, 1716-1859.* Woolwich: 1952.

Malcomson, Robert. *Historical Dictionary of the War of 1812.* Lanham: 2006.

Norman, C.B. *Battle Honours of the British Army from Tangier 1662, to the Commencement of the Reign of Edward VII.* London: 1911.

The Royal Military Calendar, or Army Service and Commission Book. London: 1815. 5 vols.

Sawicki, James. *Infantry Regiments of the US Army.* Dumfries, VA: 1981.

Sutherland, Stuart, ed., *His Majesty's Gentlemen: A Directory of British Regular Army Officers of the War of 1812.* Toronto: 2000.

Swinson, Arthur. *A Register of the Regiments and Corps of the British Army.* London: 1972.

Wickes, H.L. *Regiments of Foot. A Historical Record of all the foot regiments of the British Army.* Southampton: 1974.

Other Books

Adams, Henry. *History of the United States during the Administration of James Madison.* New York: 4 vols., 1930.

Ammon, Harry. *James Monroe: The Quest for National Unity.* New York: 1971.

Ansley, Norman. *Vergennes, Vermont and the War of 1812. The Battle of Lake Champlain.* Severna Park: 1999.

Anonymous. *A Brief Sketch of the Services of John G. Watmough, during and subsequent to the Campaigns of 1814-1815.* Philadelphia: 1838.

———. *Memoir of Colonel William McRee, U.S.E.* Wilmington: 1843.

Armstrong, John. *Notices of the War of 1812.* New York: 2 vols., 1840.

Arthur, Brian. *How Britain Won the War of 1812: The Royal Navy's Blockades of the United States, 1812-1815.* Woodbridge: 2011.

Babcock, Louis L. *The War of 1812 on the Niagara Frontier.* Buffalo: 1927.

Baynham, Henry. *From the Lower Deck: The Old Navy, 1780-1840.* London: 1972.

Bilow, Jack. *A War of 1812 Death Register.* Plattsburgh: 2011.

Blackmore, Howard. *British Military Firearms, 1650-1850.* London: 1961.

Book of Common Prayer. Episcopalian Church. Boston: 1789.

Calwell, Charles. "The Sacking of Ciudad Rodrigo, Badajoz and San Sebastian," *Blackwood's Magazine*, September 1913.

Chartrand, René. *Uniforms and Equipment of the United States Forces in the War of 1812.* Youngstown: 1992.

Courten, Antoine de. *Canada 1812-1814: Fighting the British Banner. The Swiss Regiments de Watteville and de Meuron on the Fronts of Niagara and Montreal.* Montreal: 2009.

Crisman, Kenneth. *The Eagle: An American Brig on Lake Champlain during the War of 1812.* Annapolis: 1987.

Dibdin, Thomas, ed. *Songs, Naval and National of the Late Charles Dibdin.* London: 1841.

Elting, John. *Amateurs to Arms: A Military History of the War of 1812.* Chapel Hill: 1991.

Eschelman, Ralph. *In Full Glory Reflected: Discovering the War of 1812 in the Chesapeake.* Annapolis: 2012.

Everest, Allan. *The War of 1812 in the Champlain Valley.* Syracuse: 1981.

Fredriksen, John C. *The United States Army of the War of 1812.* Jefferson: 2009.

George, Christopher. *Terror in the Chesapeake: The War of 1812 on the Bay*. Shippensburg: 2001.

Goodspeed, Donald. *Battle Royal: A History of The Royal Regiment of Canada, 1862-1962*. Toronto: 1962.

Graves, Dianne. *In the Midst of Alarms: The Untold Story of Women and the War of 1812*. Montreal: 2007.

Graves, Donald E. *Where Right and Glory Lead: The Battle of Lundy's Lane, 1814*. Toronto: 1997.

———. *Field of Glory: The Battle of Crysler's Farm, 1813*. Toronto: 1999.

———. *Fix Bayonets! A Royal Welch Fusilier at War, 1795-1815*. Toronto; 2006.

Grodzinski, John. *Defender of Canada: Sir George Prevost and the War of 1812*. Norman: 2013.

Hamilton, Hugh. *History of Norfolk County, Massachusetts*. Philadelphia: 1884.

Hart, Roger. *England Expects*. London: 1972.

Hicks, James. *Notes on U.S. Ordnance*. Mount Vernon: 1940

Hinton, Harwood. *The Military Career of John Ellis Wool, 1812-1863*. Madison: 1960.

Herkalo, Keith. *The Battles at Plattsburgh, September 11, 1814*. Charleston: 2012.

Hickey, Donald R. *The War of 1812: A Forgotten Conflict*. Chicago: 1989, revised 2012.

Hitsman, J.M. *The Incredible War of 1812: A Military History*. Toronto: 1965, revised 1999.

Hughes, B.P. *Firepower, Weapons Effectiveness on the Battlefield, 1630-1850*. London: 1974.

Johnston, Winston. *The Glengarry Light Infantry, 1812-1816*. Charlottetown, 1998.

Jones, Thomas. *History of the Sieges Carried on by the Army under the Duke of Wellington, in Spain, during the Years 1811 to 1814*. London: 3 vols. 1846.

Kert, Faye. *Pride and Prejudice: Privateering and Naval Prize in Atlantic Canada in the War of 1812*. St. John's: 1997.

Lambert, Andrew. *The Challenge: America, Britain and the War of 1812*. London: 2012.

Languth, A.L. *Union 1812: The Americans Who Fought the Second War of Independence*. New York: 2006.

Livingston, John, ed. *Portraits of Eminent Americans, now living....* New York: 1854.

Lossing, Benson. *Pictorial Field-Book of the War of 1812*. New York: 1869.

Malcomson, Robert. *Lords of the Lake*. Toronto: 1998.

———. *Warships of the Great Lakes, 1754-1834*. London: 2001.

———. *Historical Dictionary of the War of 1812*. Lanham: 2006.

Martens, Georg von. *A Compendium of the Law of Nations*. London: 1802.

McAfee, Robert. *History of the Late War in the Western Country*. Bowling Green: 1919.

McCarty, William. *Songs, Odes and Other Poems of National Subject*. N.p.: 1842.

McDonald. John. *Biographical Sketches of General Nathaniel Massie, General Duncan McArthur and General Simon Kenton*. Dayton: 1851.

McTaggart, John, ed. *The Scottish Gallovidian Encyclopedia*. London: 1878.

Moller, George Moller. *American Military Shoulder Arms. Volume II. From the 1790s to the End of the Flintlock Period*. Author's publication, 2011.

Morris, John. *Sword of the Border: Major General Jacob Jennings Brown, 1775-1828*. Kent: 2000.

Muir, R.C. *The Early Political and Military History of Burford*. Quebec: 1913.

Napier, William. *History of the War in the Peninsula and the South of France ...* London: 1840.

Nichols, Roger L. *Black Hawk and the Warrior's Path*. Arlington Heights: 1992.

Oman, Charles. *History of the Peninsular War*, vol. IV. Oxford: 1902.

———. *Wellington's Army, 1809-1814*. London: 1913.

Owen, David. *Fort Erie (1764-1823): An Historical Guide*. Fort Erie: 1988.

Owen, E.A. *Pioneer Sketches of the Long Point Settlement*. Toronto: 1898.

Palmer, Roy. *The Rambling Soldier: Life in the Lower Ranks, 1750-1900, through Soldier's Songs and Writing*. London: 1985.

Platt, George. *The Platt Lineage: A Genealogical Research and Record*. New York: 1891.

Pope, Dudley. *England Expects: Nelson and the Trafalgar Campaign*. London: 1959.

Quimby, Robert. *The U.S. Army in the War of 1812: An Operational and Command Study*. Lansing: 2 vols, 1998.

Rammage, Stewart. *The Militia Stood Alone: Malcolm's Mills, 6 November 1814*. Summerland: 2000.

Reilly, Robin. *The British at the Gates: The New Orleans Campaign in the War of 1812*. Toronto: 2002.

Roosevelt, Theodore. *The Naval War of 1812*. New York: 1902.

Riley, Jonathon. *A Matter of Honour: The Life, Campaigns and Generalship of Isaac Brock*. Montreal: 2012.

Sailly, Peter. *History of Plattsburgh, N.Y.* Plattsburgh: 1877.

Sheppard, George. *Plunder, Profit and Paroles: A Social HIstory of the War of 1812 in Upper Canada*. Montreal: 1994.

Shield, Joseph W. *From Flintlock to M1*. New York: 1954.

Silver, James. *Edmund Pendleton Gaines. Frontier General*. Baton Rouge: 1949.

Skaggs, David. *Thomas Macdonough: Master of Command in the Early U.S. Navy*. Annapolis: 2003.

———. *Oliver Hazard Perry: Honor, Courage and Patriotism in the Early U.S. Navy*. Annapolis: 2006.

Skeen, Carl. *John Armstrong Jr. 1758-1843: A Biography*. Syracuse: 1982.

Stagg, John. *Mr. Madison's War: Politics, Diplomacy, and Warfare in the Early American Republic, 1783-1830*. Princeton: 1983.

———. *The War of 1812: Conflict for a Continent*. Cambridge: 2012.

Stanhope, Phillip. *Notes of Conversations with the Duke of Wellington*. London: 1866.

Stanley, George. *The War of 1812: Land Operations*. Ottawa: 1983. .

Stott, Glenn. *Greater Evils: The War of 1812 in Southwestern Ontario*. Arkona: 2001.

Sullivan, Neil and David Martin. *A History of the Town of Chazy, Clinton County, New York*. A.P.:, 1970.

Thorman, George and Frank Clark, eds. *Garret Oakes, Tales of a Pioneer*. Elgin: 1991.

Tucker,Spencer. *Arming the Fleet: U.S. Navy Ordnance in the Muzzle-Loading Era*. Annapolis, 1989.

Wallace, A. Bryce. *History of Fort Wayne from the Earliest Known Accounts of the Past to the Present Period*. Fort Wayne: 1868.

Whitehorne, Joseph. *While Washington Burned. The Battle for Fort Erie, 1814*. Baltimore: 1992.

———. *The Battle for Baltimore 1814*. Baltimore: 1997.

Winstock, Lewis. *Songs & Music of the Redcoats, A History of the War Music of the British Army, 1642-1902*. London: 1970.

Articles

Anonymous, "Biographical Sketch of Major Thomas Biddle," *Illinois Monthly Magazine*, vol. 1, 557.

Antal, Sandor, "The River Raisin! Anatomy of a Demon Myth," *War of 1812 Magazine* (online) Issue 10 (Oct 2008)

Armstrong, John. *Notice of Mr. Adams' Eulogiium on the Life and Character of James Monroe*. Washington: 1832.

Barker, A.S. "An Incident from the War of 1812," *Navy* (1914).

Foreman, Carolyn T. "General William Goldsmith Belknap, Commandant at Fort Gibson, Fort Washita and Fort Smith," *Chronicles of Oklahoma*, vol. 20, no. 2 (June 1942).

Garrod, Martin. "Amphibious Warfare: Why?," *Journal of the Royal United Services Institute*, 113, (Winter 1988).

Graves, Donald E. "'Dry Books of Tactics': U.S. Infantry Manuals of the War of 1812 and after," Part I, *Military Historian*, vol. 38, no. 2 (Summer, 1986); Part II, vol. 38, no. 4 (Winter, 1986).

———. "From Steuben to Scott. The Adoption of French Infantry Tactics by the U.S. Army, 1807-1816," *Acta of the International Commission of Military History*, no. 13, (Helsinki, 1991), 223-235.

———. "William Drummond and the Battle of Fort Erie, " *Canadian Military History* 1 (1992), 1-18.

———. "'The Redcoats are Coming!': British Troop Movements to North America in 1814," *Journal of the War of 1812*, vol. 6, no. 5 (Summer 2001).

———. "'The Finest Army ever to Campaign on American Soil,' The Organizaiton, Strength, Composition, and Losses of the British Land Forces during the Plattsburgh Campaign," September 1814, *Journal of the War of 1812*, vol. 7, no. 4 (2003).

———. "The Hard School of War. A Collective Biography of the General Officers of the United States Army in the War of 1812. Part II. The Class of 1813," *War of 1812 Magazine (online)*, Issue No. 3 (June 2006).

Laws, M.E.S. "The Royal Artillery at Martinique 1809," *Journal of the Royal Artillery Institute*, 78, no. 1 (Jan 1950).

Malcomson, Robert. "HMS St. Lawrence: The Freshwater First-Rate," *Mariner's Mirror*, vol. 83 (1997).

———. "Dobbs and the Royal Navy at Niagara," *Fortress Niagara*, (June 2000).

Melhorn, Donald. "'A Splendid Man:' Richardson, Fort Meigs and Metoss," *Northwest Ohio Quarterly*, vol. 69, no. 3 (Summer 1997).

Smith, Eric M. "Leaders Who Lost: Case Studies of Command under Stress," *Military Review*, 61 (Apr 1981).

Stacey, C.P. "An American Plan for a Canadian Campaign," *American Historical Review*, vol. 46 (1941).

Stagg, John. "The Politics of Ending the War of 1812," in R.A. Bowler, ed., *War Along the Niagara: Essays on the War of 1812 and Its Legacy* (Lewiston, 1991).

Williams, Glenn. "The Bladensburg Races," *Military History Quarterly*, vol. 12, no. 1 (1999).

Index

DON'T MISS THE COMPANION VOLUMES TO
AND ALL THEIR GLORY PAST...

FIELD OF GLORY
THE BATTLE OF CRYSLER'S FARM, 1813

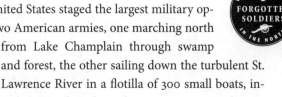

In the autumn of 1813, the United States staged the largest military operation of the War of 1812. Two American armies, one marching north

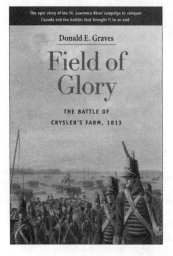

from Lake Champlain through swamp and forest, the other sailing down the turbulent St. Lawrence River in a flotilla of 300 small boats, invaded Canada – their objective, to capture the city of Montreal and thus sever the supply line between Lower and Upper Canada.

For the people of British North America, it was their darkest hour and many were convinced the Americans would prevail and they would shortly become citizens of the newest states in the union. Their fears were laid to rest when outnumbered British and Canadian troops and aboriginal warriors were victorious in two important military actions – the battle of Chateauguay in late October and, above all, the battle of Crysler's Farm fought on a muddy farm field beside the St. Lawrence River on 11 November 1813.

An epic of long marches and hard fighting, of courage and cowardice, *Field of Glory* is a fascinating panorama of one of the most dramatic periods in North American history. It is the first book in Donald E. Graves's masterful trilogy, "Forgotten Soldiers: The War of 1812 in the North."

"Graves … is a first-rate battlefield historian, and he weaves masterfully through the fog of war…. Canada would almost certainly not exist today had the day turned out otherwise."
Brian Bethune, *Maclean's* magazine

"Donald E. Graves may be the most competent of the modern Canadian military historians. His preference … has been to bore into a single battle and relate it in great detail. … an excellent account in the finest traditions of military history."
C. Edward Skeen, *Journal of American History*

"Graves has a marvellous ability to marshal many facts without interrupting the flow of his narrative. For history buffs, everything he writes is well worth reading."
Chris Raible, *Beaver: Canada's History Magazine*

WHERE RIGHT AND GLORY LEAD!
THE BATTLE OF LUNDY'S LANE, 1814

Eight months after the disastrous St. Lawrence campaign of 1813, a renewed American army led by Major General Jacob Brown took

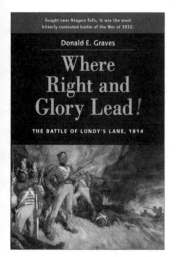

the field again. The centrepiece of *Where Right and Glory Lead!* is a detailed analysis of the battle of Lundy's Lane, one of the most hard-fought military actions to take place in North America. On a summer evening in July, 5,500 American, British and Canadian soldiers struggled desperately within sight of Niagara Falls in a close-range battle that raged on into the dark. The two armies fought each other to a standstill, and who won has long been a matter of dispute.

In his analysis of this still-controversial action, Donald E. Graves narrates the background and events of the 1814 Niagara campaign and provides a thorough examination of the weaponry, tactics and personalities of the opposing armies. The result is possibly the most thorough analysis of a musket-period action yet to appear in print, and an engrossing sequel to *Field of Glory*.

"*Where Right and Glory Lead!* is how military history should be written – deeply and carefully researched, salted with common sense, and put into a prose that stands you in a firing line that is fraying thinner by the minute.…"

John Elting, author of *Swords Around a Throne: Napoleon's Grand Armée* and *Amateurs to Arms: A Military History of the War of 1812*

"A vivid and scholarly account of … a desperate and extraordinary night battle, written by a master of the military techniques of the day. … an enjoyable and compelling read."

Piers Mackesy, author of *The War for America, 1775-83, War Without Victory: The Downfall of Pitt* and *British Victory in Egypt, 1801*

"Read Donald Graves's brilliant and exciting and sometimes surprising interpretation of the greatest battle ever to have taken place on Canadian soil."

Michael Power, *Brock Review*

To see all the books on the War of 1812 published by Robin Brass Studio, and many other fine military history titles, go to
www.robinbrassstudio.com

Donald E. Graves, one of Canada's best known military historians, is the author, co-author or editor of twenty full-length books dealing primarily with the War of 1812 and the Second World War. His detailed studies on the battles of Lundy's Lane *(Where Right and Glory Lead!)* and Crysler's Farm *(Field of Glory)* are classics of musket-period warfare. His most recent book is *Blood and Steel: The Wehrmacht Archive: Normandy 1944* and he is currently working on a study of the Niagara campaign of 1813.

Donald Graves is the managing director of Ensign Heritage Group, a consulting firm that provides military historical expertise to historic sites, government departments, film companies and individuals. He resides in the Mississippi Valley of Upper Canada with his author wife, Dianne.

Donald E. Graves is in demand as a lecturer and battlefield tour leader for the conflicts that he writes about. If you would like to have him address your group or organization, or lead a tour, contact him at his website address below.

For Donald E. Graves: www.ensigngroup.ca

www.robinbrassstudio.com